SAUDI ARABIA AND NUCLEAR WEAPONS

Nuclear proliferation in the Middle East remains an issue of concern. Saudi Arabia's actions will largely rest on Iran's decisions, and discussions and preparations within Saudi Arabia would suggest that it is ready to react to potential shifts in the region's nuclear powers.

Saudi Arabia and Nuclear Weapons uses an "inside out" approach that emphasizes the Saudis' own national interests in relation to the nuclear threat, and their understanding of the role of nuclear weapons in defense, foreign policy and the concept of deterrence. It is the first study with comprehensive use of the local Arabic-language military and civilian media to provide this understanding of official thinking and policy. The Saudi case study is contextualized against the prevailing proliferation models, to conclude that the Saudi case shares both commonalities and elements of uniqueness with other proliferation cases, implying the need for a "multi-causal" approach. Its comparative analysis also suggests potential implications applicable more broadly to the issue of nuclear proliferation.

A comprehensive study of Saudi Arabia's attitude to nuclear weapons, this book offers an exploration of nuclear proliferation that will interest students, scholars and policymakers working in Middle East studies, as well as in military and nuclear proliferation studies.

Norman Cigar is a research fellow at the Marine Corps University, from which he retired as Director of Regional Studies. His research focuses on WMD and jihadist warfare in the Middle East, and he is the author of *Saddam Hussein's Nuclear Vision: An Atomic Shield and Sword for Conquest*.

UCLA CENTER FOR MIDDLE EAST DEVELOPMENT (CMED) SERIES

Series Editors
Steven Spiegel, UCLA
Elizabeth Matthews, California State University, San Marcos

The *UCLA Center for Middle East Development (CMED)* series on Middle East security and cooperation is designed to present a variety of perspectives on a specific topic, such as democracy in the Middle East, dynamics of Israeli-Palestinian relations, Gulf security, and the gender factor in the Middle East. The uniqueness of the series is that the authors write from the viewpoint of a variety of countries so that no matter what the issue, articles appear from many different states, both within and beyond the region. No existing series provides a comparable, multinational collection of authors in each volume. Thus, the series presents a combination of writers from countries who, for political reasons, do not always publish in the same volume. The series features a number of sub-themes under a single heading, covering security, social, political, and economic factors affecting the Middle East.

1. The Struggle over Democracy in the Middle East
Regional politics and external policies
Edited by Nathan J. Brown and Emad El-Din Shahin

2. Women in the Middle East and North Africa
Agents of change
Edited by Fatima Sadiqi and Moha Ennaji

3. The Israel-Palestine Conflict
Parallel discourses
Edited by Elizabeth Matthews

4. Gender and Violence in the Middle East
Edited by Moha Ennaji and Fatima Sadiqi

5. Non-State Actors in the Middle East
Factors for peace and democracy
Galia Golan and Walid Salem

6. Regional Security Dialogue in the Middle East
Changes, challenges and opportunities
Edited by Chen Kane and Egle Murauskaite

7. Israeli Peacemaking Since 1967
Behind the breakthroughs and failure
Galia Golan

8. Justice and Peace in the Israeli–Palestinian Conflict
Yaacov Bar-Siman-Tov

9. The Political Ideology of Ayatollah Khamenei
Out of the mouth of the Supreme Leader of Iran
Yvette Hovsepian-Bearce

10. Saudi Arabia and Nuclear Weapons
How do countries think about the bomb?
Norman Cigar

SAUDI ARABIA AND NUCLEAR WEAPONS

How do countries think about the bomb?

Norman Cigar

LONDON AND NEW YORK

First published 2016
by Routledge
2 Park Square, Milton Park, Abingdon, Oxon OX14 4RN

and by Routledge
711 Third Avenue, New York, NY 10017

Routledge is an imprint of the Taylor & Francis Group, an informa business

© 2016 Norman Cigar

The right of Norman Cigar to be identified as author of this work has been asserted by him in accordance with sections 77 and 78 of the Copyright, Designs and Patents Act 1988.

All rights reserved. No part of this book may be reprinted or reproduced or utilized in any form or by any electronic, mechanical, or other means, now known or hereafter invented, including photocopying and recording, or in any information storage or retrieval system, without permission in writing from the publishers.

Trademark notice: Product or corporate names may be trademarks or registered trademarks, and are used only for identification and explanation without intent to infringe.

British Library Cataloguing in Publication Data
A catalogue record for this book is available from the British Library

Library of Congress Cataloging in Publication Data
Names: Cigar, Norman L., author.
 Title: Saudi Arabia and nuclear weapons : how do countries think about the bomb? / Norman Cigar.
 Description: Abingdon, Oxon ; New York, NY, : Routledge, 2016. | Series: UCLA Center for Middle East development (CMED) series ; 10 | Includes bibliographical references and index.
 Identifiers: LCCN 2015039728| ISBN 9781138643291 (hbk : alk. paper) | ISBN 9781138643307 (pbk : alk. paper) | ISBN 9781315629414 (ebk)
 Subjects: LCSH: Nuclear weapons–Saudi Arabia. | Nuclear weapons–Government policy–Saudi Arabia. | Nuclear nonproliferation–Saudi Arabia. | Saudi Arabia–Military policy. | Nuclear weapons–Iran. | Saudi Arabia–Foreign relations–Iran. | Iran–Foreign relations–Saudi Arabia.
 Classification: LCC U264.5.S28 C54 2016 | DDC 355.02/1709538–dc23
LC record available at http://lccn.loc.gov/2015039728

ISBN: 978-1-138-64329-1 (hbk)
ISBN: 978-1-138-64330-7 (pbk)
ISBN: 978-1-315-62941-4 (ebk)

Typeset in Bembo
by Taylor & Francis Books

CONTENTS

Preface   *x*

1 Introduction   1
   Bounding the problem 1
   The terms of reference and methodology 2

2 The dynamics of Saudi strategic culture and the decisionmaking process   15
   Where does Saudi thinking fit in? 15
   The decisionmaking process in Saudi Arabia 16
   The cultural facet of national security: Saudi views of Iran 21
   The centrality of regime legitimacy 24

3 Developing nuclear threat assessments   38
   Threat assessments and intelligence 38
   The evolution of Saudi nuclear threat assessments 39
   Mobilizing public opinion 43

4 Analyzing the threat in Riyadh: Why would a nuclear Iran be so dangerous?   48
   Iran's nuclear program: military or civilian? 49
   Creating a new Iranian hegemony 49
   Exporting the revolution and "offensive deterrence" 52
   Nuclear weapons and warfighting 53
   The threat to Saudi Arabia's economy 56

viii   Contents

5   Thinking in terms of solutions: How to stop Iran   61

    Doing nothing and accommodating Iran 61
    A foreign nuclear umbrella as an alternative? 63
    Considering the active options—striking or squeezing Iran's
      nuclear program? 67
    Watching and waiting 71

6   Thinking in terms of solutions: The evolution in Saudi thinking toward a nuclear option   78

    Saudi Arabia's traditional stand on nuclear weapons 78
    The shift to promoting nuclear weapons 79
    Developing the conceptual thinking and policy considerations for
      nuclear weapons 82
    Accounting for Saudi openness 89
    The potential mechanics of acquisition 90

7   Thinking about the utility of nuclear weapons: Deterrence and beyond   102

    Conceptualizing nuclear deterrence 102
    Saudi Arabia in a hostile world and the political power of
      nuclear weapons 107
    Drawing lessons from North Korea 111
    How to implement deterrence 114
    Developing the country's supporting infrastructure 117

8   Where does the civilian nuclear power sector fit in?   129

    Riyadh's civilian nuclear energy plans 129
    Nuclear energy and national security 130

9   A nuclear environment and foreign policy: Reshaping relations within the Gulf   137

    Confirming Saudi Arabia's leading role in the Gulf
      Cooperation Council 137
    Flexing a potential Saudi nuclear muscle 138
    Increasing Saudi leverage with the international community 139
    Promoting the idea of GCC union 140
    Gulf responses 141

10 The Rouhani era in Tehran and a new age of anxiety in Riyadh   149

   A new president for Iran 149
   The difficult Riyadh–Tehran–Washington triangle 151
   Iran's nuclear threat, Riyadh, and the GCC 156
   The long wait and mounting Saudi anxiety 158
   Intensifying activism abroad to influence the nuclear negotiations 163
   The April 2015 Framework Agreement and the May 2015 Camp David Summit 166
   Riyadh's continuing nuclear warnings 170

11 Coming to terms with the 14 July 2015 nuclear agreement: Saudi anxiety overcome?   186

   The July 2015 Nuclear Agreement: initial Saudi reactions 186
   The Saudi media: "debating" the Agreement 187
   The way forward 193
   Who's to blame? 195
   Closing the circle—King Salman's September 2015 visit to Washington 196

12 Conclusions and implications   212

   A Saudi nuclear path is likely … if … 212
   Saudi Arabia and proliferation models: commonalities and uniqueness 215
   Does the realist model apply? 215
   The models of restraint 217
   Saudi Arabia: a complex case 222
   International leverage on proliferation may sometimes be limited 223
   Modifying the threat environment can help 225
   Opening the door to further proliferation? 226
   Saudi nuclear proliferation: does it matter? 227

Index   *236*

PREFACE

I have always been fascinated by Saudi Arabia's rich and unique society and political system, while often finding the country's decisionmaking process mysterious and a frustrating challenge to understand, not least because of the well-known paucity of official information available. I have also been interested in the question of how a country views and decides on whether or not to become a nuclear power and all the more so when a country is as significant and has a decisionmaking system as distinctive as that of Saudi Arabia. A report I wrote that was published in 2013 by the United States Air Force Counterproliferation Center, entitled *Considering a Nuclear Gulf*, has served as the initial nucleus for the present study. I am especially grateful to two anonymous reviewers for helpful observations and advice on an early draft of this study, though any shortcomings, of course, remain entirely my own.

1
INTRODUCTION

Bounding the problem

The proliferation of nuclear weapons is likely to pose a continuing challenge to international security interests and to regional stability, and perhaps nowhere is this more evident than in the Middle East. Efforts to halt or manage this process must address how regional powers decide whether or not to acquire nuclear weapons and how they might plan to use them, although this may not always be an easy process, given the often closed nature of decisionmaking in that region. Saudi Arabia is certainly interested in the issue of nuclear weapons and may be one of those countries at least contemplating the possibility of joining the nuclear club at some time in the future, and that factor has already had an impact on its policymaking.

The thesis of this study is in itself dynamic, that is conditional and dependent on the key variable of Iran, both in the latter's behavior on the nuclear issue and, more broadly, in Iran's regional policy, although these two elements intersect to a significant degree. Specifically, the thesis is that had Iran acquired nuclear weapons at any point Saudi Arabia would also have done so, and that as long as Iran adheres to the agreement concluded in July 2015 with the 5+1 Group (the United States, Great Britain, France, China, Russia, and Germany) and does not acquire nuclear weapons for the next 15 years, very likely neither will Saudi Arabia. However, should Iran at any time decide on a nuclear breakout, then Saudi Arabia would very likely follow suit. In that sense, as long as Iran remains a non-nuclear state, this case study of Saudi Arabia will be one of the latter's non-proliferation, whereas that could change to one of proliferation if Iran—the key variable—became a nuclear state. Significantly, over the past few years Saudi Arabia has been developing the various components of the policy, public environment, legitimacy, and institutional and military infrastructure that could lay the groundwork to facilitate the option to acquire nuclear weapons at the appropriate moment if and when that decision is taken in response, in particular, as noted, to any acquisition of nuclear weapons by Iran, whether in the near or more distant future.

This study will close with the de facto U.S. confirmation in September 2015 of the Joint Comprehensive Plan of Action (hereafter the "Nuclear Agreement") concluded between Iran and the 5+1 Group in July 2015 and the September 2015 Saudi–U.S. summit. This is a logical cut-off point, as it marks the closure to a stage in the regional nuclear issue, as well as in Saudi thinking and policymaking on nuclear weapons. To be sure, in some ways, this apparently significant milestone in nuclear counterproliferation may perhaps only usher in a new phase of Saudi policy re-assessment of the changed regional security and political environment, and Riyadh can be expected to continue its contingency preparations as a precaution against any future Iranian breakout. In effect, over the past few years, one can identify a focus in Saudi Arabia on mobilizing support in both the civilian population and in the military for such an option, as one can see from the media intended for each audience. Moreover, in more tangible terms, there have been efforts ranging from securing religious approval for nuclear weapons to visibly developing the country's Strategic Rocket Force and a nascent space program. Even the promotion of nuclear power in the civilian sector can be seen, at least tangentially, as part of this process, if only by reinforcing the legitimacy and acceptance of nuclear power.

The results of this study should remain relevant as long as Riyadh believes there is a possibility of an Iranian nuclear breakout, and the focus here is on the deliberations in Saudi Arabia about nuclear-related policy options that are enduring and that illustrate what is perhaps representative of assessments and discussions within many countries who have faced or are facing the prospect of a nuclear-armed neighbor and the need to address the resulting change in the threat environment. Moreover, in tangible terms, the development by Riyadh of the basic justifications, institutional components, and political conditions for a potential nuclear capability will remain in place (and probably be developed further), available for activation if there should be a reversal at any time in the future in what appears to be Iran's present accommodating policy orientation. In addition, this study will address other parameters of Saudi thinking about nuclear threats and nuclear weapons, including the Saudi conceptualization of deterrence and the impact that a nuclear threat could have on reshaping Riyadh's relations within the Gulf.

The terms of reference and methodology

Analytical tools

Scholars have long sought to understand why some countries decide to embark on a nuclear path while others do not, and elements of the resulting approaches or models may be helpful in analyzing Saudi Arabia. Conversely, conclusions drawn from this case study may qualify or call into question at least certain facets of such models, and this study will seek to separate the commonalities which the Saudi case may share with general concepts of proliferation applicable to other similar situations from what may be specific to Saudi Arabia.

Efforts to develop a universal model to explain nuclear proliferation have deepened our understanding of the phenomenon but have not generated a complete consensus, despite a substantial scholarly literature on the subject.[1] Initially, the somewhat deterministic "realist" model was prevalent. The latter perspective of nuclear proliferation, in its essence, had focused on states as unitary actors and as the appropriate level of analysis who, when faced with international security threats (especially nuclear ones) in an anarchic world system, coupled with the absence of adequate alternative options such as reliable alliances, would respond with nuclear weapons in an almost reflexive pursuit of a balance of power as the desired end-state.[2]

Over the years, this model was weakened by the many exceptions of countries that did not follow the nuclear path as the realist model posited they would, and scholars highlighted the shortcomings of the realist approach. As will be seen throughout the following study, additional insightful models have also been developed in subsequent years as analytical and explanatory tools, usually by focusing on specific alternative facets that may have a bearing on decisionmaking in proliferation, such as domestic actors and politics, the influence of international nonproliferation regimes and standards of behavior (constructivism), degree of international economic integration, or leadership psychology. Etel Solingen, for example, developed, in particular, the idea of a country's elites' desire to integrate into the world economy as an indicator of the likelihood that a country will or will not pursue a nuclear option.[3] Maria Rost Rublee, instead, focuses attention on states that have not proliferated, highlighting the cumulative impact of international regimes on the likelihood of nuclear nonproliferation.[4] Jacques Hymans and K. P. O'Reilly, for their part, have seen as key the psychology of individual decisionmakers—and particularly of "oppositional nationalist" leaders for Hymans—who respond to national security threats based on a psychological national identity.[5]

On the other hand Peter R. Lavoy, in his perceptive overview of models, identified empirical shortcomings that certain approaches can have—shortcomings that often arise in the form of countries which do not conform to specific theories.[6] While finding the realist model too abstract and unable to explain the timing or the specific political, technical, or psychological variables which may determine decisionmaking on proliferation, at the same time—while seeing the idealist models as better at accounting for cultural and national specificities, motives, and decisionmaking styles of individual countries—he observes that such models, too, have limitations insofar as they cannot always explain why policymakers ignore associated constraints.[7] Noting that the "why" of acquisition is often intertwined with sets of macro-indicators that have been developed to help recognize decision points or stages of a process leading toward or away from proliferation, Lavoy proposed a helpful analytical tool that he called "nuclear mythmaking." This latter perspective makes possible a more inclusive analytical approach by allowing for due appreciation of genuine security threats while offering a framework by which to recognize and assess the process as a continuum toward or away from the acquisition of nuclear weapons. Specifically, Lavoy draws attention to national elites engaging in what he calls "nuclear mythmaking," that is when they:

> (1) emphasize their country's insecurity or its poor international standing; (2) portray this strategy as the best corrective for these problems; (3) articulate the political, economic, and technical feasibility of acquiring nuclear weapons; (4) successfully associate these beliefs and arguments (nuclear myths) with existing cultural norms and political priorities; and finally (5) convince senior decisionmakers to accept and act on these views.[8]

Scott D. Sagan, in a useful early critique of the conventional understanding of why countries decide to go or not to go nuclear, for his part offered a more complex perspective, identifying three alternative motivations or models—the "security model," that is recourse to nuclear weapons in order to increase security in response to foreign threats; a "domestic politics model," that is the use of nuclear weapons as a tool to advance domestic and bureaucratic interests; and a "norms model," where nuclear weapons serve as a symbol of a state's modernity and identity—and demonstrates the applicability and limitations of each of these.[9] While some cases support one or another of the models as an explanatory framework, he pointed out that others may not. Instead, he made a convincing argument for a more complex analysis requiring a range of variables. As he put it, "multicausality ... lies at the heart of nuclear proliferation. Nuclear proliferation and nuclear restraint have occurred in the past, and can occur in the future, for more than one reason: different historical cases are best explained by different causal methods."[10]

Ursula Jasper, too, rather than searching for an overarching explanatory theory, has contributed what she calls a "pragmatist" approach as an additional analytical tool, to which the present study will have recourse at times. A key element of her perceptive approach is that "the analysis of beliefs and narratives gains center stage."[11] That is, she posits that:

> we should depict a state's (non-)proliferation moves as the result of an ongoing process in which the state's identity, its role and position in the environment are discursively established and in which potential courses of action are construed ... In other words, the key to understanding why states pursue or abandon nuclear weapons programs lies in understanding the key underlying beliefs that are evident in the national "nuclear discourses."[12]

Any "model," of course, cannot have the precision or predictability of an algebraic equation where it would be sufficient to just insert well-defined values and expect a reliable and definitive answer. However, where a model can be useful is in suggesting relevant questions to ask. In that light, arguably, one can benefit from selected insights and limitations drawn from a variety of taxonomies, which can be adapted for use in analyzing the Saudi case, even if at times their tenets may be embedded only implicitly in the analysis presented here. In many ways, the present Saudi case can benefit from an approach using an amalgam of elements from all three of the models that Sagan had identified—the security model, the domestic politics model, and the norms model—and supports the utility of "multicausality" as an analytical approach. This construct is complemented by Jasper's insightful focus on the national narratives, that is on the national analysis and argumentation that is underlain by enduring identity and beliefs which operate interactively between the country's leaders and key sectors of Saudi society.

Rather than providing new theoretical insights or models, the intent of this study is more modest, namely to focus on Saudi Arabia as a significant regional actor in order to try to understand the latter specifically and the implications of its policy for the region. Nevertheless, the study will also gauge to what extent Saudi Arabia's experience conforms to or differs from prevailing theories about nuclear proliferation. To be sure, given all the variables and uncertainty surrounding both Iran's nuclear intentions and the regional situation, all one can do is forecast potential outcomes based on a study of the available data against an analytical background of Riyadh's strategic culture and political dynamics. Admittedly, even using the same available data, analysts can arrive at different conclusions with respect to Saudi Arabia. Ibrahim Al-Marashi, for example, in a well-argued essay, concluded that "There is little evidence ... that Saudi Arabia would seek to engage directly in a regional nuclear arms race."[13] In support of that position, he adduced that such factors as the degree of its international economic integration, the presence of an international regime, fear of an Israeli intervention, fear of stimulating further Iran's nuclear program, and an informal alliance with the United States "tilt[ed] decisively in the direction of Saudi nuclear restraint."[14]

The concern of this study is not just with the binary question of whether Saudi Arabia will or will not acquire nuclear weapons, although that in itself is a very important question, of course. In addition, what this study seeks to address is the impact that simply grappling with the nuclear issue has had for Saudi Arabia's political and security behavior domestically, in the region, and internationally. In particular, attention will be devoted to how Saudi Arabia has sought to interact with and, if possible, affect the key variable that Iran represents, as well as to how Riyadh may adapt in the future to a potential new regional nuclear environment.

Constructing an assessment—the available data

Over the years, a number of analysts have studied Saudi Arabia and have produced informative and insightful reports about it with respect to the nuclear issue, although often relying on inductive reasoning.[15] The thesis of this study is to be seen against a deeper background of Saudi Arabia's identity, national security culture, perceptions of its neighbors (and especially Iran), theoretical thinking about nuclear weapons, and national interests. The present study considers the issue of

Saudi Arabia and nuclear weapons by approaching the problem from the "inside-out," that is by evaluating the situation from the perspective of the players themselves, based on the Saudis' own security culture and calculus. How accurate Saudi assessments are and whether Saudi policies are optimal or pragmatic is less important than the fact that Saudis may view the situation as they do. Key to appreciating Saudi Arabia's thinking from this perspective is an analysis of how Saudis at various levels assess and articulate the situation within a framework of that country's strategic, or security, culture. At the same time, in parallel to verbal evidence, one must also take into consideration tangible measures taken that are related to the issue of nuclear weapons, such as developments in Saudi Arabia's Strategic Rocket Force, the civilian nuclear sector, or the mobilization of legitimacy in the religious establishment, and evaluate how these complement policy statements and discussions in the civilian and military media. In a way, all these components can be viewed as building blocks of a cohesive, if imperfectly visible and incomplete, policy option. As Jasper observes, the pragmatist approach which she promotes as a framework for analysis emphasizes such public narratives that "make certain events intelligible," as they present "interpretations of the self, of others, of the security environment or of the 'value' of nuclear weapons" and reveal the "self-conceptions, the ideological currents and worldviews on which the government's decision-making is based."[16]

Information on Saudi Arabia is not easily available, given the country's closed political system, and this study relies on information in the public domain and, in particular, on official declarations and on the Saudi media. To be sure, Saudi sources vary in their significance and function. Declaratory statements by officials in the government, and especially by senior members of the royal family, of course, carry the greatest weight. Political and strategic decisions are the purview of a narrow leadership elite consisting of the senior levels of the royal family, and opinions the royals express in public seldom stray from the consensus developed within the royal family.

However, the resulting official positions expressed are often scanty, opaque, and undeveloped, and information is routinely held tightly and stove-piped for security reasons or for internal political leverage. Not surprisingly, many Saudis find it puzzling that the country's appointed Consultative Council (Shura) treats its deliberations on even minor issues as secret.[17] Even well-placed Saudis may find official thinking on strategy unclear and sometimes have complained, even if obliquely, about the lack of clarity. For example, a senior planning official in the Ministry of Defense, calling for the participation of think tanks and experts in the formulation of strategy, rued that "economic, political, and security strategies are not clear, since they remain in the minds of senior men in the government; they are like senior officers who do not let junior employees in on them or in formulating them."[18] Likewise, a frustrated senior Air Defense Forces officer criticized, albeit circuitously, the lack of clear guidance for defense planning, noting that:

> What is needed is transparency and clarity by other parts of the government with respect to any information needed to draft strategy; there is a need to

overcome the resistance by some authorities about stating clearly what the assumed security threats are.[19]

Thus, one must look elsewhere for help on Saudi thinking, and the local media can provide a significant window into such thinking. Although the precise mechanics of the Saudi decisionmaking process are obscure, important decisions normally are not formulated and implemented in a vacuum, but are usually integrated into a broader context of national consensus, or at least of acquiescence, and major policy decisions normally are accompanied by extensive efforts to prepare, explain, and convince not only the domestic public but often also regional and international opinion. In some instances, the media are used to lay the groundwork for policy, as appears to have been the case here, where support for such issues as the concept of nuclear deterrence and nuclear weapons acquisition was visible in the media even before Saudi officials began to speak out on the subject.

It is in such public, though controlled, fora that major decisions and their rationale frequently are elaborated and refined by civilian and military analysts and by the government's unofficial spokesmen. Even then, the supporting analytical structure can still be incomplete and only emerge piecemeal through discussions over time, but such media writing is normally consistent and supportive of policy decisions, reflecting a general consensus that one can assume official circles mandate or at least can accept. As Saudi journalists recognize, realistically, the role of the media ordinarily is to be "the supporter of any domestic or foreign policy that the government undertakes, as it is the main vehicle to disseminate, explain, and clarify news and information."[20] The fact that the same views, presented in similar forms by various writers, often appear in print on the same day strongly suggests official encouragement and coordination. Even in cases where only one or two media sources may be cited as proof in this study, this is usually not indicative of uniqueness, as in most cases one could cite many more commentators voicing the same views, with clusters of similar opinion often appearing at the same time. This is not to say that those writing in the media necessarily know the detailed whys and wherefores of policy deliberations or plans, which are held within narrow circles. At times, in fact, the media and the pundits it features must intuit official policy based on limited guidance, although in some cases those in positions of responsibility in the media may already share the same views on an issue as the policymakers.

At times, the government may communicate official policy directly to editors or journalists. The previous monarch, King Fahd, was known to contact journalists directly to follow up on specific news items and was even known to request to see individual media items in order to act as arbiter on their suitability.[21] According to one report, under King Abd Allah, the Royal Council would issue detailed political guidance to the Ministry of Culture and Media which, in turn, would pass it on to all media outlets.[22] Before he became king, Salman also was reported to comment directly to journalists on their press articles, although one journalist hastened to add "not as a censor."[23] Illustrative of the relationship between the government and the media was an order from the King's Office in 2012 directing the local media "to desist from criticizing and to avoid making negative comments about Russian individuals, so that the interests of the Kingdom are not harmed," as Riyadh was then seeking improved relations with Moscow.[24] Such strictures apply also to Saudis writing in the foreign media and, although based abroad, Saudi-owned media outlets are also subject to control. For example, in a 2011 directive, the Saudi foreign minister instructed the minister of culture and media to alert two Saudi journalists contributing to the London-based but Saudi-owned *Al-Hayat* and *Al-Sharq Al-Awsat* dailies to stop writing anything negative about Lebanon's then prime minister, since the latter had complained.[25] In another case, an offending author was arrested after he had criticized a royal in *Al-Hayat*.[26]

While the situation has improved over the years, limits remain in place, and the government continues to exercise tight functional control over the mainstream media on significant issues—especially on national security and foreign policy—and the New York-based Committee to Protect Journalists' 2015 assessment, in fact, ranked Saudi Arabia as the third most-heavily censored country in the world.[27] The mainstream electronic media is state-owned and the state exercises firm control over the rest of media using multiple mechanisms. For example, the government appoints or at least must approve all editors of the print and electronic media. At times, royals can themselves be in charge of a newspaper, as is the case with Prince Bandar bin Khalid, who is chairman of *Al-Watan*, or Prince Turki bin Nasir bin Muhammad, who is chairman of *Jazan News*.

Censorship is practiced on a daily basis on individual articles, and editors, conscious of the potential consequences, routinely operate on the basis of self-censorship.[28] A persistent pattern of testing those limits can result in corrective measures, with an editor dismissed or a newspaper or electronic outlet shut down temporarily or permanently, or offending journalists blacklisted. Indicative of the basic media parameters, as a senior Saudi diplomat told the author, perhaps only half in jest, "If SPA [i.e. the government-run Saudi Press Agency] didn't report it, it didn't happen."[29]

Admittedly, according to some observers, the public's confidence in the mainstream Saudi media has been declining, with some Twitter posts deriding it as "caring about news of royal decrees," and there has been some shifting to the social media which young people, in particular, may find more accessible and credible.[30] The thousands of Saudi electronic blogs, websites and satellite channels run by individual tribes, as well as individual social media, while monitored, seem to be controlled considerably less tightly than is the mainstream media. Though it is more difficult, Saudi authorities even here try to exercise control, and the government can, and does, monitor and shut down Twitter accounts, for various reasons, while in 2015 the country's senior clerics joined in condemning those who used the social media for purposes they defined as contravening Islamic law.[31] Offenders can be dealt with harshly, such as the initiator of a liberal forum, Raif Badawi, who in May 2014 was sentenced to 10 years in prison, 1,000 lashes, and a hefty fine for his online media activity. Any dissident group's media is invariably based abroad.[32] Of course, most Saudis also have access to Arabic-language satellite television programs from other countries, but at least those based in neighboring countries, such as Al-Jazira (Qatar) and Al-Arabiya (United Arab Emirates), are usually careful to avoid direct criticism of the Saudi ruling family.

While some media outlets are more daring or more conservative than others, the range remains within accepted limits. Boundaries of expression can be tested on such issues as poor housing, unemployment, high prices, or women's rights, but major national security or foreign policy issues remain a sensitive topic where public discussions are likely only with official permission. In particular, the Saudi media is notable for its avoidance of what the regime would consider embarrassing or sensitive issues, especially if they relate directly to the royal family. Individual media items can, and do, at times reflect differences on detail, focus, or emphasis, but not those on basic national security policy issues, where the principal thrust of the approach to any topic is likely to be consistent. Although one may find an occasional article that is an outlier from the norm, patterns of such an orientation are highly unlikely.

The media can also be used to send messages on sensitive issues to the informed public or to governments in friendly or hostile countries that might otherwise be embarrassing if done officially, while benefiting from a degree of plausible denial. In addition, the media can serve as a test-bed for trial balloons, introducing ideas to gauge the reaction they might generate at home or abroad. In this case, the possibility of a Saudi nuclear option was floated in the local media before it was broached openly by officials. The Saudi-owned international media, at times more adventurous than that at home, routinely also reflects official thinking on sensitive issues—especially when the author is a Saudi—and can also be used to inform and send indirect messages to, in particular, other Arab audiences.[33] When foreigners write in the Saudi press, they are subject to the same restrictions as domestic writers, although their foreign status may lend a veneer of plausible denial to their views. The reprinting of items from other countries in the Saudi media can add yet an additional layer of plausible denial.

The country's media, in many ways, can be likened to a lopsided transmission belt, serving as an informal though semi-official vehicle, presenting and promoting government policy to the public and, to a lesser degree, serving as a rudimentary barometer of public opinion through reader comments on the internet versions of the media (though not all such feedback is necessarily published). At the same time, in the absence of political parties, labor unions, free elections, or a free legislature to reflect public views, the government uses the media not only as a vehicle to communicate policy, but also as a way to foster some controlled discussions by permitting the airing of different views if there has been no decision taken yet, if the government seeks to generate ideas or, rarely, if different stands reflect divided views within government circles. Of course, such discussions are kept within accepted parameters and are not allowed to stray into criticism of the royal family or of its decisions. Likewise, the media provides information and guidance for the informal discussion sessions among family and friends—the *majlis*—that take place in the homes of the informed public. Apparently anxious to ensure that any discussions of policy—even at the lowest levels—remain within acceptable bounds, the country's *mufti*, or chief authority on religious law, in 2015 warned citizens not to criticize or spread rumors about the royals—or about clerics—in the social media and in a private *majlis*, since "undermining the leadership" would "undermine people's lives and their security."[34]

Saudi Arabia's military media, like its civilian counterpart, is also controlled from above and is used to inform military personnel of official policy. However, the military media also serves as an important professional forum to discuss and develop ideas from an expert vantage point, especially in dealing with concepts of a theoretical or technical nature, including the general outline of military doctrine, and to provide military assessments of other countries' capabilities. As such, the military media complements the civilian media and provides insights on thinking about security matters from an additional perspective. Not surprisingly, the country's military media is more secretive than its civilian counterpart and, since mid-2013, has no longer been available online or in hard copy outside of official channels. Where it is available online, as in the case of the Saudi National Guard (SANG), readers wishing to access its official journal, *Al-Haras Al-Watani*, now have to supply their military ID number and telephone number.

Saudi academics, for their part, have been well-represented in discussions on the nuclear issue, although making their contribution not in scholarly publications but, rather, in the media, where their ideas and opinions have not differed significantly from those of other writers.

Material about nuclear weapons seems to always have been especially tightly controlled in the media. For example, when a Saudi journalist writing in an Egyptian newspaper in 1990 called for Saudi Arabia to acquire nuclear weapons, Prince Sultan, the then minister of defense, had him flown back to Riyadh immediately so that he could personally upbraid him in his office. Telling the offending journalist that he had embarrassed the country by raising that issue, Prince Sultan warned him that other countries were watching closely. Perhaps to make a point, when this journalist wrote his next article on another topic, he was nevertheless arrested on Prince Sultan's orders.[35]

Significantly, on the nuclear issue, there has been an evident consensus expressed in the civilian and military media all along. If such homogeneity came about spontaneously and naturally in an independent media, that in itself would be a remarkable and important indication as to the direction of a country's thinking. As is more likely the case for Saudi Arabia, where such expressions of opinion are guided and controlled, the media still serves as an even more valuable guide to the general lines of official thinking on this issue. To be sure, as will be seen later in greater detail, in an unusual development, while in the immediate aftermath of the July 2015 Nuclear Agreement, parallel divergent views as to the import of the latter did appear for a short time in the Saudi media, which may have been a reflection of general factional tensions for other reasons that had been reported within the ruling family, or of genuine policy disagreements within the latter. Sustained coverage in the Saudi media of a topic in itself is a good indicator of official interest in an issue. The amount of attention the media devoted to nuclear weapons would spike whenever there was an increase in threat perceptions, such as in the tense 2002–2003 period preceding the invasion of Iraq, in 2006 when Iran announced a breakthrough in enriching uranium, after 2010, when the assumption that Iran was moving inexorably towards success with its nuclear program gained currency in Saudi circles, and again when a nuclear agreement became a possibility with the election of Hassan Rouhani as Iran's president in 2013, and, especially, after the July 2015 Nuclear Agreement was reached.

Notes

1 Tanya Ogilvie-White carried out a particularly comprehensive analysis of the strengths and weaknesses of various theoretical approaches in "Is There a Theory of Nuclear Proliferation? An Analysis of the Contemporary Debate," *The Nonproliferation Review*, iv, 1, Fall 1996, 43–60. Also see Barry R. Schneider, "Nuclear Proliferation and Counter-Proliferation: Policy Issues and Debates," *Mershon International Studies Review*, 38, 1994, 209–234, Jacques E. C. Hymans, "The Study of Nuclear Proliferation and Nonproliferation; Toward a New Consensus," in William C. Potter with Gaukhar Mukhatzhanova, eds, *Forecasting Nuclear Proliferation in the 21st Century: The Role of Theory*, vol. 1 (Stanford, CA: Stanford University Press, 2010), 13–37, and Nuno P. Monteiro and Alexandre Debs, "The Strategic Logic of Nuclear Proliferation," *International Security*, xxxix, 2, Fall 2014, 7–51.
2 For an elaborated version of this model by its originator, see Kenneth N. Waltz, "Toward Nuclear Peace," in Robert J. Art and Kenneth N. Waltz, eds, *The Use of Force*, 4th edition (Lanham, MD: University Press of America, 1993), 527–55.
3 Etel Solingen, *Nuclear Logics: Alternative Paths in East Asia and the Middle East* (Princeton, NJ: Princeton University Press, 2007).
4 Maria Rost Rublee, *Nonproliferation Norms: Why States Choose Nuclear Restraint* (Athens, GA: University of Georgia Press, 2009).
5 Jacques E. C. Hymans, *The Psychology of Nuclear Proliferation: Identity, Emotions, and Foreign Policy* (Cambridge: Cambridge University Press, 2006), 35–36, and K. P. O'Reilly, *Nuclear Proliferation and the Psychology of Political Leadership: Beliefs, Motivations and Perceptions* (Abingdon: Routledge, 2015).
6 Peter R. Lavoy, "Nuclear Proliferation over the Next Decade: Causes, Warning Signs, and Policy Responses," *The Nonproliferation Review*, xiii, 3, November 2006, 434–54.
7 Ibid., 434–435.
8 Ibid., 435.
9 Scott D. Sagan, "Why Do States Build Nuclear Weapons? Three Models in Search of a Bomb," *International Security*, xxi, Winter 1996–97, 54–86.
10 Ibid., 85.
11 Ursula Jasper, *The Politics of Nuclear Non-Proliferation: A Pragmatist Framework for Analysis* (Abingdon: Routledge, 2015), 2 (hereafter Jasper).
12 Ibid., 3.
13 Ibrahim Al-Marashi, "Saudi Petro-Nukes? Riyadh's Nuclear Intentions and Regime Survival Strategies," in William C. Potter with Gaukhar Mukhatzhanova, eds, *Forecasting Nuclear Proliferation in the 21st Century: A Comparative Perspective*, vol. 2 (Stanford, CA: Stanford University Press, 2010), 98.
14 Ibid., 99–100.
15 For example, Thomas W. Lippman, *Nuclear Weapons and Saudi Strategy* (Washington, DC: Middle East Institute, Policy Brief, January 2008), www.cfr.org/iran/mei-nuclear-weapons-saudi-strategy/p19916, Michael A. Levi, *Would the Saudis Go Nuclear?*

(Washington, DC: Brookings, June 2003), www.brookings.edu/research/articles/2003/06/02middleeast-levi, James A. Russell, "Nuclear Proliferation and the Middle East's Security Dilemma: The Case of Saudi Arabia," in James J. Wirtz and Peter R. Lavoy, eds, *Over the Horizon Proliferation Threats* (Stanford, CA: Stanford University Press, 2012), 47–67, and Colin H. Kahl, Melissa G. Dalton, and Matthew Irvine, *Atomic Kingdom: If Iran Builds the Bomb, Will Saudi Arabia Be Next?* (Washington, DC: Center for a New American Security, 2013), www.cnas.org/files/documents/publications/CNAS_AtomicKingdom_Kahl.pdf.

16 Jasper, 39.

17 Ali Sad Al-Musa, "Li-Ada' majlis al-shura: 'Akhiran fahimnakum'" [To the Members of the Shura: "We Have Understood You at Last"], *Al-Watan* (Abha), 27 October 2013, www.alwatan.com.sa/Articles/Detail.aspx?ArticleID=18727.

18 [Major General] Yusuf bin Ibrahim Al-Sallum (Ret), "Ru'ya istratijiya mustaqbaliya" [A Future Strategic Vision], *Al-Jazira* (Riyadh), 11 October 2005, www.al-jazirah.com/2005/20051011/rj2.htm.

19 Staff Brigadier General Muhammad bin Yahya Al-Jadii, "Idad al-istiratijiya al-askariya: Al-Tahaddiyat wa'l-suubat" [Crafting Military Strategy: The Challenges and the Difficulties], *Al-Difa Al-Jawwi* (Riyadh), 13 December 2011, www.rsadf.gov.sa/Pub_mq1T.asp?ID=6. *Al-Difa Al-Jawwi* is the Saudi Air Defense Forces' official journal.

20 Muhammad Al-Shuwayir, "Sinaat al-sawt al-ilami" [Crafting the Media Voice], *Al-Sharq* (Dammam), 11 April 2015, www.alsharq.net.sa/2015/04/11/1326254.

21 Interview with journalist Badr Ahmad Karim, "Dardasha an al-idhaa wa-wikalat al-anba'" [Chatting About Radio Broadcasting and the News Agency], *Al-Bilad* (Jeddah), 23 December 2010, www.albiladdaily.com/print.php?action=print&m=newsm&id=67550, and Mishal Al-Anazi, "Thana' al-malik Fahd bin Abd Al-Aziz ala dawrih al-idhai bi-musalsal *Sawalif Al-Nas*" [Praise for King Fahd bin Abd Al-Aziz for His Media Role in the *Sawalif Al-Nas* TV Serial], *Al-Riyadh* (Riyadh), 3 December 2010, www.al-riyadh.com/2010/12/03/article581797.html.

22 Muhammad bin Abd Allah Al-Qarni, "*Shu'un Khalijiya* taskhif kayf yudir Al-Tuwayjiri wa'l-Qahtani al-ilam al-saudi min al-diwan al-malaki" [*Shu'un Khalijiya* Reveals How Al-Tuwayjiri and Al-Qahtani Manage the Saudi Media from the Royal Council], *Shu'un Khalijiya* (Aberdeen), 20 November 2014, http://alkhaleejaffairs.org.

23 Khalid Al-Sulayman, "Salman kharij madrasat 6 muluk" [Salman Is a Graduate of the School of Six Kings], *Ukaz* (Jeddah), 26 January 2015, www.okaz.co/bwH8cdi76.

24 Telegram from the Royal Council to the Minister of Foreign Affairs and to the Ministry of Culture and Media, 26 April 2012, Top Secret and Urgent, provided by WikiLeaks, www.wikileaks.org/saudi-cables/pics/5cd308b8-e2e9-471a-bbec-38c20e569d83.jpg.

25 Message from Prince Saud Al-Faysal to the Minister of Culture and Media, 31 January 2011, provided by WikiLeaks, www.wikileaks.org/saudi-cables/doc118847.html.

26 "Iqaf al-katib Tarrad Al-Amri bi-sabab maqalih 'Al-Walid bin Talal min ayn laka hadha?'" [The Writer Tarrad Al-Umar Arrested Because of His Article 'Al-Walid bin Talal, Where Did You Get That?'], *Al-Marsd* (Riyadh), 15 November 2014, http://al-marsd.com/c-104592.

27 Committee to Protect Journalists, "10 Most Censored Countries," https://cpj.org/2015/04/10-most-censored-countries.php, and interview with Khaled Almaeena by Ben Flanagan, "Saudi Media 'Pushing Envelop' on Taboos, Says Gazette Editor," Al-Arabiya TV, 2 September 2013, http://english.alarabiya.net/en/media/2013/09/02/Saudi-media-pushing-envelop-on-taboos-says-Gazette-editor.html.

28 On censorship, including self-censorship, in the Saudi media, see John R. Bradley, *Saudi Arabia Exposed: Inside a Kingdom in Crisis* (New York: Palgrave Macmillan, 2005), 181–204.

29 Told to the author during a visit to Saudi Arabia under the auspices of the National Council on U.S.–Arab Relations, February 2000.

30 Salih Al-Musallam, "Al-Tarh al-ilami bayn al-waqi wa'l-ma'mul!" [The Rejection of the Media: Reality and What Is Desired], *Al-Sharq*, 13 April 2015, www.alsharq.net.sa/2015/04/13/1327325.

31 Jon Stone, "The Saudi Arabian Government Claims to Have Hacked 9,000 Twitter Accounts Because They Were Tweeting Porn," *The Independent* (London), 5 January 2015, www.independent.co.uk/news/world/middle-east/the-saudi-arabian-government-claims-to-have-hacked-9000-twitter-accounts-because-they-were-tweeting-porn-9958811.html?origin=inte rnalSearch, and "Wujub raf al-mukhalafat al-shariya fi wasa'il al-ilam li'l-qada'" [A Duty to Bring Contraventions of Islamic Law in the Media before the Courts], *Ukaz*, 24 June 2015, http://okaz.co/bwlgedq1a.
32 Rory Jones and Ahmed Al Omran, "Saudi Arabia Plans to Regulate Local YouTube Content," *Wall Street Journal* (New York), 24 April 2014, http://online.wsj.com/news/a rticles/SB10001424052702304518704579521463293165726#printMode.
33 In the case of the two most influential Arabic-language international newspapers, the late defense minister, Prince Sultan, owned *Al-Hayat* (one of his sons is still the publisher, and the latter's son is his deputy), while other well-placed royals, Prince Al-Walid bin Talal and Prince Faysal bin Salman (son of the current King) own *Al-Sharq Al-Awsat*.
34 Mashari Al-Karshami, "Al-Mufti yuhdhir min itlaq al-lisan fi arad al-ulama' wa'l-umara' wa-tattabu awrathim" [The Mufti Cautions against Gossiping about the Honor of the Ulama' and the Princes and Investigating Their Faults], *Al-Madina*, 12 June 2015, www.al-madina.com/printhtml/613000.
35 Zuhayr Muhammad Jamil Kutbi, "Naam namlik silahan nawawiyan" [Yes, We Have Nuclear Weapons], *Al-Khalij* (Riyadh), 7 January 2014, www.al-khaleeg.com/article-a uid-712.html.

Bibliography

Al-Marashi, Ibrahim, "Saudi Petro-Nukes? Riyadh's Nuclear Intentions and Regime Survival Strategies," in William C. Potter with Gaukhar Mukhatzhanova, eds, *Forecasting Nuclear Proliferation in the 21st Century: A Comparative Perspective*, vol. 2 (Stanford, CA: Stanford University Press, 2010), 76–99.
Bradley, John R., *Saudi Arabia Exposed: Inside a Kingdom in Crisis* (New York: Palgrave Macmillan, 2005).
Committee to Protect Journalists, "10 Most Censored Countries," https://cpj.org/2015/04/10-most-censored-countries.php.
Hymans, Jacques E. C., *The Psychology of Nuclear Proliferation: Identity, Emotions, and Foreign Policy* (Cambridge: Cambridge University Press, 2006).
Hymans, Jacques E. C., "The Study of Nuclear Proliferation and Nonproliferation: Toward a New Consensus," in William C. Potter with Gaukhar Mukhatzhanova, eds, *Forecasting Nuclear Proliferation in the 21st Century: The Role of Theory*, vol. 1 (Stanford, CA: Stanford University Press, 2010), 13–37.
Jasper, Ursula, *The Politics of Nuclear Non-Proliferation: A Pragmatist Framework for Analysis* (Abingdon: Routledge, 2015).
Kahl, Colin H., Melissa G. Dalton and Matthew Irvine, *Atomic Kingdom: If Iran Builds the Bomb, Will Saudi Arabia Be Next?* (Washington, DC: Center for a New American Security, February 2013), available at: www.cnas.org/files/documents/publications/CNAS_Atom icKingdom_Kahl.pdf.
Lavoy, Peter R., "Nuclear Proliferation over the Next Decade: Causes, Warning Signs, and Policy Responses," *The Nonproliferation Review*, xiii, 3, November 2006, 434–454.
Levi, Michael A., "Would the Saudis Go Nuclear?" (Washington, DC: Brookings Institution, June 2003), available at: www.brookings.edu/research/articles/2003/06/02middleeast-levi.
Lippman, Thomas W., "Nuclear Weapons and Saudi Strategy" (Washington, DC: Middle East Institute, Policy Brief, January 2008), available at: www.cfr.org/iran/mei-nuclea r-weapons-saudi-strategy/p19916.

Monteiro, Nuno P. and Alexandre Debs, "The Strategic Logic of Nuclear Proliferation," *International Security*, xxxix, 2, Fall 2014, 7–51.

Ogilvie-White, Tanya, "Is There a Theory of Nuclear Proliferation? An Analysis of the Contemporary Debate," *The Nonproliferation Review*, iv, 1, Fall 1996, 43–60.

O'Reilly, K. P., *Nuclear Proliferation and the Psychology of Political Leadership: Beliefs, Motivations and Perceptions* (Abingdon: Routledge, 2015).

Rost Rublee, Maria, *Nonproliferation Norms: Why States Choose Nuclear Restraint* (Athens, GA: University of Georgia Press, 2009).

Russell, James A., "Nuclear Proliferation and the Middle East's Security Dilemma: The Case of Saudi Arabia," in James J. Wirtz and Peter R. Lavoy, eds, *Over the Horizon Proliferation Threats* (Stanford, CA: Stanford University Press, 2012), 47–67.

Sagan, Scott D., "Why Do States Build Nuclear Weapons? Three Models in Search of a Bomb," *International Security*, xxi, Winter 1996–1997, 54–86.

Schneider, Barry R., "Nuclear Proliferation and Counter-Proliferation: Policy Issues and Debates," *Mershon International Studies Review*, 38, 1994, 209–234.

Solingen, Etel, *Nuclear Logics: Alternative Paths in East Asia and the Middle East* (Princeton, NJ: Princeton University Press, 2007).

Waltz, Kenneth N., "Toward Nuclear Peace," in Robert J. Art and Kenneth N. Waltz, eds, *The Use of Force*, 4th edition (Lanham, MD: University Press of America, 1993), 527–555.

2

THE DYNAMICS OF SAUDI STRATEGIC CULTURE AND THE DECISIONMAKING PROCESS

Where does Saudi thinking fit in?

As will be seen in greater detail later in this study, the Saudi approach to nuclear weapons, to a great extent, seemingly has conformed to a classic realist tradition. Realism is not an abstract theory for most Saudis but is something that is felt as a natural, objective reality, and reflects how they interpret and react to their security environment. Saudi policymakers, as well as their co-nationals at all levels of society—whether explicitly and consciously or not—refer openly to the concepts and language of realism, with a focus on states as the relevant players, an anarchic international situation, and a balance of power as the appropriate response to such a situation.

However, the situation is more complex and, as is true for most countries, Saudi Arabia's outlook and foreign and security policies are a combination of realism and idealism, intersecting with its national strategic culture—in the sense of society's shared patterns of or a consensus on values, national interests, and threats that transcend time—to inform and determine the dynamics of the nuclear issue and to shape the responses. As Alastair Iain Johnston argued convincingly, "different states have different predominant strategic preferences that are rooted in the early or formative experiences of the state and are influenced to some degree by the philosophy, politics, culture, and cognitive characteristics of the state and its elites."[1] One could add such enduring and less malleable givens as history and geography. Evaluating national leaders or ruling elites against the background of such factors yields a more comprehensive and accurate understanding of threat perceptions and of leaders' motivations, thinking, and decisionmaking process with respect to nuclear weapons than do assumptions based solely on paradigms drawn largely from pure theory or from the experience of the superpowers. By the same token, focusing on a country's strategic culture, as Michael C. Desch and others have pointed out, need not replace the threat/interest-based realist approach but enriches and adds flexibility to its application in concrete cases.[2]

In many ways, this national security culture provides a framework for policymakers—and, by extension, to other elements in society—in which to define, understand, and assess threats to the country, and has served as the environment in which enduring paradigms are generated and expressed. Decisionmakers, of necessity, formulate paradigms or models, whether consciously or unconsciously, as Richard K. Betts notes, to make sense of problems and to organize and interpret information in order to be able to make decisions.[3] Such paradigms, once established, are likely to have a significant impact on policymaking and are hard to dislodge even in the face of contradictory evidence, something that Robert Jervis termed "premature cognitive closure." In his seminal work on decisionmaking frameworks, drawing from psychology and international relations, Jervis notes insightfully that:

> once a person has conceived of a problem in a given way, it is very hard to break out of his pattern of thought. New information, rather than calling the established subgoal into question, will be interpreted within the old framework.[4]

Realpolitik and ideology intertwine to generate Saudi Arabia's strategic culture and, as an influential Saudi observer noted, the two combine to serve as the basis for the country's decisionmaking.[5] The issue of nuclear weapons is no exception to this analytical framework in Saudi Arabia, and the credibility and import of policy statements and initiatives can best be appreciated by placing them within the broader context of Saudi Arabia's strategic culture and of the latter's relationship to decisionmaking.

The decisionmaking process in Saudi Arabia

Saudi Arabia, in some ways, approaches a realist model, with "the state" as a unitary decisionmaking entity, given the lack of genuine public debate and an apparent absence of influence by other socio-political sectors in the system—whether the bureaucracy, military, or public—on the basic aspects of the military nuclear issue. True, at least below the surface, there can often be divisions, and debate is permitted on such policy matters as education, social services, or even the civil nuclear project. However, this is ordinarily not true for national security matters and does not seem to have been the case with the military nuclear issue, as there appeared to be a consensus or, in any event, this was apparently a case where dissent was not allowed, thus situating Riyadh to a certain extent into the pattern of a cohesive state as the actor that is assumed by realist theory.

The locus of decisionmaking on national security issues lies, essentially, within the top stratum of the royal family. However, ever since the death in 1953 of King Abd Al-Aziz (founder of the modern Saudi state), the ruling system has exhibited at least a rough if fluctuating form of polyarchy—in the sense posited by Robert Dahl with multiple centers of power or influence—albeit in Saudi Arabia it is a polyarchy limited largely to the royal family, with senior royals ordinarily developing individual power bases, whether within or outside the formal government structure, thereby providing balance and encouraging consultation in decisionmaking.[6]

Nevertheless, in such a system, the level of analysis needed to determine influence on decisionmaking may not always be clear, given the blurring between the concept and interests of state and royal family which is perhaps not surprising in the patrimonial structure that characterizes the country's socio-political system, where patron–client interactions and personal loyalties often trump institutions and official hierarchies.[7] Some individuals in the royal family, in fact, may have access to information and wield influence not based on holding any official title or position but perhaps because of their reputation within the family or their membership in a specific family coterie. To be sure, most of the country's perhaps 10,000 princes are outside the immediate circles of national decisionmaking, but even some of the latter may have a power base somewhere in the military, bureaucracy, business, or the sports sector (as do some princesses in the parallel female arenas) and may have influence on specific issues, although ordinarily they will seek to attach themselves to a patron in the top ranks of royal decisionmakers to exert that influence. Key agencies connected with national security (Ministry of Defense, Ministry of the Interior, Intelligence Agency, Ministry of Foreign Affairs, Saudi Arabian National Guard—SANG, King Abdulaziz City for Science and Technology) as well as local governorships are now or have traditionally been headed by a prince, with additional princes as deputies in several other key ministries and agencies, but tight royal control is exercised even over those sectors of the system which may have a non-royal at the top.

Given the blurring between personal and institutional interests, one cannot be certain at what level Saudi policymakers may be operating on an issue. For example, hypothetically, one would not expect the SANG, whose main mission is domestic security and which operates largely as a land force, to have a strong interest in and be a supporter of nuclear weapons, yet its official journal indicated such an interest and support repeatedly over the years. However, personal status may have mattered more than an institutional one, as the commander of the SANG until 2010 had been King Abd Allah, who would have had a broader national perspective than as simply a military service commander. He was then succeeded in the same post by his son, Prince Mitib, who very likely aspired to accede to the throne himself and, towards the end of his father's reign, had begun to exert himself at a higher than military service institutional level by dealing with national policy issues, including with foreign representatives.

Whatever the power balance among various individuals, responsibility for major national security decisions, nevertheless, is highly concentrated and, indeed, the Al Saud traditionally have fostered an identification and equation of the state with their family or even with an individual ruler, and have governed their subjects in a paternalistic fashion. Characteristically, in his speech introducing the new budget in

December 2012, King Abd Allah addressed the Saudis as "my sons and daughters" and characterized their well-being as "my personal obligation and trusteeship toward you."[8] Not coincidentally, after King Abd Allah's recovery from surgery, a Saudi newspaper headline read "The King's Recovery Is the Nation's Recovery."[9] As one provincial newspaper put it on the country's National Day, "this wonderful entity—nation, abilities, blessings, steadfastness of religion— ... all of that in totality is the Al Saud."[10] And, an ad which the Bin Ladin conglomerate sponsored in the SANG's official journal on the occasion of the country's National Day in 2012 congratulated the King, the Crown Prince, the Saudi people, and "the noble ruling family" as a separate category representing the nation. Indeed, one of King Abd Allah's advisers specifically equated royal family and country, as he observed that "the unity and cohesion of this blessed country comes from the unity and cohesion of the noble ruling family."[11]

In a sense, the Al Saud "own" Saudi Arabia. That appears to be a common view in the country, and probably not only among those who are disaffected. As a source critical of the Al Saud put it, "The Al Saud harbor no doubt whatsoever that the country—all that is beneath the ground and all that moves above it—is their private property, with no need to justify that."[12] The Al Saud stress that it was they who created the country—a first version in the eighteenth century and, in 1903, the current entity in the person of their ancestor King Abd Al-Aziz Al Saud—and who named it after themselves. Reminders of this national narrative are promoted constantly. According to the official discourse, in fact, between the early days of Islam under Muhammad and the creation of the Saudi state there had been only primordial chaos. King Salman, then the country's Minister of Defense and Crown Prince, compared the current Saudi state to "the first Islamic state," i.e. the one that Muhammad had established, and was proud that the Saudis had "restored to the Arabian Peninsula the security and stability that it had lacked for many centuries." He emphasized that prior to the Saudi state every region and tribe had been a state unto itself and at war with all the others.[13] A military writer, typically, focused on the country's "heroic leaders," and stressed that before the creation of the Saudi state "there was no identity or political unity;" instead, there was only "a complete absence of security ... while the terrible triad of hunger, fear, and disease ran roughshod over the Peninsula."[14] This identification of the royal family with the nation was underlined, again, during a Ramadan reception, when a member of the Shura Council addressed King Abd Allah on behalf of the visiting delegation of the country's senior officials and notables by acknowledging that the King's father had returned to the Peninsula its dignity in the form of "an Arab Saudi state, the first independent state in the Arabian Peninsula."[15] The royal family portrays itself as having created not only the country but also a civilized society and a national identity. As Prince Khalid Al-Faysal, governor of Mecca, remarked, thanks to King Abd Al-Aziz (the father of all the succeeding monarchs and the grandfather of many of today's most senior princes), the latter's creation of a unified country "succeeded in transforming the Arabian Peninsula from a society of wars and strife to a civilized society representing a unique model of success in the modern era."[16]

In the process, the same dignitary asserted that King Abd Al-Aziz had fashioned a unity of identity, so that now there was "a Saudi person, a Saudi way of thinking, a Saudi language, and a Saudi national dress."[17]

Indeed, Saudi ideology reinforces a sense of uniqueness, especially as the very creation of the Saudi state is seen as having been "a miracle" wrought by the Al Saud family.[18] In fact, Prince Khalid Al-Faysal noted that "Saudi man is different from other individuals, since God had him dwell in the neighborhood of His age-old house to which Muslims face five times a day [for prayer]," and that Saudi Arabia would still retain Islam even if all others abandoned it.[19] Saudi exceptionalism was often seen as embodied in particular in the royal family and, typically, praising the King's "decisive victories [in Yemen] thanks to resolute decisions," a Saudi commentator interpreted that as "incontrovertible proof and an unequivocal sign that God is protecting this country," as well as a proof of "its leadership's determination to defend religion and nation."[20] Indeed, a member of the Shura Council claimed that the Saudi leadership had created a civilization for its people that had become the model for the rest of the Middle East.[21] A journalist, likewise, affirmed that "without the least doubt our kingdom is unlike any other kingdom and our inspired king is unlike any other king."[22]

Traditionally, consensus within the royal family has been a fundamental principle of Saudi decisionmaking. While individuals at the top of the royal family clearly exert the greatest influence, they do so within a wider family framework, so that changes in policy perspectives are usually gradual rather than abrupt. Perhaps inspired by senior princes as a reminder to the rest of princes, an account in a Saudi daily described the assembly of princes waiting to welcome the remains of Crown Prince Sultan, who had died in New York, and emphasized the royal family's internal cohesion. As the article noted, "this family knows that its unity and cohesion … are the yardstick for preparing for crises, emergencies, and sudden shocks." Pointing to the regimes that were then falling in the region as part of the Arab Spring, the writer identified as the reason for their demise "personal objectives and individual desires." The article stressed that, instead, "the secret of success for nations … is in the ruling family's internal cohesion," and—perhaps prescriptively—praised how the young princes respected their elders in the Saudi royal family.[23]

While there may be individual positions within the royal family on a particular issue on national security, if individual differences of views on the nuclear issue exist, they have not been apparent. Almost assuredly, there must have been lengthy discussions within the top strata of the royal family on this issue over the years, no doubt with the participation of political advisers and technical and military experts. If so, such discussions seem to have been conducted within narrow circles and held tightly, thereby also limiting the input of outside ideas and often operating on a limited intelligence base. Decisionmaking about nuclear issues apparently has been no exception to this general pattern of secretiveness, the near-impossibility of identifying who actually contributed or made relevant decisions, or the exact process and timeline involved. Nor can specific decision points be determined, and their record may well only consist of verbal exchanges rather than having been documented for posterity. All we can say is that decisionmaking on the military nuclear issue probably has not been based on plurality input—as has been the case in Iran, where different constituencies have had at times clashing positions on the issue, as was made clear during and after the nuclear negotiating process with the international community—at least not beyond a narrow circle of players within the royal family.

The death of King Abd Allah in January 2015 and the advent of his successor, Crown Prince Salman, did change the complexion of the ruling team and, to some extent, the royal governing style. In fact, King Salman's accession to the throne was accompanied by a silent palace coup of sorts, where most of the old regime's stalwarts were replaced by members of Salman's immediate family or loyal retainers. While the replacement of a previous monarch's loyalists with one's own is normal procedure, this time the traditional balance of the country's royal polyarchy may have been compromised, with an unprecedented degree of concentration of power within the King's immediate circle. That could spark political turbulence in the future, but power is likely to remain within the family. Significantly, the King's 30-year-old son, Prince Muhammad, became Minister of Defense, chairman of the Royal Court, and Special Adviser to the King and, shortly thereafter, Deputy Crown Prince. And, the new King also appointed commoners as Minister of Education, Minister of Foreign Affairs, and head of the country's General Intelligence Directorate, ordinarily the preserves of princes, thus ensuring a greater degree of control by the ruler. While royals were still well represented in the Foreign Ministry at the deputy minister level, that, too, may well change, as suggested by the public criticism in the wake of the July 2015 Nuclear Agreement with Iran of the ineffectiveness of the Foreign Ministry in influencing foreign governments, as will be seen later. In any event, one of the late King Abd Allah's sons, Prince Abd Al-Aziz, although still a deputy Minister of Foreign Affairs, had already become less prominent, and was reportedly excluded from the talks with the visiting U.S. Secretary of State John Kerry in May 2015, even though all the other Foreign Ministry officials were highlighted.[24] Moreover, in May 2015, the national petroleum company, Saudi Aramco, was removed from the Ministry of Petroleum and restructured under a new governing Supreme Council, with Prince Muhammad bin Salman as chairman, assuring greater palace control over the country's economy, as well as Prince Muhammad's direct access to a source of substantial income.[25] In addition, the country's National Security Council was dissolved, eliminating the influential Prince Bandar bin Sultan, who had been in charge of that body since its inception. This move was accompanied by the elimination of a number of other government entities and their consolidation into two new bodies: the Council of Political and Security Affairs (headed by the Minister of the Interior, Prince Muhammad bin Nayif, but also with Prince Muhammad bin Salman and seven other ministers as members), and the Council of Economics and Development Affairs (also tasked with coordinating—and controlling—several relevant ministries), with Prince Muhammad bin Salman as the latter Council's head. Observers have often suggested that the elderly king has health issues and is not the decisive and proactive leader depicted in the Saudi media, as was the case during Operation Decisive Storm against Yemen, and that his son Prince Muhammad has even greater influence than would otherwise be the case, including in all negotiations abroad with the major powers.[26] Conversely, the commander of the National Guard (which had been raised to the level of a separate ministry during the previous reign), Prince Mitib (the late king's son), has been sidelined, and it may only be a matter of time before the Guard is subordinated to the Ministry of Defense.[27]

Although the key decisionmaking personalities, and their advisers, may have changed, and while the new leadership team has engaged in greater diplomatic and military activism, the monarchy, as one would expect, has always been careful to promote an image of continuity in governance and stability, attributing that to the cohesion of the royal family. The royal family even insists that it has the same values as it had in the eighteenth century, when the first Saudi state was established.[28] Significantly, one press editorial characterized the succession process following King Abd Allah's death using the Arabic expression equivalent to "The king is dead, long live the king!"[29] When the new monarch ascended to the throne, the media continued to highlight those traditional themes, noting that Salman had already been at the center of all the previous king's decisions and that all policies were the country's policies, not those of individuals.[30] Specifically, in terms of thinking and policy on the nuclear issue, it is doubtful whether the dynastic turmoil has had any significant impact, as this issue has remained a central concern of Saudi policy, while the overall national consensus that has been forged over the years has been preserved.

The cultural facet of national security: Saudi views of Iran

Although for Saudi Arabia, as in any country, the proportion of ideology to realpolitik involved in formulating policy may well vary depending on the issue and the time, virtually anything dealing with Iran, in particular, will be marked by a disproportionate element of ideology colored by history, religion, ethnicity, and culture. As Jasper has pointed out perceptively, such internalized patterns of thought are also guides to action.[31] It is this ideological background that contributes to Saudi perceptions of an existential struggle with Iran in which the Arabs' identity and very existence are at stake and that has contributed to shaping Saudi perceptions of and prescriptions for how to deal with an environment containing a nuclear Iran. As a Saudi academic who specializes in nuclear strategy saw it, based on its Shia identity and Persian nationalism, Iran intended to dominate the Middle East and become the leader of the Islamic world. Therefore, in his view, "those who would be harmed by these 'objectives' also have the right to resist with all possible means in defense of their own existence, their interests, and their identity."[32]

In effect, Saudi Arabia's ruling elite and religious establishment display a deep-seated aversion to anything related to Iran's official Shia doctrine, not only because of theological differences but also in terms of seeing that version of Islam as a sociopolitical and philosophical threat to the very ideological foundations and legitimacy of the Saudi system.[33] This antipathy, moreover, is shared widely by all levels of Saudi society (at least among the Sunnis). The Saudi media on a daily basis—and especially when bilateral relations are poor—has depicted Iran's policies in terms of the latter's Shia doctrine, using such religious terms as "dissimulation" (*taqiya*) or "sectarian policy" (*ta'ifi*) in a derogatory manner, or purports to trace back Iran's alleged treachery and hostility to anything Arab and "genuinely" Islamic (i.e. Sunni) to the early days of Islamic history.[34] Saudi disdain for the Shia extends to the domestic Shia community, which has been traditionally maltreated, as well as to Shia communities elsewhere in the Middle East, although Saudi diatribes against Iran can be especially harsh on this score because of the additional element of interstate competition. Indeed, Saudis will also accuse Iranians of having "distorted" Islam while the Saudis propagate "genuine" Islam, and the Arabs in general are said to be "better Muslims" than the Iranians.[35] Saudis routinely also have posited an enduring "Persian personality," one only superficially overlain by Islam, and one senior Saudi military officer accused "the Safavid, recusant [*rafidi*, i.e. Shia] regime in Iran" of "giving the appearance in public of being Islamic, while in secret it is Islam's fiercest enemy."[36] A Saudi royal even accused the Shia tradition of being "deviant" and imbued with esoteric "Hermeticism, that is pagan beliefs and doctrines."[37] And, Saudis go so far as to accuse the Iranians of still being crypto-Zoroastrians (the prevailing religion in Iran before the advent of Islam), with one academic even fulminating that "The Great Satan [i.e. the United States] is gratified by the fact that the fire-worshippers are still keeping their sacred fire alive and still adhere to their beliefs, and that Islam in Tehran is only a political program and not a religion and a Lord to be worshipped."[38] Typically, when Iran released a movie in 2015 about Muhammad's life, Saudi clerics found such a portrayal on the screen to be shocking, and mounted a vigorous campaign in the media to condemn it, again often bringing up Iran's alleged Zoroastrian roots.[39]

This doctrinal component is buttressed, and aggravated, by a Saudi antipathy on an ethnic-cultural-national level, with the Saudis ready to attribute ethnicity as an auxiliary explanatory tool for Iranian policy. One commentator equated Iran's "nationalist addiction" to "one who is addicted to drugs" and stressed that Iranian policy would not change no matter who was in charge in Tehran because "it is not likely that that mentality … will change."[40] Saudis even saw treachery as a congenital feature embedded in the Iranians' genes.[41] The Saudi media routinely uses the Persian term *mellali* (national) in a pejorative sense when referring to anything Iranian or to *shuubiya*, a historical term relating to displays of hostility to anything Arab by non-Arabs.[42] Indeed, some attributed an alleged sense of Persian superiority and resulting haughtiness and aggressiveness by Iran because the latter "hates the Arabs."[43] As Saudis often put it, Iran's intent is "to destroy the Arabs," including by using "Persianized Arabs" [i.e. the Arab Shia] as subversives.[44] Shia Arabs are often termed "Iranian nationalists" in the Saudi media, and fears are expressed that Syria and Iraq will be "Persianized."[45] The Saudis regularly use the term "Safavid" in a pejorative sense to refer to the Iranians, hearkening back to the Iranian dynasty under which the Shia form of Islam became the country's official doctrine in the sixteenth century. As one senior Saudi military officer saw it, "The Safavid Persian regime's animosity toward the Arabs is an inherited enmity, one characterized by having existed from time immemorial and whose character is eternal."[46] Indeed, the editor of *Al-Riyadh* daily attributed to Iran a permanent "racism," and held that anyone who believed that co-existence between the Arabs and "Iran's Aryans" was possible "is ignorant of the historical nature of its causes whose roots go back to [Iran's] basic mentality."[47] As a result, for many Saudis, such enduring cultural characteristics as Persian nationalism and Shia doctrine predispose Iran to expansion and interference in neighboring countries, and make genuine change in Iranian policy unlikely.[48]

Iran, for its part, has often reciprocated, attributing Saudi policy to the latter's religious ideology, and specifically to what the Iranians call "Wahhabism" after the strict religious movement which has served as the ideological foundation for the Saudi state. Typically, a prominent cleric, Ahmad Khatami, declared in a sermon that "Wahhabism means barbarism and the nurturing of terrorists and killers."[49] The political adviser to the commander of Iran's Revolutionary Guards, likewise, denounced "the *jahili* [i.e. pre-Islamic] Al Saud regime."[50]

Such stereotypes serve as a fund of convenient ready-made insults to be used as the situation requires. Beyond that function, however, these stereotypes help shape Saudi paradigms and serve as an ingrained default analytical framework by which to interpret data and understand Iranian policies, thereby increasing the predisposition of most Saudis to see real or imagined threats from that quarter and to react accordingly. For the Saudi leadership, such cultural sensitivities no doubt serve as a powerful tool with which to mobilize public support against Iran and to justify hardline policies. In the case of the Saudi leadership, however, realpolitik and regime survival probably trump cultural or ideological sensitivities and, were the prospects for change in Iranian policy seen by the Saudi leadership as realistic, the latter would probably subordinate or mute such ideological considerations in the interest of foreign policy. Such an attitude should not be viewed as simply cynicism on the part of the decisionmakers so much as the latter's ability to prioritize interests, an attribute that is key for all policymakers. Even then, however, any recrudescence of political or security challenges emanating from Iran would trigger a recourse to the traditional and familiar cultural/religious/ethnic paradigms embedded just below the surface in the Saudi belief system to serve as a facile explanation of events and as a guide to further action. In the event, as long as Riyadh believes there is a threat of Iran's acquiring nuclear weapons and as long as there is a confrontation with Iran that threatens Saudi interests, more traditional realpolitik state-interests and the enduring ideological strand of Saudi concern will combine in a reinforcing pattern and contribute to greater Saudi suspicion and to a more assertive policy.

The centrality of regime legitimacy

Perhaps the key element in understanding Saudi Arabia's strategic culture from the perspective of the country's rulers is that of the essential need to maintain legitimacy both within the royal family—where competition and positioning for influence and for the future among cliques and individuals can be intense—and of the royal family in society as a whole. In Saudi Arabia's case, legitimacy depends on an aggregate collection of security, economic, religious, and symbolic elements in relation to the existing system, which is embodied in the monarchy, and intersects directly with concrete threats.

Despite the concentration of power within the royal family, the domestic political process is an interactive one to some extent, as Saudi policymakers cannot ignore the impact of their decisions on wider circles of society, even if this factor is indirect and political participation by other sectors of society is latent or passive, with such considerations acting as an implicit limiting feature that policymakers have to factor into their assumptions. Saudi society, in fact, is quite heterogeneous, and is marked by a mosaic of regional, tribal, and sectarian loyalties, and even national origins, an atomized situation that the regime has at times fostered—as in the case of the tribal sector— as a way to facilitate control and to hinder the development of cohesive societal opposition.[51] Although subordinate centers of influence—such as the clerics, the business community, bureaucrats, the tribes, journalists, academics, or the military— do exist and can play a role in certain policy areas, they are under various degrees of control by the royal family, are also fragmented, and may exert influence on specific issues indirectly, often through patrons who are members of the royal family.

The impact of the government/royal family, in any case, is extensive, not only in policy but in people's everyday lives, with only 18 percent of the country's locals, to take just one example, working in the private sector labor force, but even there the line between private and government/royal family is fuzzy, with princes functioning as businessmen and firms, in practice, often having to accept a prince as a business associate, even if only as a silent partner.[52] Opinions which the military representatives voice on policy issues in general are, if anything, even more tightly controlled than those by their civilian counterparts. At least overtly, the military remains apolitical, is not encouraged to display initiative, and is under the close control and scrutiny of the royal family, with members of the latter and its loyal retainers in key command positions and with rising princes even in the lower officer ranks, although the latter often may have more influence than their commoner superior officers. On the nuclear issue, the Saudi military does not appear to have been an actor of influence as much as a technical adviser and a booster following policy leads from above. If there has been any diversity in opinion on the nuclear issue in the broader body politic—representing factional, tribal, professional, or bureaucratic interests—it has not been evident, and there have not been any structured public debates. What one sees in public is a consensus, which may be genuine to a significant degree, the result of effective shaping by a system which controls the principal mechanisms of information and persuasion.

In order to safeguard royal legitimacy, on which this system ultimately depends, policy decisions and initiatives must take into account or at least anticipate and manipulate the latent or active demands and expectations of such sectors in society.[53] Although a public consensus is not vital in decisionmaking on key national security matters in Saudi Arabia—whether on nuclear weapons or on other similar issues—it is no doubt welcome and desirable for policymakers to have a supportive consensus or at least acquiescence, as that facilitates their task and safeguards royal legitimacy. In a way, given the absence of mechanisms to define and determine the degree of legitimacy it is a case of assumed legitimacy, a factor steeped in uncertainty that is perhaps more evident in its absence or disappearance than in its presence, and a factor which requires constant precautionary measures. Legitimacy in Saudi Arabia comprises an interconnected amalgam of elements. Characteristically, an academic identified as the foundation of "our dear King" Salman's legitimacy the continuation of all of the royal family's "political, economic, security, social, and development achievements."[54] Specifically, in the context of the nuclear issue, these requirements mean providing for the defense of the Kingdom and the region from similar threats, as this is vital for the royal family to be able to ensure a safe and secure environment, fulfill its religious obligations, and provide an expected level of economic well-being for the population.

Defense of the realm

Saudis accept traditional concepts of national defense, that is to defend the nation and its society or, as one military writer put it, Saudi Arabia's defense strategy emanates from a duty to "preserve national security and to safeguard to the utmost society and to meet challenges and threats of all types and from all sources."[55] The royal family, specifically, no doubt feels it has to be perceived by the domestic public as defending effectively the country for which the Al Saud feel proprietary responsibility. As an editorial in the Royal Saudi Land Forces' journal noted, "the top priority for the Servant of the Two Holy Shrines (Khadim Al-Haramayn) [i.e. the King] and for his faithful Crown Prince is to ensure that the nation remains secure."[56]

Domestic dissidents, such as the apparently foreign-based Hijaz regional independence movement, in fact, have used the potential for an Iranian atom bomb as a lever to criticize the Saudi government for the alleged lack of an adequate response to that threat to the country. As an anonymous writer on the Al-Hijaz website complained:

> Oh Saudis, did you feel as I did bitterness and as being duped when I heard [Iran's president Mahmoud] Ahmadinejad announce to the world that Iran had become the world's eighth nuclear power? ... I read the pride in every Iranian's eyes. I saw Ahmadinejad hold his head up high. On the contrary I, as a Saudi, was tormented by feelings of bitterness, anguish, and disappointment. I felt a lump in my throat raising the question: "What do we lack as Saudis in

order to become a nuclear power and to be proud of that in front of the world?" Why, why? … Here, as a Saudi citizen, I ask King Abd Allah "Why do we place our security, our holy places, and our very existence in the hands of others?"… We only want to be able to hold our heads up high before the world and to hear you, the Servant of the Two Holy Shrines, announce to the entire world that we have become the ninth nuclear power in the world.[57]

Questions and reproaches stemming from the nuclear threat to Saudi Arabia could even come from the country's liberal establishment, however limited the latter may be, as in the case of Abd Al-Aziz Al-Khamis, director of the Saudi Human Rights Center and a frequent critic of the regime. Seeing in Iran's quest for nuclear weapons a factor which would change the regional balance of power, Al-Khamis noted on a Yemen-based website that it "has become a duty entrusted to and thrust on the shoulders of the Saudi state to move expeditiously to also acquire nuclear weapons, in order to warn off any enemy, whether in the East or in the West."[58] Throughout the article there was a sense of implicit blame directed at the Saudi rulers for what the author interpreted as an inadequate response, as he remarked on "the indifference and slowness which impair Saudi actions to strengthen the country's military agencies," contrasting the lethargy on his side of the Gulf with the military activism on the Iranian side. In his view, Saudis now were allegedly afraid, "and are even losing their patience with the suspicious sluggishness with which the organs of the GCC, and above all Saudi Arabia, confront the destruction planned for the latter and its people." His recommendation was that "it is high time to acquire nuclear weapons and that task falls on the shoulders of Saudi Arabia, and in the shortest time possible; otherwise, one day we will lament the time when there existed an Arab Gulf and an Arabian Peninsula."[59]

What is more, the Saudi leadership must be seen to provide protection, insofar as possible, with local capabilities rather than depending on non-Muslims. Visible reliance on a non-Muslim country to defend the Saudi Holy Land could be used as a club by domestic and regional critics and at least raise questions about the regime's legitimacy and about its effectiveness in light of its massive spending on defense. Indeed, one of the stated objectives, or benefits, of Riyadh's acquisition of the CSS-2 surface-to-surface missiles (SSMs) in 1988, according to then-Minister of Defense Prince Sultan, had been that that initiative had proved that Riyadh was not a hostage to the United States in acquiring weaponry.[60] Significantly, Saudi Arabia's acceptance of a large U.S. military presence in the wake of Iraq's invasion of Kuwait in 1990 appears to have been the catalyst for Usama Bin Ladin's shift to open dissidence, and that presence on Saudi soil long remained a staple Al-Qaida propaganda theme. Accusing King Fahd (d. 2005) of having transformed the country into "an American protectorate," Bin Ladin (d. 2011) in 1995 asked himself who could be trusted to provide security: "Is it the regime which reduced the country to a state of permanent military weakness in order to permit the importation of Crusader and Jewish forces to defile the holy places?"[61] When he declared a jihad against U.S. forces in Saudi Arabia the following year, this again was a major theme, as Bin Ladin accused the Saudi rulers of having permitted "Crusader American forces" to stay in the country for years and maintained that, as a result, "people ask themselves: 'Why even have this regime?'"[62]

Admittedly, criticism by such extremist dissidents probably has limited real impact at present. However, the Al Saud may fear that such criticism potentially could come to give voice to broader feelings of dissatisfaction if they are validated by a perceived failure by the royal family to provide adequately for the country's defense. And, even if representing only a marginal slice of Saudi society, such criticism could be embarrassing to the Saudi ruling system and add pressure on decisionmakers as they deal with the nuclear issue.

Defense of the region

In addition, Saudi Arabia has a self-view as the principal Arab state with a unique mission in the Gulf and beyond, and the Saudis believe—and the royal family promotes—that their country's exceptionalism entails a natural leadership role.[63] For example, Prince Mitib, writing while he was still Deputy Commander of the SANG, argued that based on its "Arab and Islamic principles," Saudi Arabia has "historical responsibilities as a state that has political, economic, geographic, and moral prominence such as few other countries have."[64] In fact, as the Saudi media put it, Riyadh is "the center of Arab decisionmaking and the hub of the Islamic world."[65] As one Saudi journalist even claimed, Saudi Arabia is "the eastern gateway of the Arab world, defending the latter and its interests."[66]

Saudi Arabia's image as the regional leader also implies an obligation to provide for its neighbors' protection. As an editorial in a special issue of *Al-Haras Al-Watani* in honor of King Abd Allah highlighted, the Saudi monarch was seen as having broad defense responsibilities extending well beyond Saudi Arabia. According to this journal, "history had a rendezvous with a great leader ... someone whose destiny it is to defend the Kingdom, Islam, and the Arabs."[67] In such a context, an inability to do so would reflect negatively on the royal family's credibility and legitimacy. With the great diminution of the influence of Egypt, Iraq, and Syria on the Arab political horizon due to their internal turmoil, Saudi Arabia has also highlighted its own increased leadership role in defense. A Saudi military journal provided a typical overview of the official self-perception in this domain, linking the country's "leadership role in the Islamic world ... [and] its leading role in the Arab world, which stems from its being one of the largest Arab countries and having the greatest capabilities and prestige."[68] As one senior military officer saw it, Saudi Arabia "plays a pivotal and leading role in guaranteeing the security and stability of the region."[69]

Defense of the Umma

More broadly, Saudis view their country as having a special place and responsibility in the Islamic world, as was the case of a member of the Shura Council who saw the Kingdom as "the undisputed leader of the Islamic world."[70] The Saudis often remind themselves and the world that their country is:

> the Muslims' *qibla* [i.e. the geographic focus for prayer], the cradle of Islam, the bearer of the banner of Islam, and the defender of the causes of Arabness and of the Muslims in both material and moral terms in all quarters and all lands.[71]

In particular, the Saudis stress their role as the defender of the Islamic holy places. As the late King Fahd lectured Egypt's President Husni Mubarak in 1991:

> My brother, we in the Kingdom of Saudi Arabia have a special character, as is well known: God placed us in the service of Islam and the Muslims and in the service of God's holy dwelling and of Mecca and Medina, the location where the inspiration descended and the starting point of the message.[72]

According to one Saudi royal official, "The Muslims of the entire world are the concerns of the rulers and ulama' of the Kingdom of Saudi Arabia" and his country is "the spearhead of the defense of Muslim doctrine."[73] And, as King Abd Allah stressed—in a speech delivered in 2011 on behalf of the ailing monarch by the governor of Mecca, Prince Khalid Al-Faysal—"The Kingdom is faithful to its religious and historical duty ... to serve Islam ... and to proclaim and defend it in all corners of the world."[74] The Saudi military recognizes this as one of its basic missions.[75] As a well-placed Saudi military adviser remarked, it was "God's will" that the Kingdom was the structure that "supports all the Muslims ... and is the Umma's pillar."[76]

As King Salman, shortly after ascending to the throne, again reminded the participants of an international conference held in Mecca, "The Kingdom of Saudi Arabia considers as its greatest responsibility the security of God's abode [i.e. Mecca] and the site of the exile of God's prophet [i.e. Medina]."[77] In effect, the Saudi monarch is the personal self-proclaimed defender of Islam, with an earlier monarch, King Fahd, having adopted the title of Servant of the Two Holy Shrines, while the Saudi regime has long relied on the support of the domestic religious establishment for the political system. At the heart of this symbiotic relationship, the Saudi religious establishment is quick to highlight the Al Saud family's personal religious legitimacy and responsibilities. Typically, a member of the country's Council of Senior Ulama' remarked, "This blessed state, the state of the Al Saud, is a state of orthodoxy (*tawhid*), religious outreach (*dawa*), and rule by the undefiled religious law (*sharia*) ... and was established by a religious covenant (*baya shariya*)."[78] Indicative of the centrality of this facet of legitimacy was the fierce Saudi defense of the country's—and of the royal family's—ability and exclusive right to administer the Pilgrimage in response to foreign criticism after the collapse of a construction crane and a stampede during the 2015 Pilgrimage that had caused perhaps thousands of deaths.[79]

As such, the royal family must also be seen as an effective protector against all threats to Islam, and specifically to the Holy Shrines, whether from Israel or Shia Iran—which many in the Saudi religious establishment view as existential threats to Sunni Islam, doubly dangerous in the case of the latter because of its rival claim to religious legitimacy. Not coincidentally, an article in the Saudi press that dealt with the Iranian threat pointedly referred to King Abd Allah as "the Umma's shepherd" (*rai*).[80] Significantly, the religious aspect, often intertwined with the defense of Saudi territory, can act as both a stimulant and a justification for major arms acquisitions. For example, this linkage was invoked in 1990 to justify Saudi Arabia's recently-purchased SSMs, as Prince Sultan associated their acquisition to:

> the interrelated objectives of the defense and security of [Saudi Arabia's] holy places and of the just causes of the Arab and Islamic Umma, which constitute complementary facets ... these requirements are then translated into the selection of the types of weapons that correspond to those facets.[81]

Likewise, as King Fahd explained at the time, "it is not strange at all if the Kingdom of Saudi Arabia buys defensive weapons in order to protect its religion and its country. That is the reason why the Kingdom of Saudi Arabia knocks on the doors of countries of the world in one manner or another, so that it can benefit from the type of advanced weaponry that has an impact and value."[82] Again, he highlighted the same facet of legitimacy, alluding to the right "to exercise our sovereignty on our own territory and to defend the nation and the holy places for all Muslims."[83] Since Saudi Arabia was the location of Mecca and Medina, resulting in the concomitant need to protect millions of pilgrims, as well as being the leader of the Islamic world, a Saudi columnist, typically, asked rhetorically "Is this not enough justification for Saudi Arabia to acquire whatever weapons," concluding that, since many countries already had nuclear weapons then "Saudi Arabia is even more deserving of the same weapon."[84]

Defense of the economic pillar of legitimacy

In many ways, the economic pillar of the Al Saud's legitimacy is also tied to the defense of the realm from foreign threats and, in particular, from Iran, as will be discussed later. To a significant extent, the royal family has identified economic development with itself and the line between private royal wealth and that of the state is often blurred. The legitimacy of the existing system, one can argue, relies on an implicit social contract with the population to share the oil and gas wealth which the royal family controls, while the royal family claims the credit, and therefore also the responsibility, for the people's economic well-being. The media constantly reminds audiences that it is "the heroic leaders" who have created "abundance," as did the military media on the country's National Day.[85] Another typical article in the military media concluded that:

> Saudi citizens are very much aware of the achievements which are being attained day after day in every aspect of their lives; the enlightened leadership has devoted all its efforts and time and has mobilized all of the country's potential and wealth in order to raise the standard of living of Saudi citizens.[86]

As a leading Saudi businessman also waxed eloquently of the relationship between the country's rulers and society:

> there is no doubt that our dear Kingdom's path of development is witness to the natural result of one of the wonderful illustrations of the cohesion between ruler and ruled … the leadership … has never wavered in its zeal to stand by its sons, the citizens, and to fulfill their desires and needs to ensure a life of plenty and of dignity.[87]

On the country's National Day, King Salman's son, Prince Sultan, likewise, reminded his audience that it was "this noble state" (or dynasty—*dawla*) that not only unified the country but also "made it possible for society to strut its peace, security, and wealth" (*al-thara'*).[88]

Although significant socio-economic problems—including unemployment, corruption, and high prices for food, housing, medical care, and weddings—have at times frayed this unspoken, but nevertheless real, social compact, enough of the population still share in the benefits to ensure stability for now. However, sufficient national income is vital for the system to remain viable, especially given rising expectations and a burgeoning population. The Saudi rulers have been particularly sensitive to this facet of their legitimacy in the atmosphere of the popular unrest throughout the region in connection with the Arab Spring, as they succeeded in staving off discontent at home—in part at least—by being able to open the country's ample coffers for large-scale salary raises, bonuses, an economic stimulus to business, and various other material incentives, while a more recent decline in oil income has reduced such financial flexibility. Over the longer term, such legitimacy will also hinge on the success of the country's ambitious economic development plans for a post-oil era, which will also depend on a secure national and regional environment.

Notes

1 Alastair Iain Johnston, "Thinking about Strategic Culture," *International Security*, xix, 4, Spring 1995, 34.
2 Michael C. Desch, "Culture Clash: Assessing the Importance of Ideas in Security Studies," *International Security*, xxiii, 1, Summer 1998, 141–70; also see Susan C. Schneider and Arnoud de Meyer, "Interpreting and Responding to Strategic Issues: The Impact of National Culture," *Strategic Management Journal*, xii, 4, May, 1991, 307–320, and Jeffrey S. Lantis, "Strategic Culture and National Security Policy," *International Studies Review*, iv, 3, Autumn 2002, 87–113.
3 "Preconceptions cannot be abolished; it is in one sense just another word for 'model' or 'paradigm'—a construct used to simplify reality, which any thinker needs in order to

cope with complexity." "Analysis, War, and Decisions: Why Intelligence Failures Are Inevitable," *World Politics*, xxxi, October 1978, 83–84. Such paradigms correspond to Jasper's terms "set of beliefs or narrative," which she deems significant, as "it limits and facilitates a specific course of action." *The Politics of Non-Proliferation*, 26–27.
4 Robert Jervis, *Perception and Misperception in International Politics* (Princeton, NJ: Princeton University Press, 1976), 412.
5 Muhammad bin Abd Al-Latif Al Al-Shaykh, "Kayf yusna al-qarar al-siyasi fi Al-Saudiya?" [How Are Political Decisions Made in Saudi Arabia?], *Al-Sharq Al-Awsat*, 18 April 2005, www.aawsat.com/print.asp?did=294244&issueno=9638. His term for realpolitik was "interest."
6 Robert Dahl, *Polyarchy: Participation and Opposition* (New Haven, CT: Yale University Press, 1971).
7 Indicative of the porous line between private and state, the Minister of Defense and Deputy Crown Prince, Prince Muhammad bin Salman, in 2015 donated 50 million Riyals ($13.3 million) of his own money to the armed forces' welfare fund, "'Khilafat Al-Ghazi' yamnah al-itminan li-usar al-mudafiin an al-watan" [The "Holy Warrior's Caliphate" Provides Peace of Mind to the Families of the Nation's Defenders], *Al-Madina*, 17 July 2015, www.al-madina.com/printhtml/619355.
8 "Khadim al-haramayn yar'as jalsat majlis al-wuzara' wa-yuqirr akbar mizaniya fi tarikh Al-Mamlaka" [The Servant of the Two Holy Shrines Chairs a Meeting of the Council of Ministers and Unveils the Largest Budget in the Kingdom's History], *Al-Riyadh*, 30 December 2012, www.al-riyadh.com/2012/12/30/article797098.html.
9 "Shifa' al-malik shifa' al-watan," *Al-Madina*, 29 November 2012, www.al-madina.com/node/416893.
10 Khalaf Al-Hashar, "Yawm al-watan al-80 am wa-Al Saud" [The National Day, Year 80, and the Al Saud], *Ha'il* (Ha'il), 21 January 2013, www.hailnews.net/hail/article-action-show-id-2284.htm.
11 Interview with Prince Mansur bin Nasir by Ali Al-Maqbali, "Mustashar khadim al-haramayn al-sharifayn al-amir Mansur bin Nasir: Hadha ma taallumtuh fi madrasat al-malik" [The Adviser to the Servant of the Two Noble Holy Places Prince Mansur bin Nasir: This Is What I Have Learned from the King's School], *Al-Rajul* (Riyadh), 27 November 2014, www.arrajol.com.
12 "Kayf yufakkir Al Saud" [How the Al Saud Think], Najran Land website, 15 April 2003, http://najranland.8m.com/book.htm. Also see Jeff Gerth, "Saudi Stability Hit by Heavy Spending over Last Decade," *New York Times*, 22 August 1993, www.nytimes.com/1993/08/22/world/saudi-stability-hit-by-heavy-spending-over-last-decade.html?pagewanted=3&pagewanted=print. Most frequently, such criticism is found as anecdotes in blogs, as when a prince, in a dispute with one of the tribes, was allegedly to have said "They have forgotten that this land and everything on it is our property," Al-Shabaka Al-Libaraliya Al-Hurra forum, 1 April 2011, https://libral.org/vb/showthread.php?t=62895&page=3. In practical terms, individual members of the royal family do own enormous swathes of the country's land area.
13 Prince Salman's speech reported in "Al-Amir Salman: La tujad usra aw qabila fi hadhihi al-bilad illa wa-li-aba'iha aw ajdadha musharaka faila fi tawhid al-watan" [Prince Salman: There Is Not a Single Family Or Tribe in This Country Whose Fathers or Grandfathers Did Not Make a Direct Contribution to the Nation's Unification], *Al-Marsad*, 31 March 2011, www.al-marsd.com.
14 Brigadier General Salih bin Ibrahim Al-Tasan, "Fi dhikra yawmna al-watani" [Celebrating Our National Day], *Al-Difa* (Riyadh), September 2011, 55. *Al-Difa* is the official journal of the Ministry of Defense (hereafter Al-Tasan, "Fi dhikra").
15 "Talaqqi tahani al-umara' wa'l-ulama' wa-kibar al-mas'ulin wa-jam min al-muwatinin" [Receiving Congratulations from the Governors, Ulama', Senior Officials, and a Group of Citizens], *Al-Nadwa* (Mecca), 16 August 2012, www.alnadwah.com.sa (hereafter "Talaqqi tahani al-umara'").

16 Abd Allah Al-Dawsi reporting the latter's speech, "Khalid Al-Faysal: Amalt wa-asart mulukan mundh ahd al-malik Abd Al-Aziz hatta al-malik Abd Allah" [Khalid Al-Faysal: I Worked with and Was a Contemporary of Kings from the Time of King Abd Al-Aziz to That of King Abd Allah], *Al-Nadwa*, 28 February 2012, www.alnadwah.com.sa.
17 "Talaqqi tahani al-umara'."
18 Turki Abd Allah Al-Sudayri, "Ma al-amir Salman fi haqa'iq tarikh" [With Prince Salman on Historical Facts], *Al-Riyadh*, 6 February 2012, www.alriyadh.com/2012/02/06/article707389.html.
19 Mirza Al-Khuwaylidi, "Khalid Al-Faysal yadu al-muthaqqafin 'li-izalat al-dabab' khilal faaliyat suq Ukaz" [Khalid Al-Faysal Calls on the Intellectuals to "Clear Away the Fog" during the Ukaz Market Ceremonies], *Al-Sharq Al-Awsat*, 13 August 2015, http://aawsat.com/node/428986.
20 Sulayman bin Abd Allah Aba Al-Khayl, "Al-Awamir al-malakiya: Hikmat al-qa'id min qa'id al-hikma fi tarsikh al-qiyada wa-istishraf al-mustaqbal wa-ikhtiyar al-akfa' wa'l-afdal" [The Royal Commands: The Leader's Wisdom from Wisdom's Leader in Embedding the Leadership and Forecasting the Future and Selecting What Is Most Useful and Best], *Al-Jazira*, 4 May 2015, www.al-jazirah.com/2015/20150504/av8.htm.
21 Zaynab Abu Talib, "Iran wa-tasdir thawrat al-qalaqil" [Iran and the Export of the Revolution of Disorders], *Al-Jazira*, 3 June 2015, www.al-jazirah.com/2015/20150603/fe4.htm.
22 Muhammad Khidr Arif, "Mamlaka la ka'l-mamalik" [A Kingdom Like No Other], *Al-Madina*, 10 June 2015, www.al-madina.com/printhtml/612528.
23 Ahmad Al-Jamia, "Bayt Al Saud min al-dakhil takwin istithna'i hubb wa-wafa' wa-taqdir" [The Al Saud from the Inside: A Unique Structure, Love, Loyalty, and Respect], *Al-Riyadh*, 26 October 2011, www.alriyadh.com/2011/10/26/article678858.html.
24 "Al-Amir Abd Al-Aziz bin Abd Allah yaghib kulliyan an mubahathat Kerry wa'l-Jubayr fa-hal istaqal aw ufiya min mansibih ka-na'ib li-wazir al-kharijiya?" [Prince Abd Al-Aziz bin Abd Allah Was Completely Absent from the Talks between Kerry and Al-Jubeir; Did He Resign or Was He Fired from His Post as Deputy Foreign Minister?], *Ra'y Al-Yawm* (London), 7 May 2015, www.raialyoum.com/?p=254232.
25 Simeon Kerr, Anjli Raval, and David Sheppard, "Saudi Prince Sees Power Grow in Oil Restructuring," *Financial Times*, 1 May 2015, www.ft.com/cms/s/0/d3b1af6c-f014-11e4-aee0-00144feab7de.html.
26 For example, Christi Parsons and Kathleen Hennessey, "Obama, Senior Delegation Meet with Saudi Arabia's King Salman," *Los Angeles Times*, 27 January 2015, www.latimes.com/world/middleeast/la-fg-obama-saudi-king-20150127-story.html, Krishnadev Calamur, "Who Is the New Saudi King?" *NPR*, 23 January 2015, www.npr.org/sections/thetwo-way/2015/01/23/379362258/who-is-the-new-saudi-king, and Justin Fox, "Running the Saudi Family Business," *Bloomberg View*, 11 February 2015, www.bloombergview.com/articles/2015-01-23/king-salman-leads-saudi-arabia-oil-kingdom-family-business.
27 Bruce Riedel, "What's Ahead for Saudi Arabia?" *Al-Monitor* (Washington, DC), 9 June 2015, www.al-monitor.com/pulse/originals/2015/06/saud-arabia-monarchy.html#.
28 Ahmad Muhammad Al-Tawyan, "Dawlat Abd Al-Aziz fi ahd Salman" [Abd Al-Aziz's State in Salman's Reign], *Al-Jazira*, 7 May 2015, www.al-jazirah.com/2015/20150507/ar3.htm.
29 Makarim Subhi Batarji, "Al-Watan fi aydin amina" [The Nation Is in Safe Hands], *Ukaz*, 6 February 2015, www.okaz.co/bwH9udjEs.
30 Yusuf bin Muhammad Al-Atiq, "Tamasuk bayt al-hukm al-saudi; ind al-mu'arrikhin al-sirr" [The Ruling Family's Cohesion; The Historians Have the Secret], *Al-Jazira*, 10 May 2015, www.al-jazirah.com/2015/20150510/wo3.htm, Ahmad Al-Farraj, "Muluk Al Saud ... wa'l-intihaziyun!" [The Al Saud Monarchs ... and the Opportunists!], *Al-Jazira*, 4 May 2015, www.al-jazirah.com/2015/20150505/ln19.htm, and Ali bin Hamad Al-Khashiban, "Mu'assasat al-hukm fi al-mamlaka" [The Ruling System in the Kingdom], *Al-Riyadh*, 4 May 2015, www.alriyadh.com/1045091.

31 "Action … takes place largely on the basis of internalized rules of behavioral patterns. Culture and traditions, for example, provide stable webs of meaning that actors can draw upon in their day-to-day routines and dealings." Ursula Jasper, *The Politics of Nuclear Non-Proliferation: A Pragmatist Framework for Analysis*, 33.
32 Sadaqa Yahya Fadil, "Madha turid Iran al-khumayniya?" [What Does Khomeini's Iran Want?], *Ukaz*, 23 August 2015, http://okaz.co/bwljrdt3v.
33 One Iraqi Shia cleric, in fact, was miffed that numerous blatantly anti-Shia dissertations were accepted at Saudi institutes of higher learning, "Al-Qubanchi: *Al-Sayf al-batir fi qat riqab al-shia al-kawafir* huwa unwan risalat majistayr fi Al-Saudiya" [Al-Qubanchi: *The Sharp Sword for the Cutting Off the Heads of the Infidel Shia* Is the Title of an M.A. Thesis in Saudi Arabia], *Khabar* (Baghdad), 3 July 2015, www.khabaar.net/index.php/permalink/48676.html.
34 For example, imputing *taqiya* to Iran's dissimulation during negotiations, Imad Ahmad Al-Alim, "Al-Gharb wa'l-ittifaq ma Iran" [The West and the Agreement with Iran], *Al-Jazira*, 12 January 2015, www.al-jazirah.com/2015/20150112/rj11.htm, and, likewise, seemingly more moderate Iranian clerics are accused of merely practicing *taqiya*, Muhammad Al Al-Shaykh, "Li'l-ra'is Obama an Iran aqul" [I Am Telling President Obama about Iran], *Al-Jazira*, 2 June 2015, www.al-jazirah.com/2015/20150602/lp7.htm.
35 Major General Salama bin Hadhdhal Bin Saidan (Ret.), "Al-Alaqa ma Iran wa-hatmiyat al-muwajaha" [The Relationship with Iran and the Inevitability of a Confrontation], part 2, *Al-Jazira*, 15 May 2015, www.al-jazirah.com/2015/20150515/ar8.htm (hereafter Bin Saidan, "Al-Alaqa," part 2), and Said Al-Farha Al-Ghamdi, "Iran bad ittifaqiyat al-itar ma 5+1" [Iran after the 5+1 Framework Agreement], *Al-Madina*, 6 April 2015, www.al-madina.com/printhtml/599150.
36 Major General Salama bin Hadhdhal Bin Saidan (Ret.), "Al-Alaqa ma Iran wa-hatmiyat al-muwajaha" [The Relationship with Iran and the Inevitability of a Confrontation], part 1, *Al-Jazira*, 14 May 2015, www.al-jazirah.com/2015/20150514/ar10.htm.
37 Prince Faysal bin Mishal bin Saud bin Abd Al-Aziz, "Al-Abad al-tarikhiya li'l-ida' ala al-salafiya" [The Historical Dimensions of Hostility to the Salafiya], *Al-Jazira*, 10 September 2015, www.al-jazirah.com/2015/20150910/ar9.htm. He is the governor of Al-Qasim province.
38 Mutlaq bin Saud Al-Mtiri, "Al-Shaytan al-akbar wa-ibadat al-nar" [The Great Satan and Fire-Worship], *Al-Riyadh*, 14 March 2015, www.alriyadh.com/1029795.
39 For example, Ahmad Ghallab, "Mufti Al-Saudiya li'l-*Hayat*: Film *Muhammad* al-irani majusi fajir" [Saudi Arabia's Mufti to *Al-Hayat*: The Iranian Movie *Muhammad* Is Brazenly Zoroastrian], *Al-Hayat* (Saudi edition), 2 September 2015, http://alhayat.com/Articles/10927800.
40 Saud Katib, "Madha sa-tafal Iran al-an?" [What Will Iran Do Next?], *Al-Madina*, 8 April 2015, www.al-madina.com/printhtml/599551.
41 Jasir Abd Al-Aziz Al-Jasir, "Al-Tarikh sa-yadhkur muwajahat al-hazm li-jinat al-ghadar" [History Will Remember Operation Decisive Storm's Resistance to the Genes of Betrayal], *Al-Jazira*, 21 July 2015, www.al-jazirah.com.sa/2015/20150721/du16.htm.
42 Bin Saidan, "Al-Alaqa," part 2, and Fayiz bin Abd Allah Al-Shihri, "Ta'ammulat fi al-shakhsiya al-farisiya" [Reflections on the Persian Personality], *Al-Riyadh*, 13 April 2015, www.alriyadh.com/1038725 (hereafter Al-Shihri "Ta'ammulat"). The term *shu'ubiya* refers to the reaction, beginning in the ninth century, on the part of non-Arab Muslims—particularly the Persians—to Arab cultural and political hegemony, Jafar Jamshidian Tehrani, *Shu'ubiyya: Independence Movements in Iran* (n.p.: CreateSpace Self-published, 2014).
43 Al-Shihri "Ta'ammulat".
44 Muhammad Abd Allah Al-Uwayn, "Al-Mukhattat al-irani al-la'im didd al-arab!" [The Reprehensible Iranian Plot against the Arabs!], *Al-Jazira*, 13 April 2015, www.al-jazirah.com/2015/20150413/ln30.htm, and Muhammad Al Al-Shaykh, "Muzayadat al-arab adhnab al-furs" [Raising the Bidding by the Arabs Who Are the Persians' Accessories], *Al-Jazira*, 5 April 2015, www.al-jazirah.com/2015/20150405/lp7.htm.

45 Yusuf Al-Kuwaylit, "Furs wa-arab fi sira al-huwiyat al-qawmiya!" [Persians and Arabs Engaged in a Struggle of National Identities!], *Al-Riyadh*, 1 March 2015, www.alriyadh.com/1025918.
46 Major General Salama bin Hadhdhal Bin Saidan (Ret.), "Tabadul al-istiqrar ma Iran bayn ida'ha al-mawruth wa-ahdiha al-mankuth" [Mutual Stability with Iran in Light of Its Historical Enmity and Its Broken Promises], *Al-Jazira*, part 1, 29 May 2015, www.al-jazirah.com/sa/2015/20150529/ar3.htm.
47 Yusuf Al-Kuwaylit, "Ma Amrika sadaqat am imla'at?" [Genuine Friendship Or Superficiality with America?], *Al-Riyadh*, 7 December 2014, www.alriyadh.com/1001037.
48 For example, Ali Al-Khashiban, "Iran al-raghiba fi qatl ada'iha wa-taghryir al-alam hawlaha" [The Iran That Wants to Kill Its Enemies and Change the World Around It], *Al-Riyadh*, 14 April 2014, www.alriyadh.com/926797.
49 "Khatib jumat Tihran: Inn al-wahhabiya tani al-wihshiya" [The Friday Preacher of Tehran: Wahhabism Means Barbarism], *Tabnak* (Tehran), 7 November 2014, www.tabnak.ir/ar/print/22854.
50 "Mustashar qa'id al-haras al-thawri: Nizham Al Saud al-jahili yafham lughat al-tahdid afdal min al-lugha al-diblumasiya" [The Adviser to the Commander of Iran's Revolutionary Guards: The Jahili Al Saud Regime Understands the Language of Threats Better Than It Does the Language of Diplomacy], Tasnim Agency (Tehran), 1 October 2015, www.tasnimnews.com/arabic/Home?Single/876562.
51 See Norman Cigar, "Tribes, Society and the State in Saudi Arabia: Change and Continuity and the Implications for Security and Stability," *The Maghreb Review*, xxxvi, 3–4, 2011, 211–263.
52 See for example Steffen Hertog, *Princes, Brokers, and Bureaucrats: Oil and the State in Saudi Arabia* (Ithaca, NY: Cornell University Press, 2011), 3–4, 21–22, and Tim Niblock and Monica Malik, *The Political Economy of Saudi Arabia* (Abingdon: Routledge, 2007), 152–53. On the 18 percent figure, *EY: Growth Drivers: Understanding the Opportunities and Challenges for Businesses in the GCC* (McLean, VA: Ernst & Young, 2014), 7.
53 For perceptive overviews of the Saudi political system, see Tim Niblock, *Saudi Arabia: Power, Legitimacy and Survival* (London and New York: Routledge, 2006), 1–18, and Bertelsmann Stiftung, *BTI 2012 Saudi Arabia Country Report* (Gütersloh, Germany: Bertelsmann Stiftung, 2012), www.bti-project.org/fileadmin/Inhalte/reports/2012/pdf/BTI%202012%20Saudi%20Arabia.pdf.
54 Muhsin Al-Shaykh Al Hassan, "Fi ahd al-malik Salman azm wa-hazm wa-istiqrar" [In the Reign of King Salman: Decisiveness, Resolve, and Stability], *Al-Jazira*, 27 September 2015, www.al-jazirah.com/2015/20150927/ym6.htm.
55 Prince Staff Major Muhammad bin Abd Al-Aziz bin Muhammad Al Saud, "Asifat al-hazm min manzhur al-istratijia al-difaiya li'l-mamlaka" [Operation Decisive Storm as Seen from the Perspective of the Kingdom's Defense Strategy], *Al-Riyadh*, 14 April 2015, www.alriyadh.com/1039041.
56 "Al-Ru'ya al-istratijiya li'l-qiyada al-saudiya nahw watan amin wa-Khalij mustaqirr" [The Saudi Leadership's Strategic View of a Secure Country and a Stable Gulf], *Al-Barriya* (Riyadh), 27 October 2010, http://RSLF.GOV.SA/English/AlBarriyaMagazine/ArticleSharingDocs/368110ef-abc2-a309-338e212fc9ff.doc. *Al-Barriya* is the official journal of the Royal Saudi Land Forces.
57 Nawawiyun saudiyun [Saudi Nuclear Guys], "Marra ukhra ma al-qunbula al-nawawiya al-saudiya wa-lakin bi-shakl mukhtalif" [Once Again on the Saudi Atom Bomb But This Time in a Different Way], *Al-Hijaz* (London?), www.alhejazi.net/seyasah/014206.htm.
58 Abd Al-Aziz Al-Khamis, "Han waqt al-silah al-nawawi al-saudi" [The Time Has Come for a Saudi Nuclear Weapon], *Ibda* (Sanaa), 23 February 2012, http://ebdaa.com/?act=artc&id=5577&print=1.
59 Ibid.
60 Interview with Prince Sultan by Muhammad Abd Al-Mawla and Muhammad Ghabris, "Hadith wazir al-difa al-saudi ila *Al-Sayyad*" [Interview with the Saudi Minister of Defense to *Al-Sayyad*], *Al-Sayyad* (Beirut), 29 April 1988, 35.

61 Usama Bin Ladin, "Khitab ila Abi Raghal, Fahd bin Abd Al-Aziz Al Saud" [Letter to Abu Raghal, Fahd bin Abd Al-Aziz Al Saud], 5 Rabi I 1416/3 August 1995, Minbar Al-Tawhid Wa'l-Jihad website, www.tawhed.ws/r?i=oxyobqbh. Abu Raghal had served the invading the Ethiopians as a guide on their way to attack Mecca in the pre-Islamic period, and is viewed in Arab culture as the archetypical traitor.
62 Usama Bin Ladin, "Ilan al-jihad ala al-amrikan al-muhtallin li-Bilad Al-Haramayn" [Declaration of the Jihad Against the Americans Occupying the Land of the Two Holy Shrines], 1 Rabi II 1416/15 August 1996, Minbar Al-Tawhid Wa'l-Jihad website, www.tawhed.ws/r?i=1502092b.
63 Badr Al-Amir, "Al-Saudiya fi tawrha al-jadid" [Saudi Arabia in Its New Role], Al-Watan, 20 April 2015, www.alwatan.com.sa/Articles/Detail.aspx?ArticleID=25960.
64 Prince Mitib bin Abd Allah, "Al-Dawr al-saudi wa-thabat muntalaqatih" [The Saudi Role and the Firmness of Its Principles], Majallat Kulliyat Al-Malik Khalid Al-Askariya (Riyadh), 1 November 2010, www.kkmaq.gov.sa/detail.asp?InNewsItemID=371633&InTemplateKey=print. Majallat Kulliyat Al-Malik Khalid Al-Askariya is the official journal of the Saudi National Guard's military academy.
65 Jasir Al-Jasir, "Al-Saudiya min dun ritush" [Saudi Arabia as It Is], Al-Hayat, 18 February 2015, http://alhayat.com/Opinion/Jasser-AlJasser/7487551.
66 Muhammad Al-Said, "Al-Riyadh al-bawwaba al-sharqiya li'l-alam al-arabi" [Riyadh Is the Eastern Gateway of the Arab World], Al-Hayat (Saudi edition), 2 October 2015, www.al-hayat.com/Opinion/Mohammed-Al-Saed/11405291.
67 The Editor, "Mawid ma al-tarikh: 7 sanawat hafila bi'l-injaz wa'l-ijaz" [Rendezvous with History: Seven Years Jam-packed with Success and with What Is Unrivalled], Al-Haras Al-Watani (Riyadh), Rajab 1433/June 2012, 22. Al-Haras Al-Watani is the Saudi National Guard's official journal.
68 Abd Al-Azhim Mahmud Hanafi, "Al-Dawr al-qiyadi li'l-Mamlaka taht qiyadat khadim al-haramayn al-sharifayn" [The Kingdom's Leading Role under the Leadership of the Servant of the Two Holy Shrines], Majallat Kulliyat Al-Malik Khalid Al-Askariya, 21 June 2011, www.kkmaq.gov.sa/detail.ap?InNewsItemID=393304&InTemplateKey=print.
69 Staff Brigadier General Zhafir bin Ali Al-Shihri, "Istratijiyat Al-Mamlaka li-muwajahat al-mutaghayyirat al-duwaliya wa'l-iqlimiya li-tahqiq al-amn al-watani" [The Kingdom's Strategy to Deal with International and Regional Changes in Order to Achieve National Security], Al-Difa, January 2007, 65.
70 Zaynab Abu Talib, "Iran wa-tasdir thawrat al-qalaqil" [Iran and the Export of the Revolution of Disorders], Al-Jazira, 3 June 2015, www.al-jazirah.com/2015/20150603/fe4.htm.
71 Hamad bin Abd Allah Al-Luhaydan, "Majlis al-taawun al-khaliji yathbut faaliyathu" [The Gulf Cooperation Council Confirms Its Effectiveness], Al-Riyadh, 13 May 2011, www.alriyadh.com/2011/05/13/article632204.html, and Farraj Al-Aqla, "Al-Quwwa al-istiratijiya li-mashru al-tadamun al-islami" [The Strategy Power of the Plan for Islamic Solidarity], Al-Riyadh, 17 April 2015, www.alriyadh.com/1040047.
72 King Fahd quoted in press conference, Al-Riyadh, 31 January 1991, 2.
73 Prince Faysal bin Mishal bin Saud bin Abd Al-Aziz, "Al-Abad al-tarikhiya li'l-ida' ala al-salafiya" [The Historical Dimensions of Hostility to the Salafiya], Al-Jazira, 10 September 2015, www.al-jazirah.com/2015/20150910/ar9.htm. After a career in the Ministry of Defense, Prince Faysal is now governor of Al-Qasim province.
74 Reported by Wa'il Al-Lahibi and Khalid Abd Allah, "Fi kalima alqaha niyabatan anhu amir Makka Al-Mukarrama khilal mu'tamar al-dawa al-islamiya 'Al-Hadir wa'l-mustaqbal'" [In A Speech Delivered for Him by the Governor of Mecca the Venerable During the Conference on Islamic Outreach "Present and Future"], Al-Riyadh, 1 November 2011, www.alriyadh.com/2011/11/01/article680041.html.
75 See, for example, Al-Jadii, "Idad al-istiratijiya."
76 Staff Major General Anwar Ishqi (Ret.), "Al-Jamia tastadif muhadara" [The University Hosts a Lecture], King Faisal University website, 27 February 2015, www.kfu.edu.sa.

77 "Al-Malik Salman: Al-Mamlaka mas'uliyatha al-kubra al-muhafazha ala bayt Allah wa-mahjar rasul Allah wa-amn al-hujjaj wa'l-mutamirin wa'l-zuwwar" [King Salman: The Kingdom's Greatest Responsibility Is Security for God's Abode and the Exile Site of God's Prophet, and for the Safety of Those Performing the Hajj and the Umra, and Visitors], *Al-Jazira*, 27 February 2015, www.al-jazirah.com/2015/20150227/ln67.htm.
78 Shaykh Salih bin Fawzan Al-Fawzan, "Hadhihi al-bilad wa-hadhihi al-dawla al-saudiya" [This Country and this Saudi State], *Al-Riyadh*, 27 March 2013, www.alriyadh.com/2013/03/27/article820830.html.
79 Although officially the government announced over 700 deaths, the Deputy Minister of Health acknowledged that over 4,000 had died, whereupon the Ministry of Health website was promptly shut down, but not before it was cached, "Na'ib wazir al-sihha: Irtifa adad wafiyat al-tadafu fi Mina ila 4173 shakhsan" [The Deputy Minister: The Number of Deaths from the Stampede at Mina Rises to 4,173], Ministry of Health website, 29 September 2015, http://webcache.googleusercontent.com/search?q=cache:LachvJcmuesJ:press.moh.gov.sa/showdetails.asp%3Fartid%3D149170%26artype%3D1+&cd=4&hl=en&ct=clnk&gl=us.
80 Salih bin Hammud Al-Qaran, "Iran wa-qad takashshafat nawayaha al-adaniya" [Iran's Aggressive Intentions Finally Revealed], *Al-Jazira*, 9 September 2011, www.al-jazirah.com.sa/20111109/rj4.htm.
81 Interview with Prince Sultan, "Al-Alam al-arabi yamurr bi-marhala harija" [The Arab World Is Going through a Sensitive Period], *Al-Hawadith* (Beirut), 27 April 1990, 18 (hereafter Prince Sultan, "Al-Alam al-arabi").
82 Interview with King Fahd, "Khadim al-haramayn yaltaqi bi-mansubi wa-talabat far jamiat Al-Imam Saud al-islamiya bi'l-Qasim" [The Servant of the Two Holy Shrines Meets with the Staff and Students of the Branch of the Imam Saud Islamic University in Al-Qasim], *Ukaz*, 9 April 1988, 7.
83 Quoted in "Mustaiddun li-muwajahat ayy tari' lan nasmah bi-ayy tadakhkhul fi shu'unna" [We Are Prepared to Confront Any Contingency and We Will Not Permit Any Interference in Our Affairs], *Ukaz*, 29 March 1988, 3.
84 Salih Matar Al-Ghamdi, "Al-Saudiya awla bi'l-silah al-nawawi!" [Saudi Arabia Is More Deserving of Nuclear Weapons!], *Sabq* (Riyadh), 6 November 2013, http://sabq.org/js1aCd.
85 Al-Tasan, "Fi dhikra," 55.
86 Staff Lieutenant General Husayn bin Abd Allah Al-Qabil, "Ajmal ibarat al-thana' li-qiyadatna al-hakima" [The Highest Praise for Our Wise Leaders], *Al-Difa*, May 2011, 12.
87 Fahd Al-Dalani, "Al-Rajul al-mukhlis al-ladhi nadhar nafsah li-khidmat dinih wa-watanih" [The Righteous Man Who Has Devoted Himself to His Religion and Nation], *Al-Riyadh*, 15 January 2007, www.alriyadh.com/2007/01/15/article216480.html.
88 "Sultan bin Salman: Al-Saudiyun wazhzhafu al-naft li-bina' al-insan wa-tanmiyat al-makan wa-ghars al-muwatana qadiya asasiya" [Sultan bin Salman: The Saudis Used Oil to Develop the People and the Country and Instilling Patriotism Is a Fundamental Task], *Al-Riyadh*, 14 October 2015, www.alriyadh.com/1090998.

Bibliography

Bertelsmann Stiftung, *BTI 2012 Saudi Arabia Country Report* (Gütersloh, Germany: Bertelsmann Stiftung, 2012), available at: www.bti-project.org/fileadmin/Inhalte/reports/2012/pdf/BTI%202012%20Saudi%20Arabia.pdf.
Betts, Richard K., "Analysis, War, and Decisions: Why Intelligence Failures Are Inevitable," *World Politics*, xxxi, October 1978, 61–89.
Cigar, Norman, "Tribes, Society and the State in Saudi Arabia: Change and Continuity and the Implications for Security and Stability," *The Maghreb Review*, xxxvi, 3–4, 2011, 211–263.

Dahl, Robert, *Polyarchy: Participation and Opposition* (New Haven, CT: Yale University Press, 1971).
Desch, Michael C., "Culture Clash: Assessing the Importance of Ideas in Security Studies," *International Security*, xxiii, 1, Summer 1998, 141–170.
Hertog, Steffen, *Princes, Brokers, and Bureaucrats: Oil and the State in Saudi Arabia*, (Ithaca, NY: Cornell University Press, 2011).
Jasper, Ursula, *The Politics of Nuclear Non-Proliferation: A Pragmatist Framework for Analysis* (Abingdon: Routledge, 2015).
Johnston, Alastair Iain, "Thinking about Strategic Culture," *International Security*, xix, 4, Spring 1995, 32–64.
Lantis, Jeffrey S., "Strategic Culture and National Security Policy," *International Studies Review*, iv, 3, Autumn 2002, 87–113.
Niblock, Tim, *Saudi Arabia: Power, Legitimacy and Survival* (London and New York: Routledge, 2006).
Niblock, Tim and Monica Malik, *The Political Economy of Saudi Arabia* (Abingdon: Routledge, 2007).
Schneider, Susan C. and Arnoud de Meyer, "Interpreting and Responding to Strategic Issues: The Impact of National Culture," *Strategic Management Journal*, xii, 4, May 1991, 307–320.

3
DEVELOPING NUCLEAR THREAT ASSESSMENTS

Threat assessments and intelligence

In many ways, defense policy in Saudi Arabia is threat-based, in that it responds to perceived threats, and considerations surrounding nuclear weapons are no exception to that mechanism. That is, to a great extent, the Kingdom's defense policy must address such manifest challenges or potentially face the consequences of a loss or at least a diminution of the ruling system's legitimacy if it fails to do so. Traditionally, Saudi policymakers have operated on the basis of their perception of being surrounded by active or potential threats, which have varied over the years. In more recent times, the trend emanating from Saudi Arabia has been that of an integrated message at all levels indicating a perception, in particular, of the nuclear element as a key facet of that threat. Furthermore, the threat that has often been projected is one that Saudis have deemed as unacceptable, as it would imperil vital national interests, and one that could not be ignored.

Specifically on developing a nuclear threat assessment, Saudi Arabia has had to rely on limited intelligence. Political and technical intelligence on the capability and progress of Iran's nuclear program—which Saudi Arabia needs in order to develop its assessments and plans—appears to have come predominantly from foreign sources, whether from the International Atomic Energy Agency, the United Nations, foreign governments, or the foreign media, many of whose reports are cited in the Saudi media. In fact, if the Saudi Foreign Ministry documents made public in 2015 by WikiLeaks are any indication, a significant part of embassy reporting from abroad relies on reading the local press rather than engaging in deeper intelligence collection or analysis. Other information or perspectives on Iran's policy may also have come from those who have broken with the Tehran government. Moreover, the few think tanks that do exist in Saudi Arabia play a very restricted role in influencing policy. As one Saudi think tank director and retired general lamented, ideally think tanks should have the initiative and innovate plans and strategies which they would then present to the government, as in the United States, rather than, as he implied, is the case in Saudi Arabia, where a think tank "is [just] told to do [something]."[1] However effectively the Saudi intelligence process may work, the Saudi discourse has been suffused with the implicit given that Iran would be fully capable of eventually implementing its nuclear project successfully, although the assessment of Iran's technical and political timetable for achieving its goal has contained considerable uncertainty, as has been true of the foreign estimates on which such Saudi judgments must rely.

The evolution of Saudi nuclear threat assessments

Riyadh's understanding of the nuclear threat has shifted over time in reaction to regional developments, with a change in focus from Israel to Iran, although the process was neither linear nor complete.

The long-standing Israeli nuclear threat

Not surprisingly, Israel figured most prominently in this respect in the past, given its imposing nuclear capabilities and the presence of unresolved Arab–Israeli issues. Calls for a counterweight to Israel's nuclear weapons had long been a staple in public Saudi discourse—even if not expressed openly by policymakers—at least in the views of a portion of the country's "informed public," those who are interested in current affairs, insofar as one can judge based on the positions articulated by Saudi pundits in public, and that thus presumably did not contradict official thinking. Tellingly, in a telephone conversation between Saudi Arabia's King Fahd and Egypt's President Husni Mubarak in July 1990—which was intercepted by Iraqi Intelligence—King Fahd had remarked that "Israel ... is now our main concern; they possess 200 nuclear warheads and 47 atom bombs and are committed to using them against us and against our Palestinian brothers."[2]

In the past, Saudi policymakers could rely, especially in terms of public perceptions, on the fact that there was or would be an "Arab" balance with Israel, thanks to Saddam Husayn's efforts in the nuclear field, which at certain phases reportedly had benefited from Saudi encouragement. In fact, there had long been reports of Saudi financial support for Iraq's nuclear effort. For example, Sad Al-Bazzaz, a senior figure in the Iraqi media world and a Saddam regime insider, noted that after Israel had destroyed the Osirak nuclear reactor in Iraq in 1981, Saudi Arabia's King Khalid had been prepared to finance the reactor's reconstruction, allegedly to the tune of $300 million, although the offer was never implemented, since France refused to rebuild the reactor.[3] However, according to information provided by a defecting Saudi diplomat, Muhammad Al-Khilaywi, Saudi Arabia reportedly did actually help finance Saddam Husayn's nuclear program at one time.[4] That option, of course, had ended with the Gulf War.

Subsequently, in 1992, a Saudi academic specializing in nuclear strategy—and later member of the Shura Council—had called for "an assured Islamic nuclear deterrent to neutralize Israeli nuclear power," noting that without such a deterrent a country would be "at the mercy of an adversary."[5] Speaking of nuclear weapons, the same Saudi commentator fifteen years later still believed that "anyone who does not possess such weapons while his adversary does will be, most often, at the mercy of his enemy and vulnerable to blackmail."[6] In fact, when Libya's leader Muammar Qaddafi relinquished his nuclear weapons program in December 2003, a Saudi military journal carried a lengthy analytical article which took the Libyan leader to task for doing so. The article concluded that "despite the expected positive effects of this decision for Libya, the international and regional effects will not be of the same sort, as the negative effects will be dominant, especially those with respect to the unity of Arab action and the future of the Arab-Zionist conflict."[7] Blaming Libya's "eagerness to please [the United States] at whatever cost," the author cited as negative consequences of Libya's deal the validation for the United States of the principle of preventive war, a situation not supportive of stability but favoring the establishment of U.S. hegemony, the marginalization and subversion of international agencies, the embarrassment of Pakistan for its support to Libya's nuclear program, and the ensuing pressure on other Middle East states to sign the Non-Proliferation Treaty. Most importantly, there would now be a further erosion of the balance of power in the Middle East in Israel's favor, as a potential deterrent in the Arab camp was removed, which would "confirm and solidify Israel's regional position" and facilitate the United States' wider plan of enabling Israel to play the role of a regional great power.[8] Speaking in terms of being able to pressure Israel to accept a nuclear-free zone, another article in the same military journal in 2004 rued the failure of Iraq, Libya, and even Iran to pursue a nuclear program, as this "helped to weaken the three Arab [sic] countries' power … and lost cards to use to pressure and negotiate."[9]

Understandably, until a few years ago, the prevailing Saudi view continued to view Israel as the dominant nuclear threat. For example, Prince Muqrin, as then-head of Saudi Intelligence, asserted in 2006 that "Israel's possession of a nuclear arsenal is considered the biggest permanent strategic threat to Gulf security in the short and mid-term."[10] And, added Prince Muqrin, it was Israel's nuclear arsenal that had spurred Iran to also embark on its quest for nuclear weapons.[11] During the same period, a special dossier devoted to the nuclear threat in the official journal of the Shura Council focused solely on Israel.[12]

As Saudi Arabia's powerful minister of the interior and crown prince, the late Prince Nayif (d. 2012), also noted in 2006, Israel's possession of nuclear weapons "is justification for every country to think about acquiring nuclear weapons."[13] Elaborating on such perceptions, a typical opinion piece from this time-frame in a Saudi-owned daily warned that Israel put the Middle East at the mercy of its nuclear weapons, and that it was prepared to launch a nuclear first strike "even if it was not threatened by an Arab or Iranian attack using nuclear, chemical, or biological weapons."[14] The article then wondered skeptically "are the chemical and biological weapons which the Arabs do possess really a deterrent against Israel or Iran?" In that writer's view, "the Arabs" clearly needed to acquire a nuclear deterrent, and he suggested in a round-about way that Arab leaders must consider that option. He provided an answer to his own rhetorical question:

> the people in the cave are asleep, assuming that a philosophy of living in caves, deserted places, and caverns suffices for defense and protection and that there is no need to incommode the negotiators simply by raising the question of the legitimate Arab security, which is being threatened.[15]

The Saudi press, for its part, focused in particular on the combination of Israel as an "expansionist state" and its nuclear arsenal, which "places the Middle East countries under the pressing threat of [Israel's] nuclear weapons."[16]

Perhaps a more immediate lesson learned by Riyadh from the Israeli experience was that thanks to its nuclear deterrent Tel-Aviv could enforce the status quo on its own terms.[17] In the context of the concept of nuclear-supported hegemony, Saudi observers have often referred to the negative model to avoid seeing this repeated, that is Israel's use of its undeclared nuclear arsenal to establish and maintain a political situation to its favor, one highly detrimental to Arab interests. As one editor saw it, Israel in fact saw no need at all to negotiate with the Arabs thanks to its nuclear weapons.[18] In particular, the Israeli experience convinced the Saudis that a country can use its nuclear deterrent to keep territory it may have seized. As the editor of the *Al-Jazira* daily saw it, "Israel, with the West's help, acquired the nuclear weapons which it now uses to hold on to what it plundered from the Arabs and [this weapon] will serve as their 'deterrent' if [the Arabs] attempt to regain their rights."[19]

A Saudi observer even praised Israel sarcastically for its nuclear development: "Of course, one cannot blame Israel for seeking to hurt us with 400 atom bombs; rather, the rebuke should be to the Arab states which have ignored for so long the deterrent role of long-range missiles."[20] Citing Israel's large nuclear arsenal, another Saudi writer noted that "The Arabs' situation today in terms of power is enough to make friends cry and enemies rejoice!"[21] As a Saudi columnist remarked, "to embark on a confrontation with America or Israel without possessing a deterrent is a type of political suicide."[22] An academic, for his part, concluded that "no one who is fair can be forced to accept the principle of the unilateral possession by that criminal entity Israel of the advantage of a nuclear deterrent poised against the entire Umma." His corollary was that "it is therefore vital for Arab national security and to guarantee the success of peaceful Arab development policies that there be an Arab (or an Islamic) nuclear deterrent to confront Israel in order to neutralize the latter's frightening nuclear deterrent."[23]

Refocusing to Iran

By 2006, however, the impending nuclear threat from Iran progressively was joining that from Israel. Discussions began to appear in the Saudi media during the latter half of that decade as to which country—Israel or Iran—posed the greater threat as a nuclear power and where the Saudi defense focus should be.

Moreover, as Saudi Arabia increasingly came to believe that Iran was approaching nuclear status, attention began to shift to the latter as a more immediate and in key ways a more pernicious threat than Israel was. Paradoxically, although Iran was to become the focus of Riyadh's thinking in terms of the latter's own potential acquisition of nuclear weapons, this has not been a symmetric correlation in the sense that Iran almost assuredly did not embark on or continue its own quest for nuclear weapons with Saudi Arabia uppermost in mind. Rather, it is much more likely that Tehran's motivation in becoming a nuclear power would have been generated by concerns about U.S. intervention, or even an Israeli attack, a concern probably reinforced by the U.S./NATO operation against the Qaddafi regime in Libya in 2011, which observers in many other countries believed would not have occurred had the latter retained its nuclear program.

To be sure, Saudi Arabia had viewed Iran as a threat ever since the Islamic Revolution in 1979. However, Iran's possible acquisition of nuclear weapons would have raised that threat to a new level. As one retired Saudi military officer put it, "Iran's desperate and constant attempts to acquire nuclear weapons" had merely mutated "the Iranian threat to a new garb." Chief among the consequences of becoming a nuclear power in his view was the ability to "apply one's pressure and one's demands on an adversary."[24] To make his point, the author quoted Arabic poetry to that effect: "the strong rule in every land, so that the weak are not allowed their rights," which is reminiscent of Thucydides' classic Melian Dialogue: "The strong do as they can and the weak suffer what they must." Reflecting the same viewpoint, an opinion piece by a liberal Saudi academic likewise argued that "it is vital to have a nuclear deterrent, whatever the cost. For us, it is not just one of a number of options but rather an inevitable necessity in a world that only understands the logic of power."[25] Another commentator, who writes often on defense issues, even posited that Turkey could easily develop nuclear weapons, further complicating the Arabs' position in the "survival of the strongest" struggle, since "one of the elements of that survival ... is acquiring a nuclear weapons deterrent either by purchase from others ... or by developing [it]."[26]

Foreign Minister Prince Saud Al-Faysal put the nuclear threat in perspective in 2009, noting that Israel's nuclear arsenal had been a threat for decades already, but that if Iran now also acquired nuclear weapons that would "upset the traditional balance between the countries of the Gulf to Iran's favor." As he saw it:

> we have every legitimate right to express our legitimate concern and our justified fears of any developments that lead to the proliferation of WMD in the Gulf region ... and we also have the right to confirm our categorical rejection of any unilateral hegemony and influence at the expense of our states, peoples, and interests, or of any plans which transform our countries and peoples into chess pawns.[27]

Developing nuclear threat assessments 43

In 2011, Prince Turki Al-Faysal, likewise, was to declare openly in his speech at a conference in Riyadh in 2011 that "Israel, at least in the near future, is not at the forefront in the consideration of a nuclear option by the Kingdom and the Gulf states."[28]

Mobilizing public opinion

Addressing the Saudi public

Saudi policymakers, in their efforts to rank-order the threat to Saudi Arabia, have had to be careful so as not to blatantly contradict long-held popular views of a looming Israeli nuclear threat. Such perceptions are still deeply ingrained in Saudi opinion at all levels and, moreover, dismissals of the Israeli threat could prove embarrassing not only in domestic opinion but also among wider Arab circles. As one military observer noted, Israel's monopoly of nuclear weapons represents "a permanent element of threat to the Arab world."[29] Even as much of the Saudi media was shifting its focus to Iran, one Saudi commentator—a member of the Shura Council—nevertheless reminded his readers in 2009 that Israel was still an active nuclear threat, using its nuclear monopoly to blackmail not only the Arabs but Europe and Asia as well, and that any Israeli use of nuclear weapons in war would cause "great destruction" in the region.[30] Israel's assumed possession of nuclear weapons for decades has led to entrenched Saudi perceptions, at least in public opinion, of a continuing active Israeli nuclear threat, and any future Iranian threat would only join, rather than displace, the existing Israeli one for the public. Thus, one Saudi academic in 2006 typically characterized "the Arabs [as] between the pincers of the Israeli and of the Iranian nuclear deterrents."[31] Such perceptions persisted and, in 2010, another journalist spoke of the Arabs as living "between the two halves of a pincer, one of which is Iran ... in connection with its nuclear program, and the other of which is Israel."[32]

Significantly, when a columnist in 2011 sought to mobilize support against Iran, he may have gone too far for public opinion by essentially dismissing any Israeli threat, nuclear or otherwise.[33] The resulting readers' comments were scathing, reminding him that Israel still posed just as much of a threat as before and taking him to task for practically ignoring that threat. In the wake of the popular furor, he was forced to pen another article two days later, admitting that he had received many critical messages, but suggesting that he may have been reflecting official views in his original article, as he noted that "what I wrote was not my personal airing of the replacement of Israeli hostility by Iranian hostility."[34] He reassured readers that his earlier article did not mean that he was ignoring the Israeli threat, but he emphasized that Israel had also never attacked the Gulf states, and that he thought it necessary to underline the immediacy of the Iranian threat.

Ultimately, although the Saudis continued to see a dual nuclear threat from both Israel and Iran, the balance in emphasis clearly shifted toward Iran, as the Israeli nuclear threat was downgraded to more of a residual threat. Some have been very blunt, with an author promoted by the Saudi military concluding in 2014 that "Iranian nuclear weapons are a greater threat than those of Israel," and that Iranian nuclear weapons, indeed, will represent "*the* greatest threat to Arab national security."[35] In some ways, it is true, placing Iran in greater prominence may have been more acceptable and less controversial in the international arena as the proximate potential catalyst for Saudi Arabia's consideration of its own nuclear weapons rather than would have been true of a public focus on Israel. Likewise, Saudi policymakers might have assumed that a focus on Iran in this context might minimize Israeli opposition to a Saudi nuclear option. Nevertheless, to be sure, Saudis also continued to view Israel as a long-term threat, even accusing the latter of scheming with Iran to partition the Middle East between them.[36] Illustrating the continued official dual threat focus—even if more recently a noticeably uneven one—Prince Turki Al-Faysal asked in 2011: "What would be wrong with acquiring a nuclear force" to confront Iran "or [to confront] the Israeli nuclear force?"[37]

Shaping regional threat perceptions

The Saudis also sought to convince regional publics that a nuclear-armed Iran indeed had become a greater threat than Israel, which was important to Riyadh in terms of being seen as fulfilling its role of regional defender. As one editorial complained, some Arabs outside the Gulf still saw a nuclear Iran in positive terms as a balance to Israel, but the article insisted that Iran would only target the Gulf—rather than targeting Israel—and would "transform the region into a political hostage" and, therefore, constituted the greater threat.[38] Other Saudis labeled such views which presumed that Iranian nuclear weapons were a balance to Israel's as only "a hypothesis" and as "just an impossible hope."[39]

However, convincing Arab audiences that the Iranian nuclear program represented the greater threat has not always been easy. According to one Saudi opinion article from 2011, "some Arab observers" continued to view Iran's nuclear program in terms of a balance to Israel's arsenal and as a means to regain Palestinian rights. However, the writer argued that Iran was not genuinely interested in the Arab–Israeli conflict. Rather, Iran's "feverish effort to complete its nuclear program makes its intention plain that it will continue its confrontational and destructive policy against its peaceful Arab neighbors."[40] And, he concluded:

> no Arab denies … that the Zionists are our top enemy; that is true, but the mistake I want to address is that of glossing over another rogue state [i.e. Iran] on the brink of adding to its criminal record with WMD so that it can carry out its destructive plan in the region.[41]

A military study also took to task "some who hope" that Iran would balance Israel: "the truth, instead, is that it is not Israel which will feel directly the danger of [Iran's] nuclear weapons, but rather it is the Arab states of the Gulf who will fall within the danger zone of Iran's blackmail."[42] Significantly, a lone academic who did continue to express the opinion that an Iranian nuclear capability was desirable as a way to balance Israel often also defends Shia positions publicly, but he has had his website closed down by the Saudi authorities and, in this case, was forced to voice his controversial views in a Kuwaiti newspaper.[43]

Notes

1 Interview with Staff Major General Anwar Majid Ishqi (Ret.) by Walid Diyab and Ahmad Abd Al-Hamid, "Ra'is Markaz Al-Sharq Al-Awsat Li'l-Dirasat Al-Istratijiya: Iran nimr min waraq" [The Director of the Middle East Center for Strategic Studies: Iran Is a Paper Tiger], *Akhbar Al-Khalij* (Manama), 20 May 2015, www.akhbar-alkhaleej.com/13182/article_touch/19174.html.
2 The intercepted conversation is one of the Iraqi documents captured in 2003, transcript in SH-MICN-D-000–839_TF, 28 July 1990, Conflict Records Research Center, Washington, DC.
3 Sad Al-Bazzaz, *Harb talid ukhra* [One War Engenders Another], 2nd edition, (Amman, Jordan: Al-ahliya li'l-nashr wa'l-tawzi, 1992) 202.
4 Paul Lewis, "Defector Says Saudis Sought Nuclear Arms," *New York Times*, 7 August 1994, A20.
5 Sadaqa Yahya Fadil, "Al-Qunbula al-nawawiya al-islamiya bayn al-hulm wa'l-kabus" [The Islamic Atom Bomb Either Dream or Nightmare], *Ukaz*, 1 May 1992, 8.
6 Sadaqa Yahya Fadil, "Istikhdam al-silah al-nawawi … al-maful al-khafiy" [Using Nuclear Weapons… the Hidden Impact], *Ukaz*, 25 March 2007, www.okaz.com.sa/okaz/osf/20070325/PrinCon2007032597841.htm (hereafter Fadil, "Istikhdam al-silah").
7 Yusuf Kamil Khattab, "Qarar Libiya al-takhalli an aslihat al-damar al-shamil: abaduh wa-natai'jhu" [Libya's Decision to Relinquish WMD: Its Dimensions and Results], *Majallat Kulliyat Al-Malik Khalid Al-Askariya*, March 2004, 38.
8 Ibid., 35–38.
9 Hay'at Al-Tahrir [Editorial Board], "Hal yusbih Al-Sharq Al-Awsat mintaqa khaliya min aslihat al-damar al-shamil?" [Will the Middle East Become a Region Free of Weapons of Mass Destruction?], *Majallat Kulliyat Al-Malik Khalid Al-Askariya*, March 2004, 45. Iran had just signed the Additional Protocol to its NPT safeguards agreement, granting expanded international inspection rights, and the Saudis at the time apparently believed this marked the end to Iran's pursuit of nuclear weapons.
10 "Al-Amir Muqrin: Al-Nizaat al-madhhabiya wa'l-tasalluh al-nawawi yuhaddidan amn Al-Khalij" [Prince Muqrin: Ideological Conflicts and Nuclear Arms Acquisitions Threaten Security in the Gulf], *Ukaz*, 9 December 2006, www.okaz.com.sa.
11 Ibid.
12 Ahmad Muharram Najib, "Al-Silah al-nawawi yaqud" [Nuclear Weapons Rule], *Majallat Al-Shura*, Dhu al-hijja 1427/December 2006–January 2007, 32–41.
13 Prince Nayif quoted in a press conference in Tunisia, "Imtilak 'Isra'il' silahan nawawiyan yuti mubarriran li-ayy dawla li-an tufakkir bi'l-husul alayh" [Israel's Possession of Nuclear Weapons Gives Any Country the Justification to Also Think about Acquiring Them], *Al-Riyadh*, 2 February 2006, www.alriyadh.com/2006/02/02/article127533.html.
14 Ghassan Al-Imam, "Al-amn al-qawmi al-arabi wa'l-qunbula al-iraniya" [Arab National Security and the Iranian Bomb], *Al-Sharq Al-Awsat*, 10 May 2005, www.aawsat.com/print.asp?did=298477&issueno=9660.
15 Ibid.
16 Ali Abbud Madi, "Nam annaha al-khatar al-akbar" [Yes, It Is the Greater Threat], *Al-Riyadh*, 16 November 2003, www.alriyadh.com/2003/11/16/article18406.html.
17 Jasir Abd Al-Aziz Al-Jasir, "Naam li-silah nawawi khaliji" [Yes to a Gulf Nuclear Weapon], *Al-Jazira*, 7 December 2011, www.al-jazirah.com/2011/20111207/du8.htm (hereafter Al-Jasir, "Naam li-silah").

18 Yusuf Al-Kuwaylit, "La-yakun amn Isra'il waraqat al-musawama al-arabiya" [Let Israel's Security Be the Arab Negotiating Card], *Al-Riyadh*, 4 December 2001, www.alriyadh.com/2001/12/04/article30286.html.
19 Al-Jasir, "Naam li-silah."
20 Fahd Amir Al-Ahmadi, "Sahh al-nawm ya arab wasalat al-arbami'a!" [Hope You Have Slept Enough, Oh Arabs; the Fourteen Hundreds Have Arrived], *Al-Riyadh*, 13 July 2002, www.alriyadh.com/2002/07/13/article26773.html. The 1400s refers to the current century in the Islamic calendar.
21 Id bin Masud Al-Juhani, "Hal yufiq al-arab ala hadir al-quwwa al-isra'iliya?" [Will the Arabs Awake from the Noise of Israeli Power?], *Al-Hayat*, 12 April 2008, http://international.daralhayat.com/print/200023/archive. The author is Director of the Arab Gulf Center for Energy and Strategic Studies.
22 Salih Al-Namla, "Kuriya, Taywan, Iran wa-tanaqud al-siyasa al-nawawiya al-amrikiya" [Korea, Taiwan, Iran, and the Contradictions of American Nuclear Policy], *Al-Riyadh*, 8 October 2003, www.alriyadh.com/2003/10/08/article19079.html.
23 Fadil, "Istikhdam al-silah."
24 Staff Major General Salama bin Hadhdhal Bin Saidan (Ret.), "Al-Tahdid al-irani fi thawbih al-jadid" [The Iranian Threat in Its New Garb], *Al-Jazira*, 16 August 2008, www.al-jazirah.com.sa/2008jaz/aug/16/ar8.htm.
25 Muhammad bin Abd Al-Latif Al Al-Shaykh, "Al-Radi al-nawawi darura la khiyar" [A Nuclear Deterrent Is a Necessity Not Just an Option], *Al-Jazira*, 13 December 2011, www.al-jazirah.com.sa/2011jaz/dec/13/1p4.htm.
26 Sami Said Habib, "Erdogan wa-sibaq al-tasalluh al-nawawi al-qadim" [Erdogan and the Coming Nuclear Arms Race], *Al-Madina*, 17 September 2011, www.al-madina.com/printhtml/327185.
27 "Nass kalimat al-amir Saud Al-Faysal wazir al-kharijiya al-saudiya" [The Text of the Speech by Prince Saud Al-Faysal, Saudi Arabia's Foreign Minister], *Al-Sharq Al-Awsat*, 7 January 2009, www.aawsat.com/print.asp?did=501885&issueno=10998. Saudi concerns had already sharpened due to Iran's development of SSMs some years earlier, which were also viewed within the context of Iran's intent "to become a regional great power and to be able to impose its hegemony in the region." "Wast mazid min al-tawatturat wa'l-daght al-sarukh al-irani shihab 3 yadkhul al-khidma" [Amid Increasing Tensions and Pressure the Iranian Shihab-3 Missile Enters Service], *Majallat Kulliyat Al-Malik Khalid Al-Askariya*, 1 December 2003, www.kkmaq.gov.sa/detail.asp?InNewsItemID=129818&InTemplateKey=print.
28 Reported in Badr Al-Balawi, "Al-Qunbula al-nawawiya al-saudiya" [The Saudi Nuclear Weapon], *Al-Sharq* (Dammam), 14 December 2011, www.alsharq.net.sa/2011/12/14/46046.
29 Major General Muhammad Jamal Mazhlum, "Al-Amn al-qawmi al-tahaddiyat al-askariya wa-subul al-tasaddi laha" [National Security: Military Challenges and the Means to Counter Them], *Majallat Kulliyat Al-Malik Khalid Al-Askariya*, 1 June 2008, www.kkmaq.gov.sa/detail.asp?InNewsItemID=273652&InTemplateKey=print.
30 Sadaqa Yahya Fadil, "Istikhdam Isra'il li-tarsanatha al-nawawiya" [Israel's Use of Its Nuclear Arsenal], *Majallat Al-Shura*, Jumada II 1430/May–June 2009, 28.
31 Talal Salih Bannan, "Al-Arab bayn kammashat al-rub al-nawawi!" [The Arabs between the Pincers of Nuclear Terror!], *Ukaz*, 2 April 2006, www.okaz.com.sa/okaz/osf/20060402/PrinCon200604026920.htm.
32 Adnan Kamil Salah, "Al-Qadiya al-iraniya bi-ru'ya arabiya muwahhada" [The Iranian Case from a United Arab Perspective], *Al-Madina*, 7 January 2010, www.al-madina.com/print/213010.
33 Turki Abd Allah Al-Sudayri, "La-nafham shawahid al-makhatir al-qa'ima" [Let Us Understand the Evidence for the Existing Threat], *Al-Riyadh*, 15 October 2011, www.alriyadh.com/2011/10/15/article675765.print.

34 Turki Abd Allah Al-Sudayri, "Iran awwalan wa-Isra'il thaniyan" [Iran First and Israel Second], *Al-Riyadh*, 13 October 2011, www.alriyadh/com/2011/10/13/article675147.html.
35 Al-Sayyid Abu Da'ud, *Tasaud al-madd al-irani fi al-alam al-arabi* [*The Rise of Iranian Expansionism in the Arab World*] (Riyadh: Obeikan Publishing, 2014), 416. The author of the work, published in Riyadh, is given as Al-Sayyid Abu Da'ud, with no further elucidation as to his identity. This is a common name, and may be a pseudonym for a government official or for a commissioned writer, although an Egyptian political activist also bears that name.
36 Hamad Abd Allah Al-Luhaydan, "Iran wa-Isra'il wajhan li-umla wahida" [Iran and Israel: Two Sides of the Same Coin], *Al-Riyadh*, 15 May 2015, www.alriyadh.com/1048369.
37 Ali Al-Qahis, "Al-Amir Turki Al-Faysal yutalib bi-tahwil majlis al-taawun ila ittihad ashbah bi'l-urubbi wa-insha' jaysh khaliji muwahhad" [Prince Turki Al-Faysal Calls for a Transformation of the [Gulf] Cooperation Council into a Union Resembling the European Union and for the Establishment of a Unified Gulf Army], *Al-Riyadh*, 22 March 2011, www.alriyadh.com/2011/03/22/article615880.html.
38 Abd Al-Rahman Al-Rashid, "Li-hadhihi al-asbab nakhsha Iran" [These Are the Reasons Why We Fear Iran], *Al-Sharq Al-Awsat*, 18 April 2006, www.aawsat.com/leader.asp?section=3&article=358858&issueno=10003.
39 Abd Al-Munim Mustafa, "Kull shay' lam yaud kafiyan" [All of That Is Not Enough], *Al-Madina*, 14 February 2010, www.al-madina.com/print/224041.
40 Sulayman Al-Asad, "Al-Silah al-nawawi al-irani didd man?" [The Iranian Nuclear Weapon—Against Whom?], *Al-Jazira*, 26 December 2011, www.al-jazirah.com.sa/20111226/du13.htm.
41 Ibid.
42 Major General Husam Suwaylam (Ret.), "Ahdaf Iran al-siyasiya wa'l-istratijiya wa-asalib tahqiqha" [Iran's Political and Strategic Objectives and the Methods to Achieve Them], *Al-Haras Al-Watani*, part 1, August 2011, 39.
43 Man Al-Jarba, "Al-Haqq al-nawawi al-irani bayn al-naza al-madhhabiya wa'l-diniya" [Iran's Right to Nuclear Weapons Influenced by Sectarian and Religious Attitudes], *Al-Siyasa* (Kuwait), 10 January 2015, http://al-seyassah.com.

Bibliography

Abu Da'ud, Al-Sayyid, *Tasaud al-madd al-irani fi al-alam al-arabi* [*The Rise of Iranian Expansion in the Arab World*] (Riyadh: Obeikan Publishing, 2014).

Al-Bazzaz, Sad, *Harb talid ukhra* [*One War Engenders Another*], 2nd edition (Amman, Jordan: Al-ahliya li'l-nashr wa'l-tawzi, 1992).

4

ANALYZING THE THREAT IN RIYADH

Why would a nuclear Iran be so dangerous?

Not surprisingly, the Saudis devoted an increasing amount of attention to analyzing the evolving threat and its implications as Iran was seen coming closer to acquiring nuclear weapons. How Iran might use nuclear weapons and how Saudi Arabia might counter that threat elicited a considerable amount of discussion in both civilian and military circles, while Saudi policymakers and analysts focused exclusively on Iran's nuclear program from a Saudi threat perspective, with Iran seen as an aggressive state pursuing nuclear weapons as a means to increase its capability to threaten its neighbors and to impose its hegemonic control on the region. Conversely, there was no attempt by Saudi Arabia to analyze the Iranian nuclear program from Tehran's standpoint, with a regime which might have felt threatened by a U.S. military presence in the region and by the prospect at times of regime change promoted or abetted from outside, a concern very likely intensified by the events in Libya and Syria and the role played by outside support to the dissidents in those two countries.

In part, the deep and abiding cultural undercurrents have exacerbated the bilateral relationship, as the prospect of a nuclear Iran increased, interacting with the Saudis' self-identity and their country's perceived role in the Gulf, the Arab world, and the Islamic Umma. That is, the country's leadership, Saudis in general, and the religious establishment in particular, as noted earlier, view the Shia (whether in Iran or the other regional communities) with distaste and suspicion born of long-standing theological and historical differences. The intense competition for regional influence, based on state interests, complements both countries' readiness to react viscerally to each other's policies. And, to lend concrete validity to such mutual mistrust, Saudi Arabia and Iran have been engaged in a covert war in Iraq, Syria, Yemen, and Lebanon, while Riyadh has blamed the protests by the Shia majority in Bahrain on Iranian influence rather than on local grievances. Not surprisingly, Saudi assessments of a prospective Iranian nuclear capability were considered within that existing overarching threat framework. As one editorial in 2013 summed up the Saudi view, Iran was pursuing nuclear weapons to compensate for its "religious and ideological inferiority complex," and its ultimate objective was to "oblige the world to accept it on the list of great nuclear powers."[1]

Iran's nuclear program: military or civilian?

Saudi Arabia had long been convinced that Iran's nuclear program, whatever Tehran's claims, was meant for military purposes and not for civilian use. As a senior member of the royal family told the author in 2000 about Iran's claims that its nuclear program was for civilian use, "We don't believe that."[2] One observer in a Saudi-owned newspaper claimed in 2005 that Iran was merely pursuing a policy of deception similar to the one that Israel, India, and Pakistan had followed until they had developed nuclear weapons.[3] As a more recent editorial, among many articulating the Saudi consensus, noted, "Iran's repeated assurances ... that its nuclear program is not intended for the production of nuclear weapons ... is hard to believe."[4] Saudi doubts about the civilian nature of the Iranian nuclear program, despite Tehran's assurances, continued unabated.[5] Arguments by Iran that it needed nuclear power to generate electricity were dismissed out of hand, even though Saudi Arabia has made similar arguments about impending energy shortages in advocating its own civilian nuclear program. As the editor of one Saudi daily put it, Iran is "a state with enormous reserves of oil and gas, but has used [this argument] in order to achieve other objectives."[6] Saudis also saw the boundaries between a civilian program in Iran and the militarization of such capabilities as tenuous. Even if initially Iran's nuclear program was civilian, Saudis continued to believe that a conversion to military use would only be a matter of time and that this would be an easy step. A Saudi pundit, for example, felt that as long as Iran was allowed to retain its nuclear infrastructure "no one can guarantee that this program will not be converted from a peaceful one to a military one," since he believed that "the technical boundary between civilian and military is insignificant."[7] In fact, the whole thrust of Saudi analysis and policy planning has always been based on the conviction that Iran has pursued a nuclear option specifically for military purposes.

Creating a new Iranian hegemony

As many in Saudi Arabia saw it, Iran would be able to translate its nuclear weapons into considerable, and perhaps decisive, clout in the region. A consensus emerged in Saudi Arabia that Iran was not likely to use a new nuclear capability against Israel because of the latter's overwhelming overmatch and U.S. support. Significantly, a retired Saudi general, asked: "What will the Iranian regime now be able to do if it acquires nuclear weapons?" According to that officer, what was of particular concern about Iran's acquisition of nuclear weapons was that, unlike some other nuclear powers, "the difference is that in the case of Iran it has become clear that the latter has a geo-political plan for expansion."[8] As another retired Saudi military officer saw it, acquiring nuclear weapons would enable Iran to "consolidate its security, extend its influence, and break the international isolation which has beset it since the Revolution."[9] Suggestive of Saudi military thinking, or at least of the intellectual atmosphere encouraged internally, was one of the books promoted and made available within the Saudi officer corps, which deals with Iranian policy, including the nuclear factor.[10] A key intent of the book was to counter the perception that Iran's acquisition of nuclear weapons would contribute to a greater deterrent balance against Israel, from which the Arabs would also benefit. Rather, in the book's view, Iran would not use nuclear weapons against Israel but would use them, instead, to dominate the Arabs, a strategy which the book's author claims should be seen in the context of what he terms Iran's driving policy of expansion.[11]

According to another Saudi observer, "the Iranian nuclear bomb has only one objective, namely that of dominance by a new Persian Empire over Asia and the Arab and Islamic worlds," which he saw as replacing in a way the earlier Ottoman Empire, and, as he put it, the intent was to "spread this new Persian Empire's political and religious culture."[12] An editorial claimed that a nuclear Iran was merely following in the footsteps of the Shah, who had hoped the nuclear program he had initiated would enable Iran to become the "policeman of the Gulf."[13] Some went further back in history, as a journalist, who interpreted the objective "for the Persians to enslave the Arabs and to take revenge against the latter," warned that "what was taken in the past by means of preaching religion would now be retrieved by means of nuclear weapons and intercontinental missiles."[14] A 2011 report in a Saudi-owned newspaper commenting on a meeting between the defense ministers of Saudi Arabia and Kuwait noted that, according to unnamed sources, the GCC viewed Iran's recent refusal to allow international inspection of its nuclear program with "extreme concern" and that all "understood very clearly" that if Iran reached the stage of manufacturing an atom bomb that:

> will lead to a redrawing of the map of the Middle East region and, as a result, to a change in the balance of military power in the region, opening the way for Tehran to extend and expand its political and military influence [and] for the "Persianization" of the Gulf as a first phase.[15]

Similarly, a Saudi military study posited that Iran was seeking nuclear weapons "in order to safeguard its regional role, and to expand that role so that the Islamic Republic's presence is at a level no less prominent than that of India, Israel, or Pakistan."[16] Saudi observers frequently concluded that a nuclear Iran, indeed, would be able to "change the map."[17] Another Saudi study specifically linked Iran's potential acquisition of nuclear weapons to a new ability to establish its hegemony in the region by changing borders, partitioning existing states into mini-states, and turning the Arab states into satellites.[18] As that observer saw it, "we can confirm that when the production of Iranian nuclear weapons is complete they will not be directed against Israel at all ... Rather, they will be used to threaten and blackmail the Arab states, starting with those in the Gulf."[19]

A Saudi pundit, likewise, characterized the Gulf countries—with their key assets along the coast—as "becoming the hostage of Iran's ambitions" once the latter acquired nuclear weapons. Seeking to "transform the region and to exercise its hegemony, once it acquires nuclear weapons [Iran] will be able to accomplish what it has so far been unable to do, and without dropping a single atom bomb."[20] Another editorial stressed that Iran would use its nuclear weapons to extract "major concessions, that is to turn the region into a hostage to the conduct of Iranian policy."[21] Iran's nuclear weapons would also be used "to frighten and then attrit the Arab states in an arms race [as the latter try] to achieve a nuclear balance."[22] Some Saudis speculated that Iran might not even declare it had nuclear weapons but might rely on a strategy of ambivalence.[23] And, even if Iran acquired sufficient enriched uranium for only one nuclear bomb at first, it could wait until it had accumulated enough material for "a small arsenal" before proceeding to weaponization, since "a single nuclear weapon is not useful in establishing a nuclear deterrence balance."[24]

Yet another article in the military media focused on the implications for affecting the Gulf countries' decisionmaking once Iran became a nuclear power, noting that:

> the intent in [Iran's] acquiring this [nuclear] weapon is to blackmail the Gulf countries and to score political gains ... which will limit the independence of political decisionmaking in the Gulf in general terms, and which will impose on the GCC countries a new security reality in both regional and domestic terms.[25]

As another Saudi observer put it, Iran's "hegemony will be entrenched and will become a tangible reality when it acquires nuclear weapons."[26] Indeed, Iran would then use the new capability to demand from the West a new strategic deal which would recognize Iran's dominant role in Gulf security and a recognition of the legitimacy of its regime.[27] Saudis emphasized not only the material character but also the psychological aspect of nuclear weapons as part of a new strategic equation. One writer highlighted that "the psychological dividing line between nuclear and conventional weapons is enormous, despite the increase in the lethality of modern conventional weapons."[28] Some Saudis felt that simply living next door to a nuclear-armed Iran could unhinge the regional balance by pulling the GCC apart as a result of what one might term the "avalanche syndrome." That is one could equate such a situation to living in the shadow of a snow-covered mountain, when one might unconsciously start to tip-toe even inside one's own house out of concern about triggering an avalanche. The GCC's smaller members, in particular, intimidated by Iran's hegemony and conscious of their vulnerability, might become wary of irritating Iran and drift into the latter's orbit. As one Saudi commentator warned, "There is a concern that some of the Gulf states, acting out of fear, will prefer to lie down under Iran's nuclear wing. If that happens, the Gulf states' orientation will change, thereby creating a split in the Arab world."[29]

Exporting the revolution and "offensive deterrence"

Riyadh has long been apprehensive about what a Saudi editorial emphasizing Iran as the primary nuclear threat characterized as Tehran's ability to use "sectarian differences as justification and then as [potential] for incitement," referring to Iran's alleged involvement with Shia communities in Iraq, Kuwait, Bahrain, and Lebanon.[30] Riyadh also appeared concerned about its own indigenous Shia communities in the oil-rich Eastern Province and along the southern border with Yemen, attributing discontent there not to the long-standing discriminatory treatment at the hands of the Saudi government but to Iranian instigation. Saudi policymakers and public opinion became increasingly concerned about what was viewed as Iran's capability to incite and support the Shia communities in the region after the unrest in Bahrain in 2011, which Riyadh blamed on Iran. As the Saudi Land Force's journal saw it, Iran would utilize its nuclear status "to blackmail the Arab states beginning with the Gulf states in order to incite and support Iran's extended hands [i.e. the Shia communities] inside those states on a continuous basis in order to carry out Iranian plans."[31] One political commentator argued that Iran was already planting agents in the Gulf "in order to destabilize the Gulf."[32] Another commentator writing in the Saudi military academy's official journal, likewise focused on Iran's exploitation of the local Shia communities as part of its "interference" in the Gulf states, which he compared to that of the United States in Iraq and Afghanistan.[33]

While the current Iranian threat was already viewed with concern, Iran's acquisition of nuclear weapons was seen as increasing that threat exponentially. Typically, according to a retired senior Saudi military officer, "acquiring a nuclear deterrent is what will provide it [i.e. Iran] the appropriate conditions to export and impose the Revolution."[34] As a Saudi opinion piece saw it, as dangerous as the threat that Iran posed already by its creation of "a fifth column" in the region that "the threat today cannot be compared in any way to the threat in the future when [Iran] acquires nuclear weapons."[35] As another Saudi military overview concluded, Iran's objective was to establish its hegemony over the entire Middle East and some countries in Central and South Asia, and especially where there were Shia communities, by exporting its revolution, as it had been trying to do even without nuclear weapons.[36] The study assessed that the only element of Iran's national power that had been missing was the nuclear one, which was now said to be on its way. Even those Saudis who dismissed Iran's saber-rattling as largely bluster were concerned that the acquisition of nuclear weapons by the latter would change the regional military equation decisively.[37]

It was, in particular, this Iran/domestic Shia threat backed up by a nuclear deterrent that Saudi official circles viewed as the most lethal likely combination. Specifically, according to one military study, "if Iran acquires nuclear weapons that will provide it with an ideal military screen (*ghita'*) with which to carry out that mission [i.e. of exporting the Revolution]."[38] That is, the perception has been that Iran could use its nuclear weapons as a deterrent against regional or international retaliation for an aggressive policy directed against the Arab Gulf states while using conventional or unconventional means. A retired Saudi general likewise dismissed the idea that nuclear weapons were only a doomsday weapon, arguing that Iran would use them to establish its hegemony, as Israel had done.[39] And a Saudi academic posited that Iran, even with a small number of nuclear weapons at first, would already be in a position to exercise deterrence.[40] Iraqi military thinkers had already discussed years earlier this aspect of using nuclear weapons as a screen against retaliation and had labeled such a strategy "offensive deterrence" (*al-rad al-hujumi*).[41]

Saudis feared that Iran, as a nuclear power, might also be emboldened to engage in conventional military operations at a more intensive level than at present and that even the Great Powers might be more acquiescent to a nuclear-armed Iran. Addressing Iran's future nuclear capability, one Saudi observer noted that "Iran dreams of completely deterring the United States and of obliging the latter to defer to Iran's interests."[42] In concrete terms, an editorial, for example, stressed that even the Great Powers would not risk war against a nuclear state, noting that "even if tomorrow Iran undertook to occupy Bahrain—which is something only too possible—or if its militias seized southern Iraq, there would be no Great Power that would dare to prevent Iran from doing so by military means."[43] Another article in a Saudi-owned newspaper, typically, argued that thanks to nuclear weapons Iran would be able to expand and even occupy Kuwait.[44] However, others believed that Iranian aggression would likely not take the form of a ground or amphibious invasion, for which Iran has limited capabilities. Rather, many Saudis assessed that Iran would most likely have recourse to its air, naval, and SSM assets in any confrontation with its neighbors. Iran had already publicized explicitly a potential target list on the Saudi side of the Gulf in a conventional confrontation—including oil facilities, cities, power stations, and ports—many of which are vulnerable and whose loss would threaten Saudi Arabia's vital interests, and such information was often communicated to the Saudi public by its own media to highlight the threat.[45]

Nuclear weapons and warfighting

But, apart from acquiring nuclear weapons as a deterrent and political lever, might Iran also resort to nuclear weapons in a warfighting mode? Even if the Saudis recognized that Iran's use of nuclear weapons in a war was a far less likely contingency than its use of these weapons to support its use of conventional force at lower levels, they did not, and could not, dismiss that possibility entirely.

Some Western scholars, such as Nina Tannenwald, have deemed it unlikely that nuclear weapons would be used in warfighting because of self-imposed "normative prescriptions" that have "delegitimize[d] nuclear weapons as weapons of war."[46] Likewise, some Saudi observers also concluded that Iran was unlikely to use nuclear weapons in a war against the Arab states, but for a different reason, namely because that would also threaten the Shia communities living in those countries.[47] However, there were also Saudi "pessimists," that is those who did not exclude the possibility that Iran might use a nuclear capability in a warfighting mode. Thus, commentators dismissed those who felt that Iran would not use nuclear weapons against an Arab state just because it was Muslim by pointing out that the Iranians had already used chemical weapons in the Iran–Iraq War against Iraq, while others thought the Iranians might have recourse to nuclear weapons because they were "crazy chauvinists ... thirsting for blood."[48]

However low the probability of a nuclear war, some—and perhaps even most—Saudis did not dismiss that offhand. Certainly, most Saudis believed that Israel "would not hesitate to use whatever WMD it has, including nuclear weapons, in any future war with the Arabs" not only as a last resort but even in other situations, such as not being able to deal with a conventional Arab attack.[49] At least one Saudi commentator, in fact, felt that Israel also would have no qualms about targeting large Arab cities and the industrial and oil infrastructure, as well as military facilities, with its nuclear weapons.[50] More recently, Tel-Aviv had shown a more relaxed attitude about discussing its nuclear program and, for example, in 2013 Avraham Burg (former Speaker of the Knesset), had been quite unambiguous on this issue, as had been the Israeli media.[51] This openness seemed only to reinforce Saudi fears, as some interpreted that this meant that Israel had now shifted from a policy of nuclear deterrence to one of first-strike.[52] A prominent Saudi commentator, likewise, was insistent that not only would Iran use an atom bomb to deter the Great Powers so that it would have a free hand in the Middle East but that "it may also use that [bomb] in a war against a neighbor such as Saudi Arabia."[53]

Even Saudi Arabia's Foreign Minister, Prince Saud Al-Faysal, was not reassuring on this count, when he observed in 2010 with regard to the Iranian nuclear program that "history shows that no weapon has entered the region without its ending up being used."[54] Some believed that Iranian leaders could miscalculate and that such human errors could result in a nuclear war.[55] Other observers considered that Iran was willing to use, or at least to threaten to use, nuclear weapons, based on the latter's eschatological worldview and desire to bring about the reappearance of the occulted Imam of Shia doctrine.[56] One Saudi pundit in 2013 was skeptical that deterrence would work with Iran, since he claimed that the Iranian leadership was unpredictable, and that even potential alternatives to the current leadership believed in the return of the awaited Mahdi and might be willing to hasten the process at any cost. The editorial concluded by asking "How, then, can we trust a nuclear Iran?"[57]

Still other Saudis also feared that Iran was not a rational actor, suggesting that the Iranian leadership suffered from mental problems.[58] As a Saudi commentator also asked plaintively in a discussion on nuclear weapons, "is it possible for us to imagine how our current human era will be described if a fool one day commits the fatal error of pushing the button?"[59] Yet another opinion piece in 2008 also focused on the uncertainties of the Iranian leadership's perceptions of the nuclear factor. As that writer saw it:

> We are confronted by two possibilities: either we believe and trust that the Iranian leadership understands the risks and is governed by logic and will not cause the death of a million human beings in order to win a war which could be decided instead peacefully ... but that means that we have not learned our lesson from Saddam Hussein or ... the other possibility is that we do not trust anyone.[60]

The same essayist, for his part, concluded that "we cannot build our future by trusting in good intentions; the past has taught us not to trust any leader." And, he also interjected the element of imponderable cultural considerations that had to be factored into the risk assessment of nuclear war, namely that some "thoughtless leaders" in Israel or Iran might actually view a nuclear war as hastening the coming of the Messiah or the Mahdi, respectively.[61]

The above 2008 opinion piece then asked against whom Iran might use its nuclear weapons. Even in case of a confrontation with the United States, Iran was judged as unlikely to strike the United States with its nuclear weapons. Instead, if Iran wanted to hit at U.S. interests indirectly, the writer posited that although either Israel or the Gulf could be direct targets, Israel too was unlikely because of its ability to retaliate. He concluded that "Therefore, that leaves Iran with virtually a single target if it wanted to harm the United States and minimize the risk of retaliation: the Gulf."[62] Likewise, a Saudi military journal rejected the likelihood that Iran would strike either the United States or Israel with its nuclear weapons, given the overmatch it would face. In light of that factor, the writer argued that "the clearest and most feasible objective of a war, in the thinking of Iran's leaders, would be to embark on a war against the Arabs and, in particular, against the Gulf states."[63] Another editorial also derided "some Arabs ... who believe that the use of nuclear weapons against them would be impossible as long as they themselves did not have [such weapons]," labeling such attitudes as "naiveté," and assessing that Israel would have used that capability in 1973, as would have Iran or Iraq during the Iran–Iraq War.[64] Indeed, the same writer maintained that "Iran's arming itself with the bomb might entice it in the future to use it, not against nuclear-armed Israel but, rather, against the Sunni Arab states who do not possess a strategic weapon capable of deterring or responding."[65]

A Saudi military writer, as his contribution, discussed the categories of potential targets in any first strike—which he believed would be focused on counter-force military targets—if ever there should be a nuclear war. In his view:

> For those countries possessing nuclear weapons, there is a whole other target set for selection, focusing on a strategy of striking the enemy's standing forces, provided there are forces that are vulnerable to a first strike, which would give an advantage for taking the initiative to the party initiating the war. This strategy is directed against military targets only, and he who has the capability to launch a first-strike must calculate whether he has the ability to destroy every missile in the other party's arsenal. Otherwise, the result can be a guaranteed disaster.[66]

Although Iran was not specifically mentioned in this assessment, given the ongoing Saudi preoccupations with the threat posed by a potential Iranian nuclear capability, the assumed linkage for Saudi military readers was no doubt clear.

The threat to Saudi Arabia's economy

Saudi decisionmakers have also been concerned that an assertive nuclear-armed Iran could easily threaten the economic pillar of the ruling family's legitimacy and, in particular, the energy sector upon which Saudi Arabia's national income and stability depend. Even before Iran might become a nuclear power, the Saudis feared that strikes by the United States or Israel intended to prevent Iran from acquiring that nuclear capability could have led the latter to unleash a costly attack aimed at Saudi Arabia's economy, as Iran had threatened to do in retaliation for any strike against its nuclear program. In particular, Saudi and other Gulf oil and gas facilities and export mechanisms, of course, are especially vulnerable to such attacks. Even the "soft power" option of punishing sanctions put in place, while less confrontational than a military strike, it was feared, might elicit a forceful Iranian response if the Iranian regime believed its stability was being undermined. However, the tangible steps Iran took were only in the form of warnings, such as forays by Iranian naval vessels near Saudi oil facilities and a suspected cyber attack on Aramco, Saudi Arabia's national oil company.[67]

Saudis were unsure about the likelihood and feasibility of Iran's carrying through with its repeated threats to close the Straits of Hormuz, which could disrupt—even if not stop—oil exports from Saudi Arabia, with some hoping that the West would not accept such a significant economic challenge. Despite being a supporter of harsh sanctions to pressure Iran on the nuclear issue, one Saudi newspaper editor worried that Iran could even resort to "committing suicide by closing and mining the Straits of Hormuz" in a situation fraught with uncertainty.[68] Indeed, one Saudi commentator warned Iran that if the latter closed the Straits the West would react by striking Iran with nuclear weapons, and then destroy the regime and occupy the country.[69] However, given the widespread assumption in Saudi Arabia that not even a Great Power would confront a country that had nuclear weapons, the implicit assumption was that if Iran actually acquired that capability it could pose a more credible threat to close the Straits of Hormuz than it could now. As a writer in a Saudi military journal feared—although projecting such views as being felt in Israel—a nuclear-armed Iran could thereby control oil in the Gulf, thereby giving it a decisive voice on production and pricing.[70] In the event, Riyadh began preparing to revitalize the pipeline to the Red Sea that it had used to bypass the Straits of Hormuz during the Iran–Iraq War in case shipping through the Gulf was disrupted again in any way.[71] And, later, it even considered building a canal—the Salman Canal—connecting the Gulf and the Arabian Sea through Yemen or Oman.[72]

Notes

1 Yusuf Al-Kuwaylit, "Al-Shaykh al-shija" [The Brave Shaykh], *Al-Riyadh*, 11 February 2013, www.alriyadh.com/2013/02/11/article809304.html (hereafter Al-Kuwaylit, "Al-Shaykh").
2 Told to the author during a visit to Saudi Arabia under the auspices of The National Council on U.S.–Arab Relations, February 2000.
3 Ghassan Al-Imam, "Al-amn al-qawmi al-arabi wa'l-qunbula al-iraniya" [Arab National Security and the Iranian Bomb], *Al-Sharq Al-Awsat*, 10 May 2005, www.aawsat.com/print.asp?did=298477&issueno=9660 (hereafter Al-Imam, "Al-amn al-qawmi").
4 "Al-Tasrihat wahdaha la takfi!" [Declarations Alone Are Not Enough!], *Al-Madina*, 5 September 2011, www.al-madina.com/node/324918.
5 Yusuf Al-Kuwaylit, "Al-Khalij wa-kabus al-makhawif" [The Gulf and the Nightmare of Horrors], *Al-Riyadh*, 8 December 2012, www.alriyadh.com/2012/12/08/article790854.html.
6 Ibid.
7 Ahmad Al-Ahmad, "Al-Barnamaj al-nawawi al-khaliji: Hal han al-waqt?" [The Gulf Nuclear Program: Has the Time Come?], *Al-Riyadh*, 5 April 2015, www.alriyadh.com/1036368.
8 Major General Husam Suwaylam (Ret.), "Ahdaf Iran al-siyasiya wa'l-istratijiya wa-asalib tahqiqha," [Iran's Political and Strategic Objectives and the Methods to Achieve Them], *Al-Haras Al-Watani*, part 1, August 2011, 36.
9 Staff Major General Salama bin Hadhdhal Bin Saidan (Ret.), "Al-Tahdid al-irani fi thawbih al-jadid" [The Iranian Threat in Its New Garb], *Al-Jazira*, 16 August 2008, www.al-jazirah.com.sa/2008jaz/aug/16/ar8.htm (hereafter Bin Saidan, "Al-Tahdid al-irani").
10 Al-Sayyid Abu Da'ud, *Tasaud al-madd al-irani fi al-alam al-arabi* [*The Rise of Iranian Expansionism in the Arab World*] (Riyadh: Obeikan Publishing, 2014).
11 Ibid., 409.
12 Editorial "Qunbulat Iran 'al-muntazhara' didd man ya-tura?" [I Wonder, Against Whom Is Iran's 'Expected' Bomb?], *Al-Watan*, 9 January 2012, www.alwatan.com.sa/Articles/detail.aspx?ArticleId=7992 (hereafter "Qunbulat Iran").
13 Al-Kuwaylit, "Al-Shaykh."
14 Muhammad Al-Harbi, "Sharr Iran akbar min quwwatha" [Iran's Evil Is Even Greater Than Its Power], *Ukaz*, 14 October 2011, www.okaz.com.sa/new/Issues/20111014/PrintCon20111014451120.htm.
15 Sultan Abd Allah, "Nawawi Iran yutghi al-amuhadathat Salman-Jabir fi Al-Riyad" [Iran's Nuclear [Program] Dominates the Salman-Jabir Talks in Riyadh], *Ilaf*, 20 November 2011, www.elaph.com.
16 Hay'at Al-Tahrir [Editorial Board], "Al-Mashru al-irani al-iqlimi wa'l-nawawi" [The Iranian Regional Project and the Nuclear [Program]], *MajallatKulliyat Al-Malik Khalid Al-Askariya*, 1 June 2009, www.kkmaq.gov.sa/detail.asp?InNewsItemID=319120&InTemplateKey=print.
17 For example, Bayyina Al-Milhim, "Kharitat Iran ... izalat al-arab am izalat Isra'il?" [Iran's Roadmap: The Elimination of the Arabs or of Israel?], *Anba'ukum* (Riyadh), 12 June 2011, www.anbacom.com/print.php?action=print&m=articlesm&id=8269, and Usama Said Al-Qahtani, "Hal tamlik Iran al-qunbula?" [Will Iran Get the Bomb?], *Al-Watan*, 9 March 2012, www.alwatan.com.sa/Articles/Detail.aspx?ArticleId=9890.
18 Suwaylam, "Ahdaf Iran," 33–34.
19 Ibid., 37.
20 Abd Al-Rahman Al-Rashid, "Lasna kha'ifin min qunbulat Iran al-nawawiya" [We Are Not Afraid of Iran's Atom Bomb], *Al-Sharq Al-Awsat*, 21 February 2010, www.aawsat.com/leader.asp?section=3&article=558022&issueno=11408 (hereafter Al-Rashid, "Lasnakha'ifin").
21 Abd Al-Rahman Al-Rashid, "Li-hadhihi al-asbab nakhsha Iran" [These Are the Reasons Why We Fear Iran], *Al-Sharq Al-Awsat*, 18 April 2006, www.aawsat.com/leader.asp?section=3&article=358858&issueno=10003.
22 Suwaylam, "Ahdaf Iran," 37.

23 Abd Al-Jalil Zayd Al-Marhun, "Al-Nawawi al-irani ... ayn yattajih?" [Iran's Nuclear Program ... Where Is It Headed?], *Al-Riyadh*, 7 June 2013, www.alriyadh.com/2013/06/07/article841654.html.
24 Ibid.
25 "Al-Ru'ya al-istratijiya li'l-qiyada al-saudiya nahw watan amin wa-Khalij mustaqirr" [The Saudi Leadership's Strategic View of a Secure Country and a Stable Gulf], *Al-Barriya*, 27 October 2010, http://RSLF.GOV.SA/English/AlBarriyaMagazine/ArticleSharing Docs/368110ef-abc2-a309-338e212fc9ff.doc.
26 Abd Al-Aziz Al-Suwayd, "Ahyanan ... istikbar wa-salaf siyasi" [Sometimes ... Arrogance and Political Bragging], *Al-Hayat* (Saudi edition), 21 February 2012, http://ksa/da ralhayat.com/ksaarticle/353250.
27 Suwaylam, "Ahdaf Iran," 35.
28 Abd Al-Jalil Zayd Al-Marhun, "Al-Alam al-thalith wa-mudilat al-intishar al-nawawi" [The Third World and the Problem of Nuclear Proliferation], *Al-Riyadh*, 15 June 2001, www.alriyadh.com/2001/06/15/article32562.html (hereafter Al-Marhun, "Al-Alam al-thalith").
29 Fa'iq Fahim, "Duwal majlis al-taawun al-khaliji wa'l-tahaddi al-nawawi al-irani" [The Gulf Cooperation Council States and the Iranian Nuclear Challenge], *Al-Iqtisadiya* (Riyadh), 25 June 2011, www.aleqt.com/2011/06/25/article_552510.print (hereafter Fahim, "Duwalmajlis al-taawun al-khaliji").
30 Turki Abd Allah Al-Sudayri, "Iran awwalan wa-Isra'il thaniyan" [Iran First and Israel Second], *Al-Riyadh*, 13 October 2011, www.alriyadh.com/2011/10/13/article675147.html.
31 Ibid.
32 Sultan Abd Al-Aziz Al-Anqari, "Ghawwasat Iran fi'l-Bahr Al-Ahmar" [Iranian Submarines in the Red Sea], *Al-Madina*, 10 June 2011, www.al-madina.com/print/308754 (hereafter Al-Anqari, "Ghawwasat Iran").
33 Bassam Al-Asali, "Al-Tahaddiyat al-iraniya wa'l-amn al-arabi" [The Iranian Challenges and Arab Security], *Majallat Kulliyat Al-Malik Khalid Al-Askariya*, 21 June 2011, www.kkmaq.gov.sa/detail.asp?InNewsItemID=393305&InTemplateKey=print. (hereafter Al-Asali, "Al-Tahaddiyat al-iraniya").
34 Bin Saidan, "Al-Tahdid al-irani."
35 Khalid Al-Sulayman, "Al-Radikaliya al-nawawiya!" [Nuclear Radicalism!], *Ukaz*, 6 December 2011, www.okaz.com.sa/new/Issues/20111206/PrinCon20111206461025.htm. Other Saudi sources have also highlighted this concern, Abd Al-Munim Mustafa, "Kull shay' lam yaud kafiyan" [All of That Is Not Enough], *Al-Madina*, 14 February 2010, www.al-madina.com/print/224041, and Jasir Al-Jasir, "Al-Saudiya nawawiyan" [A Nuclear Saudi Arabia], *Al-Sharq* (Dammam), 25 February 2012, www.alsharq.net.sa/2012/02/25/138984 (hereafter Al-Jasir, "Al-Saudiya nawawiyan").
36 Suwaylam, "Ahdaf Iran," 30–31.
37 Nasir Al-Sirami, "Al-Tahdidat al-iraniya waqaha am daf?" [Are the Iranian Threats Arrogance or Weakness?], *Al-Jazira*, 17 January 2012, www.al-jazirah.com/20120117/ar6.htm.
38 Suwaylam, "Ahdaf Iran," 36. Similar ideas were expressed by Yusuf al-Kuwaylit, "Sibaq al-tasalluh bayn al-rad wa-makhawif al-hurub" [The Arms Race between Deterrence and the Fear of War], *Al-Riyadh*, 20 September 2010, www.alriyadh.com/2010/09/20/article561050.html.
39 Brigadier General Ali bin Hasan Al-Tawati (Ret.), "Hal falan tukhifna al-harb al-nawawiya?" [Does Nuclear War Really Frighten Us?], *Ukaz*, 30 July 2015, http://okaz.co/bwlhWdsKw.
40 Hamad bin Abd Allah Al-Luhaydan, "Al-Matami wa'l-tawajjuhat al-askariya al-iraniya" [Iranian Ambitions and Military Bearings], *Al-Riyadh*, 6 September 2013, www.alriyadh.com/865450.
41 See Norman Cigar, *Saddam Hussein's Nuclear Vision: An Atomic Shield and Sword for Conquest* (Quantico, VA: Marine Corps University Press, 2011), 25–30.

42 Ibid.
43 Al-Rashid, "Lasna kha'ifin."
44 Huda Al-Husayni, "Iran al-nawawiya tuidihya' al-imbiraturiya al-farisiya" [A Nuclear Iran Will Revive the Persian Empire], *Al-Sharq Al-Awsat*, 26 January 2006, www.aawsat.com/print.asp?did=345175&issueno=9921. This became a common theme in Saudi discourse, as in Al-Anqari, "Ghawwasat Iran."
45 For example, "Iran tuhaddid bi-imtar duwal Al-Khalij al-mutaawina ma Amirikabi'l-sawarikh" [Iran Threatens to Rain Missiles on any Gulf State Cooperating with America], *Al-Sharq Al-Awsat*, 11 June 2007, www.aawsat.com/print.asp?did=423146&issueno=10422.
46 Nina Tannenwald, "The Nuclear Taboo: The United States and the Normative Basis of Nuclear Non-Use," *International Organization*, lviii, 3, Summer 1999, 435.
47 Suhayla Zayn Al-Abidin Hammad, "Al-Ijtima al-tashawuri li-duwal al-20 wa-tajrid al-mintaqa min al-silah al-nawawi" [The Consultative Meeting of the G20 and Clearing the Region of Nuclear Weapons], *Al-Madina*, 6 March 2012, www.al-madina.com/printhtml/362496.
48 Al-Imam, "Al-amn al-qawmi," Editorial "Al-Khatar al-nawawi haqiqa wa-laysa mujarrad tahwil" [The Nuclear Menace Is a Real One and Not Just a Bogeyman], *Al-Watan*, 9 November 2012, www.alwatan.com.sa/Editors_Note/Deafult.aspx, and Sufuq Al-Shammari, "Hal tusaddiqun Iran?" [Do You Believe Iran?], *Al-Riyadh*, 14 April 2015, www.alriyadh.com/1039006.
49 Yusuf Kamil Khattab, "Qira'a fi al-malaff al-nawawi al-isra'ili" [An Analysis of the Israeli Nuclear Program], *Majallat Kulliyat Al-Malik Khalid Al-Askariya*, 1 December 2002, 62.
50 Id bin Masud Al-Juhani, "Al-quwwa al-salam wa'l-nasr" [Power, Peace, and Victory], *Al-Hayat*, 21 February 2009, www.daralhayat.net/actions/print.php.
51 Gavriel Fiske, "Avraham Burg Panned for Breaking 'Nuclear Ambiguity'" *The Times of Israel* (Jerusalem), 8 December 2013, www.timesofisrael.com/avraham-burg-panned-for-breaking-nuclear-ambiguity/#ixzz3BX4E1XFe, Reuven Pedatzur, "Israel's Rearguard Battle for Nuclear Ambiguity," *Haaretz* (Tel-Aviv), 23 September 2013, www.haaretz.com/opinion/.premium-1.548309, and Amir Oren, "Israeli Nuclear Ambiguity as an Illusion," *Haaretz*, 5 January 2014, www.haaretz.com/opinion/.premium-1.566994.
52 Talal Salih Bannan, "Ilan Isra'il dawla nawawiya!" [Proclaiming Israel a Nuclear State!], *Ukaz*, 3 June 2014, www.okaz.com.sa/new/Issues/20140603/Princon20140603703592.htm.
53 Abd Al-Rahman Al-Rashid, "Al-Qunbula al-nawawiya al-saudiya" [A Saudi Atom Bomb], *Al-Sharq Al-Awsat*, 16 November 2013, http://aawsat.com/node/9752.
54 Prince Saud Al-Faysal, speaking at a press conference in Riyadh, 15 February 2010, "Al-Mu'tamar al-suhufi al-mushtarak li-sahib al-sumuww al-malaki al-amir Saud Al-Faysal ma maali wazirat al-kharijiya al-amirikiya" [Joint Press Conference with His Royal Highness Prince Saud Al-Faysal and Her Excellency the American Secretary of State], Saudi Foreign Ministry website, www.mofa.gov.sa/Minister/PressConferences/Pages/NewsArticleID105722.aspx.
55 Khalis Halabi, "Madha law imtalakat Iran silah al-shaytan?" [What If Iran Acquired the Devil's Weapon?], *Al-Watan*, 2 August 2010, www.alwatan.com.sa/Articles/detail.aspx?ArticleId=1551.
56 Abd Al-Aziz Al-Khamis, "Han waqt al-silah al-nawawi al-saudi" [The Time Has Come for a Saudi Nuclear Weapon], *Ibda*, 23 February 2012, http://ebdaa.com/?act=artc&id=5577&print=1. This concern was also stressed in Al-Jasir, "Al-Saudiyanawawiyan."
57 Abd Al-Rahman Al-Rashid, "Isra'il tashinn harb Al-Khalij al-muqbila!" [Israel Will Spark the Next Gulf War!], *Al-Sharq Al-Awsat*, 18 April 2013, www.aawsat.com.
58 "Qunbulat Iran."
59 Muhammad Sadiq Diyab, "Madha law daghat ahmaq ala zurar?" [What If a Fool Pressed the Button?], *Al-Sharq Al-Awsat*, 3 June 2009, http://archive.aawsat.com/leader.asp?section=3&issueno=11145&article=521831.

60 Abd Al-Rahman Al-Rashid, "Ala man tarmi Iran qunbulatha al-nawawiya?" [On Whom Would Iran Drop Its Atom Bomb?], *Al-Sharq Al-Awsat*, 26 November 2008, www.aawsat.com/print.asp?did=495492&issueno=10956.
61 Ibid.
62 Ibid. The same idea was developed in Hamad bin Abd Allah Al-Luhaydan, "Abad al-tasalluh al-nawawi wa-tadaiyatih" [Dimensions of Nuclear Arming and of Its Consequences], *Al-Riyadh*, 29 May 2009, www.alriyadh.com/2009/05/29/article433463.html.
63 Al-Asali, "Al-Tahaddiyat al-iraniya." Other journalists shared this view, such as Adnan Kamil Salah, "Tasawwaru uhlumu udu!" [Imagine, Dream, Pray!], *Al-Madina*, 13 May 2010, www.al-madina.com/print/247504 (hereafter Salah, "Tasawwaru").
64 Ghassan Al-Imam, "Qanabil nawawiya li'l-aghrad al-silmiya!" [Nuclear Bombs for Peaceful Purposes], *Al-Sharq Al-Awsat*, 11 May 2010, www.aawsat.com/print.asp?did=569092&issueno=11487.
65 Ibid.
66 Staff Major General Khidr Al-Dahrawi (Ret.), "Al-Ahdaf al-akthar taarrudan li'l-hajamat al-jawwiyawa'l-sarukhiya fi halat al-harb" [The Targets Most at Risk to Air and Missile Attacks in Case of War], *Majallat Kulliyat Al-Malik Khalid Al-Askariya*, 21 June 2011, www.kkmaq.gov.sa/detail.asp?InNewsItemID=393312&InTemplateKey=print.
67 Muhammad Al-Tayir, "Al-Rashid: Tihran arsalat qawarib musallaha li-mintaqa qariba min abar al-naft al-saudiya" [Al-Rashid: Tehran Sent Armed Vessels to an Area Near the Saudi Oil Fields], *Sabq* (Riyadh), 21 January 2012, http://sabq.org/58bfde, and Ibrahim Al-Athimin, "Al-Saudiya-Iran-Al-Saudiya wa'l-asliha al-saybaraniya" [Saudi Arabia-Iran-Saudi Arabia and Cyber Weapons], *Al-Yawm*, 12 December 2012, www.alyaum.com/News/mobile/art/65454.html.
68 Yusuf Al-Kuwaylit, "Ma hiya dawafi al-munawarat al-askariya fi Al-Khalij?" [What Are the Motives for the Military Exercises in the Gulf?], *Al-Riyadh*, 18 December 2012, www.alriyadh.com/2012/09/18/article769115.html.
69 Isam Al-Zamil, "Iran wa-imdadat al-naft" [Iran and Oil Supplies], *Al-Yawm*, 2 January 2012, www.alyaum.com/News/art/39772.html.
70 Sayyid Isa Muhammad, "Al-Sira al-irani-al-isra'ili" [The Iranian–Israeli Conflict], *Majallat Kulliyat Al-Malik Khalid Al-Askariya*, 1 December 2009, www.kkmaq.gov.sa/detail.asp?InNewsItemID=342409&InTemplateKey=print.
71 "Khabir: Imkaniyat ziyadat al-taqa al-istiabiya li'l-khatt al-qadim ila 1.65 milyun barmil; Al-Saudiya tuid ta'hil khatt al-naft al-badil li-Hurmuz" [An Expert: It Is Possible to Increase the Capacity of the Old Pipeline to 1.65 Million Barrels; Saudi Arabia Again Activates the Alternate Pipeline to Hormuz], *Al-Arabiya TV*, 29 June 2012, www.alarabiya.net/save_print.php?print=1&cont_id=223395, and Abd Al-Wahhab Al-Sadun, "Al-Tahdidat al-iraniya bi-ighlaq Madyaq Hormuz farqaat ilamiya" [The Iranians' Threat to Close the Straits of Hormuz Is a Media Red Herring], *Al-Iqtisadiya*, 11 March 2015, www.aleqt.com/2015/03/11/article_938822.html.
72 Fahd Al-Ta'if, "Ibn Umar yudih tafasil 'Qanat Salman': Sa-tuid al-hayat li'l-Rub Al-Khali" [Ibn Umar Clarifies Details about the "Salman Canal": It Will Bring Life Back to the Rub Al-Khali], *Sabq*, 2 September 2015, http://sabq.org/SNFgde?printing=.

Bibliography

Cigar, Norman, *Saddam Hussein's Nuclear Vision: An Atomic Shield and Sword for Conquest* (Quantico, VA: Marine Corps University Press, 2011).

Tannenwald, Nina, "The Nuclear Taboo: The United States and the Normative Basis of Nuclear Non-Use," *International Organization*, lviii, 3, Summer 1999, 433–468.

5

THINKING IN TERMS OF SOLUTIONS

How to stop Iran

A key element in Riyadh's nuclear thinking has been to prevent Iran from becoming a nuclear power and highlighting the looming Iranian problem publicly begged the question of what could be done to neutralize the nuclear threat if and when it actually came to pass. Even if not challenged openly by public opinion, any government would likely feel sensitive about providing an answer to a threat about which it had repeatedly informed, and even alarmed, the public, thereby raising the latter's level of concern. By and large, Saudi Arabia recognized that there was not much that could be done to counter the nuclear threat from Israel. It was too late for that in any case. Moreover, as noted, Israel increasingly was seen as a far less imminent threat than that emanating from Iran and, not surprisingly, the Saudis' focus has been, instead, on how to deal with Iran. Saudi Arabia hoped to avoid creating a repetition of the situation it had come to face with Israel and believed that there was still time to act. Although, realistically, Riyadh had extremely little leverage to have an impact on Iran's nuclear policy, the Saudis nevertheless engaged in intensive analysis and discussion on the likelihood and effectiveness of the various options being considered by the international community to stop Iran's march toward nuclear weapons. In particular, Saudi official spokesmen and analysts focused on the implications of such options for Saudi national interests and on how Riyadh could adapt.

Doing nothing and accommodating Iran

As for the first option, that of doing nothing and accommodating to a new situation, Saudi Arabia implicitly rejected it. To do nothing, from the Saudi perspective, would have been to abdicate any possibility of the international community's countering what was already an active threat, and one that would only increase if

Iran acquired nuclear weapons. If anything, most Saudis believed that a passive attitude would only encourage Iran in its aggressiveness.

True, some senior Saudis may have at least considered the possibility of accommodating Iran by recognizing the latter's interests. For example, in July 2011, the country's Foreign Minister, Prince Saud Al-Faysal—in a departure from the harsh rhetoric that had been emanating from Saudi Arabia—appeared to suggest that one needed to recognize Iranian interests and power when he said that "Iran is a neighboring country; if it wants a leadership role it must take into consideration the interests of the countries of the region and not [only] its own interests."[1] However, in what was a highly unusual follow-up, a Saudi academic took Prince Saud Al-Faysal to task by name publicly, noting that his remarks differed from previous positions and that it seemed that Saudi Arabia was accepting Iran's leading role in the region, and asked whether this represented a change in Saudi policy and whether Saudi Arabia was now willing to share influence in the Gulf with Iran. Indeed, he asked directly if that meant that the Gulf states now accepted Iran's leadership, if this was really Saudi policy, and if Saudi Arabia was now prepared to coexist with Iran's ambitions. Clarifying Saudi Arabia's policy and interests, the commentator stressed, instead, that "there is no substitute for Saudi Arabia and the Gulf states to be an effective player in the regional power balance equation ... and there is no excuse for asking Iran to safeguard our interests." And, he added, "I do not believe that Saudi Arabia can or will accept coexistence with a leading role or hegemony by Iran in the Gulf." Asking himself if Prince Saud Al-Faysal really meant to link a leading role for Iran in return for the latter's protecting the Gulf states' interests, he concluded that accepting such a role for Iran would represent "a revolution in Saudi policy." Instead, what Saudi Arabia had to do was ensure its own self-defense and demand that Iran end its quest for nuclear weapons.[2]

Given the context of the Saudi political system, such immediate and forceful public questioning of a senior member of the royal family probably suggests some backing from influential circles within the royal family and may have reflected differences of opinion at the top about the approach to Iran. Subsequently, Prince Saud Al-Faysal reverted to the more standard Saudi hardline as, at a GCC foreign ministers' summit held in Riyadh in November 2011, he condemned not only Iran's "persistent interference" in the affairs of neighboring states but also its pursuit of nuclear weapons, which he noted "is considered a patent threat to the security and stability of the region."[3]

Nevertheless, some elements of a Saudi carrot and stick policy, or at least a desire to avoid a direct confrontation with Iran, remained, as in February 2012 two Iranian warships deploying to the Red Sea were allowed to make a port call in Jeddah.[4] Likewise, a Saudi military journal at the end of 2012 published two articles—albeit written by foreigners—which focused on the desirability of good Arab–Iranian relations and the need to come to an understanding based on the fact that they shared a common geography, history, culture, and political, economic, and security interests, and suggested many potential joint projects, even on civilian nuclear energy.[5] The principal stumbling block, however, was said to remain the doubts around Tehran's nuclear intentions, which had to be resolved first. Urging Iran to abandon its nuclear quest, the Saudi media even appealed to Iran's purported shared interest with the Gulf countries as common victims of a supposed "vast conspiracy" by the West and Israel to spark a war between Iran and its Gulf neighbors, which would destroy both belligerents and allow Israel to dominate the region.[6]

A foreign nuclear umbrella as an alternative?

Could the provision of a nuclear umbrella by another country represent a viable policy incentive that the Saudi leadership would see as a sufficient security guarantee to preclude a nuclear option in response to an Iranian nuclear breakout? Such guarantees have been effective in limiting proliferation in several regions of the world, but the Saudi case may be less amenable to such a solution, and there has been long-standing skepticism in Riyadh about such proposals. As one Saudi political scientist put it when discussing the nuclear threats in the region, "only the Arabs themselves can defend the Arabs' security."[7]

First, it is doubtful that the Saudis would view the Pakistani nuclear deterrent as a reliable umbrella for their own security based just on religious solidarity. As a member of the royal family who was later to become Prince Sultan's adviser on national security noted, "Saudi Arabia does not accept the notion that a Pakistani bomb is an Islamic bomb. Instead, national interest is regarded as the most likely factor affecting how nuclear capabilities will be used."[8] Likewise, when then-Secretary of State Hillary Clinton floated the possibility in 2009 of an American nuclear umbrella for the Middle East, the Saudi press was skeptical at best, and even hostile, probably reflecting official views which the Saudi leadership would have been reluctant to express openly. One Saudi columnist claimed that the inclusion of Israel in such an arrangement represented a political stumbling block, and asked "Is Israel a friendly country?"—a key question for him.[9] According to the same columnist, it was Israel's nuclear weapons that were the "real threat to peace in the region." In fact, by offering protection to "friends," that limitation would even spur others to acquire nuclear weapons, as they would then feel vulnerable to attacks by a country protected by the American nuclear umbrella.[10] Another concern was that such a relationship would create an uncomfortable dependence for the junior partner. As the same writer saw the 2009 U.S. proposal:

> This situation reminds us of what happened with Europe when the Soviet Union was still in existence, when the United States extended a nuclear umbrella "with the intent of protecting its European allies from Soviet nuclear weapons." Some of the countries even today are finding it difficult to free themselves from that American domination. The same thing is happening with the countries of Eastern Europe, as the United States extends a nuclear umbrella that Washington claims is intended to protect those countries from a

nuclear Iran, but which raises concerns in Russia and in other countries, who see it as a threat to their own security.[11]

In the event, Riyadh did not need to oppose the idea officially, as Egypt's President Husni Mubarak came out against it, effectively thwarting it.[12] In the wake of the regime changes resulting from the Arab Spring, there was likely to be even less regional support or "cover" for a Saudi acceptance of an umbrella than before. Even those individuals, such as Prince Turki Al-Faysal, who had considered an American nuclear umbrella as theoretically workable, did so only on condition that the Middle East as a whole became a nuclear-free zone, including the requirement that Israel relinquish its nuclear arsenal, thereby voiding any realistic near-term possibility of such an umbrella.[13]

At the same time, there was a growing sense that the United States would simply not be able to control nuclear proliferation everywhere by using this mechanism. As a columnist in a Saudi-owned paper put it, "the world policeman [i.e. the United States] will not be able to establish a nuclear umbrella to defend its spheres of influence from threats."[14] In fact, reflecting an anarchic world system, the writer envisioned the possibility that the NPT would collapse and that the world would become a "law of the jungle" environment, which "will force 'the school principal' [i.e. the United States] to think about just protecting himself instead of worrying about protecting others."[15]

Moreover, there were also growing uncertainties about the reliability of American guarantees, with concerns about the depth of the United States' commitment to support its allies in the region. An article by an academic from the UAE, but published in a Saudi-owned newspaper, discussing the threat that Iran's quest for nuclear weapons posed to the Gulf, openly raised doubts about U.S. reliability:

> The GCC has legitimate concerns about the United States, and it is particularly not wise to rely on American protection in light of the decline of American unipolarity. There is mounting skepticism about the United States' ability and willingness to fulfill its security and stability obligations in the region over the long term ... Relying solely on the American protection services is not convincing and its date of expiration has almost been reached. What Washington offers in security and military services is no longer of the same quality as before.[16]

Such concerns were heightened in the wake of the toppling of a number of rulers during the Arab Spring. Revealingly, senior Saudi policymakers were reportedly upset by what they interpreted to have been the United States' abrupt abandonment of its close regional ally, Egyptian president Husni Mubarak, which raised doubts about the reliability of expected U.S. support and protection in other cases. Prince Turki Al-Faysal, for example, probably reflecting impressions at the senior levels of the royal family, noted that relations at the time between Saudi Arabia and the United States were "below average," among other reasons due to Saudi irritation with:

the haste with which the American leadership, for example, pushed President Husni Mubarak out of power, even before the Egyptian people had expressed their opinion ... this angered me personally ... Saudi citizens [on the contrary] are faithful to their friends and allies ... if only [President Barack Obama] had waited a little and let the Egyptian people make their own decision.

In contrast, according to Prince Turki, at the same time Saudi King Abd Allah had been providing advice to Mubarak privately, apparently on how to deal with the crisis.[17] As a commentary in the Saudi press also argued, "America is no longer a reliable friend for its strategic friends and allies, with the exception of Israel." As a result, the United States' friends in the Middle East "must look out for their own interests without reference to those of the United States." Specifically, alluding to the experience with Mubarak, the commentary concluded that "if America expects that its biggest selling point to its friends is a security umbrella, that umbrella was smashed on the banks of the Nile."[18] In late 2012, a Saudi newspaper editor raised directly the possibility of secret U.S.–Iranian talks at the expense of the Gulf countries. Although he acknowledged that "this perhaps might not be at the expense of U.S.–Gulf relations, at least for now," he also wondered "should we become prisoners of a foreign umbrella or should we [instead] take into account what is of benefit to our future by relying on ourselves?"[19]

Paradoxically, according to press reports, as prospects increased for a nuclear agreement between the international community and Iran, the United States hinted at a nuclear umbrella for the Middle East in early 2015, but the Saudi reception was no more welcoming than it had been up to then.[20] The acceptability of a defense umbrella depends in large part on the credibility of such commitments, and one academic still worried specifically that, given U.S. interests, once Iran acquired a nuclear deterrent, "U.S. guarantees will evaporate" and then America "under no circumstance will sacrifice its sons and weapons in order to protect us."[21] Significantly, a frequent theme in Saudi writing has been that even its allies are not comfortable with a total reliance on the United States. Drawing on perceived lessons from the Cold War, for example, a Saudi political scientist asserted that Great Britain and France had both pursued their own nuclear weapons programs precisely because they did not have:

> the assurance ... that Washington would come to their assistance with nuclear weapons in case they were subjected to a Soviet nuclear attack; ultimately, the United States would not sacrifice Washington or New York, for example, for the sake of defending Paris and London.[22]

A columnist, for his part, dismissed any offer of a U.S. missile defense shield as part of a conventional umbrella, seeing in such an offer a U.S. doubt as to the effectiveness of the then-impending Nuclear Agreement in preventing Tehran's acquisition of nuclear weapons. And, citing the real danger as nuclear weapons and not missiles and the need, therefore, for a foolproof defense, he reaffirmed that Iran's acquisition of nuclear weapons would set off a nuclear arms race to meet that challenge.[23] Another commentator even attributed a willingness to sell a missile defense shield as a way "under the guise of ensuring [the Gulf states] from Iran's nuclear and conventional weapons" for the United States to get Gulf money.[24] Likewise, a Saudi journalist, terming a U.S. nuclear umbrella as "unreliable," suggested buying a nuclear capability instead as a faster option.[25] Despite reassurances by President Obama at the Camp David summit in May 2015 that the United States would defend the Gulf countries against aggression, many Saudis were disappointed not only that the guarantees were not in writing but also interpreted such guarantees as not including a preventive war to thwart Iran from acquiring nuclear weapons, that is that the United States would not actually pre-empt the most significant threat to the Gulf.[26] In fact, after the Camp David summit, some in Saudi Arabia held that the time had now come for the unification of the GCC as a way to preclude the need to rely on others, since "self-reliance is the backbone of confronting any challenges" rather than "waiting for others to defend [us]."[27] And Saudi Foreign Minister Al-Jubeir made it a point to underline while on a visit to Jordan in July 2015 that although the relationship with the United States remained a strategic one, "Saudi Arabia relies on itself to protect its own interests."[28]

Furthermore, Saudis often have raised concerns about a perceived U.S. retrenchment in the region vis-à-vis Iran. Although not articulated openly in official quarters, there was an undercurrent in the Saudi media critical of the United States on that score, claiming that the latter's invasion of Iraq in 2003 had made it possible for Iran to become dominant there. Expressions such as that the United States had "delivered Iraq to Iran on a golden platter" became common, even by influential journalists close to the palace.[29] At the time of the 2013 Korean crisis, some Saudis even interpreted the commitment which the United States displayed to its regional allies as an indication that Washington differentiated between those in East Asia which "it would avoid sacrificing at any price," and countries in the Middle East, where only Israel was said to qualify for that status for the United States.[30]

Some Saudis limited themselves to raising general—but transparent—reservations about outside protectors, as did one editor, who noted pointedly when discussing the Iranian threat that "we all understand full well that ... friendships do not last forever ... and we do not trust other parties to concur with our views and objectives."[31] Others were openly alarmist, often fearing that the United States could decide to make a deal with Iran or, as one academic put it in 2010, "what if the United States decides to cooperate with Iran to divide up influence and interests in the region?"[32] Saudi journalists were already suspicious of even limited Iranian–U.S. contacts. One journalist claimed that "the Gulf states feel that the secret as well as open talks which are being conducted between Washington and Tehran do not take [the Gulf states] into consideration to any degree," which "annoys the Gulf states."[33] This skepticism was deep-seated, and even as early as 2006 a commentator worried that the United States "will inevitably act to reach an understanding [with a nuclear-armed Iran] on the Gulf's future."[34] And, with reference to Iran's future nuclear capability, the same writer had concluded that "the time has come for self-reliance ... and to create the conditions for a strategic defense balance."[35]

However, in practical terms, as emerged at a roundtable at *Al-Riyadh*'s editorial office in April 2012 between a delegation of visiting Japanese politicians and businessmen and a group of Saudi journalists, the Saudi hosts acknowledged to their guests that "the Gulf states cannot dispense with the United States, and the strategic alliance with the latter is profound and deeply-rooted ... the alliance with the United States is the best option." At the same time, nevertheless, as one of the Saudis present stressed, the Gulf countries "have a right ... to look to a variety of sources for armaments, from any country whatsoever." And, the same speaker continued, "reliance on the United States is not a completely dependable option, and the Kingdom will turn to any country with which it can cooperate."[36]

Considering the active options—striking or squeezing Iran's nuclear program?

As reports of Iranian progress in the nuclear field accumulated over the years, Saudi Arabia, as well as the international community as a whole, weighed potential active options for dealing with the emerging challenge. Although a largely passive player in this respect, apart from the diplomatic pressure it could exert, Saudi Arabia's analysis in this arena nevertheless mattered as it provides an insight into its own thinking and policy on nuclear weapons. In a way, Saudi Arabia would probably have been content to do nothing, if the problem of the Iranian threat was solved by third parties. Specifically, Riyadh followed closely the prospects for the international community to deal with Iran's nuclear program either by military strikes or by pressure using economic and political sanctions, and sought to exert what influence it could on the relevant players.

The strike option

A military strike against Iran's nuclear infrastructure, if successful, potentially could have resolved the issue permanently or at least would have postponed the necessity for Riyadh to make a decision about acquiring its own nuclear capability. However, the success of such a strike was by no means certain, while the security, political, and economic consequences in the region could have been severe. Not surprisingly, the Saudis were very interested in trying to determine the likelihood of such a strike. Informed Saudi opinion on whether or not a strike was forthcoming was often divided and continued to oscillate between the two prospects, although an evolution occurred over the years towards skepticism.

Initially, Saudi sources had suggested they were convinced that the United States would act decisively to prevent Iran's acquisition of nuclear weapons. As the SANG's journal saw it in 2006, Iran would be targeted by the United States with an air and missile attack "because the [United States] believes that Iran's acquisition of nuclear weapons and the missiles capable of delivering the latter are a direct and grave threat to its vital interests, and it will not allow that even if it requires striking dozens of facilities, sites, and military targets."[37] By 2009, however, the Saudi media had begun to suggest that the United States was still considering its options and had not made a decision yet on whether or not to strike Iran.[38]

According to foreign press reports, the Saudi leadership at least as early as 2010 was said to support strikes against Iran's nuclear facilities—including by Israel—although it could not say so in public.[39] Indications surfaced repeatedly over the years that Saudi Arabia was prepared to facilitate any Israeli attack against Iran and, in fact, reports surfaced in 2013 that Riyadh and Tel-Aviv were coordinating operational support in case of an Israeli attack on Iran.[40] Apparently, such cooperation directed at Iran continued, with accounts of secret meetings between the two countries as late as 2015.[41] Even some Saudi journalists hinted at such cooperation, with one noting his disappointment that Israel had not struck already and that were Israel to do so "more than one state in the region would facilitate and even welcome or only pretend to be angry about such an operation."[42]

However, as one would have expected, whenever hints of such support became public, the resulting reactions in the region were exploited against the Saudi regime by religious dissidents and, in particular, by domestic and regional Shia sources.[43] At least in public, Saudi decisionmakers and other senior figures sought to engage in damage control in order to respond to the negative publicity caused by the leaks, and began to express vehement opposition to such strikes against Iran. As Prince Turki Al-Faysal told a German magazine, "I have dealt with these issues all of my life and I am telling you: Saudi Arabia would never accept to allow Israel to attack any country in the area whatever that country was."[44] Likewise, reflecting this political sensitivity, Saudi Arabia strenuously denied rumors that it had handed over to the United States an Iranian nuclear scientist who had come on the Pilgrimage.[45] However, Prince Walid bin Talal, when asked in late 2013 whether the Arab states would support an Israeli strike on Iran's nuclear program, noted "Publicly, they would be against it … Privately, they would love it."[46] Although not in a government position, he often expresses opinions that Riyadh cannot voice officially.

Apart from the issue of image, Saudi policymakers quite probably were also becoming increasingly concerned about escalating Iranian threats of reprisals in case of an attack on its nuclear program. As a senior figure in the Saudi royal family remarked to the author in 2011, he was "fully against any Israeli or American" military strike, citing concerns about Iranian retaliation, as he termed Iran "a paper tiger with steel claws."[47] As one Saudi observer noted, a strike against Iran might not succeed, but would result instead in retaliation by the latter against its neighbors—which could include the targeting of vulnerable Gulf oil facilities, power grids, and water desalination plants—as well as lead to heightened Iranian support for subversion in the region.[48] Some in Saudi Arabia believed a strike would only delay Iran's progress in any case, with an end to the nuclear quest only possible through regime change, given Tehran's strong commitment to the program.[49] Others fretted whether a military strike would spark a regional war or whether Iran's nuclear program would be destroyed for good, with one editorialist noting in 2013 that "History does not permit us to sleep [soundly] by relying on this second scenario."[50]

Over the years, a gradual pessimism appeared to take over in leadership circles and the media in Riyadh, with an increasing conviction that there would not be a U.S. or Israeli military strike against Iran, or that even such a measure might prove of only limited effectiveness in derailing Iran's march toward nuclear weapons, although such assessments would fluctuate depending on varying news reports from the West. Some observers assumed that the international community as a whole simply lacked the resolve to stop Iran.[51] Still others believed that the West had concluded that it was already too late for a military strike to reverse Iran's trajectory in any case.[52] One Saudi analyst judged that the political and media escalation by the United States was intended merely to pressure Iran and to reassure the Gulf countries that the West would not abandon the region.[53] A Saudi researcher, for his part, speculated that the United States, instead, would seek to contain Iran with a Cold War-style strategy, since military action entailed too many drawbacks.[54]

Some Saudis believed that the United States would not make a final decision on whether to strike Iran in any case while it was still involved in Iraq and Afghanistan, given the potential consequences for U.S. forces in the region.[55] Others in military circles concluded that even after these wars the United States might be reluctant to act. For example, a Saudi military study in 2009 posited that, as a result of the cost of the wars in Afghanistan and Iraq, "the United States' confidence in the effectiveness of preventive wars has been shaken."[56] In particular, as another military study argued, the United States simply would not be able to undertake another war, as "the U.S. wars—against terrorism, in Iraq, and in Afghanistan—have attrited U.S. power and have made it impossible for [the United States] to attack any other country."[57] A Saudi pundit, for his part, also judged that a U.S. strike was not probable, since the state of the U.S. economy made American policymakers wary of starting a new war, although a strike by Israel might be more likely.[58] Likewise, a Saudi writer claiming to cite U.S. military experts to the effect that a strike against Iran would not be decisive in any case, concluded that "President Barack Obama is not a man who wants to embark on conflicts."[59] And, by the end of 2011, Prince Turki Al-Faysal had decided that convincing Iran to stop its nuclear program had already failed.[60]

Subsequent analysis only confirmed such judgments. One Saudi observer concluded in 2012 that "there is not a sufficient consensus [in the United States] to launch a war against Iran." According to that same author, "the Vietnam experience" and what he said were at least partial U.S. defeats in Iraq and Afghanistan "have made ... American leaders ... think long and hard and to delay making difficult decisions such as this."[61] By that time, a Saudi commentator had also determined that "the military option against [Iran] has become a remote likelihood."[62] At the end of 2012, a senior officer writing in a military journal analyzed in detail the divided opinion in both the United States and Israel—with the

United States having the final say, in his view—and concluded that Washington for now at least would hold off on a strike in order to give economic sanctions time to work.[63] By early 2013, one Saudi pundit stated openly that "Iran knows full well that hints of a military option will not be fulfilled," and even interpreted harsher warnings from President Obama during his visit to Israel in March 2013 as "empty promises," and affirmed that "I do not believe they will see the light of day."[64]

The Saudi media in general also viewed the likelihood of an Israeli strike as increasingly limited as time went by. Some initially were of the opinion that Prime Minister Benjamin Netanyahu "will not accept Iran's emergence and continuation as a nuclear power in the region."[65] However, as one observer noted in November 2011, Israeli talk of preparations to strike were little more than "bogus propaganda," ostensibly intended to divert attention from the Palestinian issue.[66] As an editorial asserted, "objective conditions and the strategic interconnection of interests among various parties bring talk of directing a military strike by Israel and its allies into the realm of the impossible."[67] Another editorial commented that, at best, the Israeli government itself was divided over whether to launch a strike.[68] Key to this view was the Saudi assumption that "Israel knows that Tehran has passed the point of vulnerability in its nuclear program."[69] Indeed, others criticized the United States and Israel for doing nothing to stop Iran, and claimed that this was part of a pattern that had also been applied to North Korea's nuclear program.[70] Alleging that Israeli and Iranian interests against the Arabs coincided, one observer held that Israeli influence exercised through the Jewish community in America—who he said had a disproportionate presence in Congress, "not to speak of their control of financial capital, centers of influence, and the media, and their dominance over most of the think tanks ... and influence over centers of decision-making"—shaped U.S. policy to work toward a secret understanding with Iran.[71]

Squeezing Iran—the soft power option

Saudi Arabia, perhaps not surprisingly, came to prefer that non-military methods, such as economic and political sanctions, succeed in stopping Iran's quest for nuclear weapons rather than seeing a military strike with its attendant risks or doing nothing. However, the Saudi media expressed lingering doubts whether international sanctions would be effective, with one editorial characterizing such efforts as "insufficient," and concluding that "this situation raises doubts about how serious the West is about dealing with the potential Iranian nuclear threat if Iran succeeds in achieving its goals."[72] In particular, there were doubts about the effectiveness of sanctions if not enforced strictly, with one editorial noting that Iran had been able to deal with sanctions during the Khomeini era while, due to Iran's increased capabilities and expected sanction-busting, "any future Western or international sanctions will be insufficient as long as major industrial nations are not serious about enforcement."[73] By 2010, some Saudis were already suggesting that even the tougher sanctions then being discussed might delay, but not prevent, Iran's going nuclear.[74]

However, with the new, more stringent, financial and oil sanctions that the United States and the European Union began applying on Iran in 2011 and 2012, Saudi Arabia appeared to become more optimistic about the prospects for the success of "soft power." In fact, a senior figure in the Saudi royal family, speaking to an American audience, stressed the desirability of "squeezing" Iran through the latter's oil sector as a way to make it more difficult for Tehran to meet its citizens' needs, to thus convince it to forgo the nuclear option.[75] Saudi Arabia supported the sanctions actively, with Prince Abd Al-Aziz bin Salman, Saudi Arabia's Deputy Minister of Petroleum and Mineral Resources, among other Saudi officials, reassuring domestic opinion and the international community that his country would ensure sufficient oil supplies to replace reduced oil deliveries from Iran, whether as a result of the embargo or if Iran tried to disrupt traffic through the Straits of Hormuz.[76]

Watching and waiting

Increasingly, Riyadh seemed to have concluded that it could do little to affect the situation in any event, and that it would be prudent to wait and see what the international community could accomplish in stopping Iran, especially after the new sanctions had begun to take effect. Over time, there developed a noticeable change in Saudi press coverage, with a decrease by mid-2012 of the earlier extensive analytical writing on Iran in the Saudi military media. In the civilian media, editorials on the Iranian nuclear threat appeared less frequently than before, although the coverage still agreed with previous positions and, in particular, with the assessment that Iran was continuing on its nuclear path. To a certain extent, at the same time, Saudi authorities may have felt that a solid analytical and political case had already been made for the domestic public and that it might now be prudent to keep a low profile while the international community exerted pressure on Iran.

With the introduction of the more rigorous sanctions, Saudi press reports began to focus on the resulting severe economic difficulties which Iran was experiencing as a result of the cutbacks in oil exports and of the financial transaction restrictions.[77] Indeed, one editorial in the influential Saudi daily *Al-Riyadh* assessed that Iran was jeopardizing its economic stability and that the resulting domestic discontent could lead to an "internal explosion." The editorial even called for, in essence, regime change through a movement similar to those elsewhere during the Arab Spring, with hopes for free elections and a pluralistic democracy.[78] Nevertheless, in time, Saudi media opinion, based on the apparent lack of progress in subsequent negotiations, began to doubt that even the economic sanctions would succeed, claiming that the Iranian regime "does not care if the people are hungry or sick" and that Tehran would continue to pursue its nuclear goals.[79] The 2013 crisis with North Korea seemed to reinforce this perception, as Saudis noted with amazement the extent to which a state was willing to sacrifice its economic well-being in order to ensure nuclear weapons for its security.[80] At the same time, there were suggestions in the Saudi-owned media that the United States had exhausted all its options with Iran and—disinclined to use military force—was now backtracking from prevention to a posture of containment, and was only looking for ways to rationalize the change.[81] In fact, one Saudi commentator evaluated that "waiting, containment, diplomacy, and sanctions have become incentives" for Iran rather than deterrents and concluded that "only a nuclear weapon deters a nuclear weapon."[82]

If Iran's progress was not to be halted by the international community, this was sure to reinforce the skepticism that some in Saudi Arabia nurtured about the international community's ability to prevent countries in general from acquiring nuclear weapons. According to an editorial in *Al-Sharq Al-Awsat* from mid-2009, for example, North Korea's experience had been said to show that the latter "was able to defy the world and to continue with its nuclear program and be neither attracted by the carrot nor frightened by the stick," and the writer had pointed out that "it will not be long before Iran, too, will join the nuclear club."[83] He concluded that "it will not be possible for America, or the world policeman as some view the latter, to stop the virus of nuclear proliferation."[84] As Prince Turki Al-Faysal had already maintained in December 2011, "our efforts and the world's efforts failed to convince Israel to abandon its WMD, as has also been the case with Iran's arming with the same weapons."[85] In a way, by placing its focus on the international community's efforts, the Saudi media may have been shifting the blame for any future Saudi acquisition of nuclear weapons to the United States or the West for shirking their responsibility to stop Iran's quest for nuclear weapons, with the Saudis then able to argue at some time in the future that they had had no other choice but to follow Iran's example in the wake of the international community's ineffectiveness in stopping Iran.

Notes

1 "Al-Faysal: Iran talab aqd hiwar thulathi fi Al-Kuwayt. Fa qult li-ma nuhammilha khilafatna?" [Al-Faysal: Iran Requested Tripartite Talks in Kuwait. I Said, Why Burden the Latter with Our Disputes?], *Al-Madina*, 6 July 2011, www.al-madina.com/print/313975.
2 Khalid Al-Dakhil, "Tasrihat Saud Al-Faysal: Hal taghayyar al-mawqif min al-dawr al-irani?" [Saud Al-Faysal's Declarations: Has the Position on the Iranian Role Changed?], *Al-Hayat* (Saudi edition), 10 July 2011, http://international.daralhayat.com/ksaarticle/28643.
3 "Saud Al-Faysal: Iran tuhaddid amn wa-istiqrar al-mintaqa bi-qudratha al-nawawiya" [Prince Saud: Iran Threatens the Security and Stability of the Region with Its Nuclear Capabilities], *Al-Riyadh*, 24 November 2011, www.alriyadh.com/2011/11/24/article685758.html.
4 Inidicative of the sensitivities involved, after the visit it was felt that an official explanation needed to appear in all the Saudi media to minimize the out-of-character event, claiming that the ships were only carrying naval cadets on a training cruise and that this was simply a goodwill gesture in line with common international naval conventions. "Wizarat al-difa: Al-Samah bi-ubur al-sufun al-harbiya al-iraniya yakis hirs al-mamlaka ala idamat alaqat al-sadaqa" [The Ministry of Defense: Permission for the Iranian Warships to Cross Reflects the Kingdom's Desire for Friendly Relations], *Al-Riyadh*, 26 February 2012, www.alriyadh.com/713252.

5 Ibtisam Al-Kitbi, "Al-Alaqat al-khalijiya al-iraniya darurat wa-majalat al-taawun" [Gulf–Iranian Relations: The Imperatives and Scope for Cooperation], *Al-Haras Al-Watani*, November–December 2012, 18–24, and Bashir Abd Al-Fattah, "Al-Arab wa-Iran … furas al-shiraka wa'l-taawun" [The Arabs and Iran: Opportunities for a Partnership and Cooperation], *Al-Haras Al-Watani*, November–December 2012, 26–37.
6 Hamad bin Abd Allah Al-Luhaydan, "Al-Ahdath tasir nahw tadmir Iran wa-duwal Al-Sharq Al-Awsat" [Events Are Heading Toward a Destruction of Iran and the Middle East Countries], *Al-Riyadh*, 31 May 2013, www.alriyadh.com/2013/05/31/article839788.html.
7 Talal Salih Bannan, "Al-Arab bayn kammashat al-rub al-nawawi!" [The Arabs between the Pincers of Nuclear Terror!], *Ukaz*, 2 April 2006, www.okaz.com.sa/okaz/osf/20060402/PrinCon200604026920.htm.
8 Prince Naef bin Ahmed Al Saud, "Underpinning Saudi National Security Strategy," *Joint Forces Quarterly* (Washington, DC), Autumn 2002, 130.
9 Fawzi Al-Asmar, "Amrika wa'l-mizhalla al-nawawiya" [America and the Nuclear Umbrella], *Al-Riyadh*, 18 September 2009, www.alriyadh.com/2009/09/18/article460327.html.
10 Ibid.
11 Ibid.
12 See Usama Saraya's interview with President Husni Mubarak, "Ziyarat Washington li-tarh ru'yat Misr li-tahqiq al-salam" [Visit to Washington to Present Egypt's View on Achieving Peace], *Al-Ahram* (Cairo), 17 August 2009, www.ahram.org.eg/archive/Index.asp?CurFN=fon1.htm&DID=10042.
13 Interview with Prince Turki Al-Faysal, BBC Arabic News (London), 8 July 2011, www.youtube.com/watch?=Kfw.R7j4-HwZO (hereafter Turki Al-Faysal, BBC).
14 Muhammad Sadiq Diyab, "Madha law daghat ahmaq ala zurar?" [What If a Fool Pressed the Button?], *Al-Sharq Al-Awsat*, 3 June 2009, http://archive.aawsat.com/leader.asp?section=3&issueno=11145&article=521831. (hereafter Diyab, "Madha law daghat").
15 Ibid. The writer uses the term *Harat kull min idu ilu*, a reference to a popular play in the Arab world which has become symbolic of the law of the jungle. My thanks to my wife, Nidhal, for clarifying that point.
16 Abd Al-Khaliq Abd Allah, "Sibaq al-tasalluh fi Al-Khalij Al-Arabi mukallaf lakin la mafarr" [The Arms Race in the Arab Gulf Has Been Imposed But There Is No Escaping It], *Al-Sharq Al-Awsat*, 25 November 2010, www.aawsat.com/print.asp?did=596759&issueno=11685.
17 Turki Al-Faysal, BBC.
18 Abd Allah bin Musa Al-Tayir, "Amrika al-lati lan taud" [An America That Is Gone Forever], *Al-Riyadh*, 18 June 2013, www.alriyadh.com/2013/06/18/article844720.html.
19 Yusuf Al-Kuwaylit, "Hal qawwamna alaqatna ma Amrika?" [Have We Adjusted Our Relations with America?], *Al-Riyadh*, 9 December 2012, www.alriyadh.com/2012/12/09/article791185.html.
20 Mark Landler and David E. Sanger, "Clinton Speaks of Shielding Mideast from Iran," *New York Times*, 22 July 2009, www.nytimes.com/2009/07/23/world/asia/23/diplo.html, and Joyce Karam and Muhammad Salih Sidqiyan, "Washintun tadrus khutta li-ta'min 'mizhalla nawawiya' li-duwal Al-Khalij" [Washington Is Studying a Plan for a 'Nuclear Umbrella' for the Gulf States], *Al-Hayat*, 5 March 2015, www.alhayat.com/Articles/7831182.
21 Abd Al-Rahman Al-Tariri, "Al-Ajz al-nafsi da' al-umma" [Lack of Self-Confidence Is the Umma's Malady], *Al-Iqtisadiya*, 30 April, 2015, www.aleqt.com/2015/04/30/article_953745.html.
22 Bannan, "Adw jadid."
23 Abd Al-Rahman Al-Rashid, "Al-Ittifaq al-nawawi sa-yughayyir al-mintaqa" [The Nuclear Agreement Will Change the Region], *Al-Sharq Al-Awsat*, 4 April 2015, http://aawsat.com/print/328246. Ayman Al-Hammad, "Hal yualij Washintun al-khatar al-nawawi bi-dir sarukhi?" [Will Washington Remedy the Threat with a Missile Shield?], *Al-Riyadh*, 8 May 2015, www.alriyadh.com/1046253.

24 Nasir Al-Shihri, "Hal yatajawaz qadat Al-Khalij fakhkh Camp David?" [Will the Gulf Leaders Be Able to Avoid the Camp David Trap?], *Al-Bilad*, 10 May 2015, www.albila ddaily.com.
25 "Al-Saudiya wa-Baskitan … alaqat ka'l-sakhra li-muwajahat nawawi Iran" [Saudi Arabia and Pakistan: Relations as Solid as a Rock to Confront Iran's Nuclear Weapons], *Al-Khalij Online* (Riyadh), 28 March 2015, http://alkhaleejonline.net.
26 Ibrahim bin Mahmud Al-Nahhas, "Ru'yat al-ra'is Obama li-amn Al-Khalij: Al-Salam min khilal tawazun al-quwa" [President Obama's View of Security in the Gulf: Peace through a Balance of Power], *Al-Riyadh*, 16 May 2015, www.alriyadh.com/1048588.
27 Muhammad Al-Mukhtar Al-Fal, "Zaman al-ittihad" [Time for Unification], *Ukaz*, 19 May 2015, http://okaz.co/bwlexdo41.
28 "Al-Jubayr: Al-Mamlaka lan taqif maktufat al-aydi amam 'al-shaghab' al-irani fi al-mintaqa" [Al-Jubayr: The Kingdom Will Not Remain Passive in the Face of Iranian 'Troublemaking' in the Region], *Al-Yawm*, 10 July 2015, www.alyaum.com/article/4078031.
29 For example, Badr Al-Rashid, "Al-Rabi al-arabi yatgha ala ahdath al-alam am 2011" [The Arab Spring Overshadowed Other World Events in 2011], *Al-Riyadh*, 31 December 2011, www.alriyadh.com/2011/12/31/article696623.html, and Turki Abd Allah Al-Sudayri, "Thumma madha bad?" [What Next?], *Al-Riyadh*, 17 June 2012, www.alriyadh.com/2012/07/17/article752397.html.
30 Muhammad Maruf Al-Shibani, "Muqaranatan bi-Kuriya" [Compared with Korea], *Al-Bilad*, 1 April 2013, http://albiladdaily.com/articles.php?action-show&id-14984.
31 Yusuf Al-Kuwaylit, "Kayf nakhtu bi'l-ittihad al-khaliji al-arabi" [How Do We Proceed with the Arab Gulf Union?], *Al-Riyadh*, 24 February 2012, www.alriyadh.com/2012/02/24/article712535.html (hereafter Al-Kuwaylit, "Kayf nakhtu").
32 Abd Allah Al-Qafari, "Amrika wa-Iran … madha law kan thamma safqa?" [America and Iran … What If There Were a Deal?], *Al-Riyadh*, 8 November 2010, www.alriyadh.com/2010/11/08/article575386.html.
33 Fa'iq Fahim, "Duwal majlis al-taawun al-khaliji wa'l-tahaddi al-nawawi al-irani" [The Gulf Cooperation Council States and the Iranian Nuclear Challenge], *Al-Iqtisadiya*, 25 June 2011, www.aleqt.com/2011/06/25/article_552510.print.
34 Abd Allah Al-Qafari, "Iran wa'l-Khalij madha bad dukhul Iran al-nadi al-nawawi?" [The Gulf and Iran: What Happens after Iran Joins the Nuclear Club?], *Al-Riyadh*, 17 April 2006, www.alriyadh.com/2006/04/17/article146938_s.html.
35 Ibid.
36 Ahmad Al-Jamia, "Wafd yabani yatrah tasa'ulat an mustaqbal al-takattul al-khaliji wa'l-alaqat ma Iran wa-Turkiya wa-Amrika wa-ta'thirat al-rabi al-arabi" [A Japanese Delegation Raises Questions About the Future of Gulf Blocs, Relations with Iran, Turkey, and America, and the Impact of the Arab Spring], *Al-Riyadh*, 24 April 2012, www.alriyadh.com/2012/04/24/article729874.html.
37 Brigadier General Saba' Abd Allah BaHabri (Ret.), "Al-Barnamaj al-nawawi al-irani hal yasmud amam al-mutatalabat wa'l-tahdidat al-dawliya?" [Will the Iranian Nuclear Program Withstand the International Demands and Threats?], *Al-Haras Al-Watani*, September 2005, 67.
38 Abd Al-Jalil Zayd Al-Marhun, "Amn Al-Khalij … hal min mutaghayyir amiriki jadid?" [Gulf Security: Is There an American Shift?], *Al-Riyadh*, 20 March 2009, www.alriyadh.com/2009/03/20/article417096.html (hereafter Al-Marhun, "Amn Al-Khalij").
39 David E. Sanger, James Glanz, and Jo Becker, "Around the World, Distress Over Iran," *New York Times*, 28 November 2010, www.nytimes.com, and Hugh Tomlinson, "Saudi Arabia Gives Israel Clear Skies to Attack Iranian Nuclear Sites," *The Times* (London), 12 June 2010, www.timesonline.co.uk.
40 Uzi Mahnaimi, "Two Old Foes Unite against Tehran," *Sunday Times* (London), 17 November 2013, 21.
41 Eli Lake, "Israelis and Saudis Reveal Secret Talks to Thwart Iran," *Bloomberg View*, 4 June 2015, www.bloombergview.com/articles/2015-06-04/Israelis-and-saudis-reveal-secret-

talks-to-thwart-iran, and "Report: Saudis Ready to Help Israel Attack Iran," *Israel Today* (Jerusalem), 26 February 2015, www.israeltoday.co.il/NewsItem/tabid/178/nid/26134/Default.aspx.
42 Dawud Al-Shiryan, "Netanyahu yurawwij li'l-shurti" [Netanyahu Promotes Himself as the Policeman], *Al-Hayat* (Saudi edition), 5 March 2015, www.alhayat.com/Opinion/Dawood-Al-Sheryan/7829543.
43 "Al-Ahil al-saudi alahh ala Washington li-darb Tihran" [The Saudi Ruler Pressed Washington to Strike Tehran], *Al-Haramayn website*, 11 December 2010, www.alhramain.com/hiic/index.php?sec=V1d4a1IySm5QVDA9&sub=V1cweFYwMHlUak5RVkRBOQ==&r=%7B0000B3DC35CA2C4CFF6A9734BF9C59E13/000053724F182C7DAE863/00 000009E2D0E6EE%7D&id=17384&act=show&Sectyp=219. Al-Haramayn is a dissident Saudi Shia website. Iran routinely accused Riyadh of such cooperation with Israel and, indicative of the sensitivity of the issue, the Saudi media would respond by raising countercharges that Iran and Israel were actually secret allies, Ali Al-Qahis, "Al-Alaqa al-iraniya-al-isra'iliya tahaluf sirri wa-ada' mulan" [The Iranian–Israeli Relationship: A Secret Alliance and Hostility in Public], *Al-Riyadh*, 24 August 2015, www.alriyadh.com/1075955.
44 "*Spiegel* Interview with Saudi Prince Turki bin [sic] Faisal," *Der Spiegel* (Hamburg, Germany), English edition, 12 June 2010, www.spiegel.de/international/world/0,1518, druck-733054,00.html.
45 "Riyadh Refutes Allegations by Tehran," *Arab News* (Jeddah), 10 December 2009, www.arabnews.com/services/print/print.asp?artid=129362&d=.
46 Interview with Prince Al-Walid bin Talal by Jeffrey Goldberg, "Iran Is Playing Obama, Says Savvy Saudi Prince," *Bloomberg News* (New York), 22 November 2013, www.bloomberg.com/news/print/2013-11-22/iran-is-playing-obama-says-savvy-saudi-prince.html.
47 As told to the author 8 November 2011.
48 Adnan Kamil Salah, "Al-Qadiya al-iraniya bi-ru'ya arabiya muwahhada" [The Iranian Case from a United Arab Perspective], *Al-Madina*, 7 January 2010, www.al-madina.com/print/213010 (hereafter Salah, "Al-Qadiya al-iraniya"), and Adnan Kamil Salah, "Tasawwaru uhlumu udu!" [Imagine, Dream, Pray!], *Al-Madina*, 13 May 2010, www.al-madina.com/print/247504.
49 Major General Husam Suwaylam (Ret.), "Ahdaf Iran al-siyasiya wa'l-istratijiya wa-asalib tahqiqha," [Iran's Political and Strategic Objectives and the Methods to Achieve Them], *Al-Haras Al-Watani*, part 1, August 2011, 37.
50 Abd Al-Rahman Al-Rashid, "Isra'il tashinn harb Al-Khalij al-muqbila!" [Israel Will Spark the Next Gulf War!], *Al-Sharq Al-Awsat*, 18 April 2013, www.aawsat.com.
51 Editorial, "Iran al-nawawiya" [A Nuclear Iran], *Al-Madina*, 13 July 2010, www.al-madina.com/print/256294.
52 Abd Al-Munim Mustafa, "Kull shay' lam yaud kafiyan" [All of That Is Not Enough], *Al-Madina*, 14 February 2010, www.al-madina.com/print/224041 (hereafter Mustafa, "Kull shay'").
53 Ibrahim bin Abd Allah Al-Mutrif, "Lin fat al-fawt … ma yanfa al-sawt" [Shutting the Barn Door after the Horses Have Left], *Al-Yawm*, 8 December 2011, www.alyaum.com/News/art/37586.html.
54 Dayf Allah Al-Dayan, "Al-Alaqat al-amrikiya al-iraniya al-wajh al-akhar" [U.S.–Iranian Relations: The Other Face], *Al-Bayan* (London), 1428/2009, 242, www.albayan.co.uk/Files/articleimages/takrir/4-3-2.pdf.
55 For example, Al-Marhun, "Amn Al-Khalij."
56 Hay'at Al-Tahrir [Editorial Board], "Al-Mashru al-irani al-iqlimi wa'l-nawawi" [The Iranian Regional Project and the Nuclear [Program]], *Majallat Kulliyat Al-Malik Khalid Al-Askariya*, 1 June 2009, www.kkmaq.gov.sa/detail.asp?InNewsItemID=319120&InTemplateKey=print.
57 Ayyad Al-Batniji, "Al-Siyasa al-kharijiya al-iraniya" [Iranian Foreign Policy], *Majallat Kulliyat Al-Malik Khalid Al-Askariya*, 21 June 2011, www.kkmaq.gov.sa/detail.asp?InNewsItemID=393306&InTemplateKey=print.

58 Ahmad Dayf, "Darb Iran: ma mada jiddiyat al-tahdidat?" [A Strike on Iran: How Serious Are the Threats?], *Al-Jazira*, 22 November 2011, www.al-jazirah.com.sa/20111122/du4.htm.
59 Salah, "Al-Qadiya al-iraniya." A similar opinion article by Yusuf Abd Allah Makki reinforced the view that the United States was reluctant to engage in another "military adventure," "Azmat al-malaff al-nawawi al-irani ila ayn?" [Where Is the Crisis Over the Iranian Nuclear Issue Headed?], *Al-Watan*, 23 November 2011, www.alwatan.com.sa/Articles/Detail.aspx?ArticleID=8329.
60 Salim Al-Sharif, "Turki Al-Faysal: Al-Alam fashal fi iqna Isra'il wa-Iran min 'al-nawawi' wa-khiyaratna maftuha" [Turki Al-Faysal: The World Failed to Convince Israel and Iran on the Nuclear [Issue] and Our Options Are Open], *Al-Madina*, 6 December 2011, www.al-madina.com/print/343006 (hereafter Al-Sharif, "Turki Al-Faysal").
61 Usama Said Al-Qahtani, "Hal tamlik Iran al-qunbula?" [Will Iran Get the Bomb?], *Al-Watan*, 9 March 2012, www.alwatan.com.sa/Articles/Detail.aspx?ArticleId=9890.
62 Saud Kabili, "Al-Mintaqa ala washk sibaq al-tasalluh al-nawawi" [The Region Is on the Brink of a Nuclear Arms Race], *Al-Watan*, 22 April 2012, www.alwatan.com.sa/Articles/Detail.aspx?ArticleId=10530.
63 Major General Husam Suwaylam (Ret.), "Al-Inqisamat al-amrikiya wa'l-isra'iliya hawl darb Iran" [The American and Israeli Divisions on Striking Iran], *Al-Haras Al-Watani*, November-December 2012, 44–53. This view seemed predominant in the Saudi military media, as in Brigadier General Saba' Abd Allah BaHabri (Ret.), "Li-Madha ta'akhkharu fi muhajamat al-mansha'at al-nawawiya al-iraniya?" [Why Have They Delayed Striking the Iranian Nuclear Facilities?], *Al-Haras Al-Watani*, January–February 2013, 34–39.
64 Ibrahim Al-Athimin, "Iran wa-mufawadat Kazakhstan" [Iran and the Negotiations in Kazakhstan], *Al-Yawm*, 27 February 2013, www.alyaum.com/News/art/73493.html, and Ibrahim Al-Athimin, "Iran: kalam sawwi shahi" [Iran: Like Saying Make Me Tea], *Al-Yawm*, 20 March 2013, www.alyaum.com/News/art/76170.html.
65 The same opinion was shared by Nasir Al-Shihri, "Al-Khalij wa makhatir al-mustaqbal" [The Gulf and the Perils of the Future], *Al-Bilad*, 8 March 2009, www.albiladdaily.com/print.php?action=print&m=articlesm&id=2209.
66 Uthman Al-Khuwaytir, "Isra'il wa-qunbulat Iran" [Israel and Iran's Bomb], *Al-Iqtisadiya*, 20 November 2011, www.aleqt.com/2011/11/20/article_599776.print.
67 Editorial "Malaff Iran al-nawawi mujaddadan … hal min muwajaha askariya?" [Iran's Nuclear Issue Once Again; Will There Be a Military Confrontation?], *Al-Watan*, 9 November 2011, www.alwatan.com.sa/Articles/Detail.aspx?ArticleID=8126.
68 Editorial "Al-Takhabbut al-isra'ili hawl barnamaj Iran al-nawawi" [Israeli Fumbling on Iran's Nuclear Program], *Al-Watan*, 27 April 2012, www.alwatan.com.sa/editors_note/Editor_Note_Detail.aspx?ID=739. Actually, recent revelations about Israeli government deliberations indicate that Tel-Aviv did seriously consider launching strikes against Iran but decided not to do so because of divided opinion in the government, "Barack: Netanyahu Wanted to Strike Iran in 2010 and 2011, but Colleagues Blocked Him," *Times of Israel* (Jerusalem), 21 August 2015, www.timesofisrael.com/barak-netanyahu-wanted-to-strike-iran-in-2010-and-2011-but-colleagues-blocked-him.
69 Mutlaq Saud Al-Mtiri, "Al-Khuruj an al-nass: Madha law qalat Al-Mamlaka naam" [Departing from the Script: What if the Kingdom Said Yes], *Al-Riyadh*, 25 August 2012, www.alriyadh.com/2012/08/25/article762523.html.
70 Hamad bin Abd Allah Al-Luhaydan, "Abad al-tasalluh al-nawawi wa-tadaiyatih" [Dimensions of Nuclear Arming and of Its Consequences], *Al-Riyadh*, 29 May 2009, www.alriyadh.com/2009/05/29/article433463.html.
71 Ibid.
72 Editorial, "Sibaq nawawi fi Al-Sharq Al-Awsat" [A Nuclear Arms Race in the Middle East], *Al-Madina*, 20 February 2010, www.al-madina.com/print/225775 (hereafter "Sibaq nawawi").
73 Ibid.
74 Mustafa, "Kull shay'."

75 Quantico, Virginia, 8 November 2011.
76 "Abd Al-Aziz bin Salman: Al-Mamlaka tasa li-tawfir imdadat kafiya fi suq al-naft" [Abd Al-Aziz bin Salman: The Kingdom Is Striving to Provide Sufficient Supplies on the Oil Market], *Al-Watan*, 23 February 2012, www.alwatan.com.sa.
77 For example, Mahmud Lauta, "Iran fi ma'ziq; Taraju mabiat al-naft ila 135 alf barmil yawmiyan" [Iran in Critical Situation: Reduction in Oil Sales to 135,000 Barrels per Day], *Al-Iqtisadiya*, 26 December 2012, www.aleqt.com/2012/12/26/article_719885.print.
78 Yusuf Al-Kuwaylit, "Hal najahat al-quwwa al-naima ma Iran?" [Has Soft Power Succeeded with Iran?], *Al-Riyadh*, 3 October 2012, www.alriyadh.com/2012/10/03/article773134.html.
79 Adnan Kamil Salah, "Ma al-thaman al-ladhi sayadfahu Obama li-tuhibbahu Tihran?" [What Price Is Obama Willing to Pay so that Tehran Loves Him?], *Al-Madina*, 19 February 2013, www.al-madina.com/printhtml/434687.
80 Raqiya Sulayman Al-Huwayrini, "Al-Manshud al-nawawi qabl al-khubz ahyanan!" [Sometimes Nuclear Aspirations before Bread!], *Al-Jazira*, 9 April 2013, www.al-jazirah.com/2013/20130409/ar1d.htm, and Ali Al-Jahali, "Kuriya Al-Shimaliya: 'Al-Amn muqabil al-ghidha'" [North Korea: "Security in Exchange for Food"], *Al-Iqtisadiya*, 14 April 2013, www.aleqt.com/2013/04/14/article_747226.html.
81 Amir Tahiri, "Iran wa'l-qunbula al-nawawiya: Hujaj ghayr mubashira fi Washintun" [Iran and the Atom Bomb: Indirect Excuses in Washington], *Al-Sharq Al-Awsat*, 26 April 2013, www.aawsat.com/print.asp?did=726127&issueno=12568. Analyses on Iran by Tahiri, an Iranian émigré from 1979, appear frequently in the Saudi media.
82 Yazid Bin Muhammad, "Iran al-nawawiya lan tantazhirkum … irdauha" [A Nuclear Iran Will Not Wait for You to Deter It], *Al-Watan*, 30 April 2013, www.alwatan.com.sa/Articles/Detail.aspx?ArticleID=16512.
83 Diyab, "Madha law daghat."
84 Ibid.
85 Al-Sharif, "Turki Al-Faysal."

6
THINKING IN TERMS OF SOLUTIONS
The evolution in Saudi thinking toward a nuclear option

While the Saudis may have studied the issue of nuclear weapons for many years, this was essentially in the abstract, and it was really the growing anticipated Iranian nuclear threat that gave decisive impetus to a qualitative evolution in Saudi thinking, and was to result in active planning for concrete measures in support of such thinking in case Iran's own acquisition of nuclear weapons could not be stopped.

Saudi Arabia's traditional stand on nuclear weapons

Although there had been reports as early as 1989 of attempts by the Saudis to obtain experimental nuclear reactors from China as a start toward eventually acquiring a weapons program, nothing had come of such talk.[1] Traditionally, Saudi spokesmen were always eager to disavow any interest in nuclear weapons. As far back as at least 1990, the then-Minister of Defense and eventually Crown Prince, Prince Sultan (d. 2011), himself insisted that "the Kingdom of Saudi Arabia has the capability of acquiring and developing nuclear weapons but, as is well known, the Kingdom is at the forefront of the states calling to make the Middle East a nuclear-free zone."[2] More concretely, a Saudi-owned newspaper reported that the post-Soviet Ukrainian government had proposed to Riyadh in 1994 to help the latter develop nuclear weapons, but that the then-monarch, King Fahd, had declined the offer.[3] In fact, the Saudi media would respond routinely with vehement denials to any suggestion of Saudi nuclear plans or activity. For example, in the wake of press coverage based on revelations by a defecting Saudi diplomat about his country's cooperation in that field with other countries, the Saudi media dismissed such reports as just "a press campaign targeting Saudi Arabia."[4]

Even in the more recent past, Saudi Arabia routinely would deny any intention to acquire nuclear weapons. For example, the Saudi Foreign Minister, Prince Saud Al-Faysal, when asked in 2006 whether his country would consider seeking nuclear weapons if Iran did so, replied categorically "No, we will not. We do not believe that it gives any country security to build nuclear weapons."[5] In fact, in 2006, Prince Sultan dismissed nuclear weapons as of no importance, contending that "we in the Kingdom do not need them."[6] Elsewhere, Prince Sultan sought to dispel persistent reports of Pakistani–Saudi cooperation in the nuclear field. As he put it, "Saudi Arabia categorically does not believe in nuclear means and nuclear weapons because they would annihilate human life and what was said about there being Pakistani–Saudi cooperation is completely unfounded."[7] To be sure, even then, Saudi messages at times were somewhat cryptic. For example, in December 2005, Prince Turki Al-Faysal—former Director General of Saudi Arabia's Intelligence Agency and former Ambassador to Great Britain and, at the time, Saudi Ambassador to the United States—rejected speculation that Saudi Arabia would follow suit if Iran acquired nuclear weapons, stating that the Saudis "will not follow the nuclear path under any circumstance because that would contribute to an arms race in the region." However, at the same time, he had also alerted the Saudi public that if Iran developed nuclear weapons "many neighboring states will also follow its example."[8] With an Iranian acquisition of nuclear weapons then not foreseen in the immediate future, such denials would have made sense if they were intended not to arouse international concern.

The shift to promoting nuclear weapons

However, a shift in statements by senior members of the royal family about the possibility of Saudi Arabia reacting to Iran's acquisition of nuclear weapons by also following that route began to be noticeable over the years. In general, normally reticent Saudi government officials and other public figures became increasingly willing to address that issue, even if sometimes indirectly. To be sure, nuclear weapons are a delicate topic in the international community and official references to Saudi Arabia's nuclear option remained largely in the realm of hints and allusions, often in terms of references to "the Gulf countries" or "the Arabs" as those likely to adopt a nuclear response to an Iranian nuclear threat.

Prince Turki Al-Faysal became perhaps the most visible Saudi spokesman on the regional and international scene for such an option during King Abd Allah's reign, although he had to be especially careful in his choice of words when dealing with the issue, given its sensitivity. In March 2011, at a conference organized by a high-profile research center in the United Arab Emirates (UAE), Prince Turki Al-Faysal asked openly: "What would be wrong with acquiring a nuclear force to confront the Iranian [nuclear] force if international efforts to prevent Iran's acquisition of nuclear weapons fail?"[9] A short time later, speaking to senior NATO military officials, he hinted cryptically that if Iran developed nuclear weapons then that "would compel Saudi Arabia … to pursue policies which could lead to untold and possibly dramatic consequences."[10] However, in an interview with the BBC, Prince Turki Al-Faysal specifically sought to clarify his UAE speech—in which he had perhaps been too open—and now insisted that Saudi Arabia "is not seeking to acquire nuclear weapons," but he also warned pointedly that if Iran did so Saudi Arabia's response would be "severe and resolute in order that this situation does not become a threat to its interests."[11] When pressed by the interviewer about his earlier speech, a discomfited Prince Turki cut him off, cautioning "Don't attribute words to me that I didn't say."[12]

Yet at a Gulf Cooperation Council (GCC) meeting in December 2011, when speaking of Iran's expected acquisition of nuclear weapons, Prince Turki again noted that "It is necessary and indeed it is our duty on behalf of our [GCC] nations and peoples for us to examine all possible options, including our own acquisition of the same weapons."[13] Later, Prince Turki appeared to soften his message when speaking publicly to Western audiences, placing greater emphasis on the desirability of a regional weapons of mass destruction (WMD)-free zone and a United Nations nuclear umbrella, although his precondition that both Iran and Israel forgo their nuclear programs indicated he did not see this to be a realistic option for the foreseeable future.[14] In fact, in the same speech, using language that he had used before, he suggested that if Iran did acquire nuclear weapons this "would compel other nations to pursue policies that could lead to untold and possibly dramatic consequences."

While the articulate and cosmopolitan Prince Turki Al-Faysal may have garnered the most headlines in the West, he was no black swan. Rather, his statements could be seen as part of a larger pattern, as other members of the royal family had also expressed at least implicit support for a nuclear option even years earlier. For example, Prince Naef bin Ahmed Al Saud, who eventually was to become Defense Minister Prince Sultan's adviser on national strategy, as early as 2002 had hinted that "turmoil in the Middle East could engender the sort of instability that may result in attempts to acquire WMD," citing efforts by Israel, India, Pakistan, Iran, and Iraq in that arena, and adding that "despite the lack of evidence that Riyadh may be pursuing a nuclear option, some speculate on the possibility."[15] To be sure, statements by high-ranking officials and influential members of the royal family were often vague, veiled, or ambiguous, as when Prince Muqrin, then-Director General of the country's Intelligence Agency, in 2006 had assessed at a conference in Bahrain that the proliferation of nuclear weapons in the Middle East would "also spur *moderate states in the region* to establish nuclear programs, whether covertly or openly, aimed at creating a military balance in the region" (emphasis added).[16]

Likewise, in April 2010, Prince Muqrin, speaking at the Nuclear Security Summit in Washington, DC, presented his prognosis of a nuclear arms race in the Middle East, alluding that the quest by an unnamed country for nuclear weapons "may lead once again to a return to the environment of the Cold War."[17] In December 2010, Prince Turki bin Muhammad, Saudi Arabia's Deputy Foreign Minister for Multilateral Relations, for his part, was also circumspect when he repeated his country's calls for a nuclear-free zone in the Middle East, but hinted at the same time that Iran's quest for nuclear weapons "will lead to a slide toward a nuclear arms race in the region."[18] Again, at a Gulf conference in December 2011,

Prince Muqrin told his audience that he feared Iran's nuclear polices would lead to a "return to the doctrine of balance of terror," a term commonly used in Arab discourse to refer to the nuclear deterrence characteristic of the superpower relationship during the Cold War, and cautioned enigmatically that "the Gulf states cannot simply stand by as observers" of Iran's nuclear program.[19] For his part, Prince Khalid, then Deputy Minister of Defense (and son of then-Defense Minister Prince Sultan), when asked during a visit to Kuwait in 2010 what the position of the Gulf countries would be if the nuclear issue with Iran was not resolved, answered ambiguously that "every state will then do what is in its interest."[20] Elsewhere, Prince Khalid cautioned that "a change in the balance of power" in the region "requires us to acquire power in all its forms."[21] Saudi Foreign Minister Prince Saud Al-Faysal also warned, as another round of talks between Iran and the international community was set to start in February 2013, that although Saudi Arabia favored the elimination of all WMD in the region:

> if the [Iranians] continue on the path they are now on, many other countries will also follow the same path. This is not speculation. The fact is that proliferation of nuclear weapons to any one country means the proliferation of nuclear weapons also to other countries.[22]

Over the years, senior Saudis also warned U.S. officials privately that Riyadh would follow suit if Iran acquired nuclear weapons. Sometimes this has been indirect, as when King Abd Allah informed one visiting U.S official that "if Iran gets [a] nuclear capability, all the other major countries in the region will seek it as well."[23] Perhaps the most explicit message in this vein was the private communication from King Abd Allah to veteran U.S. negotiator Dennis Ross in April 2009, when the Saudi monarch told the latter that "If they [i.e. the Iranians] get nuclear weapons, we will get nuclear weapons."[24]

Admittedly, most official statements in public have been ambiguous and suggestive more than concrete. Nevertheless, even these were unmistakable in their intent. In case any local or international audience should not understand the meaning of such veiled statements, accompanying Saudi press commentary or back-channel communications often spelled out their meaning in no uncertain terms. For example, a Saudi journalist noted that Prince Turki Al-Faysal's comments:

> at present do not go beyond oblique messages; however, these are messages that must be taken seriously, since they express the Gulf's concerns about falling behind in the nuclear arms race in the region in case the international community fails to deal with the issue.[25]

Significantly, after one such pronouncement by Prince Turki, a Saudi pundit who often writes on defense matters penned an article in the mainstream press entitled "A Reading of [Prince Turki] Al-Faysal's Statements," in which he highlighted the "extreme importance" of the prince's "official or semi-official" statements because they affirmed "absolutely clearly and plainly" Saudi Arabia's "intent to acquire nuclear weapons as a corrective to the upsetting of the … strategic nuclear deterrence equation in the region."[26] He added that "personally, I understand His Highness Prince Turki's statements as the firm Saudi decision to have nuclear weapons."[27] The same writer stressed that Prince Turki's statements were "a ray of hope" and "long-awaited" and that they had met with "broad approval within the popular strata and among the intellectual elite."[28] Likewise, an influential columnist explained that when Prince Turki and Prince Muqrin, as the past and the then-current chiefs of the country's intelligence, spoke about nuclear options he interpreted the timing and importance of their statements as "the initial indications" reflecting "a change in Saudi security options." And, based on his understanding of the message, the writer followed up by stressing the urgency for the GCC to "think about acquiring nuclear weapons."[29]

Again, reacting to Prince Turki Al-Faysal's speech, noted above, at the conference on Gulf security in December 2011, another Saudi commentator reinforced the point by explaining that what was meant was that "the Kingdom [of Saudi Arabia] may be compelled to follow the same path" as Iran and Israel.[30] Likewise, after Prince Turki Al-Faysal's cryptic speech to NATO officials in June 2011, according to British press reports, "a senior official in Riyadh who is close to the prince" interpreted his message as "We cannot live in a situation where Iran has nuclear weapons and we don't. It's as simple as that … If Iran develops a nuclear weapon, that will be unacceptable to us and we will have to follow suit."[31]

Developing the conceptual thinking and policy considerations for nuclear weapons

Over the years, as Iran announced its success with the enrichment of uranium, one could notice a development of conceptual Saudi thinking and policy considerations related to nuclear weapons. In a way, such thinking built on, fleshed out, and provided justifications and support for the positions represented by the often ambiguous warnings by Saudi political figures.

Rethinking the idea of the general desirability of nuclear weapons

Not surprisingly, as part of this intellectual process, Saudi observers often addressed the desirability of nuclear weapons in general conceptual terms, with a focus on the significance of nuclear weapons for providing national security. Other countries' experience in acquiring nuclear weapons was often portrayed in a positive light, thereby legitimizing the process itself in an indirect way. For example, one senior military writer noted that:

> we can see that many countries, especially developing ones, have spared no expense in order to acquire capabilities to ensure for themselves a position

among the world's states, as is the case of North Korea, or in order to preserve their unity or for their population's security, as is the case of Pakistan.[32]

Generalizing such experiences, this study concluded that:

> modern-day states have begun to understand clearly that their existence and ability to protect their people from any foreign aggression is intimately linked with their national security, which in turn will not be achieved except by developing weapons for security, the principal one of which is nuclear weapons, which contribute to deterring foreign aggressors.[33]

Another commentator posited that "some" understood that "the countries in the region have as their only option to follow the example of countries such as India, Pakistan, and Israel" and that merely discussing such an option openly might induce other countries—clearly intending Israel and Iran—to reconsider their policies.[34]

Proposing an "Arab" or "Gulf" deterrent

Often, the Saudi media promoted a nuclear option using circumlocutions intended not to be too provocative—such as "the Arabs" or "the Gulf countries"—as the prospective nuclear acquirer in response to nuclear threats. As early as at least 2007, the Saudi press was already writing that "there is no dispute that most of the Arabs wish that an Arab state would acquire WMD."[35] Likewise, one Saudi media commentator noted that if Iran did not agree to a nuclear-free Middle East then "there is no alternative to taking Arab decisions for self-defense whether by means of overt or covert plans" and predicted that in order to counter the Iranian threat "small and large neighboring states will also seek to acquire nuclear weapons."[36] Again, an editorial in 2010 depicting a looming dual nuclear threat from both Israel and Iran hinted that "some" assessed that "there is no alternative but to think in terms of a nuclear option" since "the existence of the Arabs between the pincers of an Israeli and an Iranian nuclear deterrent is not an option." Highlighting the need to deal with Israel's nuclear weapons, this Saudi editorialist likewise asserted that:

> the only genuine option for dealing with the conflict with Israel is Arab self-reliance, and relying above all on God. And, moreover, one of the most important elements of that self-reliance is creating a genuine nuclear deterrence balance with both Israel now and with Iran in the future, beginning with a joint decision by all the Arab states to withdraw from the current NPT which allows some countries to possess [nuclear weapons] and forbids it to others, and to Arab countries in particular and to Islamic countries in general. The combined Arab countries can cooperate in developing a peaceful and a military nuclear program.[37]

Affirming that the Arab states have the same right to self-defense as any other state, one writer added that:

> the need is increasing for a joint Arab nuclear strategy to acquire nuclear weapons, whatever the legality of the path taken to achieve that, in order to provide for deterrence and self-defense and to confront the Israeli and the Iranian [nuclear] programs.[38]

As a Saudi newspaper editor put it, "one cannot be reassured about the intent of either Israel or Iran," and the Gulf and Peninsula Arabs would find themselves "between two fires" once Iran also acquired nuclear weapons. For him, "the only plausible option for the Arab Gulf states is to begin immediately the development of a nuclear program with the intent of producing a nuclear weapon deterrent which will make us at least equal in defensive capabilities."[39] In fact, he advised that "the Gulf Arabs are in dire need of this weapon and [must acquire it] quickly, before we are subjected to the dual nuclear hegemony—Israeli hegemony and Iranian hegemony."[40]

Responding, in particular, to a projected Iranian nuclear threat, some Saudi media sources issued indirect but transparent warnings of unspecified others in the Middle East who would be likely to seek nuclear weapons if Iran did so. For example, one editorial advised that "The international community must demonstrate its will and resolve to prevent the start of a nuclear arms race in the Middle East, as it will not be possible to otherwise prevent [such a race] if Tehran enters the nuclear club."[41] As a Saudi political analyst also concluded, the Gulf states "must seek immediately and resolutely to acquire nuclear weapons, using any possible means," arguing that "it is not logical for Iran, whose objectives of expansion are well-known, to seek nuclear weapons while the Gulf states do nothing."[42]

For his part, a senior Saudi military officer noted that Iran's failure to comply with international controls of its nuclear program could "lead to a new conventional and unconventional arms race in the Gulf region."[43] Another military observer also argued that the "Gulf states ... will have to build a nuclear arsenal in order to create a balance of terror that will deter Iran from blackmailing the non-nuclear Arab and Islamic states."[44] Similarly, a Saudi newspaper editor called for a "Gulf nuclear weapon."[45] Yet another Saudi commentator argued that "the Gulf states" must create a nuclear balance in the Gulf to neutralize the Iranian nuclear threat.[46] Citing Pakistan's success in dealing with India once it had developed nuclear weapons, in 2012 a Saudi academic urged the GCC to also acquire a deterrent weapon "at whatever the cost and the sacrifices ... for the sake of future generations."[47] In 2013, a key Saudi editor expressed his concern about the looming Iranian threat to the Gulf in dire terms as "a challenge to our existence," with "the clock ticking, so that no time is left for our options except to also acquire power as quickly as possible." Addressing the Gulf states, he warned that anyone desiring peaceful coexistence with Iran would need first to create "a military and strategic balance, including the possession of nuclear weapons, whether by development or purchase," which he saw as "an option that is unavoidable, at whatever cost."[48] Realistically, of course, none of the smaller Gulf countries could have been expected to respond to Iran's nuclear arsenal with one of their own, and such calls for a "Gulf" weapon could only be interpreted as a convenient cover of plausible denial for Riyadh.

Being candid—a Saudi deterrent

Mirroring warnings from official circles, some Saudis also made the case openly for an independent Saudi nuclear deterrent. For example, as a senior military officer concluded already in 2010, "All of that [threat] makes our possession of a nuclear deterrent a necessity for our national security and for the defense of our political independence in the face of any regional or international pressure."[49] Likewise, Saudi human rights activist Abd Al-Aziz Al-Khamis, expressing his support for a national Saudi nuclear deterrent, argued for self-reliance in defense of his country's natural resources from Iranian nuclear threats, since "only our own power growing out of the people of the Gulf themselves will protect these riches, and not the West's fleets."[50] A Saudi academic, writing in the national press, inveighed against the threat from Iran's potential nuclear weapons and concluded that "only one's own brute power will deter an opponent's brute power."[51] A paper that another Saudi academic presented at a conference at the Foreign Ministry's Institute for Diplomatic Studies in Riyadh, likewise, concluded that, in view of the looming Iranian nuclear threat, "it is vital to adopt a policy of nuclear deterrence … Saudi Arabia must pursue the acquisition of nuclear weapons, even if only by purchase."[52] Though acknowledging technical and financial obstacles, as well as the likelihood of regional and international opposition in connection with a Saudi nuclear option, one Saudi media commentator concluded that, nevertheless, "some countries are willing to bear the burdens of acquiring nuclear weapons as a trade-off for the feeling of having achieved comprehensive long-term security assurance."[53] Likewise, in 2013, a prominent Saudi journalist asked rhetorically whether, if the United States "allows" Iran to develop nuclear weapons, then "does its neighbor, Saudi Arabia, not have the right to defend itself by acquiring its equivalent?"[54] Such calls continued, as a Saudi academic remarked in 2014 that "The biggest factor for a deterrent is one's own power, which an enemy must take into account one thousand times over, while weakness is one of the greatest incentives to aggression and interference in one's affairs."[55] After calling for a universal ban on WMD, one journalist warned that, however, if Saudi Arabia:

> sees those around it violating agreements and seeking to acquire any weapons that will have an impact on the region's security and stability, then [Saudi Arabia] will do likewise and acquire the weapons that are able to protect its people, the country, and its riches from those dealing in treachery and deception.[56]

More directly, another Saudi academic, discussing nuclear weapons, concluded that Saudi Arabia "needs a deterrent," because "in the regional neighborhood where it is located one cannot keep one's 'clothes clean,'" that is one has to also acquire the same capabilities as others, "so that the other side understands you have a gun hidden under your robe (*mishlah*)."[57]

Ordinary Saudis in online fora, blogs, tribal websites, and in comments which are sometimes published online to local press articles, routinely expressed strong popular support for a Saudi nuclear option. If anything, not fettered by the constraints of policy responsibility, such commentators often seem to be even more hardline and supportive of nuclear weapons than government officials or the mainstream media. For example, responding to an article discussing whether Saudi Arabia should acquire nuclear weapons, one reader noted that "If Saudi Arabia had the atom bomb that would provide the greatest security for its government, since neither America nor anyone else can harm or provoke a state which has the atom bomb."[58] Another reader held that "The Kingdom must think about and begin to acquire weapons of deterrence, and this cannot wait … at whatever the cost," while a third stated that "I am one of those supporting Saudi Arabia's acquisition of nuclear weapons, because Saudi Arabia has a trusteeship over Mecca the Venerable and Medina the Brilliant, and America one day could abandon the Kingdom."[59] As yet another reader commenting on a press article warned, "if Iran insists on nuclear weapons, there will be a nuclear arms race in the region between Iran and Saudi Arabia."[60] Another blogger, whose message went viral in Saudi Arabia, pleaded that:

> The Saudi government and [the country's] defense policymakers must begin a project to acquire nuclear weapons immediately … I beg anyone who has access to the policymakers who deal with the defense of the Kingdom to forward this request [to them] as an urgent appeal from the people, since it is our duty to defend our religion and our nation.[61]

If there are opponents in Saudi Arabia to a nuclear military option, their views have not been evident in public. It is true that there may be at least some Saudis who may be concerned about further nuclear proliferation on practical grounds. As one press report noted, "there are some Saudis who do not welcome a policy of a nuclear arms race in the region for a simple reason, namely that the states in the region do not have the technical capability for such a race."[62] One Saudi observer did express his malaise—albeit obliquely—with the wisdom of anyone trusting in nuclear weapons. Alluding to the potential destructiveness of nuclear weapons, and railing against Iran's quest for such weapons, he argued that what made the most sense was the conduct of ants who, when attacked with destructive substances by man, will not resist but will manage the situation by fleeing to another area where they can avoid death and start new colonies in order to stay alive—which is the supreme objective. He contrasted this nonconfrontational strategy with that of "some ignorant humans who adopt confrontation and resist death with death."[63]

Although directed at Iran, there were also uncomfortable implications for any other present or would-be nuclear power.

Ensuring religious legitimization

Ruling circles in Saudi Arabia have also sought to ensure support from the country's religious establishment. Although the religious perspective on nuclear weapons will be the subject of a separate monograph, what is significant here is that Saudi policymakers have sought and welcomed religious input as support for the legitimacy of the acquisition—and potential use—of nuclear weapons for its political importance.

The importance of the clerics

Such religious/ethical considerations are significant to most regimes in the region, and of capital importance to Saudi Arabia's ruling family, given the latter's foundations on a base of religious legitimacy within the country and the family's claim to their country's leadership in the Muslim world. Ensuring the clerical establishment's support by providing religious argumentation is important, in light of the role clerics play in promoting the principle of obedience to the ruler. In effect, senior clerics periodically remind the faithful, as did the Kingdom's *mufti*, that "betrayal of the ruler is equivalent to betrayal of the nation, and the nation requires obedience to the ruler… disobeying the ruler or opposing him in carrying out his policy is treason."[64] As has been true throughout Islamic history, the clerics' crafting of religious opinions is often intertwined with political considerations. Although the mainstream Saudi religious establishment is essentially an administrative arm of the regime, this is not true of all the country's clerics. Any opposition or criticism on moral grounds from this sector could prove embarrassing for the ruling family and its relationship with the public, so that this is always a closely-monitored factor.

Theology and realpolitik

In conceptual terms, Saudi clerics often address WMD as a single analytical category, rather than differentiating among different components, and their legal rulings are applicable to all such aspects of WMD, but their focus of interest is clearly on nuclear weapons, to which they devote the greatest attention. The example of one prominent cleric, A'id Al-Qarni, illustrates what is apparently the overall thinking of Saudi religious figures, and there have been no dissenters in religious circles who have expressed differing views. Already in 2002, Al-Qarni drafted a *fatwa*, or religious opinion, on the use of WMD in war, which set the tone.[65] Indicative of official approval, the document was published in several installments in a Saudi military journal, *Al-Jundi Al-Muslim*. Relying on his interpretation of legal principles and historical analogies, the thrust of the *fatwa* was that:

There is no doubt that shooting (*ramy*) is the greatest element of power and that the greatest means to terrify the enemy of God by shooting is by possessing all the weapons with which one can shoot against [those enemies], or at least the most powerful weapons. Possessing WMD—nuclear, chemical, and biological—is considered one of the means to strengthen the position of the Islamic states vis-a-vis the infidel states and to make them feared, and a means for them to ensure their survival, their status, and their stability, especially nowadays when the whole world is challenging the Muslims.[66]

Turning to the potential use of WMD, Al-Qarni notes that, of course, less powerful weapons should be used if it is possible to achieve victory thus. However, if that is not possible, or if one suspects that the enemy will do so, then the use of WMD is permissible.[67] Ultimately, Al-Qarni leaves discretionary power to the political leaders, basing his judgment on the legal principle of utility (*maslaha*), as he concluded that "it is up to the discretion of a Muslim ruler to do as he sees fit for the common good."[68]

More extreme Saudi clerical elements with jihadist ties also back the pursuit of an Islamic nuclear capability, although not necessarily a Saudi one, and refrain from giving any credit to the Al Saud. Such jihadist clerics go even further in their support for nuclear weapons than do spokesmen in the mainstream clerical establishment. For example, the Saudi cleric Nasir bin Hamad Al-Fahd, who has been linked to Al-Qaida and is now again in prison, published a widely-distributed *fatwa* giving great leeway for the use of WMD against infidels, noting that "if it is not possible to repel the infidels from the Muslims except by using these weapons [i.e. WMD] then they are permissible even if [these weapons] kill them all and destroy their agriculture and progeny."[69] While beyond the accepted bounds of the political arena in Saudi Arabia, such clerics constitute a source of criticism in the shadows that cannot be ignored entirely.

Moreover, not only can Saudi clerics provide the necessary moral backing for the government but even mainstream ones can also stray into the political arena and subtly pressure policymakers on an issue, potentially reducing the latter's room for maneuver. That is, clerics can push the nuclear issue even harder than the government may have intended and can question the policymakers' effectiveness. For example, Al-Qarni, expressing annoyance that the West arms itself while proscribing others from doing so, belittled the Arabs' alleged preoccupation with culture, and argued that the world respects a country for its power, not for its good taste.[70] Referring to nuclear weapons, he claimed that Iran "has broken the code," that is that "manufacturing a single [atom] bomb is more awe-inspiring than a hundred epics reminding us of our ancestors' glory." Indeed, as he saw it, the world respects the Great Powers specifically because they have nuclear weapons. He concluded, therefore, "Oh, Arabs, I beg you to develop the atom bomb and nuclear weapons" because "the world is run according to the law of the jungle [literally 'of the strongest']."[71]

Accounting for Saudi openness

Unlike the complete secrecy which surrounded Saudi Arabia's acquisition of the CSS-2 missiles from China in 1986, official statements and discussions about nuclear issues have been very much in evidence, although one can only speculate about the intent behind such openness. The purpose of such extensive public coverage, on the one hand, may have been to deter Iran by warning the latter that Saudi Arabia would respond in kind if Iran acquired nuclear weapons and that this would thereby set off an expensive and hazardous arms race in which any projected Iranian advantage would be neutralized. One Saudi journalist, in fact, interpreted such openness as necessary in order to convince Iran that Riyadh was not bluffing.[72] As another Saudi commentator also noted, "simply considering this [nuclear] option openly forces other countries in the region to reconsider, knowing that they cannot continue to pursue their nuclear programs while the Arabs remain in their nuclear backwardness."[73] In addition, public declarations may also have been intended to pressure the United States and the international community into being more proactive against Iran by raising the specter of runaway proliferation in the region if nothing was done. Also, the leadership no doubt wanted to reassure the public and the military that policymakers were in fact aware of the nuclear threat and were preparing to do something meaningful about it.

The visibility and frequency of discussions in the Saudi media about the nuclear issue may also indicate that Saudi policymakers wanted to ensure support within society for a potential nuclear option by giving the impression of a bottom-up demand for such a capability by raising public awareness about the potential nuclear threat. As one Saudi academic put it, "we must have a popular nuclear culture which requires, for example, extensive media coverage lasting many months on television and radio, and in newspapers and magazines ... before the axe falls on our head."[74] Highlighting what the government could portray as popular demand might serve to prepare the public by creating a consensus and allowing the royal family to gain credit for responding to society's ostensible security demands. Emphasizing the Iranian threat may also have been a means of unifying society on the basis of patriotism and religious sentiment in an effort to forestall discontent similar to that in other countries in the region as part of the Arab Spring. Moreover, discussions in the military media may have been intended to generate and spread ideas on military doctrine, as well as pursuing the same objectives as with the civilian media. From available indications, the acquisition of nuclear weapons would probably be a popular decision among Saudis in any event, and the government needed only to crystallize and channel such inchoate support rather than having to create it from scratch. In many ways, the Saudi public's available information about the Iranian threat and about nuclear weapons, although filtered and shaped to produce specific effects, builds on long-accepted popular negative cultural attitudes toward the Shia, distrust of the West, and national pride.

The potential mechanics of acquisition

There are no definitive indications as to how Saudi Arabia might acquire nuclear weapons should it choose to do so, although it would have to be either by local development or by transfer from another country.

Developing a nuclear weapons capability, of course, is not an easy process, requiring a complex technical infrastructure, skilled cadres, and effective safety and command and control mechanisms, quite apart from the necessary fissile material. Some have dismissed that possibility outright. For example, in a 2015 opinion article, U.S. pundit Fareed Zakaria stated categorically that Saudi Arabia could not do so even 10 years from now, arguing that since the country had no industry or experts, it could not develop an atomic bomb domestically and, he added, that it was "highly unlikely" that Riyadh could acquire one elsewhere, since even Pakistan would not want to become a pariah and risk sanctions by supplying one.[75] The article raised a media firestorm in Saudi Arabia, although it may have been the author's patronizing approach that commentators found most offensive, as well as what one journalist claimed were his pro-Iranian leanings.[76] One Saudi academic viewed the article as part of a media campaign by U.S. liberals to "soften American public opinion" with respect to Iran and wondered why the Saudi lobby in the United States was not being more effective with the media and politicians on such issues.[77] Other commentators focused on the substantive issues, such as one who argued that there was no linkage between, as she put it, Saudi Arabia's inability to manufacture cars (one of Zakaria's litmus tests) and an inability to acquire nuclear weapons. Reminding Zakaria that Riyadh was planning to begin an automobile industry soon, using imported technology and materials, she argued that the country could do likewise with nuclear weapons. And, significantly, citing the success of Saudi Arabia's secret original acquisition of missiles from China, she reiterated that if Iran was not thwarted in getting an atomic bomb, Saudi Arabia "will not delay long in acquiring its equivalent."[78]

Potentially, if, as a result of the Nuclear Agreement concluded in 2015, there is an extensive hiatus in Iran's development of nuclear weapons, Saudi Arabia may be tempted to use the intervening period to pursue its own domestic weapons program—whether it would be successful or not is another question—importing know-how, personnel, components, and fuel, however ambitious such an undertaking may appear. Realistically, it is probably not plausible that Saudi Arabia would be able develop nuclear weapons relying on its own domestic capabilities in the foreseeable future, given its lack of physical infrastructure and cadres in this field. For Saudi Arabia to duplicate Iran's path to nuclear weapons would require many years, and a Saudi political scientist recognized that "there is no doubt that such [nuclear] technology requires great effort and internal development in the fields of science and engineering over a long period of time in the future," noting that Iran's program had begun already some 30 years earlier.[79] One Saudi academic rued the fact that the Gulf countries—and, implicitly, also his own country—simply did not have enough qualified people even for the planned civilian nuclear program.[80]

Despite the major agreement that they help build most of Saudi Arabia's nuclear reactors, the director of Rusatom, Russia's civilian nuclear agency, likewise cautioned the Saudis that "any country starting out in the nuclear sector will find that undertaking a national nuclear program without a significant suitable nuclear base is extremely difficult."[81]

Significantly, in past years, Saudi blogs often carried postings by disillusioned students who had majored in nuclear studies—currently nuclear engineering programs exist at three Saudi universities—discouraging others from pursuing that course of study, since there were no job opportunities for such graduates. A Saudi nuclear engineer, in fact, complaining of the past neglect of nuclear studies, marked by limited budgets and facilities, noted that he had stopped teaching the subject altogether, as graduates had no work and, although he claimed that the situation had started to improve more recently, clearly the domestic cadre of nuclear experts remains small.[82] More basically, STEM studies traditionally have been neglected in Saudi Arabia to the benefit of the humanities, and especially for women students, which has often led to complaints in the local media.[83]

Rather, acquisition would almost assuredly have to occur by purchase. As one Saudi blogger in a forum connected to the Saudi Stock Exchange urged, the country should not waste its money buying expensive conventional Western arms but, instead, "for less than that, we can buy a ready-made turnkey atom bomb."[84] Another blogger, likewise, urged that:

> thanks to the wisdom and planning of our enlightened leaders, and the creative use of oil money, [we] avoid the foolishness of repeating the initial steps and instead proceed directly to a deterrent weapon which, with our money, we can afford ... we have awesome buying power.[85]

Based on history and existing connections, the most likely source for a nuclear weapon would be Pakistan, although additional know-how or technology might also be forthcoming from other countries. There has been a long-standing bilateral relationship in the field of nuclear power between Pakistan and Saudi Arabia.[86] Saudi Arabian oil and financial aid helped Pakistan overcome international sanctions following its first nuclear detonation in 1998. When the then-Defense Minister Prince Sultan visited Pakistan in 1999, he was allowed to tour the country's nuclear development facility at Kahuta—the first foreigner to do so, as the Pakistani hosts stressed—and he was briefed on the program by the country's leading nuclear scientist, A. Q. Khan, often called the father of Pakistan's atom bomb, who showed him several nuclear weapons, including a Pakistani-made Ghauri SSM equipped with a nuclear warhead.[87] Saudi sources had been anxious to downplay the visit, claiming that Prince Sultan had only visited the first part of Pakistan's nuclear reactor and not the secret parts as had been reported.[88] But another Saudi report also noted that Prince Sultan at Kahuta had "praised Dr. Abd Al-Qadir Khan and his colleagues ... for the achievement of establishing this wonderful scientific structure."[89] Prince Sultan's son and then-Deputy Minister of Defense,

Prince Khalid, was reported to have been present at a Pakistani nuclear test in October 2005.[90] In promoting a Saudi atom bomb, at least one Saudi pundit has called openly for nuclear cooperation with such countries as Pakistan to bring to fruition what he termed "this great dream."[91] In the wake of the country's 2014 Sword of Abd Allah Exercise, in fact, the local Saudi electronic media that is aimed at domestic audiences stressed that the CSS-2 that had been displayed was not only nuclear-capable but that in the audience watching the parade was the Chief of Staff of "nuclear Pakistan" and suggested that there was now a new alliance with "nuclear Pakistan."[92] Any significant influx of Pakistani nuclear experts to Saudi Arabia could certainly serve as an indicator of an impending transfer of nuclear equipment.

Perhaps understandably, whenever reports have surfaced in the foreign media about Saudi–Pakistani cooperation in the nuclear field, Saudi sources have denied them heatedly, as in a Saudi editorial following Prince Sultan's visit to Pakistan in 2006, which dismissed accounts of cooperation in the nuclear arena as "asinine allegations."[93] Prince Sultan, Minister of Defense at the time, himself rejected such reports as "baseless allegations."[94] The official organ of the Muslim World League (a Saudi-based and financed international organization), while maintaining that Saudi Arabia had a right to nuclear weapons, likewise characterized any such Western speculation about cooperation with Pakistan as "surprising" and "ridiculous." And, this same source attributed such accounts to "the Zionist lobby" and to U.S. efforts to blackmail Saudi Arabia into cooperating with the United States' Middle East policy.[95] More recently, Pakistan has joined in the denials whenever a report has surfaced involving a transfer of nuclear materials to Saudi Arabia, as was the case when Pakistan's Foreign Ministry, in November 2013, called such reports "speculative, mischievous and baseless."[96] Likewise, rebutting similar speculation arising after the visit by Prince Salman, at the time Saudi Arabia's Minister of Defense, in February 2014, the Pakistani government again issued heated denials.[97] Pakistan's Prime Minister Nawaz Sharif, likewise, assured the IAEA in 2014 that "Pakistan is a committed nuclear non-proliferation state."[98] And, yet again, when the *Sunday Times* in 2015 published another article about a Saudi–Pakistan nuclear understanding, a Saudi military spokesman categorized the report as old news and simply "speculation and rumors."[99]

To be sure, there is no hard evidence of any formal bilateral deal having been struck for nuclear weapons, although unverifiable Western media reports have surfaced periodically to that effect. For example, in 2003, an unnamed "ranking Pakistani insider" was the purported source for the reported existence of a secret agreement for "nuclear cooperation" intended to provide Saudi Arabia with nuclear weapons technology.[100] Again, an unnamed "senior U.S. official" claimed that Saudi Arabia had helped finance Pakistan's nuclear program, and suggested that Pakistan could well make nuclear weapons from its arsenal available to Saudi Arabia.[101] More recently, based on unattributed "intelligence reports," the British press also reported an alleged deal in which "the Saudi monarchy paid for up to 60% of the Pakistani nuclear [program], and in return has the option to buy a small nuclear arsenal ('five to six warheads') off the shelf if things got tough in the [neighborhood]."[102] And in 2013 there was a report yet again to that effect.[103] Suggestive, although by no means definitive, was information in the Russian press, based on unnamed Pakistani officials. According to the latter, there is a verbal agreement with Saudi Arabia on nuclear cooperation, with one Pakistani source quoted as saying "What do you think? Why would Saudi Arabia have given us so much money? It wasn't just philanthropy."[104] Perhaps a journalist who has known King Salman personally for many years and socialized with him both in Saudi Arabia and abroad may add some additional informed perspective on Saudi thinking on this issue, as he surmised in a Saudi-owned newspaper that "King Salman ... could conclude an agreement tomorrow with Pakistan to buy atom bombs from the latter ... an atom bomb would arrive in a week."[105] In fact, some Saudis have shown a particular sensitivity to what they believe are U.S. plans to disarm Pakistan, and a recurring theme for Saudi pundits has been that Washington was promoting chaos in Pakistan in order to achieve its ultimate objective, that of partitioning the country and removing its nuclear arsenal, since both the United States and Israel feared a transfer of nuclear technology to the Arabs.[106] Pakistan has reinforced such concerns, with the country's Minister of Defense in 2014 openly accusing the West of seeking to "take our nuclear weapons from us," which was reported in the Saudi media.[107]

Admittedly, the expectation that Pakistan would automatically provide nuclear weapons if asked may have become somewhat less certain in Saudi circles in the wake of Pakistan's refusal in 2015 of a Saudi request to contribute ground forces to an envisioned invasion of Yemen. This development seemed to surprise the Saudis, with one journalist, speaking specifically in the context of the recently-announced Nuclear Agreement with Iran, calling "Pakistan's neutrality" an "alarm bell" to the fact that national interests and alliances may change over time.[108] Another Saudi commentator also admitted that some of his countrymen interpreted Pakistan's negative response for troops as "a sort of betrayal" and concluded that Pakistan, a "historic ally," was still "a friend, even if no longer an ally."[109] That said, a large economic inducement might still be successful in overriding any reluctance, if there is any, in Islamabad about the transfer of nuclear technology. Significantly, Pakistan may not be overly concerned to see a nuclear Saudi Arabia, as it would balance Iran while posing no threat to Pakistan itself. As Matthew Kroenig has noted, states that cannot project power over another specific state have less to lose strategically by seeing that state acquire nuclear weapons.[110] Thus, Pakistan—which cannot project military power over Saudi Arabia even if it wanted to—could view proliferating to Saudi Arabia with relative equanimity, since it would not incur any strategic cost. And, while Pakistan of course might be liable to political and economic retaliation by the United States, that, too, would depend on the international context at the time, especially if such a transfer were to occur during the turmoil that would accompany an Iranian breakout, when any potential international reaction might well be muted and more understanding of a Saudi acquisition.

In practical terms, a very small number of warheads, or their components, could be transported fairly easily to Saudi Arabia and whether they would be traced is open to question. When Saudi Arabia embarked on its SSM program, for example, in order to allay suspicions, the Saudis told the United States that the extensive new construction work being carried out ultimately in support of the expected SSMs was for an ammunition depot, whereas for a rudimentary nuclear arsenal probably fewer new facilities would be needed.[111] All that would really be required in order to provide the desired effect is a tangible presence of what can be portrayed with at least some credibility to be a nuclear device. What might be less noticeable than transferring a ready-made bomb, of course, might be the transfer of drawings and parts for nuclear programs, as was the case with the surreptitious transfers between Pakistan and Iran in the 1980s at the hands of Pakistani scientist A. Q. Khan.[112]

In the event, it would not be necessary that any nuclear device be in a condition to be deployed or launched immediately, or that it be on ready-alert. To some extent, perceptions can be as effective as reality, as shown by the acquisition and presence even of some conventional state-of-the art equipment of which the Saudi military very likely cannot make optimal use. As Prince Bandar bin Sultan (long-time Saudi ambassador to Washington and son of the late Defense Minister, and later Director General of the Saudi Intelligence Agency), expressed the deterrent value of his country's SSMs, "the psychology behind [the missile] was more important than its capability."[113] From the Saudi perspective, a physical presence would probably be sufficient, at least initially, as an immediate psychological and political factor to reassure the country and its regional friends that Riyadh had a counterweight and deterrent to any political influence and military advantage that Iran would have gained from acquiring a nuclear arsenal. An integrated system with a launch capability, command and control, and other technical aspects to make the program genuinely credible—even if only to achieve a rudimentary and an unlikely warfighting option—could come considerably later. One Saudi journalist even suggested basing part of Pakistan's nuclear arsenal in Saudi Arabia, offering as a selling point for Islamabad that those weapons would also be safer there from Indian attacks.[114]

Iran seems to be taking the possibility of such a transfer from Pakistan to Saudi Arabia in its stride, but has reacted publicly at times to rumors of Saudi attempts to acquire nuclear weapons by purchase, as was the case after a report of a Saudi approach to Pakistan for that purpose. On that occasion, an Iranian official derided such attempts as "childish" and warned that the United States would pre-empt any transfer by mounting an air strike against Pakistan.[115] The Iranian media has at times also mocked what they concluded was Saudi Arabia's inability to develop its own nuclear weapons and its presumed dependence on Pakistan as the future supplier.

Notes

1 The reports came from Saudi defector Muhammad Al-Khilaywi; see Marie Colvin and Peter Sawyer, "Riyadh Bargained with Chinese for Nuclear Reactors," *Sunday Times*, 7 August 1994, 17.

2 Interview with Prince Sultan, "Al-Alam al-arabi yamurr bi-marhala harija" [The Arab World Is Passing through a Delicate Phase], *Al-Hawadith* (Beirut), 18–27 April 1990, 19.
3 Amir Tahiri, "*Ilaf* takshif sirran li'l-marra al-ula: Al-Saudiya rafadat silahan nawawiyan min Ukraniya" [*Ilaf* Reveals a Secret for the First Time: Saudi Arabia Rejected Nuclear Weapons from Ukraine], *Ilaf*, 4 August 2007, www.elaph.com/ElaphWeb/akhbarKhasa/2007/8/253000.htm.
4 For example, Uthman Al-Rawaf, "Madha bad iddia' ann Al-Saudiya tasa li-imtilak asliha nawawiya? As'ila tabhath an ijabat" [What Next after Claims That Saudi Arabia Is Seeking Nuclear Weapons? Questions in Need of Answers], *Al-Sharq Al-Awsat*, 26 September 2003, www.aawsat.com/print.asp?did=194802&issueno=9068.
5 Interview with Prince Saud Al-Faysal, "Changes in the Kingdom—on 'Our Timetable'" *Washington Post*, 27 February 2005, B5.
6 Prince Sultan quoted in "Al-Amir Sultan: Al-Saudiya laysat bi-haja li-asliha nawawiya" [Prince Sultan: Saudi Arabia Does Not Need Nuclear Weapons], *Al-Sharq Al-Awsat*, 19 April 2006, www.aawsat.com/print.asp?did=359013&issueno=10004.
7 Reported in Muhammad Al-Ghunayyim, "Al-Amir Sultan: Al-Mansha'at al-naftiya al-saudiya amina" [Prince Sultan: The Saudi Oil Facilities Are Secure], *Al-Riyadh*, 4 April 2006, www.alriyadh.com/2006/04/04/article143736.html.
8 "Al-Safir al-saudi lada Amirika: Al-Qaida la tazal qadira ala shann hajamat" [The Saudi Ambassador in America: Al-Qaida Is Still Capable of Launching Attacks], *Al-Sharq Al-Awsat*, 9 December 2005, www.aawsat.com/print.asp?did=337373&issueno=9873.
9 Ali Al-Qahis, "Al-Amir Turki Al-Faysal yutalib bi-tahwil majlis al-taawun ila ittihad ashbah bi'l-urubbi wa-insha' jaysh khaliji muwahhad" [Prince Turki Al-Faysal Calls for a Transformation of the [Gulf] Cooperation Council into a Union Resembling the European Union and for the Establishment of a Unified Gulf Army], *Al-Riyadh*, 22 March 2011, www.alriyadh.com/2011/03/22/article615880.html.
10 Jason Burke, "Riyadh Will Build Nuclear Weapons if Iran Gets Them, Saudi Prince Warns," *The Guardian* (London), 29 June 2011, www.guardian.co.uk/world/2011/jun/29/saudi-build-nuclear-weapons-iran/print (hereafter Burke, "Riyadh Will Build").
11 Interview with Prince Turki Al-Faysal, BBC Arabic News, 8 July 2011, www.youtube.com/watch?=Kfw.R7j4-HwZO (hereafter Turki Al-Faysal, BBC).
12 Ibid.
13 Salim Al-Sharif, "Turki Al-Faysal: Al-Alam fashal fi iqna Isra'il wa-Iran min 'al-nawawi' wa-khiyaratna maftuha" [Turki Al-Faysal: The World Failed to Convince Israel and Iran on the Nuclear [Issue] and Our Options Are Open], *Al-Madina*, 6 December 2011, www.al-madina.com/print/343006.
14 Prince Turki Al-Faysal, "Saudi Arabia's New Foreign Policy Doctrine in the Aftermath of the Arab Awakening," lecture at the Belfer Center for Science and International Affairs, Harvard University, 25 April 2013, http://live.belfercenter.org/publication/23013/prince_turki_on_saudi_arabias_role_after_arab_awakening.html?breadcrumb=%2F.
15 Prince Naef bin Ahmed Al Saud, "Underpinning Saudi National Security Strategy," *Joint Forces Quarterly*, Autumn 2002, 130.
16 "Ra'is al-mukhabarat al-saudiya akkad ann al-nawawi al-isra'ili yuthir sibaq tasalluh" [The Head of Saudi Intelligence Asserted That Israel's Nuclear Weapons Would Spur an Arms Race], *Al-Arabiya TV* (Abu Dhabi, UAE), 9 December 2006, transcript at www.alarabiya.net/articles/2006/12/09/29744.html.
17 "Ra'is al-istikhbarat al-saudiya: Imtilak Isra'il li'l-asliha al-nawawiya yushakkil aqaba asasiya amam al-istiqrar fi al-mintaqa" [The Head of Saudi Intelligence: Israel's Possession of Nuclear Weapons Presents a Fundamental Obstacle to Stability in the Region], *Al-Sharq Al-Awsat*, 15 April 2010, www.aawsat.com/print.asp?did=565347&issueno=11461.
18 Turki Al-Suhayl, "Al-Saudiya: Lan nadkhul sibaq tasalluh nawawi wa-ala Tihran taqdim damanat" [Saudi Arabia: We Will Not Enter a Nuclear Arms Race but Tehran

19 Umar Al-Zubaydi and Mashari Al-Wahbi, "Muqrin bin Abd Al-Aziz yuhdhir min sibaq tasalluh fi'l-mintaqa wa-awdat 'tawazun al-rub'" [Muqrin bin Abd Al-Aziz Warns of an Arms Race in the Region and of a Return to a 'Balance of Terror'], Al-Watan, 4 December 2011, www.alwatan.com.sa/Politics/News_Detail.aspx?Arti cleID=78218&CategoryID=1.
20 "Khalid bin Sultan: Amn Al-Kuwait min amn Al-Saudiya" [Khalid bin Sultan: Kuwait's Security Is Part of Saudi Arabia's Security], Al-Ra'y (Kuwait), 5 May 2010, www.alraimedia.com/Alrai/ArticlePrint.aspx?id=201410.
21 "Khalid bin Sultan: Taghayyur mawazin al-quwwa yaduna ila tatwir qudratna al-qitaliya wa-tahsinha" [The Change in the Balance of Power Requires Us to Develop and Improve Our Combat Capabilities], Al-Madina, 18 April 2011, www.al-madina. com/print/299303.
22 Fahd Al-Dhiyabi, "Saud Al-Faysal: Yajib tamkin al-shab al-suri min al-difa an nafsih, wa-Iran ghayr sadiqa hawl barnamijha al-nawawi" [Saud Al-Faysal: The Syrian People Must Be Empowered to Defend Themselves, and Iran Is Not Sincere about Its Nuclear Program], Al-Sharq Al-Awsat, 13 February 2013, www.aawsat.com/print.asp? did=717110&issueno=12496 (hereafter Saud Al-Faysal).
23 Cable from U.S. Embassy Riyadh, 13 December 2006, Wikileaks, http://wikileaks.org/plusd/cables/06RIYADH9078_a.html.
24 Reported in Chemi Shalev, "Dennis Ross: Saudi King Vowed to Obtain Nuclear Bomb after Iran," Haaretz, 30 May 2012, www.haaretz.com/news/diplomacy-de fense/dennis-ross-saudi-king-vowed-to-obtain-nuclear-bomb-after-iran-1.433294.
25 Saud Kabili, "Al-Mintaqa ala washk sibaq al-tasalluh al-nawawi" [The Region Is on the Brink of a Nuclear Arms Race], Al-Watan, 22 April 2012, www.alwatan.com.sa/ Articles/Detail.aspx?ArticleId=10530.
26 Sami Said Habib, "Qira'a fi tasrihat Al-Faysal" [A Reading of [Turki] Al-Faysal's Statements], Al-Madina, 10 December 2011, www.al-madina.com/print/343867.
27 Ibid.
28 Ibid. Another Saudi press analysis of Prince Turki's statements, likewise, clarified that what he meant was that if the international community failed to stop Iran, other options, including a nuclear one, would be "inevitable" for Saudi Arabia. "Khabira: Imtilak al-mamlaka li-silah nawawi yajurr al-mintaqa ila sibaq li'l-tasalluh" [An Expert: The Kingdom's Acquisition of Nuclear Weapons Will Propel the Region into an Arms Race], Al-Ikhbariya (Saudi Arabia), 5 January 2012, www.k1b1.com/print.php? action+print&m=newsm&id=18289.
29 Turki Al-Dakhil, "Al-Khalij Al-Arabi wa'l-rabi al-arabi" [The Arab Gulf and the Arab Spring], Al-Hayat, reproduced in Anba'kum, 18 December 2011, www.anbacom. com/articles.php?action=show&id=10902.
30 Prince Turki Al-Faysal's speech was reported in "Al-Faysal: Al-Saudiya qad tudtarr li-hiyazat al-silah al-nawawi" [Al-Faysal: Saudi Arabia May Be Forced to Acquire Nuclear Weapons], Al-Yawm, 6 December 2011, www.alyaum.com/News/art/37488. html. The commentary is found in Abd Al-Aziz Husayn Al-Suwaygh, "Al-Khalij wa'l-khatar al-nawawi?" [The Gulf and the Nuclear Threat], Al-Madina, part 2, 23 May 2012, www.al-madina.com/printhtml/379718.
31 Burke, "Riyadh Will Build."
32 Staff Brigadier Zayid bin Muhammad Al-Amri, "Dawafi imtilak al-qudrat al-istratijiya al-sarukhiya al-fada'iya wa'l-nawawiya" [The Incentives for Acquiring Strategic Rocket, Space, and Nuclear Capabilities], Al-Difa Al-Jawwi, December 2010, 12 (hereafter Al-Amri, "Dawafi imtilak").
33 Ibid., 15.
34 Talal Salih Bannan, "Al-Arab bayn kammashat al-rub al-nawawi!" [The Arabs between the Pincers of Nuclear Terror!], Ukaz, 2 April 2006, www.okaz.com.sa/oka z/osf/20060402/PrinCon200604026920.htm (hereafter Bannan, "Al-Arab").

35 Sadaqa Yahya Fadil, "Istikhdam al-silah al-nawawi ... al-maful al-khafiy" [Using Nuclear Weapons ... the Hidden Impact], *Ukaz*, 25 March 2007, www.okaz.com.sa/okaz/osf/20070325/PrinCon2007032597841.htm.
36 Adnan Kamil Salah, "Tasawwaru uhlumu 'udu!" [Imagine, Dream, Pray!], *Al-Madina*, 13 May 2010, www.al-madina.com/print/247504.
37 Sami Said Habib, "Al-Khiyar al-arabi al-amthal fi al-taamul ma al-malaffat al-nawawiya fi'l-mintaqa" [The Best Arab Option for Dealing with Nuclear Issues in the Region], *Al-Madina*, 13 March 2010, www.al-madina.com/node/231352.
38 Ibrahim Al-Amir, "Qunbula nawawiya wa-law sirran" [A Nuclear Bomb Even If Covertly], *Al-Watan*, 10 September 2011, www.alwatan.com.sa/Articles/Detail.aspx?ArticleID=7323 (hereafter Al-Amir, "Qunbula nawawiya").
39 Jasir Abd Al-Aziz Al-Jasir, "Naam li-silah nawawi khaliji" [Yes to a Gulf Nuclear Weapon], *Al-Jazira*, 7 December 2011, www.al-jazirah.com/2011/20111207/du8.htm (hereafter Al-Jasir, "Naam li-silah").
40 Ibid.
41 "Sibaq nawawi fi Al-Sharq Al-Awsat" [A Nuclear Arms Race in the Middle East], *Al-Madina*, 20 February 2010, www.al-madina.com/print/225775.
42 Interview with Sami Uthman, "Muhallil siyasi li'l-*Marsad*: Ala duwal Al-Khalij wa-khassatan Al-Saudiya al-say li'l-husul ala qunbula nawawiya" [A Political Analyst to *Al-Marsad*: The Gulf States, and in Particular Saudi Arabia, Must Seek to Acquire an Atom Bomb], *Al-Marsad*, 21 December 2011, www.al-marsd.com.
43 Major General Jamal Mazhlum, "Matalib duwal Al-Khalij min Iran" [The Gulf States' Demands of Iran], *Al-Jazira*, 8 October 2011, www.al-jazirah.com.sa/20111008/du11.htm.
44 Major General Husam Suwaylam (Ret.), "Ahdaf Iran al-siyasiya wa'l-istratijiya wa-asalib tahqiqha" [Iran's Political and Strategic Objectives and the Methods to Achieve Them], *Al-Haras Al-Watani*, part 1, August 2011, 37.
45 Al-Jasir, "Naam li-silah."
46 Hamad bin Abd Allah Al-Luhaydan, "Abad al-tasalluh al-nawawi wa-tadaiyatih" [Dimensions of Nuclear Arming and of Its Consequences], *Al-Riyadh*, 29 May 2009, www.alriyadh.com/2009/05/29/article433463.html (hereafter Al-Luhaydan, "Abad al-tasalluh").
47 Ali bin Fayiz Al-Juhani, "Majlis al-taawun al-khaliji wa-khiyar imtilak silah al-rad" [The GCC and the Option of Acquiring a Deterrent Weapon], *Al-Riyadh*, 11 April 2012, www.alriyadh.com/726193.
48 Yusuf Al-Kuwaylit, "Hal nu'akkid annana lasna al-ha'it al-qasir?" [Can We Confirm That We Are Not a Pushover?], *Al-Riyadh*, 23 February 2013, www.alriyadh.com/2013/02/23/article812425.html.
49 Al-Amri, "Dawafi imtilak," 15.
50 Abd Al-Aziz Al-Khamis, "Han waqt al-silah al-nawawi al-saudi" [The Time Has Come for a Saudi Nuclear Weapon], *Ibda*, 23 February 2012, http://ebdaa.com/?act=artc&id=5577&print=1.
51 Hamad bin Abd Allah Al-Luhaydan, "Al-Matami wa'l-tawajjuhat al-askariya al-iraniya" [Iranian Ambitions and Military Bearings], *Al-Riyadh*, 16 September 2013, www.alriyadh.com/865450.
52 The paper was by Abd Allah Al-Utaybi, as reported in Abd Allah bin Ibrahim Al-Askar, "Malaffat sakhina" [Hot Issues], *Al-Riyadh*, 19 January 2011, www.alriyadh.com/2011/01/19/article595966.print. (herafter Al-Askar, "Malaffat sakhina").
53 Badr Al-Balawi, "Al-Qunbula al-nawawiya al-saudiya" [A Saudi Atom Bomb], *Al-Sharq*, 14 December 2011, www.alsharq.net.sa/2011/12/14/46046.
54 Abd Al-Rahman Al-Rashid, "Al-Qunbula al-nawawiya al-saudiya" [A Saudi Atom Bomb], *Al-Sharq Al-Awsat*, 16 November 2013, http://aawsat.com/node/9752.
55 Hamad bin Abd Allah Al-Luhaydan, "Ma bayn ghazw Kuba wa-ghazw Ukraniya" [The Difference between the Invasion of Cuba and That of Ukraine], *Al-Riyadh*, 7 March 2014, www.alriyadh.com/915945.

98 The evolution in Saudi thinking

56 Salih Matar Al-Ghamdi, "Al-Saudiya awla bi'l-silah al-nawawi!" [Saudi Arabia Is More Deserving of Nuclear Weapons!], *Sabq*, 6 November 2013, http://sabq.org/js1aCd, and Abd Al-Latif Al-Mulhim, "Al-Mamlaka wa'l-silah al-nawawi" [The Kingdom and Nuclear Weapons], *Al-Yawm*, 24 March 2015, www.alyaum.com/article/405578.
57 Ali Sad Al-Musa, "Li-madha ghab su'al al-silah al-nawawi al-saudi?" [Why Is the Issue of a Saudi Nuclear Weapon Neglected?], *Al-Watan*, 23 February 2014, www.alwatan.com.sa/Articles/Detail.aspx?ArticleId=20259.
58 Comments to Hisham Munawwar, "Al-Mamlaka Al-Arabiya Al-Saudiya wa-imtilak al-silah al-nawawi: al-muawwiqat wa'l-muhaffizat" [The Kingdom of Saudi Arabia and Acquiring Nuclear Weapons: The Obstacles and the Incentives], *Al-Muslim* (Saudi Arabia), 23 Safar 1430/19 February 2009, http://almoslim.net/node/107241.
59 Ibid.
60 Comments to Khalid Al-Dakhil, "Marhalat al-hudu' wa'l-hifazh ala al-siyasa al-kharijiya" [A Quiet Phase While Maintaining the [Same] Foreign Policy], *Anba'ukum*, 21 June 2013, www.anbacom.com/print?action=print&m=articlesm&id=16877.
61 "Quwwat al-rad al-nawawi al-saudi" [Saudi Deterrent Power], *Aswaq Royal Blog*, 17 March 2003, www.aswaqroyal.com/t18351.html.
62 Al-Askar, "Malaffat sakhina."
63 Shahir Al-Nahari, "Al-Nawawi wa'l-naml" [Nuclear Weapons and Ants], *Al-Sharq* (Najran, Saudi Arabia), 16 April 2013, www.alsharq.net.sa/2013/04/16/805815.
64 Sermon by the *mufti*, Abd Al-Aziz Al Al-Shaykh, "Mufti al-mamlaka: Kashf asrar al-watan li'l-ada' min ashadd anwa al-khiyana li'l-umma" [The Kingdom's Mufti: Revealing the Country's Secrets to the Enemy Is the Most Serious Form of National Treason], the Mufti's personal website, 23 April 2015, http://mufti.af.org.sa. The religious establishment's official publication also underlies frequently the principle of obedience to the ruler as a religious duty, "Taat wulat al-amr tawq najat min al-tafarruq wa'l-tashardhum" [Obedience to the Rulers Is a Life-Saver against Divisions and Factionalism], *Al-Dawa* (Riyadh), 26 March 2015, www.alddawah.com/?p=10936.
65 A'id Al-Qarni, "Al-Hurub al-nawawiya wa'l-kimawiya wa'l-biyulujiya fi al-mizan al-fiqhi" [Nuclear, Chemical, and Biological Wars on the Scale of Religious Law], *Al-Jundi Al-Muslim* (Riyadh), 3 January 2002, http://jmuslim.naseej.com/Detail.asp?InsectionID=260&InNewsItemID=66247 (hereafter *Al-Jundi Al-Muslim*, 3 January 2002), 9 January 2002, http://jmuslim.naseej.com/Detail.asp?InNewsItemID=85963&q=, and 11 January 2002, http://jmuslim.naseej.com/Detail.asp?InNewsItemID=92526&q= (hereafter *Al-Jundi Al-Muslim*, 11 January 2002).
66 *Al-Jundi Al-Muslim*, 3 January 2002.
67 *Al-Jundi Al-Muslim*, 11 January 2002.
68 *Al-Jundi Al-Muslim*, 3 January 2002.
69 Nasir bin Hamad Al-Fahd, "Hukm istikhdam aslihat al-damar al-shamil didd al-kuffar" [Ruling on the Use of WMD against Infidels], Rabi I 1424/May 2003, http://72.29.89.164/showthread.php?t=3711&page=2.
70 A'id Al-Qarni, "Al-Gharb yujahid wa-yuharrim alayna al-jihad" [The West Goes on a Jihad But Forbids Us from Doing So], *Al-Sharq Al-Awsat*, 8 November 2011, www.aawsat.com/print.asp?did=648856&issueno=12033.
71 Ibid.
72 Zuhayr Muhammad Jamil Kutbi, "Naam namlik silahan nawawiyan" [Yes, We Have Nuclear Weapons], *Al-Khalij* (Riyadh), 7 January 2014, www.al-khaleeg.com/article-auid-712.html.
73 Bannan, "Al-Arab."
74 Abd al-Malik bin Abd Allah Al-Khayyal, "Al-Saudiya wa'l-saudiyun wa-istidadhum li'l-hurub al-nawawiya al-qadima" [Saudi Arabia and the Saudis and Their Preparation for Future Nuclear Wars], *Al-Jazira*, 9 April 2007, www.al-jazirah.com/2007/20070609/ar6.htm.
75 Fareed Zakaria, "Saudi Arabia's Bluff," *Washington Post*, 14 June 2015, A23.

76 Mashari Al-Dhaydi, "Fareed Zakariya 'habibna'" [Fareed Zakaria "Our Buddy"], *Al-Sharq Al-Awsat*, 13 June 2015, http://aawsat.com/node/383001.
77 Ahamad Al-Farraj, "Fareed Zakaria: Ayn al-lubi al-saudi?" [Fareed Zakaria: Where Is the Saudi Lobby?], *Al-Jazira*, 29 June 2015, www.al-jazirah.com/2015/20150629/ln49.htm.
78 Amal Abd Al-Aziz Al-Hazzani, "Safirat intilaq al-barnamij al-nawawi al-saudi" [The Starting Gun for the Saudi Nuclear Program], *Al-Sharq Al-Awsat*, 15 June 2015, http://aawsat.com/node/384676. In fact, in that vein, in 2015 Saudi Arabia signed an agreement with Ukraine to co-manufacture Antonov An-132 transport aircraft, "Ukraina i Saudovskaya Araviya nachnut sovmestnuyu razrabotku i proizvodstvo An-132" [Ukraine and Saudi Arabia to Begin Joint Development and Production of the An-132], *RBK News Agency* (Kiev), 13 May 2015, www.rbc.ua/rus/news/ukraina-sa udovskaya-araviya-nachnut-sovmestnuyu-1431502501.html. Moreover, another academic assured readers that there was no link between a country's level of education and its military power, Abd Al-Aziz Al-Umar, "Al-Quwwa al-talimiya wa'l-quwwa al-askariya" [Educational Power and Military Power], *Al-Jazira*, 14 June 2015, www.al-jazirah. com/sa/2015/20150614/ar7/htm.
79 Salih Abd Al-Rahman Al-Mani, "Al-Tiqniya al-nawawiya fi Al-Khalij" [Nuclear Technology in the Gulf], *Ukaz*, 16 December 2006, www.okaz.com.sa/okaz/osf/20061216/PrinCon2006121671686.htm.
80 Salih Al-Mani quoted at a roundtable, "Al-Barnamij al-nawawi al-khaliji: Li-madha wa-kayf?" [The Gulf Nuclear Program: Why and How?], *Al-Yamama* (Riyadh), 7 January 2014, www.alriyadh.com/alyamamah/article/970990.
81 Nikolai Drozdov quoted in "Taqaddum saudi rusi fi al-taawun al-nawawi" [Saudi–Russian Progress in Nuclear Cooperation], *Al-Watan*, 5 September 2015, www.alwata n.com.sa/Economy/News_Detail.aspx?ArticleID=234469&CategoryID=2.
82 Interview with Tawfiq bin Ahmad Saud Al-Qusayr by Asma' Al-Abbudi, "Ustadh al-handasa yatamanna: La budd min alla nujamil ayya quwa alamiya min ajl al-maslaha al-wataniya wa-bina' al-quwwa wa'l-taqniya" [A Professor of Engineering Expresses a Desire: We Must Not Try to Please Any World Powers When It Is a Question of Our National Interest and the Development of Our Power and Technology], *Al-Hayat* (Saudi edition), 12 January 2010, http://daharchives.alhayat.com.
83 Musa bin Isa Al-Abbus, "Al-Karasi al-ilmiya fi jamiatna" [Science Chairs in Our Universities], *Al-Jazira*, 13 April 2015, www.al-jazirah.com/2015/20150413/ar2.htm.
84 Hawamir Al-Bursa Al-Saudiya, 2 November 2010, www.hawamer.com/vb/show thread.php?t=705888&page=3.
85 "Li-madha la namlik al-silah al-nawawi?" [Why Don't We Get Nuclear Weapons?], *Jazan News*, 23 May 2006, www.jazan4u.com/vb/showthread.php?t=42590.
86 An excellent overview and analysis of the Saudi–Pakistan nuclear relationship can be found in Kimberly Van Dyke and Steve A. Yetiv, "Pakistan and Saudi Arabia: The Nuclear Nexus," *Journal of South Asian and Middle Eastern Studies*, xxxiv, 4, Summer 2011, 68–84.
87 A. Q. Khan, "My Services Are Well-Known," *The News International* (Karachi), 8 October 2012, www.thenews.com.pk/PrintEdition. aspx?ID=136329&Cat=9&dt=12/7/2012, and "Al-Amir Sultan bin Abd Al-Aziz yakhtatim jawlathu bi-ziyara najiha wa-muthmira li-Pakistan" [Prince Sultan bin Abd Al-Aziz Completes His Trip with a Successful and Productive Visit to Pakistan], *Ayn Al-Yaqin* (Riyadh), 14 May 1999, www.ainalyaqeen.com/ issues/19910514/feat3ar.htm. The English-language version of *Ayn Al-Yaqin* omitted the visit to Kahuta, perhaps indicating a desire to avoid highlighting the issue abroad.
88 "Al-Amir Sultan yanfi sai Al-Saudiya li-imtilak silah nawawi" [Prince Sultan Denies That Saudi Arabia Is Attempting to Acquire Nuclear Weapons], *Al-Sharq Al-Awsat*, 5 August 1999, 1.

89 Nasir Al-Sarami, "Sumuww al-na'ib al-thani yakhtatim ziyarathu ila Pakistan al-yawm" [His Highness the Deputy Crown Prince Concludes His Visit to Pakistan Today], *Al-Riyadh*, 9 May 1999, www.alriyadh.com/Contents/1999/09-05-1999/new.html.
90 Georges Malbrunot, "Les ambitions saoudiennes s'appuient sur le savoir-faire pakistanais" [Saudi Ambitions Rely on Pakistani Know-how], *Le Figaro* (Paris), 31 October 2010, www.lefigaro.fr/economie/2007/10/31/04001-20071031ARTFIG90143_les-ambitions_saoudiennes_s_appuient_sur_le_savoir_faire_ pakistanais.php.
91 Al-Amir, "Qunbula nawawiya."
92 Bandar Al-Dawshi, "Abr al-sarukh al-balisti Al-Saudiya tafrud halat al-samt ala al-mutarabbisin" [By Means of the Ballistic Missiles Saudi Arabia Silenced Those Who Are Lurking], *Sabq*, 30 April 2014, http://sabq.org/yGYfde.
93 "Ukdhubat aslihat al-damar" [The Lie About WMD], *Ukaz*, 18 April 2006, www.okaz.com.sa/okaz/osf/20060418/PrinCon2006041810726.htm.
94 Prince Sultan quoted at a press conference, Muhammad Al-Sanid, "Lada wusulih Al-Riyadh qadiman min Bakistan" [On His Arrival in Riyadh Returning from Pakistan], *Al-Jazira*, 17 April 2006, http://search.al-jazirah.com.sa/2006jaz/apr/17/In2t.htm.
95 Munir Hasan Munir, "Al-Qunbula al-nawawiya al-saudiya!" [The Saudi Atom Bomb!], *Al-Alam Al-Islami* (Mecca), number 1812, ca. late 2003, www.muslimworldleague.org/paper/1812/articles/p16-a2.htm.
96 "Pakistan Denies Reports of Nuclear Deal with Saudi Arabia As 'Baseless'", *Al-Arabiya TV*, 7 November 2013, http://english.alarabiya.net.
97 Mariana Baabar, "Pakistan Not Giving Saudi Arabia Nuke Technology: FO," *The International News*, 14 February 2014, www.thenews.com.pk/PrintEdition.aspx?ID=28554&Cat=13&dt=3/18/2014.
98 "Pakistan, a Committed Nuclear Non-proliferation State: Nawaz," *Dawn* (Karachi), 11 March 2014, www.dawn.com/news/1092478.
99 "Mas'ul askari Saudi yarudd li-CNN ala taqrir sayi Al-Riyadh li'l-husul ala silah nawawi min Bakistan" [A Saudi Military Official Responds to CNN about the Report That Riyadh Is Seeking to Acquire Nuclear Weapons from Pakistan], *CNN Arabic*, 19 May 2015, http://arabic.cnn.com/middleeast/2015/05/19/saudi-pakistan-nuclear-reportindex.html.
100 "Pakistan, Saudi Arabia in Secret Nuke Pact," *Washington Times*, 21 October 2003, www.washingtontimes.com/news/2003/oct/21/ 20031021-112804-8451r/print.
101 Roula Khalaf, Farhan Bokhari, and Stephen Fidler, "Saudi Money Joins Forces with Nuclear Pakistan," *Financial Times* (London), 5 August 2004, www.ft.com.
102 Julian Borger, "Pakistan's Bomb and Saudi Arabia," *Guardian*, 11 May 2011, www.guardian.co.uk, also see Hugh Tomlinson, "Saudi Arabia Threatens to Go Nuclear 'Within Weeks' If Iran Gets the Bomb," *The Times*, 10 February 2012, 23.
103 Mark Urban, "Saudi Nuclear Weapons 'On Order' from Pakistan," *BBC News*, 6 November 2013, www.bbc.co.uk/news/world-middle-east-24823846?print=true.
104 Nikolai Ivanov, "V Saudovskuyu Araviyu dostavili ballisticheskie rakety Shahin" [They Supplied Shaheen Missiles to Saudi Arabia], *Mir novostei* (Moscow), 16 November 2013, http://mirnov.ru.
105 Jihad Al-Khazin, "Utalib Al-Saudiya bi-barnamaj nawawi askari" [I Request from Saudi Arabia a Military Nuclear Program], *Al-Hayat*, 23 June 2015, http://alhayat.com/Opinion/Jihad-El-Khazen/9616428. His article was subsequently also carried by the media in Saudi Arabia. Al-Khazin, of Palestinian origin, has worked as the editor of a number of Saudi-owned newspapers in-country and abroad.
106 Sami Said Habib, "Li-madha yastahdif hilf al-atlasi Bakistan?" [Why Is NATO Targeting Pakistan?], *Al-Madina*, 3 December 2011, www.al-madina.com/print/342312, and Al-Luhaydan, "Abad al-tasalluh."
107 Tahir Hayyan, "Wazir al-difa al-bakistani: Al-Gharb yasa li-intiza silahna al-nawawi" [Pakistan's Minister of Defense: The West Wants to Take Our Nuclear Weapons from Us], *Al-Riyadh*, 8 August 2014, www.alriyadh.com/959069.

108 Mubarak Al Ati, "Al-Ittifaq al-nawawi bayn al-thawra wa'l-tharwa" [The Nuclear Agreement between Revolution and Wealth], *Sabq*, 15 July 2015, http://sabq.org/9L1aCd.
109 Mazin Al-Sudayri, "Li-madha al-rihan ala Bakistan?" [Why the Dependence on Pakistan?], *Al-Riyadh*, 22 April 2015, www.alriyadh.com/1041580.
110 "States that are less able to use conventional military power against a particular state, however, do not incur as many strategic costs when nuclear weapons spread to that particular state, and will be less likely to vigorously oppose nuclear proliferation to that state," Matthew Kroenig, "Exporting the Bomb: Why States Provide Sensitive Nuclear Assistance," *American Political Science Review*, ciii, 1, February 2009, 115.
111 Prince Bandar quoted in William Simpson, *The Prince: The Secret Story of the World's Most Intriguing Royal, Prince Bandar Bin Sultan* (New York: Regan, 2006), 156. This work is a semi-official biography based largely on interviews with Prince Bandar (hereafter Simpson, *The Prince*).
112 R. Jeffrey Smith, "Pakistani Scientist Khan Describes Iranian Efforts to Buy Nuclear Bombs," *Washington Post*, 14 March 2010, www.washingtonpost.com.
113 Prince Bandar quoted in Simpson, *The Prince*, 164.
114 Bayyina Al-Milhim, "Hal tai Amrika hajm Al-Mamlaka?" [Is America Aware of the Kingdom's Importance?], *Al-Riyadh*, 4 February 2014, www.alriyadh.com/2014/02/04/article906949.html.
115 "Mas'ul irani rafi yarudd ala masai Al-Saudiya li-shira' qunbula dharriyya" [A Senior Iranian Official Responds to Saudi Arabia's Attempts to Buy an Atom Bomb], Al-Alam TV (Tehran), 25 November 2013, www.alalam.ir/print/1537990?img=0.

Bibliography

Kroenig, Matthew, "Exporting the Bomb: Why States Provide Sensitive Nuclear Assistance," *American Political Science Review*, ciii, 1, February 2009, 113–133.
Simpson, William, *The Prince: The Secret Story of the World's Most Intriguing Royal, Prince Bandar Bin Sultan* (New York: Regan, 2006).
Van Dyke, Kimberly and Steve A. Yetiv, "Pakistan and Saudi Arabia: The Nuclear Nexus," *Journal of South Asian and Middle Eastern Studies*, xxxiv, 4, Summer 2011, 68–84.

7
THINKING ABOUT THE UTILITY OF NUCLEAR WEAPONS

Deterrence and beyond

Thinking about how to actually use nuclear weapons for defense and in foreign policy, of course, is key to any country considering the potential acquisition of such a capability. Saudi Arabia's policymakers have not suggested publicly how they might envision using a future nuclear arsenal, and if the Saudis have developed doctrinal thinking for their own forces in a nuclear environment, it is probably rudimentary. Such indications as are available have to be gleaned, instead, from discussions in the military and civilian media, although here, too, one cannot expect a clear translation of policy options into cohesive concepts and doctrine.

Conceptualizing nuclear deterrence

Saudi Arabia, although a propagator of its version of Islamic practice and a supporter of proxies in other countries as it seeks to enhance its influence and security in the region, is basically a status-quo state (although, arguably, its efforts to restore earlier statuses quo have at times been destabilizing) and would almost assuredly intend to use any nuclear arsenal in a deterrence capacity to enhance what it viewed as regional stability. Saudi commentators have stressed repeatedly this defensive aspect of nuclear doctrine as a form of reassurance for foreign and domestic publics.

A Saudi analyst encapsulated eloquently the prevailing Saudi view of the utility of nuclear weapons. As he saw it:

> the simplest option if you wish to protect yourself and fortify your nation and your people in case you are menaced by a neighbor who covets your country's riches and who has hostile intentions is for you to be able to ward him off by having defensive means at least equal to, if not better than, his, with capabilities that will deter him and make him think a thousand times before he attacks you.[1]

Another Saudi commentator stressed the unique utility of nuclear weapons within the context of deterrence, and noted that "possessing force is the most unambiguous means of preventing the use of the opponent's force; only iron counters iron."[2] Conceptually, it would seem that the military—insofar as one of the country's most prominent military thinkers is representative of such thought—accepts very much as a given a "realist" analytical framework, seeing the international system as anarchic and the use of power in order to achieve national interests rather than morality and justice as the acknowledged approach among states.

In the division between "pessimists" who, conceptually, see nuclear weapons as destabilizing, and "optimists," who see nuclear weapons as stabilizing through mutual deterrence, the Saudis tend to fall squarely in the latter camp, although, as noted already, the Saudis also have doubts about whether Iran is a rational actor relying on a calculus of balance of power, or whether that approach could be overridden by what they interpret as Iran's messianic religious tendencies. In this vein, a Saudi journalist, Hasan Ahmad Hasan Fitayhi, for example, challenged an essay by an American academic, Andrea Varisco, in which the latter had argued that the spread of nuclear weapons to small and medium powers would undermine stability in today's multipolar system. Fitayhi disagreed vehemently and held that, on the contrary, nuclear weapons would continue to serve as a stabilizing deterrent to prevent wars.[3]

The Saudis pay close attention to the history of nuclear deterrence and their understanding of other countries' experience provides insights into Saudi thinking on the role and advantages of nuclear deterrence as it might apply to their own country. What stands out in Saudi discussions within policy, military, and civilian circles is the consensus around the belief of the validity and effectiveness of nuclear deterrence. In drawing lessons learned from the past, the Saudis repeatedly have referred not only to the relationships between the United States and the Soviet Union during the Cold War, but also to Pakistan and India, and North Korea and the United States as proof that mutual nuclear deterrence is an effective mechanism to ensure security and stability.[4]

Typically, one Saudi journalist stated categorically that "nuclear weapons are the safety valve for world peace." As he saw it, mutual nuclear deterrence during the Cold War had resulted in "the nuclear paralysis ... [that] imposed peaceful coexistence between the western camp led by Washington and the eastern camp led by Moscow." And, in light of the perceived success of mutual deterrence, he expressed his absolute confidence that "the production of nuclear weapons today represents, in fact, a peaceful nuclear path."[5] As another Saudi observer saw it:

> The system of the balance of nuclear terror between the eastern and western camps was a success even with the presence of marginal nuclear powers such as Britain, France, and China in that system, since both camps had the strategic assurance that the eruption of a nuclear war between them was impossible thanks to the presence of a second-strike capability on both sides.[6]

In fact, Saudis believe that this "strategic stability" based on nuclear weapons continues to this day as the basis of the security relationship between the United States and Russia, and the difficulty in reducing the number of nuclear weapons "shows the extent to which states are [still] focused on that."[7]

Saudis also see as the key lesson from Pakistan's acquisition of nuclear weapons that the nuclear option had been the only possible response once India had developed its own nuclear program in 1974, for Pakistan had then realized that without its own nuclear deterrent India would initiate further military confrontations and that Pakistan "would perish."[8] Highlighting the success of nuclear deterrence, this same article concluded that, without a doubt, it had been Pakistan's own nuclear tests which had caused India to hesitate and back off from attacking Pakistan, and drew a parallel to Israel's nuclear threat to Saudi Arabia.[9] Although in the early stages there had been doubt in Saudi Arabia that mutual deterrence in the Pakistan–India dyad was stable and there was concern that tension between the two countries could escalate into a nuclear war, by the end of the last decade there was a growing conviction that in this case, too, nuclear deterrence had been successful and stabilizing, with nuclear weapons seen as enabling Pakistan to safeguard its independence.[10] In fact, a retired Saudi military officer writing in the media expressed his strong support for the efficacy of nuclear deterrence, calling it "a basic guarantee for stability" and successful in preventing total war, pointing specifically to the case of India and Pakistan to prove his point.[11]

Significantly, in relation to the utility of deterrence, in a 1998 opinion piece, the then-Assistant Defense Minister, Prince Khalid bin Sultan, had highlighted the U.S. strike against a suspected chemical weapons factory in Sudan, noting that Sudan had been obliged to absorb the affront to its dignity and sovereignty because "power talks."[12] That is, since Sudan could not retaliate, all it could do was to remonstrate verbally and seek sympathy, whereas had it had the means to retaliate or to threaten to do so "the language and conduct [of the United States] would have been different." He contrasted the case of Sudan with the impact of nuclear weapons in the Pakistan–India relationship, where:

> the voice of power was loud and [India] threw its weight around and threatened up until the time it heard another voice of power no weaker than its own on the opposing side [i.e. Pakistan], whereupon it moderated its language and requested a dialogue.

The cause imputed to this change in India's attitude was "the balance of power of conventional or nuclear weapons." In effect, according to Prince Khalid, in May 1998, India had conducted five nuclear tests, and had accompanied the latter with demonstrations of power and intimidation, including calls to Pakistan to negotiate, but not about the key Kashmir issue, and threatened instead to occupy the rest of the disputed province. As Prince Khalid saw it, "Power was talking, and what power—nuclear power!" However, before the end of the same month, India had been forced to moderate its tone and even became willing to discuss the future of

Kashmir, and all because Pakistan that month had exploded its first nuclear weapon. As he concluded, "a balance of nuclear terror will create peace" and "having power is vital, and a balance of power is inevitable."[13] Not surprisingly, when it came specifically to Iran, as one senior retired military officer saw it, a Saudi deterrent would likewise be needed in order to neutralize Iran's deterrent advantage, as such a capability would "constitute a counter-deterrent to an Iranian nuclear deterrent."[14]

Similarly, a Saudi military observer defined the pursuit of nuclear weapons as a quest for "the equality of deterrence so that a state can be secure from external threats, especially if it is confronted by a historic enemy," as he saw illustrated by Pakistan's deterrent against India or India's deterrent against China.[15] In general terms, Saudis also view Israel's possession of nuclear weapons as having been a factor enabling the latter to withstand international pressure to join the NPT.[16] As a senior military officer expressed it:

> Contemporary states began to realize clearly that their existence and their ability to protect their populations against any foreign aggression is tied intimately to [their] national security which, in turn, will not be achieved except by developing defensive weapons, uppermost of which are nuclear weapons, which support deterrence against foreign aggressors.[17]

In selling the concept of nuclear deterrence, a dean at the Nayif Arab University for Security Sciences (a senior academic institution run by Saudi Arabia's Ministry of the Interior) stressed the positive results of mutual nuclear deterrence in terms of facilitating peaceful coexistence, again citing the case of Pakistan and India and the United States and the Soviet Union. For him, in fact, this concept is "completely easy to understand," and he advised that "the GCC must strive to acquire a nuclear weapons deterrent ... at whatever sacrifice."[18] Otherwise, he concluded gloomily, "everyone will regret it when it will be too late." Faith in such deterrence has persisted, as Saudi academics still believe that "The biggest factor for a deterrent is one's own power, which an enemy must take into account one thousand times over, while weakness is one of the greatest incentives to aggression and interference in one's affairs," and that nuclear weapons were the basic reason why there has been no major war in the last 70 years.[19]

Here, too, Saudi Arabia's history with its SSMs may provide some glimpses into thinking on deterrence and warfighting, despite the recognized qualitative differences with nuclear weapons. Saudi Arabia used its SSMs in a deterrent mode at least three times: against any Israeli strike after the SSMs were publicized in 1988, that same year against Iran during the Iran–Iraq War, and against Iraq after the latter's invasion of Kuwait and during the subsequent Gulf War, 1990–91.[20] On the first occasion, after the presence of the SSMs was first discovered, Riyadh had become alarmed about a possible Israeli preventive strike. Although not mentioning the new missiles directly, Saudi Arabia's King Fahd condemned Israeli threats and declared that "Saudi Arabia will continue to carry through its legitimate defensive programs," warning that "we are prepared to defend our holy places."[21] The Saudi media repeated and amplified the King's message of deterrence. As one press editorial warned:

> When the Kingdom is intent on building up its independent power and might, it does so that this will be a force for peace and security that will deter others and prevent them from even thinking of attempting aggression. If they do do so, [Saudi Arabia] is able, God willing, to defend the entire country and to protect the holy places and to repay the aggressors' plots forcefully.[22]

A few days later, King Fahd, in an interview, once again alluded to the new SSMs, and threatened that Saudi Arabia:

> is not prepared to stand by idly to anyone who attacks it, [and will] use any available means. Thank God, we have weapons that I can say are if not superior to the weapons found in the rest of the region at least equal to them, whether aircraft or other weapons.[23]

As part of its deterrent effort, according to the then-Minister of Defense Prince Sultan, Saudi Arabia had also informed the United States that it would respond with all the means at its disposal to any Israeli attack and that it had placed its forces on full alert.[24]

Shortly thereafter, Riyadh severed relations with Iran, accusing the latter of subversion and, addressing specifically the ongoing Iran–Iraq War, King Fahd hinted publicly that the country's new SSMs "will be used in case of any threats against our country ... if we are forced to use our defensive power, watch out."[25] In the context of the recent escalation of the missile exchanges as part of the "War of the Cities" between the two belligerents and the venue of a Kuwaiti newspaper for the interview, the intended recipient of King Fahd's message was clearly Iran.

Again, during the Gulf War, Riyadh had recourse to its SSM capability as a deterrent, communicating by means of both clear and veiled messages directed at Saddam Husayn. For example, the Minister of Defense, Prince Sultan, warned in September 1990 that if Iraq resorted to chemical weapons:

> we are able, first of all, to thwart that before it happens, but that will make us use the fearful weapons we possess, including missiles that are able to reach the depths of Iraq. We possess the means to cause destruction, as Saddam Husayn well knows, and we all hope that we will not get to that point and I still appeal in the name of peace.[26]

The Saudi media coverage of that address, moreover, highlighted, in particular, the country's missile capability.

To be sure, Israel did not attack the SSMs and Iran did not launch its missiles against Saudi Arabia in 1988, and during the Gulf War Iraq did not use chemical weapons against Saudi Arabia—the presumed red line for Saudi retaliation. However, realistically, in all three cases, other extraneous factors (such as U.S. pressure and threats, other political considerations, or direct U.S. military protection) very likely were decisive in achieving the deterrent results rather than the Saudi SSMs themselves. Although one cannot determine the effect the Saudi SSMs had on either Israeli or Iraqi decision-making, Saudi leaders believed that their deterrence effort had been successful.[27] Those Saudis who have any reservations about the stability of deterrence are rare, and I could find only one who was concerned about the risk of miscalculation, a businessman who worried that Iran's acquisition of nuclear weapons, followed by others in the region, "raises the risk of unleashing a nuclear conflict as a realistic possibility."[28]

Moreover, there has been a Saudi consensus that deterrence clearly also contains a warfighting component. As one commentator on defense issues noted:

> the concept of strategic deterrence is an offensive military concept, meaning that if I am subjected to an attack by the other side then my response will not be to attempt to repel that attack but rather to mount an equivalent attack to the same or a greater degree of punishment against the other side.[29]

In fact, as a senior military officer took for granted, even the concepts of "preventive war" (*al-harb al-wiqa'iya*) and "pre-emptive strike" (*al-darba al-istibaqiya*)—that is to foil an imminent enemy attack—are traditional and accepted ways of waging war.[30] An unspoken but no doubt central intent of the widely-publicized anti-missile Patriot system live-fire exercise in 2009 was to stress a Saudi capability to protect its own SSM delivery force (with whatever payload) for a second strike. Although Prince Khalid denied at the time that Saudi Arabia's intent was to send a message to anyone in conjunction with that exercise, the head of the Control and Exercise Committee, Major General Salih Abd Al-Rahman Al-Suqayri, nevertheless underlined the success of the exercise in defending against incoming SSMs, clearly a reference to such threats from countries in the region.[31] Riyadh has also expressed an interest in buying the U.S.-made Terminal High-Altitude Area Defense (THAAD) anti-ballistic missile system and, after the 2015 rapprochement with Moscow, a Saudi pundit, for his part, suggested that another attraction of dealing with Russia was that the latter produces "an array of defensive rockets."[32]

Saudi Arabia in a hostile world and the political power of nuclear weapons

The reality of a state's overall power in international affairs as provided by nuclear weapons has long been a subject of Saudi interest and concern, and the Saudis have emphasized the accompanying political benefits once a state joined the nuclear club, in addition to that of defensive deterrence.

The mark of a great power

Some Saudis believe that it was the possession of nuclear weapons that enabled the Great Powers to "impose their hegemony over other states and to shape international policy according to their interests."[33] And, therefore, an aspect of the perceived utility of nuclear weapons from Saudi Arabia's perspective is that of the leverage they provide against military and political pressure even from the Great Powers. In fact, simply having nuclear weapons is seen to confer "importance and respect" to a country and to constitute a sufficient characteristic conferring Great Power status. India, for example, was said to have achieved respect and Great Power status specifically thanks to its nuclear weapons.[34] While many in Saudi Arabia view Chinese or Indian workers and products as inferior, one journalist sought to correct that impression, citing not only those two countries' economic and educational achievements but the key fact that they were nuclear powers.[35] Indeed, a Saudi journalist took his countrymen to task for still using the local expression "Do you take me for an Indian?" (idiomatic for "Do you take me for a simpleton?") as an insult, pointing out that, after all, India was a nuclear power.[36] As an academic and member of the Shura Council even saw it, "Were it not for its enormous nuclear arsenal, Russia would have become just a marginal country."[37]

According to a book published locally and promoted by the Saudi military—albeit probably penned by a non-Saudi—if "the Arabs" acquire nuclear weapons the international situation would change "dramatically," as "their importance will increase, and what they say will be listened to and their views respected, while no one will even consider oppressing them, including Israel."[38] Typically, in a message addressed to "our people in the Kingdom of Saudi Arabia," a Saudi blogger, whose message was published in a Saudi newspaper, hoped that his country would seek the help of Pakistani and Chinese experts "so that the Kingdom can become the eighth nuclear nation in the world."[39] For that blogger:

> the Kingdom, thanks to these [nuclear] weapons, will have the right to be a full member in the nuclear club and, as a consequence, will be worthy of becoming a member of the Security Council, since it will possess what the Great Powers possess, and it will be a state which must then be recognized as great and powerful.[40]

Dealing with the great powers

While by no means in the same category as the Israeli or Iranian threats, and although it is a subject not discussed frequently in public, some Saudis nevertheless feel concerns even about friendly outside powers. In a way, some Saudis simply sense such subliminal threats in an indistinct manner, sensitive to what they see as potential U.S. pressure in the future. For example, in addition to exercising defensive deterrence, the United States was also seen as using nuclear weapons in a more assertive manner, such as by coercing other countries into not opposing its policies.[41] An officer writing in a military journal, for his part, was uncomfortable in general terms, as he noted that "it is not in the interest of Arab national security that the United States continue to be alone in possessing the strongest nuclear and missile strike force so that it controls unilaterally the management of the international system," preferring instead a multipolar world.[42] And, as a Saudi proponent of nuclear weapons put it, "this call [for nuclear weapons] stems from a fear for the Arabness of the Gulf not only because of Iran and its minions but also because of Western control over the destiny of the Gulf states."[43]

More specifically, some Saudis still bring up such threats as that mooted in the United States in the wake of the 1973 October War to the effect that Washington might retaliate with a food embargo for any future Saudi oil embargo similar to the one Riyadh had implemented against most Western countries during that war.[44] However farfetched it may be, some Saudis—though very probably only a small minority, although at times that has included public figures such as the country's *mufti*—also worry that Israel and the United States might want to partition Saudi Arabia and other Arab countries and turn them into mini-states that are not a threat to Israel.[45] The mainstream Saudi press itself occasionally carries reports of conspiracies, such as one of an alleged U.S.–Israeli–Iranian plot "to weaken and bring down the Arab Umma as a whole and, in particular, the Gulf states."[46] Even a member of the royal family, the reformist Prince Talal, has himself on occasion raised this possibility as an Israeli policy goal, and he assumed that the United States would remain passive if that happened.[47] Syria and Shia quarters in Iraq have also actively fed such fears of a partition of Saudi Arabia.[48] Comments such as those by a U.S. presidential candidate in 2007 to the effect that Mecca and Medina should be held hostage to nuclear strikes against further terrorist attacks have also generated popular fear and resentment, as indicated by the Saudi media reaction at the time.[49] Such latent fears persist and are reawakened in the Saudi media from time to time by injudicious remarks or incidents in the West, one of the most recent being news of a course taught at a U.S. professional military educational institution, which reportedly had included options to "strike Mecca and Medina with nuclear weapons in order to obliterate them and to kill as many Muslims as possible."[50]

Moreover, some Saudi observers believe that the United Sates could use its nuclear weapons not only as a deterrent but also as a warfighting tool against Middle East countries in some circumstances. Particularly during the presidency of George W. Bush, Saudi observers viewed the United States as prepared to launch nuclear strikes against Iran or Syria if the latter attacked Israel with WMD.[51] And, some were convinced that the United States had also considered doing so against Libya and, later, against Syria.[52] In general, the United States was also seen as likely to consider using nuclear weapons rather than accepting a war of attrition.[53]

In that context of additional threats, nuclear weapons may be seen as an even more important guarantee of a nation's independence. An article in the Saudi press, for example, claimed that it was only thanks to its nuclear weapons that "Pakistan escaped from [America's] clutches by a miracle."[54] The same writer therefore concluded that "the possession of a nuclear deterrent by any state is a patriotic and national duty even more than being a strategic priority."[55] Another author was confident that the world would respect the Arabs if they had nuclear weapons and that it would then be possible to pressure Israel, as well Iran, into withdrawing from the disputed islands it occupies in the Gulf and from supporting the Asad regime in Syria, and to oblige the United States and the West to change their policies because "they only respect those who can rely on power when they negotiate."[56] Significantly, one of the country's few nuclear engineers, Tawfiq bin Ahmad Al-Qusayr, who has been arrested in the past for his reformist political activities, voiced his support for nuclear weapons as a deterrent against foreign intervention, claiming that the world was run according to "the law of the jungle" and, citing the lessons of the U.S. invasion of Afghanistan and Iraq, he asserted that if Iraq had had nuclear weapons a U.S. invasion would not have occurred.[57] Saudi military thinkers appear to adhere to such views of the international system as well, with one senior officer concluding that "the ability to use power to achieve national interests … and not righteousness or justice, is what distinguishes the character of the present-day state of affairs most of the time."[58]

The events in Libya related to the Arab Spring may have provided especially worrisome lessons learned relevant to proliferation, as it was widely believed in the Middle East that had Muammar Qaddafi retained his nuclear program the United States and other NATO countries would have been reluctant to become involved on behalf of the opposition that toppled his regime in 2011. Significantly, the prominent Saudi cleric Muhsin Al-Awaji was critical of NATO's military intervention against Libya, but also of Qaddafi for having surrendered his nuclear program:

> the hypocritical West has received its payment from this tyrant, since he … handed over to the West the Libyan nuclear sites and abjectly surrendered to [the West] tens of billions [of dollars], which he had taken from the mouths of the helpless Libyan people.[59]

In a more direct instance of advocacy for a nuclear deterrent based on lessons learned from Libya's experience, a Saudi columnist held that the Libyan case raised an urgent question, namely "May the Arab states possess a nuclear weapon?" Significantly, he raised doubts about whether NATO would have dared attack Libya if the latter had possessed nuclear weapons, asking "would the Europeans consider admonishing Qaddafi if he insinuated he would launch a nuclear missile against France?" Likewise, that commentator wondered whether Syria would have come under such intense international pressure had it had a nuclear capability. Maintaining that the Arab states have the same right to self-defense as any other state, the same author then concluded that:

> it is becoming increasingly necessary for a joint Arab nuclear strategy to acquire nuclear weapons, whatever the legality of the path taken to achieve

that, in order to provide for deterrence and self-defense and to confront the Israeli and the Iranian [nuclear] programs.

He called for cooperation with such countries as Pakistan to achieve what he saw as "this great dream." In the meantime, he suggested reliance on diplomatic support from other Great Powers to make possible "confronting America and Israel." However, as he remarked, "once the Arabs possess nuclear weapons they will have a different degree of influence in the international balance."[60]

Drawing lessons from North Korea

Focusing on the centrality of power politics, Saudis often have sought lessons learned for dealing with the Great Powers from the success of other small nuclear powers.

North Korea: a success story in deterrence?

For example, Saudi observers believe that North Korea provides an instructive case study since, by acquiring a nuclear deterrent, Pyongyang increased its leverage, and the latter's acquisition of nuclear weapons has been characterized in the Saudi press as having "provided [North Korea] with a powerful nuclear shield both on a regional level and beyond."[61] The Saudi media drew a stark contrast between the United States' willingness to invade Iraq in 2003 but not North Korea even though—or because—the latter had a proven WMD arsenal. For a Saudi military journal, by claiming to have nuclear weapons:

> the [North] Korean government responded in a practical way to American pressures which sought to force it to relinquish its nuclear program, at a time when it feared it would become Washington's next target after the latter finished with the Iraqi case. It thus wants to inform Washington that it is not an easy target like Iraq.[62]

As a writer in the civilian media likewise argued in 2003, "the reason [for not invading] is obvious, namely that [North] Korea has the atom bomb while Iraq only has media noise about its imaginary power." And, the article added, "The United States knows the danger of 'provoking' a nuclear country such as North Korea, and so has contented itself with verbal protests void of any meaning."[63] The author concluded that:

> the balance of terror may be one of the lessons of the war now in progress in Iraq ... What America has done may awaken dreamers and make them open their eyes to the bitter truth in our ugly world and motivate them to arm.[64]

Another observer concluded that once North Korea had acquired nuclear weapons, the United States could no longer solve the Korean issue by force and was obliged, instead, "to use the carrot with North Korea instead of the stick."[65] Based on the North Korean experience, an article in a Saudi military journal also deduced that "it appears that one of the basic principles—albeit one that has never been spoken of openly because it is not possible to do so—on which U.S. strategy is based, is that of not deciding lightly an initiative for any military action against any country which has one of the WMD (nuclear, chemical, or biological). That is what explains the fact that the United States has not attacked North Korea, which may have a respectable missile force and nuclear weapons."[66]

Following North Korea's reported nuclear test in 2006, linking the event to Iran's own quest for nuclear weapons, one Saudi observer concluded that by becoming a nuclear power North Korea had thereby "altered the balance of power and how it was to be dealt with."[67] Indeed, a Saudi columnist assessed that North Korea had successfully challenged the world and "was not frightened of the stick," and that by now "removing nuclear weapons from a country like North Korea is not feasible in practical terms, since considerations of the cost and risks would make taking such a step a major gamble whose cost most of mankind would have to pay."[68] A Saudi academic also expressed his support for nuclear weapons as a deterrent against hegemony and noted that thanks to its nuclear weapons North Korea had succeeded in thwarting U.S. plans for such hegemony, since it was henceforth impossible to threaten North Korea or to force it to be submissive. Noting that this success served as "encouragement for other new members to enter this [nuclear] club," he asked, "Will the Arabs learn that lesson?"[69] The Saudis, moreover, assumed that Iran had also internalized North Korea's message, as well as the presumed lesson of Libya's experience of having relinquished a nuclear program and thereby having made itself vulnerable to Western intervention, and that that factor shaped Iran's position of being unwilling to forego the development of nuclear weapons.[70]

North Korea has continued to propagate such ideas in the Gulf, as was the case with that country's ambassador to Kuwait, who told the Kuwaiti press that:

> we were obliged to develop nuclear weapons, since American nuclear weapons are deployed in South Korea at present ... we will not relinquish our nuclear weapons intended for the defense of our country ... we desire a dialogue with [the United States] but aggression occurs by the strong against the weak, the best examples of which are what happened to Afghanistan and Iraq.[71]

North Korean diplomats also stressed that possessing nuclear weapons had been the only deterrent that had prevented their country from suffering the same fate as Libya or Iraq, while claiming that their country could not rely even on China or Russia to defend it against the United States' nuclear weapons, thus necessitating an independent nuclear deterrent.[72]

The 2013 crisis with North Korea

Saudi Arabia, as one could expect, paid close attention to the protracted crisis that began in 2013 between the United States and North Korea, a crisis in which the latter's nuclear arsenal was a central component. As was true of the rest of the international community, Saudi Arabia at the time could not predict the outcome of the confrontation, which has continued in an uneasy, ongoing and unresolved stand-off. Although no official statements emanated from Riyadh, the Saudi media offered some potential lessons learned. First, there was concern that the United States' preoccupation with East Asian affairs stemming from the crisis with North Korea, which was so important because of its nuclear aspect, could mean that Washington would pay less attention to problems in the Middle East.[73] Another Saudi viewed North Korea's nuclear bluster in the evolving confrontation as confirmation that rights could only be seized by power, and that weakness would mean a loss of rights.[74]

Participants in the Saudi Hawamir Al-Bursa blog discussing the implications of the North Korean crisis noted that the United States had not attacked North Korea (or other nuclear powers). But, according to the bloggers, this situation also showed that the Arab world was vulnerable because it lacked nuclear weapons, as "our Arab countries have become the exemplary image of the model victim for an executioner." An accompanying undertone suggested a challenge to decision-makers, as one blogger noted sarcastically that "it is impossible that our rulers are considering developing nuclear weapons in the Gulf, because Auntie America would get mad at them."[75] Other Saudis believed that North Korea was merely saber-rattling, since it could not really match the United States in power, but still others worried that the high-risk brinkmanship might spill over into a nuclear war.[76] In particular, Saudis may have wondered what the North Korean crisis might mean for Iran's behavior. Writing in a Saudi-owned newspaper, the former head of Iraq's military intelligence warned that the effect of North Korea's readiness to engage in nuclear threats would encourage Iran to also adopt a defiant posture if it became a nuclear power.[77] A Saudi columnist, for his part, discussing Iran's nuclear ambitions, likewise equated Iran's outlook to that of North Korea, taxing both countries as "unpredictable."[78]

Significantly, Saudi opinion was often not critical of North Korea for the 2013 crisis, or at least not exclusively so. Some media articles seemed to place equal blame on the United States, or even predominantly on the latter, as they suggested that Washington had long threatened North Korea, that the United States was using the crisis as a means to pressure South Korea into buying expensive U.S. military equipment, or that it was using the crisis as a way to cement its military presence in Southeast Asia, and also raised the possibility that the U.S.-led economic embargo on North Korea perhaps in itself represented "a blatant attack."[79]

Although the potential cost of nuclear weapons has never been raised, at least insofar as Saudi Arabia would be concerned, a theme that occurred repeatedly at the time of the North Korean crisis was that of the enormous economic burden that the North Korean population has had to carry in order to pay for the country's nuclear status. Some observers, in fact, noted that the North Korean case showed that possessing nuclear technology did not automatically translate into prosperity, social progress, or achieving Great Power status.[80] It is unclear whether such writers assumed that Saudi readers might apply such criticism subtly to their own situation and national policy or whether an unintentional double standard was at play. However, other analysts expressed a grudging admiration of a nuclear North Korea, suggesting that the latter had dealt with the crisis as a Great Power would, and were sympathetic that Pyongyang was willing to sacrifice in order to "maintain its national sovereignty and independence."[81]

How to implement deterrence

There have been no official indications as to how Saudi Arabia would implement nuclear deterrence in concrete terms if it acquired nuclear weapons, but past practice and current discussions may provide some insights.

Establishing credibility

Some Saudis seem to adhere to a "fleet-in-being" view of deterrence. That is, by simply possessing nuclear weapons one gains automatic deterrence, as well as the ability to translate that deterrence into political clout, as suggested by Riyadh's view of its SSMs, with the Strategic Rocket Force's (SRF) current commander, Staff Major General Jar Allah Al-Alwit, assessing that just the SRF's "birth created fear and by its very existence it achieved deterrence."[82] For one Saudi academic, who argued in favor of acquiring nuclear weapons, in fact, military power is primarily a political weapon, and "simply having military power supports a state's position and political independence, while the politician who negotiates having only a sword will of course be weaker than his counterpart if the latter has a rifle."[83] A Saudi journalist also claimed that just knowing a country had or was seeking nuclear weapons could serve as a deterrent.[84]

However, many Saudi military thinkers, in particular, have shown that they are fully aware that an effective deterrent also requires credibility that the capability would be used and that thinking about deterrence and warfighting must exist in tandem. As a study in a Saudi military journal stressed, "the decisive factor today, as it has been throughout history, is the ability to use a weapon." It is this factor which "must constitute a deterrent to the leadership in Tehran in order to prevent that leadership from embarking on a military venture whose outcome is uncertain or to prevent it from igniting an armed conflict whose cost exceeds the value of that war."[85]

During the Gulf War, Saudi decisionmakers apparently had been prepared to launch their SSMs against Iraq. As Prince Khalid bin Sultan, at the time Commander of the Combined Forces and later to be Deputy Defense Minister, subsequently confided, "we had ... prepared an appropriate response that would have taught [Saddam Husayn] a lesson" had the latter decided to launch SSMs with chemical or biological warheads—as Prince Khalid said the Saudis fully expected.[86] True, as he added, Saudi Arabia would have launched only as a last resort—"only if all other available weapons had been used … and if this had been absolutely vital and unavoidable."[87] However, according to Prince Khalid:

> the Saudi SSMs were ready and aimed at several military targets … I remember that on one occasion the order was given for operational readiness to launch a concentrated volley against one of the targets. All that was needed was the actual order to fire.[88]

Prince Khalid, in fact, had viewed the SSMs as an effective weapon for a counterattack, what he termed the ability to "demoralize the enemy by delivering a painful and decisive blow."[89]

A retired general officer provided at least a fleeting glimpse into updated Saudi thinking about nuclear doctrine in a 2014 article. What makes his views even more interesting is the fact that he was also an adviser to the Defense Committee in the Cabinet and a former adviser to the Director of Saudi Intelligence, and is also reported to be one of King Salman's close advisers, which would at least indicate what ideas may have been circulating in policy circles.[90] He addressed Saudi Arabia's SSMs, noting that they had two functions—deterrence and offensive/warfighting functions—concluding that they could be used not only as a deterrent but also "in an offensive mode against anyone who attempts to bully the Kingdom." He spoke of the combination of SSMs and nuclear warheads as a unit, and suggested that their primary logical target would be "to completely destroy and erase the enemy's cities"—"city-busting"—but also enemy fleets, military concentrations, bases, and airfields. Assuring readers that the Kingdom did not intend to attack anyone but would only use its SSMs to defend itself and the other Gulf countries, as part of his deterrent message he also added pointedly that the SSMs cannot be countered or recalled and that they had a 99 percent success rate in striking their targets, especially as these are "the fastest and most modern [SSMs] in the world." In fact, some Saudis even saw a broad permissibility for a first-strike use. For example, one commentator suggested the need to amend the NPT so that a country would have the right to use nuclear weapons not only if another country had first used such arms against it, but also in case a country was threatened with such an attack or even if there were "strong indications" that a country's interests were to be threatened by a nuclear attack, adding "as is the case with Iran."[91]

Would Saudi Arabia declare its nuclear capability? In order for a nuclear deterrent to be effective, others must either know of or assume its existence. An undeclared capability, but one surrounded by sufficient hints signaling its existence in no uncertain terms, might prove attractive. That option would enable Saudi Arabia to use its nuclear capability for the intended deterrent role while managing or delaying, if not totally avoiding, potential discord with the international community. Perhaps, here again, Saudi Arabia's experience with its SSMs may be instructive.

Apparently, Saudi Arabia was relying on the discovery of the missiles as the preferred method of making their existence known for, according to Prince Khalid, "if it [i.e. the weapon system] was not detected by June 1989, we should consider leaking the news ourselves."[92] Prince Bandar, likewise, revealed that the original intent had been to make the CSS-2s public eventually, once the system was operational, for "that was the real value of the weapon; if no one knew about it, it could scarcely be a deterrent."[93] And, as part of a deterrent strategy, Riyadh would have to decide whether to communicate what the "red lines" might be that could trigger nuclear use or whether to rely on a significant degree of uncertainty. In fact, a Saudi journalist recently praised his country's restrained response to various media reports that Riyadh was seeking nuclear weapons as a "shrewd move … to leave interested parties wondering and questioning."[94] Moreover, one can speculate that Saudi Arabia perhaps might not limit itself to a passive sort of deterrence if and when it acquired a nuclear capability. Rather, given the prevailing view of a nuclear-armed country's relative immunity from retaliation, Riyadh might feel more confident and be tempted to play an even more assertive hand in the confrontational situations which have already developed in its shadow war against Iran in such areas as Iraq, Yemen, Lebanon, and Syria, potentially opening the door to unintended escalation.

Avoiding escalation dominance

Saudi Arabia will still face a threat from Iran whether or not the latter acquires a nuclear capability and, in any event, Saudi Arabia is not likely to rely solely on a potential future nuclear deterrent for its national security. In fact, Riyadh was said to have spent $80 billion in 2014 for conventional military equipment intended to deter Iran.[95]

As a Saudi analyst saw it, if a nuclear-armed Iran attacked the Gulf states even with just conventional weapons, no country would be able to call on foreign support because Iran's nuclear capability would serve as a deterrent to such aid.[96] In such a scenario, it would make sense to have a robust conventional capability at every level to forestall placing Saudi Arabia in an unenviable position of risking escalation dominance. Otherwise, in case of a military conflict with Iran in the future, the Saudis—should they decide to acquire nuclear weapons—might have no choice but to use nuclear weapons as the only remaining military option if they could not match Iran at lower levels of conventional force. In fact, one of the lessons a Saudi scholar highlighted from the U.S. experience was that of "developing conventional military capabilities in order to be able to engage in a limited war without having recourse to using WMD."[97] Saudi Arabia has frequently showcased its conventional defensive capabilities—and especially its air and air/missile defense systems—verbally and in field exercises, with the then-Deputy Minister of Defense Prince Khalid noting after one such high-visibility air defense exercise, that the exercise had been "a message to states which use surface-to-surface missiles to send messages [i.e. Iran] that the Kingdom has the deterrence capability against such missiles." And, he reassured his audience that "we will be fully prepared for years to come, not just for now."[98] More recently, having concluded that confrontation with Iran—based on history, culture, and national interests—is "inevitable," a retired military officer likewise argued that "the only thing that will protect [our] rights is the power that one controls and that confers deterrence in all its aspects—conventional, unconventional, and nuclear."[99]

Developing the country's supporting infrastructure

To make any future option on nuclear weapons feasible and credible, Saudi Arabia has also been developing other military capabilities that would support a nuclear program.

The Strategic Rocket Force

Saudi Arabia's Strategic Rocket Force (SRF) and the surface-to-surface missiles (SSMs) with which it is armed has long been a key element in the country's defense thinking.[100] In terms of the SRF, what is important here is the relationship of the SSMs to the broader nuclear issue. Most Saudis seem to recognize that in order for nuclear deterrence to be effective there is also a need to have a demonstrable or assumed capability to deliver the weapons. For example, one academic noted perceptively that "The possession of nuclear weapons is meaningless from a strategic point of view as long as there is not a parallel development in the system for delivering these nuclear weapons to the selected targets."[101] In all probability, the most realistic method of delivery of any nuclear weapons by Saudi Arabia would be by SSMs. Aircraft are slower, have a limited range, are too vulnerable to countermeasures and error, and pilots are too valuable, while SSMs are a more reliable vehicle for such a mission. Significantly, a retired senior military officer indicated openly the symbiotic linkage between nuclear weapons and SSMs as the preferred delivery vehicle for the latter.[102]

Saudis view nuclear weapons, SSMs, and space-based capabilities as interrelated elements of a cohesive deterrence package, as was the case with one senior military officer who spoke of "strategic power in its three dimensions: missiles, space, and nuclear."[103] In fact, Saudi media reports routinely link Iran's missile developments to the latter's projected nuclear weapons acquisition, and Saudi pundits often pair Iran's SSM and nuclear programs as a dyad.[104] As one Saudi journalist put it:

> Perhaps it is not far from most people's minds that the missiles that Iran is developing with a capability to reach long distances in space carrying a monkey or other [payloads] are in themselves messages that [Iran] has the capability to deliver its nuclear weapons at long ranges.[105]

In that vein, many Saudi observers were concerned that although Iran became willing to negotiate on its nuclear program it continued to refuse to do so as far as its SSMs were concerned, and Saudi critics often raised the issue that Iran's missile development was exempt from restrictions as an indication of Tehran's continuing nuclear intentions. As one editorial warned, Iran's refusal to include its SSMs in negotiations "will be unacceptable to either the Kingdom or to the other Gulf Arab states … and then all options will be open to the Kingdom and the other Arabs."[106] In fact, the lesson learned from that Iranian stance, according to one Saudi diplomat, was that "missile capabilities are a vital requirement for any leading country in our region that wants to protect its national security."[107]

When Saudi Arabia's first SSMs—the CSS-2 (DF-3) purchased from China—entered the country's arsenal in 1988, Riyadh had refused to allow their inspection to ensure that they were not WMD-capable. For example, according to one of Prince Sultan's sons, Faysal, when U.S. officials pressured his father—then in the United States for knee surgery—to give access to the SSMs, Prince Sultan had refused, unless Israel also agreed to allow its arsenals to be inspected, which the Saudis knew was not likely.[108] However, at the time, senior Saudi government officials had repeatedly offered assurances that the SSMs did not and would not be WMD-capable. King Fahd himself, for example, informed a Saudi audience that "we reassured anyone who asked us that the [SSMs] really do not carry nuclear or chemical warheads; rather, they are only defensive missiles and nothing else."[109] Likewise, an unnamed Saudi "official source" briefed the local media that foreign media claims that the CSS-2s were nuclear-capable had "no basis in fact and the Kingdom denies that categorically."[110]

Significantly, there are strong indications that Riyadh has recently upgraded its SSM force. In 2010, based on his work in the U.S. intelligence community, former analyst Jonathan Scherck claimed that perhaps as early as 2003 Saudi Arabia had begun acquiring the CSS-5 from China.[111] While having a shorter range than the original liquid-fuel CSS-2 that Riyadh had bought from China, the CSS-5 is more accurate and is propelled by solid fuel, making a launch quicker and less complicated. Likewise, nonproliferation expert Jeffrey Lewis, in an insightful commentary in the wake of a tantalizing photo appearing in the Saudi media in May 2013 showing models of three different SSMs, also speculated that the Saudi missile inventory included the CSS-5.[112] The message that Saudi Arabia may have wanted to send was that now potentially it had two other SSMs in addition to the CSS-2, or at least two versions of an additional SSM type. The third unidentified SSM could be the nuclear-capable solid-fuel-propelled Shaheen II made in Pakistan, a country with which Riyadh has had a long-standing military relationship. And, in early 2014, *Newsweek* reporting, based on an unnamed "well-placed intelligence source," confirmed that Saudi Arabia had indeed bought the CSS-5 from China in 2007. Ostensibly, the deal had occurred with U.S. approval, with American inspectors satisfied that the new missiles "were not designed to carry nukes."[113]

There had already been hints in the Saudi media for a number of years that the country's inventory of SSMs might have been upgraded. For example, although citing the book by Scherck as a source, in 2011 a Saudi aerospace engineer and head of the Saudi Air and Space Sciences Organization, who writes frequently on defense issues, took for granted that the CSS-5 was in the national inventory, although denying that his country had nuclear warheads for the SSMs.[114] The latter pundit, moreover, insisted that acquiring new SSMs was "a right for the Kingdom for self-defense, whether the American administration ... approves or disapproves."[115] Some participants in Saudi discussion fora assumed that it was common knowledge at least by 2012 that the country now had at least the CSS-5.[116] And, in 2014, a well-placed retired general officer discussed the CSS-5 (DF-21) nuclear-capable Chinese-made missile, hinting that this was already in the country's arsenal ("when the Kingdom acquired them"), as foreign analysts had suspected for some time.[117]

Moreover, after the April 2014 Sword of Abd Allah military exercise, when two CSS-2 missiles were displayed, the Saudi edition of the *Al-Hayat* Arabic-language daily also suggested that the CSS-2 shown was not the only SSM in the national arsenal, as it spoke of the Saudis having "the East Wind missiles and other strategic missiles."[118] Shortly thereafter, a columnist warned that, with the new challenges facing the Kingdom, the CSS-2 "is only the beginning of what Saudi policy may encompass in the upcoming period."[119] Probably as a way to underline the point to domestic audiences that their country could indeed go nuclear, the local electronic media, which is mostly read by Saudis and not by international audiences, stressed—despite all the repeated earlier denials—that the CSS-2 SSMs displayed at that exercise were "capable of carrying nuclear warheads."[120] The Saudi government was probably pleased that such publicity was further spread by foreign sources, thereby enhancing its deterrent.

Looking toward the future, in June 2015 Saudi Arabia's Foreign Minister Adil Al-Jubeir expressed his country's interest in also purchasing the Iskander SSM, to which Moscow agreed, although indications were that limited production runs and preexisting commitments to first equip Russia's armed forces with this system would rule out a near-term delivery date.[121] Although mobile and capable of carrying nuclear warheads, given the limited (280km/174miles) range of the Iskander-E export version of this system, which puts it beyond the range of most Iranian targets, it makes little military sense for Saudi Arabia and, rather, the intention may be to make a political statement in response to the missile capabilities that Iran has developed. Alternatively, it may be used as a conventional weapon against large Yemeni targets or, even if not very likely, Riyadh might be thinking of an acquisition of tactical nuclear warheads in the long term.

The SRF's supporting infrastructure has also been expanded and improved in recent years, and included the opening of a new headquarters in Riyadh in 2010 and of a new training center and school in 2011, both of which received wide media publicity. The SRF's personnel now number "in the thousands," according to the commander of the SRF.[122] There have long been calls in Saudi Arabia to acquire an autonomous domestic SSM development capability, although that would be beyond the country's capacities for the foreseeable future. However, there have also been proposals for a more realistic objective of being able to, as one

Saudi diplomat termed it, "exploit and extend" missile technology, that is, to modify existing technology which, with foreign help, is more feasible.[123]

The nascent space sector

Similarly, the Saudi military and civilian media have expressed considerable support for the country's emerging space sector, citing as benefits of space-based systems their contribution to early warning, command and control, communications, and reconnaissance and, in particular, to improved targeting.[124] Some Saudis view space capabilities as key for deterrence, even if for now in conjunction only with SSMs.[125] The Saudi military has become especially concerned about the capabilities and implications of Israel's space-based systems, which provide the latter with the ability to obtain early warning and to avoid a surprise first-strike, quite apart from the ability to spy on, and target, the Arabs.[126] One military study even urged "the Arabs" to manufacture their own satellites, citing as a side benefit the spin-off of other science-based industries, including that for the production of heavy water (which can be a key component in reactors used to produce isotopes for dual nuclear purposes).[127]

Cooperation in the space sector has expanded significantly over the past few years with Russia and other former Soviet states, and has included collaboration in research and the launching of numerous Saudi-owned space satellites. There is already a Space Research Institute as part of the King Abdulaziz City for Science and Technology and there are also plans for a new Saudi space center.

Integrating a nuclear capability into the force structure

There is no hard information about how Saudi Arabia would integrate a nuclear capability into its force structure if and when it does acquire such a capability and, at this stage, all one can do is speculate. Unquestionably, command and control would remain strictly in Saudi hands and, moreover, within the ruling family, whatever formal organizational relationships and ranks are involved. Nuclear weapons, in fact, are especially attractive in a political system such as that of Saudi Arabia, as it is a small, non-labor-intensive, highly-technical weapons system that does not over-empower a country's military on the domestic scene in the same way as a system requiring a large manpower pool might, or represent hardware that could also be used in a coup attempt or civil conflict.

Here too, Saudi Arabia's history with its SSMs may be instructive about such questions. During the Gulf War, according to Prince Khalid bin Sultan, it was King Fahd (as the King is also Commander-in-Chief of the Armed Forces) who had command and control of the SSMs, holding the ultimate say about launching and canceling launches.[128] To be sure, technical support and very probably the actual operational handling of the SSMs was in the hands of Chinese advisers, a situation that may well have continued for many years thereafter, as suggested by the fact that as late as 2006 the King awarded one of the country's highest decorations to the Chinese head of the Joint Military Committee in recognition for "strengthening friendship and cooperation." Since the ceremony was hosted by Saudi Arabia's Strategic Rocket Force, the event was clearly in connection with China's support of the CSS-2 program.[129] Similarly, command and control over a nuclear device would certainly be in Saudi hands even if foreign advisers were required to maintain and operate the actual equipment. Nuclear devices may require foreign technical support for some time to come as, in the event, the Saudis have continued to depend on foreign technical support even for key conventional sectors of their military for many years already.

It is also not clear whether nuclear weapons would be integrated with the SSMs (where it would make operational sense for them to be collocated), with the Saudi Air Force, or become a separate service, as was the case with the country's SSMs, which became the nucleus for a separate service, the Strategic Rocket Force.

Notes

1 Jasir Abd Al-Aziz Al-Jasir, "Naam li-silah nawawi khaliji" [Yes to a Gulf Nuclear Weapon], *Al-Jazira*, 7 December 2011, www.al-jazirah.com.sa/20111207/du8.htm.
2 Id bin Masud Al-Juhani, "Hal yufiq al-arab ala hadir al-quwwa al-isra'iliya?" [Will the Arabs Awake Thanks to the Noise of Israeli Power?], *Al-Hayat*, 12 April 2008, http://international.daralhayat.com/print/200023/ archive.
3 Hasan Ahmad Hasan Fitayhi, "Al-Asliha al-nawawiya" [Nuclear Weapons], *Al-Madina*, 5 November 2014, www.al-madina.com.
4 For example, the Deputy Minister of Culture Salih Al-Namla, "Pakistan wa-tajrubat al-rad al-nawawi" [Pakistan and the Experience of Nuclear Deterrence], *Al-Riyadh*, 12 June 2002, 32.
5 Rida Muhammad Lari, "Urid an aqul: Isra'il tastakhdim al-silah al-nawawi" [I Want to Say: Israel Is Using Nuclear Weapons], *Al-Riyadh*, 2 November 2006, www.alriyadh.com/2006/11/02/article198567.html.
6 Talal Salih Bannan, "Adw jadid fi al-nadi al-nawawi …ya ilahi!" [A New Member in the Nuclear Club, Oh My God!], *Ukaz*, 15 October 2006, www.okaz.com.sa/okaz/osf/20061015/PrintCon2006101555252.htm (hereafter Bannan, "Adw jadid").
7 Abd Al-Jalil Al-Marhun, "Man yarfud taqlis al-asliha al-hujumiya?" [Who Is Refusing to Reduce Offensive Weapons?], *Al-Riyadh*, 15 January 2010, www.al-riyadh.com/2010/01/15/article489828.html.
8 Fahd Amir Al-Ahmadi, "Al-Radi al-bakistani" [The Pakistani Deterrent], *Al-Riyadh*, 12 January 2002, www.alriyadh.com/2002/01/ 12/article29757.html.
9 Ibid.
10 For earlier skeptical views, see Muhammad Shuman and Uthman Anwar, "Dirasa jadida an al-sibaq al-nawawi bayn Al-Hind wa-Bakistan al-tadaiyat wa-mawqi Al-Sharq Al-Awsat" [A New Study on the Nuclear Race between India and Pakistan and the Consequences for and the Situation of the Middle East], *Al-Jazira*, 3 June 1999, www.al-jazirah.com.sa/1999jaz/jun3/wt1.htm. Also, Abd Al-Jalil Zayd Al-Marhun, "Al-Alam al-thalith wa-mudilat al-intishar al-nawawi" [The Third World and the Problem of Nuclear Proliferation], *Al-Riyadh*, 15 June 2001, www.alriyadh.com/2001/06/15/ article32562.html.
11 Colonel Ibrahim bin Sad Al Al-Mari (Ret.), "Al-Rad al-nawawi" [Nuclear Deterrence], *Al-Riyadh*, 5 January 2015, www.alriyadh.com/1010214. Also, Abd Al-Jalil

Zayd Al-Marhun, "Nahw salam muqim bayn Al-Hind wa-Bakistan" [Toward a Permanent Peace between India and Pakistan], *Al-Riyadh*, 5 June 2015, www.alriyadh.com/1054143, and for a representative view, also see Said Al-Farha Al-Ghamidi, "Khuturat al-silah al-nawawi" [The Danger of Nuclear Weapons], *Al-Madina*, 6 July 2009, http://archive.al-madina.com/node/156695.

12 Prince Khalid bin Sultan bin Abd Al-Aziz, "Al-Quwwa tatahaddath" [Power Talks], *Al-Ahram*, 2 November 1998, www.ahram.org.eg/Archive/1998/11/2/opin3.htm.

13 Ibid.

14 Major General Husam Suwaylam (Ret.), "Ahdaf Iran al-siyasiya wa'l-istratijiya wa-asalib tahqiqha," [Iran's Political and Strategic Objectives and the Methods to Achieve Them], *Al-Haras Al-Watani*, part 1, August 2011, 37.

15 Staff Brigadier Zayd bin Muhammad Al-Amri, "Dawafi imtilak al-qudrat al-istratijiya al-sarukhiya al-fada'iya wa'l-nawawiya" [The Incentives for Acquiring Strategic Rocket, Space, and Nuclear Capabilities], *Al-Difa Al-Jawwi*, December 2010, 14 (hereafter Al-Amri, "Dawafi imtilak").

16 Ma'mun Kayawan, "Kharitat aslihat al-damar al-shamil fi Al-Sharq Al-Awsat" [The Map of WMD in the Middle East], *Majallat Kulliyat Al-Malik Khalid Al-Askariya*, 1 October 2009, www.kkmaq.gov.sa/detail.asp?InNewsItemID=334526&InTemplateKey=print.

17 Al-Amri, "Dawafi imtilak," 15.

18 Ali bin Fayiz Al-Juhani, "Majlis al-taawun al-khaliji wa-khiyar imtilak silah al-rad" [The GCC and the Nuclear Weapon Deterrent Option], *Al-Riyadh*, 11 April 2012, www.alriyadh.com/2012/04/11/article726193.html.

19 Hamad Abd Allah Al-Luhaydan, "Ma bayn ghazw Kuba wa-ghazw Ukraniya" [The Difference between the Invasion of Cuba and That of Ukraine], *Al-Riyadh*, 7 March 2014, www.alriyadh.com/915945, and Talal Salih Bannan, "Silah al-salam al-fattak" [The Lethal Weapon of Peace], *Ukaz*, 8 September 2015, http://okaz.co/bwIkOdu1H.

20 See Norman Cigar, *Saudi Arabia's Strategic Rocket Force: The Silent Service* (Quantico, VA: Middle East Studies, 2014) (hereafter Cigar, *Saudi Arabia's Strategic Rocket Force*).

21 Quoted in "Mustaiddun li-muwajahat ayy tari' lan nasmah bi-ayy tadakhkhul fi shu'unna" [We Are Prepared to Confront Any Contingency and We Will Not Permit Any Interference in Our Affairs], *Ukaz*, 29 March 1988, 3.

22 Editorial, "Bi-Kull al-quwwa difaan an al-watan wa'l-muqaddasat" [With All Our Power in Defense of the Nation and the Holy Places], *Ukaz*, 29 March 1988, 5.

23 Interview with King Fahd, "Khadim al-haramayn yaltaqi bi-mansubi wa-talabat far jamiat Al-Imam Saud al-islamiya bi'l-Qasim" [The Servant of the Two Holy Shrines Meets with the Staff and Students of the Branch of the Imam Saud Islamic University in Al-Qasim], *Ukaz*, 9 April 1988, 7 (hereafter King Fahd, "Khadim al-haramayn").

24 Interview with Prince Sultan, "Al-Amir Sultan: Ishtarayna al-sawarikh min Al-Sin li-annaha dawla muhayida bayn al-imlaqayn" [Prince Sultan: We Bought the Missiles from China Because It Is a Neutral Country between the Two Giants], *Al-Sayyad* (Beirut), 29 April 1988, 33.

25 Interview with King Fahd by Ahmad Al-Jar Allah. "Al-Fahd: Anayt ka-ma law ann al-ta'ira al-makhtufa saudiya" [Fahd: I Suffered as if the Hijacked Airplane Was a Saudi One], *Al-Siyasa* (Kuwait), 28–29 April 1988, 7.

26 Speech by Prince Sultan, "Al-Amir Sultan: Quwwatna mutakamilat al-taslih wa-qadirun ala al-hasm al-sari wa-namlik sawarikh qadira ala al-tadmir" [Prince Sultan: Our Forces Are Fully Armed and We Are Able to Decide Quickly and We Possess Destructive Missiles], *Al-Riyadh*, 5 September 1990, 1, 9.

27 According to Prince Khalid bin Sultan, "Hiwar sari ma qa'id al-quwwat al-mushtaraka fi harb Al-Khalij" [A Quick Interview with the Commander of the Combined Forces During the Gulf War], *Al-Ahram*, 28 February 1992, 5 (hereafter Khalid bin Sultan, "Hiwar sari").

The utility of nuclear weapons 123

28 Adnan Kamil Salah, "Wad Iran wa-Isra'il taht mizhallat naz silah nawawi wahida" [Placing Iran and Israel under a Single Nuclear Disarmament Umbrella], *Al-Madina*, 17 December 2013, www.al-madina.com/printhtml/498590 (hereafter Salah "Wad Iran").
29 Abd Allah bin Fahd Al-Luhaydan, "Al-Difa al-istratiji wa'l-nizham al-duwali" [Strategic Defense and the World Order], *Al-Jazira*, 7 July 2000, www.al-jazirah.com/2000/20000707/ar2.htm.
30 Staff Brigadier General Abd Allah bin Mufrih Shibli, "Mafhum al-harb al-wiqa'iya wa'l-darabat al-istibaqiya" [The Meaning of Preventive War and Pre-emptive Strikes], *Al-Difa Al-Jawwi*, September 2012, 34–37. The Air Defense Forces' journal may serve at times as the surrogate professional forum also for the country's Strategic Rocket Force, since the latter does not have a journal of its own, while its officers are also educated at the Air Defense Forces' Academy.
31 Awad Mani Al-Qahtani, "Uqb riayatih faaliyat tamrin itlaq al-sawarikh al-itiradiya al-balistiya" [After He Presided over the Exercise Activities of the Launch of the Anti-Ballistic-Missile Missiles], *Al-Jazira*, 4 November 2009, www.al-jazirah.com/2009/20091104/fe15.htm (hereafter Al-Qahtani, "Uqb riayatih faaliyat tamrin").
32 Amanda Macias, "Here's How the World's Most Advanced Missile-Defense System Works," *Business Insider* (New York), 17 January 2015, www.businessinsider.com/thaad-missile-defense-system-2015-1, and Jasir Abd Al-Aziz Al-Jasir, "Basha'ir ijabiya li-ziyarat al-amir Muhammad bin Salman li-Rusiya" [Good News from Prince Muhammad bin Salman's Visit to Russia], *Al-Jazira*, 22 June 2015, www.al-jazirah.com/2015/20150622/du14.htm.
33 For example, Yusuf Makki, "Al-Arab wa'l-tiknulujiya al-nawawiya" [The Arabs and Nuclear Technology], *Al-Khalij*, 15 March 2009, www.alkhaleej.ae/portal/ab1b80b2-b23b-4e70-8021-a8af70d022d4.aspx.
34 For example, Abd Allah Mughram, "Al-Hind masna al-alam al-qadim" [India Is the World's Future Factory], *Al-Riyadh*, 22 February 2015, www.alriyadh.com/1023913, and Abd Al-Wahid Al-Hamid, "Durus min bilad Al-Hind" [Lessons from India], *Al-Jazira*, 15 October 2014, www.al-jazirah.com/2014/20141015/ln41.htm.
35 Rashid Muhammad Al-Fawzan, "Al-Sin wa'l-Hind mizan al-alam" [China and India: The World's Balancers], *Al-Riyadh*, 2 September 2015, www.alriyadh.com/1078786.
36 Ibrahim Ali Nasib, "Lay … shayifni hindi?" [Why? Do You Take Me for a Simpleton?], *Al-Madina*, 27 August 2015, www.al-madina.com.sa/printhtml/627049.
37 Sadaqa Yahya Fadil, "Rusiya wa'l-gharb al-mutanaffidh!" [Russia and a Forceful West!], *Ukaz*, 21 June 2015, http://okaz.co/bwIgbdqPT.
38 Al-Sayyid Abu Da'ud, *Tasaud al-madd al-irani fi al-alam al-arabi* [*The Rise of Iranian Expansionism in the Arab World*] (Riyadh: Obeikan Publishing, 2014), 413.
39 "Li-madha la namlik al-silah al-nawawi?" [Why Don't We Get Nuclear Weapons?], *Jazan News*, 23 May 2006, www.jazan4u.com/vb/showthread.php?t=42590.
40 Ibid.
41 Muhammad Al-Hajjar, "Sikulujiyat rad al-irhab bi'l-tahdid al-nawawi: Al-Istratijiya al-jadida al-amrikiya fi al-harb al-nafsiya" [The Psychology of Deterring Terrorism by Nuclear Threats: The New American Strategy in Psychological Warfare], *Al-Haras Al-Watani*, January 2006, 70 (hereafter Al-Hajjar, "Sikulujiyat rad al-irhab").
42 Staff Brigadier General Zhafir bin Ali Al-Shihri, *Al-Dar al-sarukhi al-amriki wa-inikasatuh al-alamiya wa'l-iqlimiya* [*The American Missile Defense Shield and Its International and Regional Impact*], supplement to *Al-Difa*, January 2008, 70.
43 Abd Al-Aziz Al-Khamis, "Han waqt al-silah al-nawawi al-saudi" [The Time Has Come for a Saudi Nuclear Weapon], *Ibda*, 23 February 2012, http://ebdaa.com/?act=artc&id=5577&print=1.
44 This fear had spurred a costly and environmentally-damaging program for self-sufficiency in grains which began to be phased out only in 2008, despite an interruption when the late Prince Nayif became Crown Prince in 2011, "Al-Amir Nayif yuwajjih bi-dirasat iadat ziraat al-qamh fi'l-mamlaka" [Prince Nayif Orders a Study to Bring Back

Wheat Farming in the Kingdom], *Sabq*, 17 December 2011, http://sabq.org/ sabq/user/news.do?id=34980&section=5&print=true. Also see Yossi Mann, "Can Saudi Arabia Feed Its People?", *Middle East Quarterly*, xxii, 2, Spring 2015, www.meforum.org/5098/can-saudi-arabia-feed-its-people.

45 Turki Al-Suhayl, "Mufti Al-Saudiya yuhadhdhir min mukhattat li-taqsim al-mintaqa ila 'duwal mutakhallifa'" [Saudi Arabia's Mufti Warns of a Plan to Partition the Region into "Backward States"], *Al-Sharq Al-Awsat*, 5 February 2011, www.aawsat.com/print.asp?did=606976&issueno=11757, and Sami Zayn Al-Abidin Hammad, "Kayf tuhkam Amrika?" [How Is America Governed?], part 60, *Al-Bilad*, 17 December 2010, www.albiladdaily.com/ print.php?action=print&m=articlesm&id=8410.

46 For example, "Duwal Al-Khalij wa'l-difa an al-nafs" [The Gulf States and Self-defense], *Al-Madina*, 26 May 2011, www.al-madina.com/print/305799. Also, Sultan Abd al-Aziz Al-Anqari, "Abd Allah bin Abd Al-Aziz wa-tanqiyat al-ajwa' al-arabiya" [Abd Allah bin Abd Al-Aziz and Clearing the Arab Air], *Al-Madina*, 6 August 2010, www.al-madina.com/print/259378.

47 "Al-Amir Talal Al Saud: Hunak mukhattat Qatari sahyuni li-darb Suriya" [Prince Talal Al Saud: There Is a Qatari-Zionist Plan to Strike Syria], *Watan* (Amman), 1 December 2011, http://watnnews.net/Print.aspx? PageID=3&NewsID=38070.

48 "Masadir amirikiya tatahaddath an mashru li-taqsim Al-Saudiya ila thalath duwaylat" [American Sources Talk of a Plan to Partition Saudi Arabia into Three Mini-States], *Buratha News Agency* (Iraq), 15 May 2011, www.burathanews.com/index_lite.php?show=news&action=print&id=125057, and Yusuf Al-Kuwaylit, "Kam yamlik Nasr Allah min qunbula nawawiya?" [How Many Atom Bombs Does Nasr Allah Have?], *Al-Riyadh*, 4 June 2011, www.alriyadh.com/2011/06/04/article638360.html.

49 Such fears can resurface even long after the event, "Ra'is al-majlis al-baladi fi Makka: Al-Makan muqaddas laysa fa-qat lada al-muslimin" [The Head of the City Council of Mecca: The Site Is Holy Not Only to Muslims], *Al-Watan*, 4 May 2010, www.alwatan.comsa./News/newsPrinting/newsPrinting.asp?Issueno-2511&id=18002.

50 "'Bomb Mecca' Minhaj yatimm tadrisuh li'l-zhubbat al-amrikiyin hawl mahw Makka wa'l-Madina bi'l-qanabil al-nawawiya!" ["Bomb Mecca": The Program Being Taught to American Officers to Obliterate Mecca and Medina with Atom Bombs!], *Al-Marsad*, 12 May 2012, www.al-marsd.com.

51 Al-Hajjar, "Sikulujiyat rad al-irhab," 70.

52 For example, Sami Said Habib, "Hal sa-yajlib Al-Qadhdhafi ala Libiya qasfan nawawiyan?" [Will Qaddafi Bring on A Nuclear Strike against Libya?], *Al-Madina*, 26 May 2011, www.al-madina.com/node/296506, and Sami Said Habib, "Hal nahnu bi-sadad harb alamiya?" [Are We Facing a World War?], *Al-Madina*, 9 September 2013, www.al-madina.com/ node/47706.

53 Al-Hajjar, "Sikulujiyat rad al-irhab," 70.

54 Bannan, "Adw jadid."

55 Ibid.

56 Muhammad Al-Mansur Al-Hazimi, "La yafull al-hadid illa al-hadid" [Only Iron Blunts Iron], *Jazan News*, 15 November 2012, www.jazannews.org/articles.php?action=print&m=&id=2177.

57 Interview with Tawfiq bin Ahmad Saud Al-Qusayr by Asma' Al-Abbudi, "Ustadh al-handasa yatamanna: La budd min alla nujamil ayya quwa alamiya min ajl al-maslaha al-wataniya wa-bina' al-quwwa wa'l-taqniya" [A Professor of Engineering Expresses a Desire: We Must Not try to Please Any World Powers When It Is a Question of Our National Interest and the Development of Our Power and Technology], *Al-Hayat* (Saudi edition), 12 January 2010, http://daharchives.alhayat.com.

58 Staff Brigadier Zayid bin Muhammad Al-Amri, "Mafhum al-quwwa wa'l-qudra fi al-fikr al-istratiji" [The Concept of Strength and Power in Strategic Thought] *Al-Difa Al-Jawwi*, September 2010, 22.

59 Muhsin Al-Awaji, "Wa-hal yalid al-khinzir illa khinzir" [Can a Pig Give Birth to Anything but a Pig?], 21 February 2011, Al-Awaji's website, www.mohsenalawaji.com.

60 Ibrahim Al-Amir, "Qunbula nawawiya wa-law sirran" [A Nuclear Bomb Even If Only in Secret], *Al-Watan*, 10 September 2011, www.alwatan.com.sa/Articles/Detail.aspx?ArticleID=7323.
61 Bannan, "Adw jadid."
62 "Kuriya Al-Shimaliya tatarif bi-imtilakha asliha nawawiya" [North Korea Admits to Having Nuclear Weapons], *Majallat Kulliyat Al-Malik Khalid Al-Askariya*, 1 March 2003, www.kkmaq.gov.sa/detail.asp? InNewsItemID=105721&InTemplateKey=print.
63 Abd Al-Wahid Al-Hamid, "Haqa'iq murra fi alam bashsh" [Bitter Truths in a Happy World], *Al-Riyadh*, 9 April 2003, www.alriyadh.com/ 2003/04/09/article22250.html.
64 Ibid.
65 Bannan, "Adw jadid."
66 Haytham Al-Kaylani, "Al-Azma al-kuriya" [The Korean Crisis], *Majallat Kulliyat Al-Malik Khalid Al-Askariya*, December 2002, 78.
67 Prince Khalid bin Abd Allah bin Fahd Al Saud, "Al-Sibaq al-nawawi al-irani" [The Iranian Nuclear Race], *Al-Jazira*, 13 April 2006, www.al-jazirah.com/2006/20060413/rj1.htm.
68 Muhammad Sadiq Diyab, "Madha law daghat ahmaq ala zurar?" [What If a Fool Pressed the Button?], *Al-Sharq Al-Awsat*, 3 June 2009, http://archive.aawsat.com/leader.asp?section=3&issueno=11145&article=521831.
69 Yusuf Makki, "Al-Rad al-nawawi fi muwajahat siyasat al-haymana" [The Nuclear Deterrent against the Policy of Hegemony], *Al-Tajdid Al-Arabi* (Saudi Arabia), 18 October 2006, www.arabrenewal.org/articles136/1/CaNIU.
70 Adnan Kamil Salah, "Iran wa-harb al-thalathin sana al-islamiya" [Iran and the Islamic Thirty Years' War], *Al-Madina*, 9 December 2014, www.al-madina.com.node/574590.
71 Interview with Ho Jong, "Jong li'l-Anba': 'Ujbirna ala imtilak al-silah al-nawawi li-wujud silah amiriki mumathil fi Kuriya Al-Janubiya wallad adam thiqa mutlaqa'" [Jong to *Al-Anba'*: 'We Were Obliged to Acquire Nuclear Weapons Due to the Presence of Similar American Weapons in South Korea Which Engendered a Lack of General Trust'], *Al-Anba'* (Kuwait), 20 February 2011, www.alanba.com.ku/Absolute NMNEW/templates/print-articleid=173538&zoneid=14.
72 "Ra'is al-tahrir istaqbal safir Kuriya Al-Shimaliya" [The Editor Hosts North Korea's Ambassador], *Al-Anba'*, 21 January 2015, www.alanba.com.kw/ar/kuwait-news/official/531175/21-01-2015.
73 Editorial "Al-Niza al-kuri wa-tahmish qadaya al-arab" [The Korean Dispute and the Marginalization of Arab Issues], *Al-Watan*, 2 April 2013, www.alwatan.com.sa/Editors_Note/Editor_Note_Detail.aspx?ID=1082.
74 Muhammad Maruf Al-Shibani, "Durus min Kuriya" [Lessons from Korea], *Al-Bilad*, 6 April 2013, www.albiladdaily.com/print.php?action=print&m=articlesm&id=15026.
75 Hawamir Al-Bursa Al-Saudiya, 4 April 2013, www.hawamer.com/vb/showthread.php?t=1217053.
76 Yusuf Al-Kuwaylit, "Man sa-yamhu Amrika—Kuriya Al-Shimaliya am Iran?" [Who Will Obliterate America—North Korea or Iran?], *Al-Riyadh*, 1 April 2013, www.alriyadh.com/2013/04/01/article822202.html, Salih Bakr Al-Tayyar, "Hal tashal Kuriya Al-Shimaliya fatil harb nawawiya?" [Will North Korea Light the Fuse for a Nuclear War?], *Al-Bilad*, 21 March 2013, www.albiladdaily.com/print.php?action=print&articlem&id=14889, and Sami Said Habib, "Amrika wa-Kuriya Al-Shimaliya wa'l-lib bi'l-nar al-nawawiya" [America, North Korea, and Playing with Nuclear Fire], *Al-Madina*, 6 April 2013, www.al-madina.com.sa/node/444779?risala.
77 Wafiq Al-Samarra'i, "Hal istaslamat Amirika amam al-nawawi al-irani?" [Has the United States Caved In to the Iranian Nuke?], *Al-Sharq Al-Awsat*, 29 March 2012, www.aawsat.com/print.asp?did=722648&issueno=12540.
78 Abd Al-Rahman Al-Rashid, "Isra'il tashinn harb Al-Khalij al-muqbila!" [Israel Will Spark the Next Gulf War!], *Al-Sharq Al-Awsat*, 18 April 2013, http://archive.aawsat.com/leader.asp?issueno=12560&article=725026.

79 Salim bin Ahmad Sahab, "Azmat Kuriya Al-Shimaliya: zawbaa am thawra?" [The North Korean Crisis: Storm or Revolution?], *Al-Madina*, 8 April 2013, www.al-madina.com/printhtml/445094, Ayman Al-Hammad, "La-nuqaddim al-jazara li-Biyungh Yangh" [Let Us Offer a Carrot to Pyongyang], *Al-Riyadh*, 12 April 2013, www.alriyadh.com/2013/04/12/article825396.html, Fahd Amir Al-Ahmadi, "Khamsat durus min Kuriya Al-Shimaliya" [Five Lessons from North Korea], *Al-Riyadh*, 17 April 2013, www.alriyadh.com/2013/04/17/article826999.html (hereafter Al-Ahmadi, "Khamsat durus"), and Rakan Al-Majali, "Al-Bashariya al-mankuba bi-shurur al-qatl wa'l-ibada wa'l-damar" [Humanity Afflicted by the Evils of Death, Extermination, and Destruction], *Al-Riyadh*, 19 April 2013, www.alriyadh.com/2013/04/19/article827250.html.
80 For example, Turki al-Dakhil, "Al-Mulhaq al-kajwal" [The Casually-dressed Attaché], *Al-Riyadh*, 17 April 2013, www.alriyadh.com/2013/04/17/article827039.html, and Al-Ahmadi, "Khamsat durus."
81 Alyan Alyan, "Maghza wa-abad al-tasid al-nawawi al-kuri al-shimali" [The Meaning and Dimensions of the North Korean Nuclear Escalation], *Al-Bilad*, 21 April 2013, www.albiladdaily.com/print.php?action=print&m=articlesm&id=15146.
82 Reported in Turki Al-Suhayyil, "Al-Saudiya: Al-Amir Khalid bin Sultan yaftatih mansha'at al-sawarikh al-istratijiya" [Saudi Arabia: Prince Khalid bin Sultan Inaugurates a Strategic Rocket Facility], *Al-Sharq Al-Awsat*, 3 March 2010, www.aawsat.com/print.asp?did=559516&issueno=11418.
83 Al-Amri, "Dawafi imtilak," 15.
84 Fahd Amir Al-Ahmadi, "Wa-ma alladhi yamna imtilakna silahan nawawiyan?" [What Prevents Us from Acquiring Nuclear Weapons?], *Al-Riyadh*, 18 February 2014, www.alriyadh.com/2014/02/18/article911241.html (hereafter Al-Ahmadi, "Wa-ma").
85 Bassam Al-Asali, "Al-Tahaddiyat al-iraniya wa'l-amn al-arabi" [Iranian Challenges and Arab Security], *Majallat Kulliyat Al-Malik Khalid Al-Askariya*, 21 June 2011, www.kkmaq.gov.sa/detail.asp?InNewsItemID=393305&InTemplateKey=print.
86 HRH General Khaled Bin Sultan, *Desert Warrior* (London: HarperCollins, 1995), 145 (hereafter Khaled, *Desert Warrior*).
87 Ibid.
88 Ibid.
89 Ibid.
90 Staff Major General Anwar bin Majid Ishqi (Ret.) quoted in Ali Bin Gharsan, "Riyah Al-Sharq tuazziz tarsanat al-rad wa'l-'dabbaba al-ta'ira' hujumiya mudammira" [The East Wind Strengthens the Deterrent Arsenal and the "Flying Tank" Is a Devastating Offensive Weapon], *Ukaz*, 18 September 2014, www.okaz.co/bwFJGdcuG. "East Wind" is another name for the CSS-2 (hereafter Ishqi, "Riyah Al-Sharq").
91 Tariq Al-Buaynayn, "Shukran Iran … al-nawawi al-saudi qariban" [Thank You Iran … A Saudi Nuclear Weapon Is Coming Soon], *Al-Sharq*, 11 April 2015, www.alsharq.net.sa/2015/04/10/1325731.
92 Khaled, *Desert Warrior*, 150.
93 Prince Bandar quoted in William Simpson, *The Prince: The Secret Story of the World's Most Intriguing Royal, Prince Bandar Bin Sultan* (New York: Regan, 2006), 156.
94 Al-Ahmadi, "Wa-ma."
95 Mark Mazzetti and Helene Cooper, "Sale of U.S. Arms Fuels the Wars of Arab States," *New York Times*, 18 April 2015, A1.
96 Al-Rashid, "Isra'il tashinn."
97 Abd Al-Jalil Zayd Al-Marhun, "Amn Al-Khalij … hal min mutaghayyir amiriki jadid?" [Gulf Security … Is There an American Shift?], *Al-Riyadh*, 20 March 2009, www.alriyadh.com/2009/03/20/article417096.html.
98 Prince Khalid quoted in Al-Qahtani, "Uqb riayatih faaliyat tamrin."

99 Major General Salama bin Hadhdhal Bin Saidan (Ret.), "Al-Alaqa ma Iran wa-hatmiyat al-muwajaha" [The Relationship with Iran and the Inevitability of a Confrontation], part 2, *Al-Jazira*, 15 May 2015, www.al-jazirah.com/2015/20150515/ar8.htm.
100 See Cigar, *Saudi Arabia's Strategic Rocket Force*.
101 Talal Salih Bannan, "Al-Arab bayn kammashat al-rub al-nawawi!" [The Arabs between the Pincers of Nuclear Terror!], *Ukaz*, 2 April 2006, www.okaz.com.sa/okaz/osf/20060402/PrinCon200604026920.htm.
102 Major General Salama bin Hadhdhal Bin Saidan (Ret.), "Tabadul al-istiqrar ma Iran bayn ida'ha al-mawruth wa-ahdiha al-mankuth" [Mutual Stability with Iran in Light of Its Historical Enmity and Its Broken Promises], *Al-Jazira*, part 1, 29 May 2015, www.al-jazirah.com/sa/2015/20150529/ar3.htm.
103 Al-Amri, "Dawafi imtilak," 15.
104 For example, Muhammad Ali Al-Buraydi, "Sawarikh Iran wa-qitat Al-Khalij" [Iran's Missiles and the Gulf's Scaredy Cats], *Al-Sharq* (Najran), 5 February 2013, www.alsharq.net.sa/2013/02/05/707819, and Jasir Abd Al-Aziz Al-Jasir, "Al-Malaff al-nawawi al-irani ala tawulat Camp David" [The Iranian Nuclear Program on the Table at Camp David], *Al-Jazira*, 12 May 2015, www.al-jazirah.com.sa/2015/20150512/dul2.htm.
105 Al-Ahmadi, "Wa-ma."
106 "Al-Jadid fi al-alaqat al-saudiya al-amrikiya" [What Is New in Saudi–U.S. Relations], *Ukaz*, 19 May 2015, http://okaz.com/bwlexdo46, Mustafa Al-Tarhuni, "Muhadathat Iran al-nawawiya wa-aqabat al-sawarikh" [Iran's Nuclear Negotiations and the Missile Obstacle], *Al-Madina*, 13 April 2014, www.al-madina.com/printhml/524239, and Jasir Abd Al-Aziz Al-Jasir, "Al-Uyun al-gharbiya tughammad an al-ghubar al-nawawi al-irani" [The West's Eyes Are Blinded by Iran's Nuclear Dust], *Al-Jazira*, 23 February 2014, www.al-jazirah.com/2014/20140223/du6.htm.
107 Isam Aman Allah Bukhari, "Taht zhilal al-sawarikh" [Under the Shadow of Missiles], *Al-Riyadh*, 5 September 2014, www.alriyadh.com/973270 (hereafter Bukhari, "Taht zhilal").
108 Prince Faysal quoted in "Rakab sayyarat Datsun li-ziyarat marid" [He Rode in a Datsun Car to Go Visit a Sick Man], *Sabq*, 24 October 2011, http://sabq.org/sabq/user/news.do?id=32236&section=5&print=true.
109 King Fahd, "Khadim al-haramayn," 7.
110 "Hasalna ala sawarikh mutafawwiqa li'l-difa an muqaddasatna" [We Acquired Advanced Missiles in Order to Defend Our Holy Places], *Ukaz*, 20 March 1988, 1.
111 Jonathan Scherck, *Patriot Lost* (Los Angeles: The Author, 2010), 75, 96–7, passim. For an informed analysis of Scherck's claims, see Jeffrey Lewis, "Saudi Missile Claims," *Arms Control Wonk blog*, 8 June 2010, http://lewis.armscontrolwonk.com/archive/2761/china-and-saudi-bms.
112 Jeffrey Lewis, "Saudi Arabia's Strategic Dyad," *Arms Control Wonk blog*, 15 July 2013, http://armscontrolwonk.com/archive/6688/saudi-arabias-strategic-dyad.
113 Jeff Stein, "The CIA Was Saudi Arabia's Personal Shopper," *Newsweek* (New York), 29 January 2014, http://mag.newsweek.com/2014/01/31/cia-saudi-arabias-personal-shopper.htm.
114 Sami Said Habib, "Qira'a fi tasrihat Al-Faysal" [An Analysis of [Turki] Al-Faysal's Statements], *Al-Madina*, 10 December 2011, www.al-madina.com/print/343867.
115 Ibid.
116 "Al-Tarsana al-sarukhiya bi'l-Mamlaka Al-Arabiya Al-Saudiya" [The Missile Arsenal in the Kingdom of Saudi Arabia], Arar forum (Arar, Saudi Arabia), 14 December 2012, www.alshmaly.net/vb/showthread.php?=86914.
117 Ishqi, "Riyah Al-Sharq."
118 Ahmad Ghallab, "Al-Saudiya tastarid quwwatha amam al-alam bi-Sayf Abd Allah" [Saudi Arabia Displays Its Power to the World with the Sword of Abd Allah Exercise], *Al-Hayat* (Saudi edition), 29 April 2014, http://alhayat.com/Articles/20544569.

119 Ayman Al-Hammad, "Madha bad Riyah Al-Sharq?" [What Is Next After the East Wind?], *Al-Riyadh*, 13 May 2014, www.alriyadh.com/935367.
120 For example, "Li-awwal marra sawarikh Riyah Al-Sharq al-qadira ala haml ru'us nawawiya bi munawarat 'Sayf Abd-Allah'" [For the First Time in the Sword of Abd-Allah Exercise the East Wind Missiles That Are Nuclear-Capable], *Tawasul* (Riyadh), 30 April 2014, http://twasul.info/55974, "Al-Salmi: Sayf Abd-Allah tabath rasa'il mutaaddida" [Al-Salmi: Sword of Abd-Allah Sends Multiple Messages], *Arkan* (Saudi Arabia), 30 April 2014, www.arkan-news.com/?p=1556, Salih Al-Quthami, "Zhuhur sawarikh Riyah Al-Sharq li-awwal marra tuthlij sudur al-saudiyin" [The Appearance of the East Wind Missiles for the First Time Delights the Saudis], *Sada* (Saudi Arabia), 29 April 2014, www.slaati.com/2014/04/29/p181530.html, or "Al-Saudiya tastakhdim silah jadid li-awwal marra fi munawarat askariya" [Saudi Arabia Uses New Weapons for the First Time in Military Exercises], *Al-Rajul*, 1 May 2014, www.arrajol.com.
121 "Ziyarat waliy waliy al-ahd li-Musku" [The Deputy Crown Prince's Visit to Moscow], *Al-Riyadh*, 20 June 2015, www.alriyadh.com/1058324, "Saudovskaya Araviya zakupit komplesy 'Iskander'" [Saudi Arabia Is Buying the Iskander System], *Rossiiskaya gazeta* (Moscow), 3 July 2015, www.rg.ru/2015/07/03/iskander2-site.html, and Yurii Zaishanev and Andrei Rezchikov, "Saudovskaya Araviya 'Iskandery' srazu ne poluchit" [Saudi Arabia Will Not Receive the Iskander Immediately], *Vzglyad* (Moscow), 11 August 2015, http://vz.ru/politics/2015/8/11760678.html.
122 Staff Major General Jar Allah Al-Alwit, quoted in Turki Al-Suhayl, "Al-Saudiya: Al-Amir Khalid bin Sultan yaftatih mansha'at al-sawarikh al-istratijiya" [Saudi Arabia: Prince Khalid bin Sultan Opens Strategic Rocket Facilities], *Al-Sharq Al-Awsat*, 3 March 2010, www.aawsat.com/print.asp?did=559516&issueno=11418.
123 Bukhari, "Taht zhilal."
124 Al-Amri, "Dawafi imtilak," 13.
125 Fawaz Hamad Al-Fawaz, "Alamat fi al-amn al-watani" [The Characteristics of National Security], *Al-Iqtisadiya*, 21 November 2006, www.aleqt.com/2006/11/21/article_7059.print.
126 Hamid Hawran, "Al-Tajassus al-fada'i: uyun Isra'il tulahiq al-arab" [Space Espionage: Israel's Eyes Pursue the Arabs], *Majallat Kulliyat Al-Malik Khalid Al-Askariya*, 1 June 2010, www.kkmaq.gov.sa/detail.asp?InNewsItemID=360638&InTemplateKey=print.
127 Ibid.
128 Khalid bin Sultan, "Hiwar sari," 5.
129 "Khalid bin Sultan yuqallid al-fariq al-awwal Li An Dong wisam al-malik Abd Al-Aziz min al-daraja al-mumtaza" [Khalid bin Sultan Awards Lieutenant General Li An Dong the King Abd Al-Aziz Medal, Exceptional Class], *Al-Madina*, 6 October 2006, www.al-madina.com/print/267573.

Bibliography

Abu Da'ud, Al-Sayyid, *Tasaud al-madd al-irani fi al-alam al-arabi* [*The Rise of Iranian Expansion in the Arab World*] (Riyadh: Obeikan Publishing, 2014).
Cigar, Norman, *Saudi Arabia's Strategic Rocket Force: The Silent Service* (Quantico, VA: Middle East Studies, 2014).
HRH GeneralKhaledBin Sultan, *Desert Warrior* (London: HarperCollins, 1995).
Mann, Yossi, "Can Saudi Arabia Feed Its People?" *Middle East Quarterly*, xxii, 2, Spring 2015, www.meforum.org/5098/can-saudi-arabia-feed-its-people.
Simpson, William, *The Prince: The Secret Story of the World's Most Intriguing Royal, Prince Bandar Bin Sultan* (New York: Regan, 2006).

8

WHERE DOES THE CIVILIAN NUCLEAR POWER SECTOR FIT IN?

In parallel with the increased attention that Saudi Arabia has paid to nuclear weapons, there has also been progress in the civilian nuclear sector which, to some extent at least, may be seen as a related facet of the nuclear military option. Saudi discussions about civilian nuclear power provide some insights into the Saudi understanding of nuclear power in general, and official support for nuclear power can be viewed as the government's commitment to the nuclear idea overall. The primary mover for a civilian capability, to be sure, has been a recognized need for future energy supplies. In effect, the Saudi media has been filled frequently with legitimate concern and even dire predictions about the growing proportion of domestic oil production consumed for local power generation and the future depletion of oil reserves. Promoters of a civilian nuclear option have focused on the many potential benefits of nuclear power for medicine, agriculture, transportation, industry, power generation, and water purification, as well as the creation of thousands of new jobs.[1]

Riyadh's civilian nuclear energy plans

Riyadh has proposed ambitious plans entailing 16 nuclear reactors by 2030, to be devoted mainly to the generation of electricity and water purification, as the central part of a strategy focused on renewable energy. There is to be an initial five-year study and planning cycle, to be followed by a five-year building phase.[2] The King Abd Allah Complex for Nuclear and Renewable Energy, which is to oversee research, planning, and management of the country's nuclear activities, was established in April 2010, and Riyadh has reached agreements for cooperation on nuclear development with such countries as Pakistan, the United States, China, Russia, Ukraine, Kazakhstan, Argentina, France, and South Korea.

True, in the case of a civilian nuclear option—unlike that of the military option—frequent doubts have been aired in the Saudi media as to its desirability, although there was no structured public debate, and we are not privy to the discussions that may have occurred within government circles. The focus of those who were unconvinced about the wisdom of pursuing a nuclear option varied, as they have argued over the years about the high cost of reactors and nuclear fuel, the risk of accidents, or the preferability of other alternative forms of energy, such as solar.[3] One critic of the Saudi nuclear power program, who was a proponent of solar energy instead, even sought to tap into fears of giving greater leverage to the West, as he argued that the country would become dependent on the West for uranium to fuel its planned reactors, and he assessed that "If we begin to rely on others for energy, that opens the door to blackmail!"[4] Evidently, such doubts have not had an impact on policy decisions, as one journalist supportive of nuclear power pointed out already in 2012 that "avoiding nuclear power is just not in the cards," while major deals to construct reactors were concluded in 2015.[5]

Nuclear energy and national security

For the vast majority of voices in the Saudi media, nuclear power in itself is viewed as an element of national pride and as evidence of modernity and, perhaps not coincidentally, the logo of the Saudi Ministry of Higher Education is built around the symbol of an atom. As one commentator noted, praising King Abd Allah for his vision, the civilian nuclear sector will "raise Saudi society toward the knowledge society in the century of knowledge-based economies."[6]

In addition, reflecting the psychological facet of nuclear power, Saudi observers often also explicitly conflate the development of a civilian nuclear sector with national security and the balance of power in the region, with its impact somehow perceived and promoted as a quasi-military factor. In fact, one Saudi proponent of civilian nuclear projects in the Gulf openly claimed that countries such as Saudi Arabia, Kuwait, or the UAE did not need nuclear capabilities for energy since they were already major oil producers, but that a civilian nuclear program was part of the local response to the threat from Iran.[7] One well-placed observer praised Riyadh's decision to embark on its civilian nuclear program, seeing this as "a requirement in order to create a nuclear balance in the Middle East region, since it is not logical that Israel and Iran enjoy a monopoly in this sphere."[8] As another commentator put it, in order to protect Saudi Arabia's national security, even if Iran initially acquired only a civilian nuclear program that alone should spur Riyadh to develop its own equivalent.[9] A Saudi academic at Umm Al-Qura University in Mecca also linked the Gulf countries' own civilian nuclear programs to their "fears about Iran's nuclear ambitions and the growth of Tehran's nuclear influence."[10] As a Saudi academic saw it, a peaceful nuclear capability somehow would endow the GCC countries with the ability to "withstand the demands of Israel and Iran."[11] And, he added, if the GCC countries adopt nuclear power for peaceful purposes:

they will thereby augment their power, which will be added to their oil, economic, and strategic power, which will provide them a powerful dynamism that will enable them to demand from Israel and Iran a WMD-free zone in the Middle East. This will not happen unless the other parties are convinced that the GCC and the Arab states have entered the appropriate path to mastering nuclear technology for peaceful purposes.[12]

Indeed, in a somewhat far-fetched argument in favor of a civilian nuclear program, a writer in a Saudi military journal even posited that such a capability would enable his country to be a major international player, with Mecca as the center of the world. Paraphrasing Halford Mackinder's nineteenth-century geopolitical argument about the dominance of the Heartland, he identified Saudi Arabia as the latter and, by extension, as the actor destined to rule the world, "provided it has the other elements of power."[13] A Saudi editorial saw nuclear power as a lever for Riyadh to exert its influence over its neighbors, as he called for merging the other nuclear programs in the GCC as part of the broader unification which Saudi Arabia has promoted, although apparently there has not been any response in that vein from any of the other member states.[14] Likewise, a Saudi academic reminded readers that the individual Gulf states have few cadres in the nuclear field and should therefore pool their resources, implicitly under Saudi patronage.[15]

Frequently, there were military overtones when Saudi analysts discussed civilian nuclear programs. One Saudi commentator, for example, seemed to be concerned about the potential diversion of a civilian program to military uses. Claiming that it is easy to use spent material from civilian facilities for nuclear weapons, he worried that "many countries seek to establish a nuclear reactor to generate electricity … but the fear of their neighbors' arming quickly causes them to rush toward military escalation." However, he attributed such intentions only to unspecified neighbors, and very probably meant Iran. The same source also worried that civilian reactors—although he mentions only those in other countries—would be able to produce spent plutonium sufficient for numerous atom bombs.[16] Likewise, a Saudi editorial raised the possibility that Iran could use its existing civilian nuclear reactor at Bushehr as a weapon of war by releasing nuclear material on purpose to pollute the Gulf in order to disrupt shipping and contaminate water for desalination plants.[17]

Others were even more explicit in blurring the civilian and military benefits of nuclear power specifically in terms of Saudi Arabia and, at times, it appears that Saudi discussions about civilian nuclear power have really been surrogate discussions about nuclear weapons. For example, one Saudi observer noted that if Saudi Arabia, or Egypt, established peaceful nuclear programs "that will pave the way for the development of nuclear weapons."[18] In fact, one the country's few nuclear engineers, Tawfiq bin Ahmad Al-Qusayir, in a 2009 discussion of Saudi Arabia's options for nuclear development, noting that Iran already had "thousands" of nuclear experts and that its claims of a peaceful nuclear program were "baloney" (*kalam fadi*), therefore urged Saudi Arabia to develop its own nuclear program. He maintained that it was a vital requirement for Saudi Arabia to produce its own nuclear fuel and, "if we want [this fuel] to be useable for a weapon," it will be necessary to enrich uranium found locally in the Tabuk area. His apparent intent for a civilian nuclear program was clearly military, as he concluded that

> The only practical solution to this crisis [i.e. of Iran's pursuit of nuclear weapons] is for the Gulf countries to seek in a serious manner and urgently to develop strategic deterrence means of their own in order to remedy the deterioration in the balance of power.[19]

Similarly, a retired senior military officer encouraged the development of a civilian nuclear capability, one which, however, he saw as "having the possibility of being used for military purposes in case of need."[20] Another academic, concerned that "our neighbor, Safavid Iran, is seeking to acquire nuclear weapons surreptitiously and by inveigling the duplicitous West led by the United States," called bluntly on "the Gulf states" to acquire "peaceful nuclear programs equivalent to the Iranian program, which can be transformed, if required by the interests of those [Gulf] states, into military programs." Citing the benefits of a recently-concluded nuclear agreement with South Korea in terms of developing a nuclear infrastructure, know-how, and the personnel base necessary to run nuclear reactors, he added that "I am afraid we will wake up one day and see that Iran has joined Israel [i.e. as a nuclear power]," and therefore he proposed the urgent development of a "Gulf" nuclear capability "Now, now, not tomorrow!" as a counterweight.[21] A Saudi academic, for his part, suggested a phased approach: "We must act quickly, as others have done. First, we acquire peaceful nuclear technology. If [the Iranians] escalate, then we escalate and then, if necessary, also [acquire] the most up-to-date [nuclear] arms technology."[22] Yet another observer, in fact, openly claimed that the nuclear deal with South Korea was "a strong indicator" of Saudi Arabia's resolute intent to acquire nuclear weapons if Iran did.[23]

A senior Saudi military officer, for his part, made perhaps the most unambiguous case suggesting that the capabilities that a civilian nuclear program would develop could also support a military nuclear program. In a thinly-veiled—and at times explicit—article, he promoted the development of the country's civilian nuclear sector as a path to eventual weaponization. Although much of his discussion dealt with the civilian nuclear sector, the very title of his article—"The Scientific Path to Acquiring Strategic Nuclear Weapons"—and the fact that it was also richly illustrated with multiple nuclear mushroom clouds, left little doubt to the reader as to the ultimate intent.[24] He noted that many countries dream of entering the nuclear club, which he saw as "a legitimate dream," and he stressed the importance of technology transfer, specifically integrating know-how and equipment and training local cadres, not just buying a capability.[25] Furthermore, he cautioned that in developing a civilian nuclear sector one of the requirements was that of "geographic strategic depth," that is, room that "will permit a country to work in complete secrecy and where its nuclear reactors will be safe from hostile attacks."[26]

The author acknowledged that foreign help would be needed if Saudi Arabia was to one day be able to develop its own nuclear weapons, and he noted that the help in the civilian nuclear field that had been received recently from countries such as China, North Korea, Italy, France, and Germany would be useful to that end. As he saw it, the development of the civilian nuclear sector would not only provide research reactors, but also develop cadres who could manage a reactor and conduct R&D and, in general, create an appropriate working environment. Although, as he recognized, Saudi Arabia would need time to arrive at such a juncture, nevertheless "we say that it is critically imperative to acquire these strategic capabilities right now in order to preserve the regional balance which, if lost, will be hard to restore."[27]

Civilians have also posited a linkage between the civilian military spheres of nuclear programs. For example, stressing self-reliance in the nuclear field, one Saudi editor urged that Saudi Arabia prepare itself for acquiring nuclear weapons—if that should become necessary—by building civilian nuclear reactors, implying a transition from one sphere to the other, and suggested that the lack of local expertise be filled by foreigners.[28] A Saudi analyst at the London-based Gulf Center for Strategic Studies (which is reportedly funded by the Bahrain government), for his part, noted that, since "the Arabs" faced a nuclear threat, their strategy should be "based on possessing nuclear technology, for it is their right—if they want to maintain the security of their countries—to acquire that technology without confusion or fear of a reaction from other countries that deny them such technology." And, linking that requirement with a security strategy, he urged unambiguously that Saudi Arabia develop a civilian nuclear sector, and suggested "perhaps converting it to a military program in the future the same way as other nuclear states in the world [have done]."[29] Likewise, a Saudi cleric, Awad Al-Qarni, associated the need to develop a civilian nuclear sector with a military strategy, arguing that the region was unstable and that countries hostile to Saudi Arabia have nuclear programs and are on their way to acquiring nuclear weapons so that it was therefore "imperative for the Kingdom to have its own nuclear program."[30]

While one might impute such views to some civilians' limited understanding of the nuclear process, at the same time such a public linkage would represent a sensitive political issue and would certainly seem to be a theme that is at least not officially proscribed. At the very least, there may be an official desire to give the public the impression that a civilian nuclear program provides a balancing counter to any Iranian nuclear capability and the political influence that such a capability is expected to generate. All this is not to say that the Saudi civilian nuclear sector would necessarily be misused for military purposes. One must remember that the covert conversion of fissile materials to military use presents significant technical difficulties, and especially so if effective international controls are exercised to prevent the diversion of spent fuel.[31] Rather, where there could well be a crossover between the civilian nuclear sector and a military program may be if the civilian nuclear sector over the longer term is used as a support element for maintaining and expanding an acquired military nuclear capability. That is, a civilian nuclear sector could provide ancillary infrastructure and trained personnel, as well as serve as a source for acquiring dual-use technology, components, and expertise which could also be applied to developing or maintaining nuclear weapons.[32] For example, the creation of a civilian nuclear sector could help form and sustain a cadre of nuclear experts—both Saudi and foreign—who could function in either sphere. King Abd Al-Aziz University (which has the only department of nuclear engineering in the country), other institutions with nuclear engineering courses, and the nuclear physics programs at three other Saudi universities already prepare both academics and technicians who could participate as dual-program personnel, as will the planned nuclear research center at King Abd Al-Aziz University—which is envisioned to also include many foreign experts.[33] Over the past few years, virtually every Saudi university has sought to recruit faculty in nuclear physics, although there is no indication as to how successful that effort has been. In addition, Saudi students are pursuing nuclear studies abroad in a number of countries.

To be sure, in early 2015, in the wake of lower oil prices and reduced national income, there were reports that Saudi Arabia would postpone its nuclear and solar energy projects.[34] However, as will be seen below, the contracts signed for eighteen nuclear reactors as part of Riyadh's negotiations with Russia and France in June 2015 suggest that political reasons may well trump strictly economic concerns and that the original development schedule may have been revived. In fact, for some in Saudi Arabia, a willingness to help develop a Saudi nuclear sector became a litmus test for how good an ally another state was, and some expressed disappointment with the United States after the Camp David summit of May 2015 for not having done so, and contrasted that with the subsequent Russian and French willingness to be more forthcoming in that area.[35]

Notes

1 For example, Malha Abd Allah, "Al-Siyasa al-saudiya tahkumha al-mabadi' wa-qiyam al-haqq" [Saudi Policy Is Governed by Principles and Just Standards], *Al-Yawm*, 18 April 2013, www.alyaum.com/News/art/79481.html.
2 Ali Sharaya, "Al-Saudiya: 16 mufail nawawi tatakallaf 3000 milyar riyal hatta am 2030" [Saudi Arabia: 16 Nuclear Reactors Costing 300 Billion Riyals by 2030], *Al-Sharq Al-Awsat*, 31 May 2011, www.aawsat.com/ print.asp?did=624264&issueno=11872.
3 See, for example, Muhammad bin Ibrahim Al-Jar Allah, "Al-Taqa al-nawawiya ma laha wa-ma alayha bayn al-ams wa'l-yawm" [Nuclear Energy: Arguments For and Against, Past and Present], *Al-Qafila* (Dammam), 2003, faculty.kfum.edu.sa. Also, Fahd Al-Thunayan, "Iqtisadiyun yantaqidun tawajjuh Al-Mamlaka ila al-taqa al-nawawiya bi-sabab taklifatha al-aliya" [Economists Criticize the Kingdom's Move to Nuclear Power Because of Its Cost], *Al-Riyadh*, 10 March 2012, www.alriyadh.com/2012/03/10/article716911.html, and Uthman Al-Khuwaytir, "Al-Taqa al-shamsiya awwalan" [Solar Energy First], *Al-Iqtisadiya*, 24 June 2012, www.aleqt.com/2012/06/24/article_669486.print.
4 Sufuq Al-Shammari, "Intabihu hatta la nakun rahina li-intiqamhim!" [Be Careful So That We Do Not Become Hostages to Their Retaliation!], *Al-Riyadh*, 18 September 2012, www.alriyadh.com/2012/09/18/article 769149.html.
5 Ihsan Ali Al-Hulaygi, "Al-Taqa al-dharriya … saudiya" [Saudi Nuclear Power], *Al-Yawm*, 14 March 2012, www.alyaum.com/News/art/ 45509.html. Yet, proponents of solar rather than nuclear power were allowed to continue their campaign into 2015,

Uthman Al-Khuwaytir, "Al-Taqa al-shamsiya al-masar al-sahih" [Solar Power Is the Right Way to Go], *Al-Iqtisadiya*, 26 July 2015, www.aleqt.com/2015/07/26/article_976155.html.
6 Sami Said Habib, "Al-Taqa al-dharriya ra'ida fi ittijah takamul al-tiqniyat al-istratijiya bi'l-Mamlaka" [Atomic Energy Leads the Way in Complementing Strategic Technologies in the Kingdom], *Al-Madina*, 24 April 2010, www.al-madina.com/print/242524.
7 Abd Al-Rahman Al-Turayri, "Al-Khalij arabi am farisi?" [The Gulf: Arab or Persian?], *Al-Iqtisadiya*, 23 August 2011, www.aleqt.com/2011/08/23/article_572330.print.
8 [Prince] Badr bin Saud, "Al-Nawawi al-saudi" [The Saudi Nuclear Weapon], Al-Arabiya TV, 4 September 2014, www.alarabiya.net, and Aruba Al-Manif, "Al-Hulm al-khaliji al-nawawi" [The Gulf Nuclear Dream], *Al-Jazira*, 29 November 2014, www.al-jazirah.com/2014/20141129/ar7.htm.
9 Salih Matar Al-Ghamdi, "Al-Saudiya awla bi'l-silah al-nawawi!" [Saudi Arabia Is More Deserving of Nuclear Weapons!], *Sabq*, 6 November 2013, http://sabq.org/js1aCd, and Abd al-Wahid Hamid, "Mufailat nawawiya saudiya li-ma la?" [Saudi Nuclear Reactors—Why Not?], *Al-Jazira*, 18 April 2015, www.al-jazirah.com/2015/20150418/ln.52.htm.
10 Lecture by Abd Al-Hafizh Abd Al-Rahman Mahbub, "Muhaddadat bina' amn khaliji jadid" [Defining the Creation of a New Gulf Security], *Umm Al-Qura lecture website*, http://uqu.edu.sa/page/ar/77553.
11 Id bin Masud Al-Juhani, "Hal yufiq al-arab ala hadir al-quwwa al-isra'iliya?" [Will the Arabs Awake from the Noise of Israeli Power?], *Al-Hayat*, 12 April 2008, http://international.daralhayat.com/print/200023/archive.
12 Ibid.
13 Yusuf bin Ibrahim Al-Sallum, "Al-Abad al-istratijiya li-quwwat Al-Mamlaka Al-Arabiya Al-Saudiya al-mutasaida" [The Strategic Dimensions of the Kingdom of Saudi Arabia's Growing Power], *Al-Haras Al-Watani*, 1 June 2006, http://haras.naseej.com.
14 Yusuf Al-Kuwaylit, "Kayf nakhtu bi'l-ittihad al-khaliji al-arabi" [How Do We Proceed with the Arab Gulf and Union?], *Al-Riyadh*, 24 February 2012, www.alriyadh.com/2012/02/24/article712535.html.
15 Salih Abd Al-Rahman Al-Mani, "Al-Tiqniya al-nawawiya fi Al-Khalij" [Nuclear Technology in the Gulf], *Ukaz*, 16 December 2006, www.okaz.com.sa/okaz/osf/20061216/PrinCon2006121671686.htm.
16 Mazin Abd Al-Razzaq Balayla, "Wa-Akhiran madina li'l-taqa al-dharriya" [Finally, A Complex for Nuclear Energy], *Al-Madina*, 23 April 2010, www.al-madina.com/node/242201.
17 Yusuf Al-Kuwaylit, "Man yahmi bi'at Al-Khalij min Iran?" [Who Will Protect the Gulf's Environment from Iran?], *Al-Riyadh*, 16 October 2012, www.alriyadh.com/2012/10/16/article776630.html.
18 Muhammad Al-Mansur Al-Hazimi, "La yafull al-hadid illa al-hadid" [Only Iron Blunts Iron], *Jazan News*, 15 November 2012, www.jazannews.org/articles.php?action=print&m=&id=2177.
19 Lecture by Tawfiq bin Ahmad Al-Qusayyir, "Al-Nashatat al-nawawiya fi mintaqat Al-Khalij" [Nuclear Activity in the Gulf Region], delivered at the Umari Forum (Riyadh), 6 March 2009, recording at http://omaryforum.com/play.php?catsmktba=9.
20 Staff Major General Salama Hadhdhal Bin Saidan (Ret.), "Al-Tahdid al-irani fi thawbih al-jadid" [The Iranian Threat in Its New Garb], *Al-Jazira*, 16 August 2008, www.al-jazirah.com.sa/2008jaz/aug/16/ar8.htm.
21 Sad bin Abd Al-Qadir Al-Quwai, "Al-Ittifaq al-nawawi bayn al-makasib wa-hajm al-tanazulat!" [Weighing the Benefits of the Nuclear Agreement and the Extent of the Concessions], *Al-Jazira*, 17 April 2015, www.al-jazirah.com/2015/20150417/du5.htm.
22 Yusuf Abd Allah Makki, "Malaffat sakhina wa-maayir muzdawija" [Hot Issues and Double Standards], *Al-Watan*, 19 October 2013, www.alwatan.com.sa/Articles/Detail.aspx?ArticleID=18761.

23 Tariq Al-Buaynayn, "Shukran Iran … al-nawawi al-saudi qariban" [Thank You Iran … A Saudi Nuclear Weapon Is Coming Soon], *Al-Sharq*, 11 April 2015, www.alsharq.net.sa/2015/04/10/1325731.
24 Staff Brigadier General Zayd bin Muhammad Hasan Al-Amri, "Al-Tariqa al-ilmiya li-imtilak al-asliha al-istratijiya al-nawawiya" [The Scientific Path to Acquiring Strategic Nuclear Weapons], *Al-Difa Al-Jawwi*, March 2011, 24–29 (hereafter Al-Amri, "Al-Tariqa al-ilmiya").
25 Ibid., 24; also see Nayif Al-Wayil, "Al-Nawawi al-saudi hulm mashru li-mustaqbal taqa akthar ishraqan wa-aminan" [The Saudi Nuclear Program Is a Dream for a Program for a More Brilliant and More Secure Energy Future], *Al-Riyadh*, 22 June 2015, www.alriyadh.com/1058888.
26 Al-Amri, "Al-Tariqa al-ilmiya," 27.
27 Ibid., 29.
28 Yusuf Al-Kuwaylit, "Al-Khalij al-ari wa-Iran al-nawawiya" [The Exposed Gulf and a Nuclear Iran], *Al-Riyadh*, 26 November 2014, www.alriyadh.com/997663.
29 Quoted in "Al-Karra al-nawawiya ishkaliyat al-tahdid wa-ghatrasat al-quwwa" [The Nuclear Comeback: The Ambiguity of the Threat and the Arrogance of Power], *Al-Yawm*, 18 April 2013, www.alyaum.com/article/3079481.
30 "Awad Al-Qarni: Al-Saudiya fi ashadd al-haja li-mufailat nawawiya" [Awad Al-Qarni: Saudi Arabia Has a Pressing Need for Nuclear Reactors], *Akhbar Al-Khalij* (Great Britain), 10 May 2015, http://alkhaleejonline.net.
31 Paul I. Bernstein and Nima Gerami, *Proliferation Risks of Civilian Nuclear Power Programs*, Proceedings (Washington, DC: Center for the Study of Weapons of Mass Destruction, June 2012), http://wmdcenter.dodlive.mil/ files/2012/06/CSWMD-Proceedings-3-FINAL.pdf.
32 Matthew Fuhrmann focuses on the potential threat of such an overlap in civilian and military programs through the acquisition of dual-use technology and expertise, "Spreading Temptation: Proliferation and Peaceful Nuclear Cooperation Agreements," *International Security*, xxxiv, 1, Summer 2009, 7–41.
33 Samir Al-Saadi, "KAU Campus to Get Nuclear Research Center, Says Tayeb," *Arab News*, 2 November 2008, www.arabnews.com/services/print/print.asp?artid=113728&d=. See also, "Baramij li'l-majistayr wa'l-dukturah wa-khutat mustaqbaliya tamuha" [Masters and Doctoral Programs and Ambitious Plans for the Future], *Al-Watan*, 4 May 2010, www.alwatan.com.sa/news/newsPrinting.asp?issueno=2921&id=76519.
34 "Saudi Arabia's Nuclear, Renewable Energy Plans Pushed Back," Reuters, 19 January 2015, www.reuters.com/assets/print?aid=USL6N0UY2LS201150119.
35 Saud Al-Riyas, "Al-Ittifaq al-mudhill hafla min naw akhar" [The Demeaning Agreement: A Party of a Different Kind], *Al-Hayat* (Saudi edition), 15 July 2015, http://alhayat.com/Opinions/Saud-Al-Rias/9989245.

Bibliography

Bernstein, Paul I. and Nima Gerami, *Proliferation Risks of Civilian Nuclear Power Programs*, Proceedings (Washington, DC: Center for the Study of Weapons of Mass Destruction, June 2012), http://wmdcenter.dodlive.mil/files/2012/06/CSWMD-Proceedings-3-FINAL.pdf.
Fuhrmann, Matthew, "Spreading Temptation: Proliferation and Peaceful Nuclear Cooperation Agreements," *International Security*, xxxiv, 1, Summer 2009, 7–41.

9

A NUCLEAR ENVIRONMENT AND FOREIGN POLICY

Reshaping relations within the Gulf

In a sense, the shadow of nuclear proliferation has already stimulated potential geo-strategic change in the Gulf. For Saudi Arabia, a key policy concern related to the Iranian threat and, in particular, to the potential nuclear aspect of that threat, has been Riyadh's perceived need to reconsider and refashion its relationship with its smaller neighbors in the Gulf Cooperation Council (GCC). Apparently seeing the evolving threat situation both as a challenge and an opportunity, Saudi Arabia sought to translate its own present and future military clout into greater political influence in the immediate region. According to a Saudi military journal, the essential impetus for such a development within the GCC was the need to "confront the inequality in the balance of terror resulting from the existence of a nuclear power in the Middle East, namely Israel, and of a regional power doing its utmost to develop nuclear weapons [i.e. Iran]."[1] Although the Iranian threat to the Gulf, from the Saudi perspective, encompasses a number of aspects, the nuclear factor has received a significant amount of emphasis and at times has been the linchpin of Riyadh's strategy for an envisioned new relationship within the GCC.

Confirming Saudi Arabia's leading role in the Gulf Cooperation Council

In concrete terms, against a backdrop of increased perceived threats, Riyadh has promoted a new vision for the GCC, one centered on unprecedented integration which, unavoidably, would occur under Saudi Arabia's aegis. Thanks to its relatively greater size, wealth, and human and technical resources in comparison to the other GCC states, Saudi Arabia is the natural leader of that key regional organization, and Saudis sometimes refer to their country as "the Gulf states' elder sister," albeit not without discomfort for some of its smaller neighbors.[2] A writer in a

Saudi military journal, discussing recent developments, depicted Riyadh's leadership role as central from the GCC's very creation:

> the Kingdom of Saudi Arabia was the main partner in bringing about a developed institutional framework which would concretize the aspirations of the sons of the region into a collective entity with which they could confront the challenges of preserving security, achieving development, and structuring and developing mutual cooperation.[3]

Predictably, another writer in the same journal emphasized Saudi Arabia's "political role in Gulf politics as a leading state which bears most of [the Gulf's] burden."[4]

Saudis, as one might expect, also stress their country's unique importance for the GCC's security, with one Saudi press commentary claiming that Saudi Arabia, "thanks to its regional and international standing and to the wisdom of its leaders, represents the strategic depth" of the GCC.[5] As a senior Saudi military officer saw it, Saudi Arabia "plays a pivotal and leading role in guaranteeing the security and stability of the region."[6] Another senior military officer, a member of the royal family, echoed this view: "Our country has become ... a pivotal axis for the states of the region ... the sad recent events in Bahrain confirm our country's leading role and its ability to assume an important role in guaranteeing the region's security and stability."[7] And, in arguing for unification, one Saudi commentator pointedly reminded readers that his country was already the GCC's "political representative."[8]

Flexing a potential Saudi nuclear muscle

In concrete terms, Saudi Arabia hinted it could provide at least an informal nuclear umbrella to the rest of the GCC if the situation reached a nuclear stage. For example, noting that his country was "the representative of the Gulf region," one prominent Saudi journalist asked "what if Riyadh acquired a nuclear weapon to confront Iran as part of that [regional] equation of balance?"[9] Likewise, a Saudi academic, writing in a Bahraini newspaper, warned that governments in the Gulf would not enjoy security unless they "sought to acquire nuclear weapons," further appealing to his audience's pride by adding that "we are not just shepherds; we have dreams too; we are a civilized people," clearly alluding to the one GCC country that had that capability.[10] Saudi sources have also argued that their country's size would even provide strategic depth and refuge for the GCC population in case there were nuclear leaks from Iran's nuclear facilities.[11] Expressions of doubt about the reliability of outside guarantees often went hand-in-hand with the promotion in Saudi circles of a greater degree of GCC unification, as was the case with one editorialist writing in favor of a unified GCC, when he asserted that "regional powers [i.e. Iran] will not find a deterrent to reduce the impact of their ambitions of expansion except by confronting these [ambitions] with a barrier of [GCC] unity."[12] As another Saudi editor put it, while calling for greater GCC unity in the face of a potential Iranian nuclear threat, "the defense [of the Gulf] must not be decided by outside states."[13] Similarly, when speaking of the potential Iranian nuclear threat, yet another Saudi observer noted that "the West cannot always be relied upon, and those in the Gulf are the ones best suited to defend their own security."[14]

Saudi Arabia again reminded its neighbors of such an offer during the Saudi "Sword of Abd Allah" exercise in April 2014, when the country's nuclear-capable CSS-2 missiles were showcased for the first time, as many pundits in the Saudi media pointed out that the exercise had a message for Saudi Arabia's neighbors, namely that Riyadh could provide an effective security umbrella for them. According to one commentator, with that exercise, "Saudi Arabia has become a different country, one that has military deterrent power for all, and not just for its immediate neighbors," and, moreover, "everyone has understood the message that the Kingdom is capable of defending its own holy lands as well as its allies in the region."[15] Another journalist, likewise, concluded that the exercise was intended to show that Saudi Arabia "has the ability to slap down any transgressor who thinks he can violate the security and stability of our country and of the brotherly Gulf countries."[16]

Some of the GCC states, particularly those which feel a direct threat from Iran or which are most heavily influenced by Riyadh, did recognize the need for a friendly nuclear deterrent should Iran acquire the atom bomb. In practical terms, such a deterrent could only be achieved by the GCC's biggest member, Saudi Arabia. For example, in 2012 the King of Bahrain hinted at his support for Saudi Arabia's nuclear option at a press conference, as he warned that "although today we miss Egypt's and Syria's absence, if Iran develops the atom bomb there is no doubt that the Arab countries will also acquire it."[17] In the context, it would hardly have been missed by a regional audience that only one other Arab state could realistically be assumed to be able to fill that role in confronting Iran—Saudi Arabia. As an editorial in the Kuwaiti press urging the acquisition of a nuclear deterrent to respond to Iran also acknowledged, a nuclear establishment requires depth for physical space and security, "such as the Suman Desert in the Kingdom of Saudi Arabia."[18]

Increasing Saudi leverage with the international community

While perhaps a secondary consideration for Riyadh in mobilizing regional approval for a Saudi nuclear deterrent, such support could provide further legitimacy for the Saudi leadership with its own public to pursue the nuclear option when and if it decides to do so. Such support from the smaller GCC states would no doubt also be welcome in Riyadh in order to provide to the latter greater political leverage with the international community with respect to a nuclear option. As one retired senior Saudi officer put it, "he who desires to affirm his presence and influence on the world stage will find that the most appropriate approach is to first solidify his presence on the regional stage and in the Arab and

Islamic circles."[19] Clearly, a GCC consensus could facilitate international acceptance of Saudi nuclear weapons. As a Saudi journalist recognized, "I imagine that the hardest phase if the Kingdom or another Gulf state acts to acquire WMD would be that of getting international agreement." However, he continued, "if there were a consensus and solidarity in diplomacy among the Gulf countries for one of the countries to acquire them [i.e. WMD], there is no doubt that this would contribute to strengthening that country's negotiating position with the international community."[20]

Promoting the idea of GCC union

Not surprisingly, it has been Saudi Arabia which has taken the lead in efforts to reshape the future of the GCC, and has generated sweeping proposals for a significantly greater degree of unification which, if implemented, would mark the greatest change in the structure of that organization since its creation in 1981.

The overall threat context provided the framework for a tangible plan for union from Saudi Arabia, and Prince Turki Al-Faysal broached the subject of union at least as early as March 2011 in a major speech which he delivered at a conference in Abu Dhabi, and which focused on Gulf security, linking unity specifically to the Iranian nuclear threat.[21] At the December 2011 GCC Summit, held in Riyadh, King Abd Allah formally called for movement toward "a single entity." The final communiqué proposed a standardization of financial practices, greater coordination in defense matters, and other secondary agreements, while an accompanying joint "Riyadh Declaration"—citing "changing conditions, challenges, and threats"—set even loftier goals, and specifically a transition of the GCC "from the stage of cooperation to that of a union." The latter declaration spelled out concrete areas for integration to be studied, including a customs union, a common currency, a joint market, coordinated diplomacy, and "close ties, cooperation, and rapprochement" in education, the media, sports, and even the Boy Scouts.[22]

In his keynote speech focusing on Iran's nuclear program at a conference on Gulf affairs held in Riyadh in December 2011, Prince Turki Al-Faysal presented in detail his vision of a more unified GCC in all spheres as a necessary counter to the Iranian threat. His proposal went far beyond any previous ones, as he advocated "the establishment of a unified Arabian Peninsula, with an elected Shura for the single state, a unified military, a unified economy, a single currency, a unified school syllabus, and unified energy and petro-chemical industries."[23] At a conference held in Riyadh in April 2012, a stand-in for the ailing Foreign Minister Prince Saud Al-Faysal called for "transitioning from the cooperation to the union phase."[24] Prince Salman, then Saudi Arabia's Defense Minister, based on his reading of history, also foresaw the development of the GCC into a unified entity— one no doubt under Saudi leadership—for he touted Saudi Arabia's experience as the first state to have become unified in the Arabian Peninsula since the early days of Islam.[25] The effort to promote unity soon became identified with King Abd Allah personally, placing considerable Saudi prestige on the line.

The Saudi media, as one might expect, supported such proposals for unification enthusiastically, as when a commentator close to the palace termed GCC unification "what minds dream about and that which the requirements of the present situation dictate," while he praised King Abd Allah as "a man of history" for proposing this initiative.[26] Another Saudi press commentary appealed for the establishment of a single federal or confederal political entity resembling the United States, Canada, or Mexico.[27] As a Saudi military journal acknowledged, what King Abd Allah's plan meant was that "The givens of the strategic situation in the Gulf region point to an enlargement of the Saudi role, based on the wise vision of the Servant of the Two Holy Shrines."[28]

Gulf responses

Acknowledging a growing threat

To be sure, policymakers and the media in at least some of the GCC states at the time conceded the need for a major role by Saudi Arabia in Gulf security, with the Qatari-born Secretary General of the GCC, Abd Al-Rahman Al-Atiya, depicting Saudi Arabia as "the basic pillar of the GCC and someone who is able to protect the latter's territory, skies, and borders."[29] Many Kuwaitis—especially those in the country's Sunni community—as was the case with one local politician, also readily acknowledged that Saudi Arabia is "Kuwait's strategic depth."[30]

However, Riyadh's political task has been a delicate one—to act as the GCC's big brother without frightening and alienating the smaller members. To be sure, the ominous threat situation at the time resulted in an unusual degree of receptiveness on the part of the smaller GCC states to at least greater coordination. Indeed, the joint communiqué following the GCC summit in Riyadh in December 2011 highlighted:

> the adoption of the initiative [proposed] by the Servant of the Two Holy Shrines to transition from the phase of cooperation to that of unification, so that the GCC's entities form a single entity which will bring about good and repel evil in response to the aspirations of the GCC countries' citizens and in order to deal with the challenges which these countries face.[31]

This situation stood in stark contrast to that of earlier GCC summits, when some of the member states had been openly disinclined to confront Iran. At the December 2005 summit, for example, there had been no consensus on even mentioning Iran's nuclear weapons in the final communiqué, apparently much to the dismay of the Saudis.[32]

Since then, there have been discussions on enjoined defense, security, and foreign policies, and integration in such as areas as air defense and early warning; the creation of a combined defense council; and also calls for a standing combined force under Saudi leadership; and in 2012 the creation of a joint nuclear radiation monitoring center was announced. Recognizing the growing threat, not only from Iran's potential nuclear weapons but also from its appeal to the local Shia communities, some of the GCC states—and especially Bahrain and some quarters in Kuwait (countries that have large Shia populations of their own and feel most vulnerable to Iran)—displayed unusual deference to Saudi leadership, enabling Saudi Arabia to gain increasing support for its regional leadership. As an editorial by an unnamed former Kuwaiti diplomat noted, Saudi Arabia had replaced Egypt as the "powerbroker" (*wasit*) in the region.[33] Bahrain's Prime Minister, Prince Khalifa bin Salman, for his part, welcomed warmly the Saudi king's call for a unified GCC, and stressed that "we look forward to the unification of the Gulf as soon as possible."[34]

Dissonant views on the nuclear issue

However, Saudi Arabia did not always find it easy to translate its talk of the Iranian threat, offers of a future nuclear umbrella, and promotion of a more unified GCC into universal acquiescence, as some of the member states became increasingly uncomfortable with Saudi Arabia's growing clout and pressure for unity. Clearly, in some states there was a more nuanced perception of the Iranian threat, and there may have been a reluctance to provoke Iran by being seen as supporting a confrontational Saudi approach to relations with their neighbor across the Gulf, and even more so if nuclear weapons were involved. As a result, some in the GCC were anything but receptive to the Saudi unification initiative, differing with Riyadh on the nuclear threat assessment and on potential remedies. As a Kuwaiti editorial complained about such doubters, "it appears that some officials in some of the GCC states can be described as not comprehending the extent of the Iranian threat."[35] The Gulf's Shia communities, as one could expect, were especially opposed to closer ties to Saudi Arabia, as was Oman, which traditionally has had good relations with Iran.

Fahd bin Mahmud Al Said, Oman's Deputy Minister for Cabinet Affairs, for example, emphasized a more benign view of Iran than that which Saudi Arabia had been promoting, as he noted in 2011 that "geography is determinant in the region and Iran, despite everything, is a neighboring state and we cannot change that reality, and the GCC states do not want our region to be one of tension."[36] Not surprisingly, speaking the following year about King Abd Allah's proposal for Gulf unification, Oman's Foreign Minister, Yusuf Bin Alawi, likewise, noted that:

> in our view, the energy that was put into the [original] framework of the GCC is still the foundation and we have not developed to where we are thinking of anything else ... The situation around us does not require [anything else] and neither do we; maybe the next generation might be able to accomplish that.[37]

Dubai, one of the constituent emirates within the UAE, with its long-standing economic relationship with Iran, too, expressed a less alarmist view of Iran than that projected by Saudi Arabia. For example, Shaykh Muhammad bin Rashid Al-Maktum, the ruler of Dubai, remained unconvinced as late as 2011 that Iran was developing nuclear weapons, as he noted in an interview with CNN that:

> Iran is our neighbor, they are Muslim and we lived next to each other for thousands and thousands years. I don't believe that Iran will get a nuclear weapon, I don't think so. What can Iran do with the nuclear weapon? Will they hit Israel? How many Palestinians will die? And do you think if Iran hit Israel, Iran will be safe? They will be gone the next day.[38]

Indicative of such differing perspectives, by 2014, Qatari opinion was upbeat about the possibility of negotiating a genuine agreement on Iran's nuclear program, in stark contrast to views in Riyadh.[39] Significantly, an analyst from the UAE, while acknowledging the need for a nuclear deterrent, apparently did not view Saudi Arabia as the only option, as he posited as early as 2009 that such a deterrent "could be local, Arab, or international, or even by means of a [broader] nuclear umbrella for the defense of the Gulf."[40] He even openly expressed a willingness to "accept in principle a nuclear umbrella from a country such as the United States."[41] In fact, advocating nuclear weapons for Saudi Arabia too visibly by Saudi spokesmen in neighboring countries became somewhat sensitive at times. Thus, a Saudi political analyst's scheduled appearance on a Kuwaiti TV program was canceled after his views, fervently in favor of a Saudi nuclear deterrent, were previewed by the show's producers.[42] Nevertheless, Saudis continued to represent even in 2015 Iran's existing nuclear reactors as sufficient reason for complete GCC unification, citing the purported shared negative GCC views of the Iranian reactors as a key common unifying factor.[43]

Sensitivity to potential Saudi hegemony

Moreover, there have been lingering suspicions in some GCC states of creeping Saudi hegemony under the guise of unification and of offers of a nuclear umbrella. As part of the process of proposed unification, Prince Turki Al-Faysal had called for the unavoidable need for member states to compromise some national sovereignty.[44] The Saudis appeared to have been surprised by the lack of enthusiasm they encountered, despite their portrayal of the looming Iranian threat, and Saudi Foreign Minister Saud Al-Faysal found it necessary in 2012 to allay fears of Saudi domination, assuring Gulf audiences that "it must be clear to all that union will not violate in any way the sovereignty of any of the member states."[45]

No doubt seeking to counter concerns on that score from some of the other GCC states, the Saudi media also sought to dispel the doubts that some had voiced about the wisdom of unification. One Saudi editor taxed as "not correct" the apprehension in some states to the effect that "unification may end their independence." He stressed that states could still retain their individual domestic policies, even as he compounded GCC fears by noting that "strategic projects" such as roads, electric power establishments, railroads, the import and export sectors, energy, and arms purchases would be "subordinated to greater coordination." In particular, he emphasized "the nationalization of [the petrochemical] industry and other sources of energy, whether nuclear or other" and that the transition from present-day cooperation to unity would lead to "a strong entity."[46] However, as a Saudi columnist acknowledged, some—albeit, as he saw it, only a minority—in the GCC were "unenthusiastic" about union, due to the small states' fear of losing relative influence.[47]

Usually, those wary of greater GCC unification expressed their concern officially in indirect terms, as did Shaykh Muhammad bin Rashid Al Maktum, ruler of Dubai and the UAE's Prime Minister and Vice President, who emphasized such terms as "cooperation and complementarity" rather than union, in a communiqué released as he arrived in Riyadh for the December 2011 GCC summit.[48] Likewise, Fahd bin Mahmud Al Said, Oman's Deputy Minister for Cabinet Affairs, noted after the same summit that the experience of the European Union demonstrated that monetary unification should not be hasty, and that the Saudi-promoted expansion of the GCC with the proposed admission of Jordan and Morocco "requires time" and "many preliminary steps."[49] Later, the Omani Foreign Minister was quoted as concluding curtly that "There is no union."[50] Even a pro-Saudi Kuwaiti politician admitted to the Saudi press that one could explain recent Kuwaiti accommodation of Iran, at least in part, as "a reaction to what [Kuwaitis] consider 'Saudi interference' in [Kuwait's] internal affairs and [Saudi] efforts to recruit the [Kuwaiti] tribes."[51]

While Bahrain, understandably due to the minority Sunni regime's need for Saudi support, continued to second Saudi proposals energetically, elsewhere in the GCC support for union never gained traction. A Bahraini academic, writing in a Saudi newspaper, was appalled by the prevailing attitude at a conference of Gulf intellectuals in November 2012 dealing with a potential GCC union. As he noted, the presenters had begun with discussing the potential benefits but "then suddenly switched to doubts about [the union's] success and to laying out the obstacles," while commentators "criticized extremely bitterly the direction and achievements of the GCC over the past three decades, and even ridiculed the very idea of union."[52] At the GCC summit in Bahrain the following month, while the Bahraini foreign minister noted blandly that "not one state said it did not want to enter a union," he also admitted that progress might appear slow, since "every state's views must be considered."[53] Despite the Saudis' positive "spin" on the summit, the final communiqué, while acknowledging the Iranian nuclear threat, spoke pointedly of "cooperation" more than once, not of union.[54] Again, the December 2014 GCC summit held in Doha was a disappointment for the Saudis in terms of progress toward unification, with one journalist concluding that it was "the same old record" of just verbal support, and reminded the other states that King Abd Allah was, after all, "the father of all the Arabs."[55] Subsequent friction between Saudi Arabia and Qatar, as well as Oman's more independent policy toward Iran, would soon put a stop to any further progress toward unification, at least for the time being.

Saudi Arabia may have concluded from its disappointing experience with the GCC that translating its talk of a nuclear threat and of its own nuclear—or implied nuclear—clout and its offers of a future nuclear umbrella into influence with its neighbors was not necessarily an automatic process. It is uncertain whether the outlook in the smaller GCC states would change if and when Iran actually acquired nuclear weapons, and in what direction—whether that would move them toward greater cohesion with Saudi Arabia or in a centrifugal pattern, with accommodation of Iran. In the end, however, the smaller GCC states' views would not be likely to sway Saudi Arabia's own views on nuclear weapons.

Notes

1 Abd Al-Azhim Mahmud Hanafi, "Al-Dawr al-qiyadi li'l-Mamlaka taht qiyadat khadim al-haramayn al-sharifayn" [The Kingdom's Leading Role under the Leadership of the Servant of the Two Holy Shrines], *Majallat Kulliyat Al-Malik Khalid Al-Askariya*, 21 June 2011, www.kkmaq.gov.sa/detail.ap?InNewsItemID=393304&InTemplateKey=print (hereafter Hanafi, "Al-Dawr al-qiyadi").
2 Badr Al-Balawi, "Al-Qunbula al-nawawiya al-saudiya" [The Saudi Nuclear Weapon], *Al-Sharq*, 14 December 2011, www.alsharq.net.sa/2011/12/14/46046. (hereafter Al-Balawi, "Al-Qunbula al-nawawiya").
3 Major General Isa bin Ibrahim Al-Rashid, Commandant of the Saudi National War College, "Majlis al-taawun wa'l-radd al-hasim" [The GCC and the Resolute Response], *Majallat Kulliyat Al-Malik Khalid Al-Askariya*, 21 June 2011, www.kkmaq.gov.sa/detail. ap?InNewsItemID=393296&InTemplateKey=print.
4 Hanafi, "Al-Dawr al-qiyadi."
5 "Abr tabanniha li'l-adid min qararat al-qimam al-khalijiya li-tawthiq awasir al-ukhuwwa bayn al-shuub Al-Mamlaka sahamat bi-dawr bariz fi tahqiq ahdaf Majlis Al-Taawun wa-taziz al-amal al-mushtarak" [By Adopting Many of the Gulf Summits' Decisions to Strengthen the Bonds of Brotherhood among Peoples the Kingdom Played a Key Role in Achieving the GCC's Objectives and in Solidifying Joint Activity], *Al-Riyadh*, 7 December 2011, www.alriyadh.com/2011/12/17/article692411.html.
6 Staff Brigadier General Zhafir bin Ali Al-Shihri, "Istratijiyat Al-Mamlaka li-muwajahat al-mutaghayyirat al-duwaliya wa'l-iqlimiya li-tahqiq al-amn al-watani" [The Kingdom's Strategy to Deal with International and Regional Changes in Order to Ensure National Security], *Al-Difa*, January 2007, 65.
7 Staff Major General [Prince] Bandar bin Abd Allah bin Turki Al Saud, "Hadha al-yawm al-khalid fi tarikhna al-majid" [This Memorable Day in Our Glorious History], *Al-Difa*, September 2011, 81.
8 Khalid bin Fayhan Al-Zatar, "Al-Taqarub al-amriki al-irani wa'l-duwal al-khalijiya" [The U.S.–Iranian Rapprochement and the Gulf States], *Al-Jazira*, 30 November 2013, www.al-jazirah.com/2013/20131130/rj10.htm.
9 Abd Al-Rahman Rashid, "Raddan ala Iran: qunbulatan saudiya wa-misriya" [In Response to Iran: Two Bombs, a Saudi One and an Egyptian One], *Al-Sharq Al-Awsat*, 13 April 2006, www.aawsat.com/print.asp?did=358088&issueno=9998.
10 Tariq Al Shaykhan Al-Shammari, "Al-Silah al-nawawi al-khaliji" [The Gulf Nuclear Weapon], *Al-Bilad* (Manama), 10 September 2011, www.albiladpress.com/column1294 2-8462.html.
11 Dr. Al-Qasim and Dr. Al-Anazi, "Al-Ittihad fi kiyan wahid yulabi al-tumuhat al-khalijiya wa'l-mamlaka umq istratiji li-duwal Al-Khalij" [Unification in a Single Entity Responds to Gulf Desires and the Kingdom Is the Strategic Depth for the Gulf States], *Al-Jazira*, 22 December 2011, www.al-jazirah.com/20111222/In1.htm (hereafter Al-Qasim and Al-Anazi, "Al-Ittihad").

12 Muhammad Al-Rumayhi, "Ittihad duwal Al-Khalij Al-Arabi wa-tahammul al-makhatir" [The States of the Arab Gulf and Taking on the Burden of Risk], *Al-Sharq Al-Awsat*, 28 February 2012, www.aawsat.com/print.asp?did=665686&issueno=12145. (hereafter Al-Rumayhi, "Ittihad duwal Al-Khalij").
13 Yusuf Al-Kuwaylit, "Hal nu'akkid annana lasna al-ha'it al-qasir?" [Can We Confirm That We Are Not a Pushover?], *Al-Riyadh*, 23 February 2013, www.alriyadh.com/2013/02/23/article812425.html.
14 Abd Al-Rahman Al-Turayri, "Al-Khalij arabi am farisi?" [The Gulf: Arab or Persian?], *Al-Iqtisadiya*, 23 August 2011, www.aleqt.com/2011/08/23/article_572330.print.
15 Bandar Al-Dawshi, "Abr al-sarukh al-balisti Al-Saudiya tafrud halat al-samt ala al-mutarabbisin" [By Means of the Ballistic Missiles Saudi Arabia Silenced Those Who Are Lurking], *Sabq*, 30 April 2014, http://sabq.org/yGYfde.
16 Yasir Al-Ghaslan, "Kaff Sayf Abd Allah" [The Slap of the Sword of Abd Allah], *Al-Watan*, 1 May 2014, www.alwatan.com.sa/Articles/Detail.aspx?ArticleId=21160.
17 Reported in Sultan Al-Qahtani, "Malik Al-Bahrain yulinha bi-saraha: 'Mawaqif al-bad fi Al-Kuwait kha'iba" [The King of Bahrain Says It Openly: "The Positions of Some in Kuwait Are Disappointing"], *Ilaf*, 29 February 2012, www.elaph.com.
18 Abd Al-Latif Sayf Al-Utaybi, "Mahattat Al-Suman li'l-taqa al-nawawiya" [Al-Suman Nuclear Power Station], *Al-Qabas* (Kuwait), 12 December 2011, www.alqabas.com.kw/ArticlePrint.aspx?id=695181&mode=print (hereafter Al-Utaybi, "Mahattat Al-Suman").
19 Staff Major General Salama bin Hadhdhal Bin Saidan (Ret.), "Al-Ibtiad an al-waqi bayn halat al-jawaz wa'l-iman fi al-nashaz" [Acquiring Perspective on the Situation: What Is Permitted and What Will Make It Worse], *Al-Jazira*, 1 October 2008, www.al-jazirah.com.sa/2008/20081001/ar5.htm.
20 Al-Balawi, "Al-Qunbula al-nawawiya."
21 Ali Al-Qahis, "Al-Amir Turki Al-Faysal yutalib bi-tahwil majlis al-taawun ila ittihad ashbah bi'l-urubbi wa-insha' jaysh khaliji muwahhad" [Prince Turki Al-Faysal Calls for a Transformation of the [Gulf] Cooperation Council into a Union Resembling the European Union and for the Establishment of a Unified Gulf Army], *Al-Riyadh*, 22 March 2011, www.alriyadh.com/2011/03/22/article615880.html (hereafter "Al-Amir Turki Al-Faysal yutalib").
22 "Nass al-bayan al-khitami" [Text of the Final Communique], *Al-Sharq Al-Awsat*, 21 December 2011, www.aawsat.com//print.asp?did=655296&issueno=12076, and Ayman Al-Hammad, Nayif Al-Wayil, and Bayyina Al-Milhim, "Al-Qada al-khalijiyun yakhtatimun ijtimaat dawrathim al-32" [The Gulf Leaders Conclude the Meetings of Their 32nd Session], *Al-Riyadh*, 21 December 2011, www.alriyadh.com/2011/12/21/article693500.html (hereafter Al-Hammad, "Al-Qada al-khalijiyun").
23 Salim Al-Sharif, "Turki Al-Faysal: Al-Alam fashal fi iqna Isra'il wa-Iran min 'al-nawawi' wa-khiyaratna maftuha" [Turki Al-Faysal: The World Failed to Convince Israel and Iran on the Nuclear [Issue] and Our Options Are Open], *Al-Madina*, 6 December 2011, www.al-madina.com/print/343006.
24 "Saud Al-Faysal: Al-Tahdidat tastadi al-amal al-jadd li'l-tahawwul min sayghat al-taawun ila sayghat al-ittihad" [Saud Al-Faysal: The Threat Requires Serious Efforts to Transition from the Cooperation Model to the Union Model], *Al-Madina*, 28 April 2012, www.al-madina.com/printhtml/374157.
25 "Al-Amir Salman: Al-Shabab al-saudi ladayh namadhij min al-tarikh al-watani tubriz ma qam bih al-aba' wa'l-ajdad min juhud ashamat fi tawhid al-bilad" [Prince Salman: Saudi Youth Have Examples from National History That Highlight Our Fathers' and Ancestors' Efforts Which Contributed to the Unification of the Country], *Al-Sharq Al-Awsat*, 5 February 2012, www.aawsat.com/print.asp?did=662105&issueno=12122.
26 Turki Abd Allah Al-Sudayri, "Mantiqi wa-waqii wa-daruri al-wusul ila ittihad Al-Khalij" [Achieving a United Gulf Is Logical, Realistic, and Necessary], *Al-Riyadh*, 21 December 2011, www.alriyadh.com/2011/12/21/article693501.html.
27 Al-Qasim and Al-Anazi, "Al-Ittihad."
28 Hanafi, "Al-Dawr al-qiyadi."

29 Quoted in Hani Al-Fardan, "Iqtarahatha Al-Bahrayn wa-aqarraha qadat Al-Khalij fi Al-Kuwait" [Bahrain Proposed It and the Gulf Leadership Confirmed It in Kuwait], *Al-Wasat* (Manama), 3 January 2010, www.alwasatnews.com//2676/news/print/358170/1.html.
30 "Al-Jasim mutanaqqidan al-hukuma al-kuwaitiya: Al-Saudiya tumaththil al-umq al-istratiji li'l-Kuwayt wa-laysat Iran" [Al-Jasim Criticizing the Kuwaiti Government: Saudi Arabia Represents Kuwait's Strategic Depth, Not Iran], *Jazan News*, 13 March 2010, www.jazannews.org/newsphp?action=print&m=id=2973 (hereafter "Al-Jasim mutanaqqidan"). Likewise, "Al-Nufudh al-farisi fi Al-Iraq yataazham" [Persian Influence in Iraq Is Growing], *Al-Watan* (Kuwait), 23 November 2011, http://alwatan.tt/printarticle.aspx?Id=153450&iYearQuarter=0.
31 Reported in Al-Hammad, "Al-Qada al-khalijiyun."
32 Information about the discord in the closed sessions seems to have been leaked to a Saudi-owned newspaper, which highlighted the absence of any mention of Iran's nuclear issue in the final communique and criticized the "minimal results" achieved at that summit, Zuhayr Al-Harithi, "Iran wa-duwal Al-Khalij … tura li-madha yaqlaq al-khalijiyyun?" [Iran and the Gulf States … Is It a Wonder Why Those in the Gulf Are Worried?], *Al-Sharq Al-Awsat*, 22 December 2005, www.aawsat.com/print.asp?did=339444&issueno=9886.
33 "Al-Siyasa al-kharijiya al-saudiya fi'l-waqt al-rahin" [Current Saudi Foreign Policy], *Al-Siyasa*, 9 May 2011, www.al-seyassah.com/ArticleView/tabid/59/smid/438/ArticleID/138658/reftab/94/Default.aspx.
34 "Khalifa bin Salman: Natatalla li'l-ittihad al-khaliji al-yawm qabl al-ghad" [Khalifa bin Salman: We Look Forward to the Unification of the Gulf as Soon as Possible], *Al-Watan*, 18 January 2012, www1.alwatan.com.sa/Politics/News_Detail.aspx?ArticleID=83409&CategoryID=1.
35 Al-Utaybi, "Mahattat Al-Suman."
36 Quoted in "Jalalat al-sultan yusharik fi amal al-qimma al-khalijiya wa-yu'akkid: 'Yatawajjab alayna muwasalat al-amal al-da'ib wa'l-juhud al-mushtaraka li-taziz awasir al-taawun'" [His Highness the Sultan Participates in the Work of the Gulf Summit and Confirms: "We Must Continue Tirelessly Our Activity and Joint Efforts to Strengthen the Bonds of Cooperation"], *Al-Watan* (Muscat, Oman), 20 December 2011, www.alwatan.com (hereafter "Jalalat al-sultan").
37 Interview with Yusuf Bin Alawi by Jabir Al-Harami, "Wazir kharijiyat Uman: Dam Al-Khalij lana shiraka wa-lays ataya" [The Gulf Is Our Support as a Partnership Not in Handouts], *Al-Sharq* (Doha, Qatar), 20 March 2012, www.al-sharq.com.
38 Interview with Shaykh Muhammad by Erin Burnett, "Transcript of Shaikh Mohammed's interview with CNN," *Khaleej Times* (Dubai, UAE), 6 December 2011, www.khaleejtimes.com/DisplayArticle08.asp?xfile=data/theuae/2011/December/theuae_December178.xml&section=theuae.
39 For example, "Hall al-khilafat hawl nawawi Iran bi'l-hiwar wa'l-diblumasiya" [Resolving Differences on Iran's Nuclear Program through Dialog and Diplomacy], *Al-Arab* (Doha), 6 March 2014, www.alarab.qa/details.php?issueID=2278&&artid=285578.
40 Abd Al-Khaliq Abd Allah quoted in Hayyan Nuyuf and Mustafa Sulayman, "Talabu bi-wujud mizhalla li-himayat al-mintaqa" [They Asked for an Umbrella to Defend the Region], Al-Arabiya TV, 10 October 2009, transcript at www.alarabiya.net/mob/ar/866684.html.
41 Ibid.
42 Interview with Sami Uthman, "Muhallil siyasi li'*l-Marsad*: Ala duwal Al-Khalij wa-khassatan Al-Saudiya al-say li'l-husul ala qunbula nawawiya" [A Political Analyst to *Al-Marsad*: The Gulf States, and in Particular Saudi Arabia, Must Seek to Acquire an Atom Bomb], *Al-Marsad*, 21 December 2011, www.al-marsd.com.
43 Musaid Al-Asimi, "Didd al-ittihad al-khaliji" [Against the Gulf Union], *Al-Watan*, 6 May 2015, www.alwatan.com.sa/Articles/Detail.aspx?ArticleID=26173.
44 "Al-Amir Turki Al-Faysal yutalib."

45 Reported in Ayman Al-Hammad, "Al-Amir Saud Al-Faysal muftatihan ijtima al-wizari al-khaliji fi Al-Riyadh" [Prince Saud Al-Faysal Opens a Meeting of the Gulf Ministers in Riyadh], *Al-Riyadh*, 5 March 2012, www.alriyadh.com/2012/03/05/article715301.html.
46 Yusuf Al-Kuwaylit, "Kayf nakhtu bi'l-ittihad al-khaliji al-arabi" [How Do We Proceed with the Arab Gulf and Union?], *Al-Riyadh*, 24 February 2012, www.alriyadh.com/2012/02/24/article712535.html.
47 Al-Rumayhi, "Ittihad duwal Al-Khalij."
48 "Muhammad bin Rashid yasil ila Al-Riyadh" [Muhammad bin Rashid Arrives in Riyadh], *Al-Ittihad* (Abu Dhabi), 20 December 2011, www.alittihad.ae/print.php?id=117659&y=2011.
49 "Jalalat al-sultan."
50 "Yusuf Bin Alawi: La yujad ittihad khaliji siwa fi uqul al-suhufiyin fa-qat!" [Yusuf Bin Alawi: There Is No Gulf Union Except in the Minds of Journalists], *Al-Wisam* (Saudi Arabia), 4 June 2012, http://alwesam.org/news.php?action=print&m=m+id5209.
51 "Al-Jasim mutanaqqidan."
52 Abd Allah Al-Madani, "Mashru al-ittihad al-khaliji marra ukhra" [The Gulf Union Plan, Yet Again], *Al-Iqtisadiya*, 4 November 2012, www.aleqt.com/2012/11/04/article_706621.print.
53 Ayman Al-Hammad and Abd Allah Al-Hasani, "Wazir al-kharijiya al-bahrayni wa-amin amm al-taawun fi mu'tamar sahafi: Fikrat al-ittihad maqbula min al-jami wa-la mawqif khalijiyan min al-ikhwan" [Bahrain's Foreign Minister and the GCC's Secretary General: The Idea of Union Is Acceptable to All and There Is No Gulf Position on the [Muslim] Brotherhood], *Al-Riyadh*, 26 December 2012, www.alriyadh.com/2012/12/26/article796055.html.
54 Ibid.
55 Saud Al-Riyas, "Mufaja'at al-qimma … la mufaja'a!" [The Surprise from the Summit… No Surprise!], *Al-Hayat*, 11 December 2014, www.alhayat.com.

10

THE ROUHANI ERA IN TEHRAN AND A NEW AGE OF ANXIETY IN RIYADH

A new president for Iran

Apparently feeling the effect of the stringent economic sanctions, Iran had agreed to re-engage in negotiations on the nuclear issue with the international community (in the form of the five permanent members of the UN Security Council plus Germany, known as the 5+1 Group) in 2012, but all three rounds of talks had ended inconclusively by July 2012. When these talks with Iran reconvened in February 2013 in Kazakhstan, Saudi observers, typically, were highly doubtful there would be any genuine progress. One commentator predicted that "the negotiations … will lead to a dead-end," since "from the beginning of the negotiations [Iran's] approach has been a tactical one characterized by gaining time in order to speed up its nuclear development."[1] Even so, the Saudi media still expressed displeasure—although attributing such concerns to other Gulf diplomats—that the Gulf countries did not have a role, and claimed that the GCC countries "do not hide their concern that a deal will be reached at the expense of their regional security and of their strategic interests."[2] Saudi Arabia's Foreign Minister, Prince Saud Al-Faysal, for his part, feared some compromise between the 5+1 Group and Iran, and went out of his way to reiterate his country's position: "We are not looking for appeasement or an arrangement between Iran and anybody with whom it negotiates. What we want, instead, is a solution that prevents the spread of nuclear weapons in the Middle East."[3]

However, as a result of the June 2013 presidential elections in Iran, in which Hassan Rouhani emerged victorious, new hope arose in the international community for a resolution of the Iranian nuclear impasse. The Iranian rapprochement with the international community and the actual and potential results of the developing situation took Riyadh by surprise and generated urgent soul-searching about the fundamentals of Saudi Arabia's security foundations. To a great extent, the deeply-rooted paradigms that Saudi Arabia had developed over the years about Iran, Saudi Arabia's self-identity and role in the region, and thinking about nuclear weapons provided the framework by which Riyadh evaluated this evolving situation and shaped its policy responses.

Evaluating President Rouhani: low Saudi expectations

Official Saudi circles were generally circumspect about developments, but the national media was almost obsessively focused on the events related to Iran and on their implications, continuing familiar themes while also developing some new ones. Even before the June 2013 Iranian elections, Saudis had not been optimistic that there would be genuine change on the nuclear issue no matter who succeeded outgoing Iranian President Mahmoud Ahmadinejad.[4] Assessing President Rouhani, pundits in the Saudi media often argued that while some saw him as a reformist, that may have been true only in relative terms in comparison to his bellicose predecessor and that despite his peaceable personality and moderate statements and outreach to Saudi Arabia, Iran's policies of expansion and its quest for nuclear weapons were part of that country's enduring national strategy dating back to the Shah's era and were unlikely to change.[5] As one journalist asked rhetorically, "is there anyone who can be considered a 'moderate' president in Iran?"[6] The Saudi media even accused Rouhani of following a policy of *taqiya*, or religious dissimulation, although that is a Shia religious term, that is that he was concealing his true objectives with his public policy overtures, and attributed to Iran "skill at deception in all its dealings."[7]

Many in Saudi Arabia predicted that any potential change would be only one in style, with the intention of improving Iran's public image, and the Saudi media often set long lists of litmus tests for Rouhani by which to prove whether he was really a moderate, stipulations that would have entailed a wholesale reversal of most of Iran's long-standing national policies, of which opening the country to full-scale IAEA supervision of its nuclear sector was only one criterion.[8] In the end, Saudis argued that in any case it was Iran's Supreme Guide, Sayyed Ali Khamene'i, who held the real power in the country and that he would continue the existing policies.[9]

Fretting and adjusting to the new direction in Iran's policy

The Saudi media interpreted Tehran's new-found flexibility and decision to seek a diplomatic solution, or "dovishness" (*hama'imiya*) as the media termed it, to a desire to have the potentially destabilizing economic sanctions lifted and to avert a possible U.S. military strike following the experience in Syria, when a U.S. strike against the Asad regime, due to the latter's reported use of chemical weapons, had appeared imminent at times. And Saudi observers also attributed Iran's more cooperative approach to a desire to take advantage of what they disparagingly called President Obama's accommodating "weakness and indecisiveness."[10] In fact, the Saudi media labeled Iran's outreach in such distrustful terms as "putting on sheep's clothing," using "soft language," and adopting "finesse."[11] In using what one commentator termed simply "different means," Tehran's ultimate objective was still seen in Riyadh as the preservation of the gains it had already made in the nuclear field.[12] Saudi skepticism of Iran continued unabated, with assessments that Iran's longstanding hostility toward the United States would not really change but would be in abeyance until Tehran had achieved its objective, specifically that of acquiring nuclear weapons, with an underlying theme that a naïve Washington was being duped.[13]

There was a noticeable increase in media coverage, as one would expect, whenever there were new developments, such as a new round of talks with Iran. Although there was very limited official Saudi commentary on President Rouhani's initial outreach to the United States and the visible political progress that was being made by the fall of 2013, the Saudi media displayed a suspicious and guarded attitude. Most Saudi media commentary continued to mirror Saudi Foreign Minister Prince Saud Al-Faysal's October 2013 announcement in which he had welcomed the change in government in Tehran, his skepticism evident, however, as he also depreciated Iran's revised policy as simply "a new Iranian tune."[14] He also had demanded deeds as well as words. Otherwise, he warned, if the Iranian outreach "is not translated into deeds, it will remain just empty words and have no impact."

Throughout the extended negotiating process, the Saudis expressed serious doubts about the reliability of any agreement that might emerge. In this atmosphere of anxiety, any negative indication from Iran was sufficient to further amplify Riyadh's skepticism. Thus, when in June 2014 Khamene'i gave a sermon outlining Iran's nuclear achievements and red lines, one Saudi newspaper concluded that he had now revealed Iran's "true objectives."[15] In fact, a common theme all along in the Saudi narrative, reflecting a Saudi lack of trust in Iran, was that the latter would not adhere to any agreement it signed. The U.S. assumption that Iran would really stop its nuclear program was portrayed as merely "a hope" that was said to have "a snowball's chance in hell" of succeeding.[16] Here too, the North Korean experience was brought up as a model, this time as that of successful cheating on a nuclear program, a model which many Saudis were convinced Iran would follow.[17] Other Saudis worried that even an agreement that had been signed in good faith might not be reliable, as the successor to Iran's aging Supreme Guide Khamene'i could decide to discard any agreement made by his predecessor.[18] In fact, many Saudis were concerned that even the protracted negotiations between the United States and Iran would give the latter the time it needed to complete its nuclear program.[19]

The difficult Riyadh–Tehran–Washington triangle

The unease with American policy

At least to some extent, Riyadh's approach to nuclear weapons during the Rouhani era must be seen against a background of broader regional events and of Saudi

Arabia's relationship with the United States. The evolving worrying rapprochement between Washington and Tehran, from Riyadh's perspective, was simply the latest episode in a series of recent disappointments with American policy, including the latter's position on Egypt, Iraq, Bahrain, Syria, and Palestine, as well as its lack of support for a WMD-free zone in the Middle East that would include Israel. By late 2013, Saudi Arabia was expressing its alarm and anger visibly to the United States. For example, Riyadh declined a seat as a non-permanent member of the United Nations Security Council, while the Saudi media unleashed a torrent of articles suggesting that the Obama Administration was not a reliable friend. Some Saudis began to label U.S. policy as "fumbling," "vacillating," and "confusing," or as one of "broken promises."[20]

With respect to Iran, some described America's emerging policy as "a shock to its friends" and expressed their indignation, arguing that Saudi Arabia was not "a banana republic" to be treated thus.[21] Still others castigated U.S. policy as now based on "empty threats" against Iran and believed they saw "an unprecedented position," "a total reversal in policy," and "unexplainable conduct," trends that were raising "fundamental questions" in Saudi Arabia, the United States' "oldest friend and ally."[22] Talk in the press became frequent about how the United States was unreliable and, typically, one editorial warned that if anyone depended on Washington's "friendship and goodwill" for security, that was "a strategic mistake," as the United States had allegedly "often abandoned its friends and allies."[23] In fact, many Saudis began to worry publicly that a U.S.–Iranian rapprochement could signal a historic reversal of American policy in the Middle East, with Washington seeing Iran, rather than the Arabs, as its partner of choice. Saudis also feared that a secret broader U.S.–Iranian deal was in the offing, as part of which Washington might even recognize Iran as a nuclear power and acknowledge its traditional role as the "Gulf policeman" that is the hegemonic power in the Gulf, in order to balance Saudi Arabia and Turkey.[24] In this atmosphere, the Saudi media expressed concern all along that it would be "the Arabs" or "the Gulf" who would pay the price of a possible U.S.–Iranian, or even of an Iranian–Israeli, deal.[25] The frequency of such themes in the media suggests that it reflected official thinking, even if the Saudi authorities did not voice such worries publicly. To be sure, real as it was, Riyadh's distress during this period of negotiations with Tehran did not mean that Saudi Arabia's relationship with the United States was in danger of ending anytime soon. However, press and popular criticism of the United States was becoming so pronounced that the Saudi government may have thought it prudent to rein it in somewhat. In effect, in late October 2013, the political editor of the country's leading daily, *Al-Riyadh*, reminded readers that although the U.S.–Saudi bilateral relationship was "vulnerable to shocks" nevertheless "no one expects the relationship to collapse," given the robust economic, security, and political interests that bind the two countries together.[26]

Assessing the 2013 Geneva Interim Agreement

The Geneva Interim Agreement that was reached between the 5+1 Group and Iran on 24 November 2013, which provided for a 6-month suspension of activity in certain portions of Iran's nuclear program in return for the easing of economic sanctions, contributed to a growing optimism in the international community that a permanent deal could eventually be reached. For the Saudis, however, the Interim Agreement was visibly troubling, and Riyadh sought to gauge what it would mean for Iran's nuclear program and, as a corollary, for Saudi Arabia's strategy. Even as the Geneva talks were still in progress, one Saudi academic had predicted that "in a very few years [Iran] will enter the international nuclear club" and "the world's nations [will] reap the results of their relaxed attitude and lack of resolve."[27] And, a Saudi newspaper warned that any compromise solution would only "open the door to nuclear proliferation in the region [by states] seeking security from Iran's approaching nuclear threats," a thinly-veiled suggestion that Riyadh would then also have to think about going nuclear.[28] Perhaps more to the point, the day before the Geneva Interim Agreement was announced officially, Saudi Arabia's Ambassador to the United Kingdom, Prince Muhammad bin Nawaf (who was also King Abd Allah's nephew), castigated what he called Washington's "rush" to deal with Iran as "incomprehensible," labeling it "appeasement," and warning that "we are not going to sit idly by and receive a threat there and not think seriously how we can best defend our country and our region." When pressed as to whether that meant that Saudi Arabia would also seek nuclear weapons he was non-committal: "Let's just leave it there, all options are available."[29]

The Saudi media, for its part, overwhelmingly was skeptical or negative, and openly so, perhaps indicating what the country's government really believed. Typically, Saudis commentators stressed that the Geneva Agreement was just a temporary respite designed to buy Tehran time during which Iran could rebuild its depleted treasury, since Iran could not be trusted. Pointing to what was seen as Iran's unchanged regional policy, Saudi observers concluded that Tehran had not really changed, and that its willingness to negotiate was merely "a game."[30] One journalist, reflecting the Saudi consensus, asked rhetorically, "Have the Iranians suddenly changed their strategy? And, therefore, can we trust Rouhani's statement when he says 'The government will never seek to acquire nuclear weapons under any circumstance?' The direct reply in no uncertain terms is 'No.'"[31] In any case, as he saw it, Rouhani was only an administrative official, with the religious Supreme Guide Khamene'i holding the real power, and the latter was likely to replace President Rouhani with another president when the current policy had run its course. And, as he concluded, nuclear weapons "without a doubt are a strategic objective that the Iranians will not abandon." At best, according to another journalist, Iran, by playing a "cat and mouse game," might stop just short of weaponizing a nuclear capability for now, but nevertheless would still have developed an advantage over its Gulf neighbors.[32] In particular, according to a Saudi academic who writes on defense issues, while Iran might postpone the actual production of a nuclear weapon, it would use any agreement moratorium to further develop its scientific and technical capabilities in support of that goal, aided by the additional funds it would now have available. In his view, although an agreement could result in a delay, the ancillary progress during this period would mean that a nuclear weapon would be on the shelf in all but name, to be produced when the time was appropriate.[33] One Saudi pundit, for his part, responded to the Interim Agreement by urging that immediate steps be taken to work toward using "nuclear power" and to publicize such steps. Although the terminology he used was ambivalent, the intent to create a balance in the military nuclear field with Iran and the title of the article, "The Gulf Atom Bomb and the Sunni Shield," left little to the imagination.[34]

In some ways, the Saudis looked at the Interim Agreement as tangible proof that President Obama had caved in, achieving only a "fragile agreement," while having capitulated from a "red line" to a "soft pink line."[35] There was also surprise at how quickly the agreement had come about, and additional discomfort when it was confirmed that there had been secret meetings on the nuclear issue between the United States and Iran extending back to even when President Rouhani's predecessor, President Ahmadinejad, had been in power.[36] At the very least, some Saudis even feared that Iran had been willing to sign the Interim Agreement "so that it will leave [the GCC states] naked to face Iran's growing nuclear power and its ambitions, which it does not hide."[37] True, one prominent Saudi journalist, noting that his countrymen now felt "isolated … anxious … and threatened," tried to reassure them. Although he hoped the Interim Agreement could lead to a permanent peace, he nevertheless also acknowledged that it was "unhealthy to rely solely on the United States," conversely noting that Saudi Arabia was not alone and that it had other allies, such as Turkey and Egypt, although that was probably of small comfort to his readers.[38] In the wake of the Interim Agreement, in fact, many Saudis became even less hopeful than they had been before. The Saudi press overall became much more openly alarmist, and some Saudis now thought that their earlier fears that the United States might be prepared to "sacrifice its historic allies" had been justified; and the Saudi media, in fact, made it a point to warn that the Kingdom was independent and that it would follow its own interests.[39] Prince Turki Al-Faysal, serving frequently as a bellwether for official Saudi views during King Abd Allah's reign, for his part suggested that there was now "mistrust" in Saudi ruling circles about the U.S. Administration, and he spoke of a "retreating America."[40]

Riyadh's continuing unease

President Obama's one-day fence-mending visit to Saudi Arabia in March 2014 was apparently intended to reassure his Saudi hosts as to America's continuing commitment to their country, with the latter reciprocating with assurances of the basic soundness of the bilateral relationship.[41] U.S. Secretary of State John Kerry's visit to Riyadh in April 2014 evidently had the same intent of reassuring the Saudis. However, while the public speeches by the Saudi hosts on both occasions were guarded and diplomatic, accompanying press commentary explained, in blunter language, what the hosts' intent had been (and what the latter may have said in private). For example, one commentator, describing the meeting with

President Obama as "frank," noted that the King had expressed forcefully to his visitor not only his dismay at the ineffectiveness of U.S. policy on the Palestinian issue and the need to exert pressure on Israel, and the U.S. "abandonment of the Syrian people," but also his desire that Riyadh be informed about the guarantees that Iran had provided with respect to its nuclear program.[42] Further, perhaps reflecting official views, the same commentator went on to criticize President Obama as being "naïve" for his allegedly "unjustified rush" to make a deal with Tehran and warned that Saudi Arabia "will not place all its eggs in one basket [i.e. the United States]."

The Saudi media continued to lambast the U.S. President as gullible and U.S. policy as unclear and confused, and as one sending "the wrong signals to both its allies and adversaries."[43] Claiming that negotiations with Iran were "a waste of time" and accusing the United States of "not doing anything" to stop Iran from acquiring nuclear weapons, one Saudi academic believed that this was intentional as part of a shift in U.S. regional policy. He even accused the United States of wanting to divide and weaken the Arabs in order to subjugate them. And, he asked rhetorically "Is America on the verge of sacrificing its historical strategic ties with the Arab Gulf countries and, in particular, with Saudi Arabia, because the current situation obliges it to do so?"[44] With the Arab world in disarray, and reviving an earlier theme, the same author further claimed that the Arabs now found themselves "between two rapacious and racist countries, the sectarian Shia Persian state on one side and the Zionist Jewish state on the other."

Saudi anxiety spiked openly amid rumors that a deal had been reached at Riyadh's expense. For example, an editorial in *Al-Riyadh* even wondered if there had been "secret deals made under the table" between Iran and the West, "raising doubts among the states who are in conflict with Iran, and who fear that this bartering is not it their interest."[45] In fact, one could interpret the timing and the display of the Saudi SSMs as part of the large-scale Sword of Abd Allah military exercise conducted in April 2014, just after the visits by Obama and Kerry, as reflecting continuing Riyadh's lack of complete confidence in U.S. guarantees on Iran. Commenting on the exercise, an editor concluded that such shows of force were needed because "no country has guarantees in these changing political times," and coupled that assessment with a renewed emphasis that what had worked to stabilize the post-war world had been nuclear deterrence, adding that "he who has a deterrent has power."[46] At times, the Saudis even interpreted U.S. policy on Syria or Ukraine as concrete evidence of U.S. weakness, with one critic assessing that "The crisis in Ukraine has exposed the United States' weakness with respect to Russia, which feeds off the American weakness."[47] A member of the Shura Council shortly thereafter taxed President Obama's policy as one of "capitulation" in the region as a whole and charged it with contributing to instability.[48]

Again, after Secretary of Defense Chuck Hagel had participated in a summit of GCC defense ministers hosted in Jeddah in May 2014 and had reiterated the United States' commitment to the defense of the Gulf, Saudi press commentary continued to voice persistent concerns. For example, one commentator fretted that despite these verbal reassurances Washington had abandoned talk of a missile defense shield for the Gulf against the Iranian threat and, instead, was now focused on a U.S.–Iranian rapprochement, while the GCC (read Saudi Arabia) wanted the United States instead to "put pressure on Iran in order to compel the latter to embark on a more peaceful policy," specifically with regard to the nuclear issue and to Iran's interference in other countries.[49] The Saudi media continued to air such differences, as a typical commentary complained about U.S. regional policy and, in particular, expressed discontent with Washington's policy toward Iran, which that writer termed "a startling détente," while even in late August 2014 another editorialist expressed his suspicion of "an under-the-table" U.S.–Iran rapprochement and his "mistrust of any move that the United States makes."[50] Some even imputed the course of events, which they viewed as U.S. partiality toward Iran, to the alleged ethnic origins or linkages by marriage of some U.S. officials.[51] The Saudis were also irritated that they, as an interested party, were being excluded from the negotiations, although they sometimes expressed this in terms of deploring the absence of GCC participation. An editorial in *Al-Riyadh* in November 2014 crystallized Saudi unease about the ongoing negotiations, regretting that "our interests, our security, and our future are in someone else's hands."[52]

Iran's nuclear threat, Riyadh, and the GCC

Iran's re-emergence on the international stage also presented a challenge to Saudi Arabia's relationships within the GCC, especially in light of Riyadh's continuing fears about Iran's nuclear program, as well as about Tehran's activist regional policies. For most Saudis, their country remains the self-evident choice to lead the region in confronting the Iranian threat. In part, the dire Saudi warnings about a continuing Iranian threat and, in particular, of its nuclear component, were directed not only at a domestic audience but also as a caution to Riyadh's GCC fellow-members that the threat had not gone away. As a Saudi journalist, writing in a Qatari daily, reminded his readers in March 2014, in light of the continuing threat there was still a "necessity for one to have weapons of mass deterrence in order to respond against one's adversary effectively on the battlefield."[53] The advice stood in stark contrast to the official upbeat Qatari view at the time of the negotiating process on Iran's nuclear program, which saw it as a success and felt optimistic that it would lead to a permanent solution.[54]

Furthermore, Saudi Arabia no doubt also wanted to remind its neighbors that it should have the leading role in the GCC. The Saudi media, typically, reflected its annoyance with Oman's role as the go-between in arranging and hosting the initial meetings between Washington and Tehran, stressing that it was Saudi Arabia, not Oman with its "passive" foreign policy style, who should have been the one playing the key role in any negotiations.[55] At the same time, Riyadh expressed its discomfort with what it interpreted as Iran's recent efforts to divide the GCC— which the Saudis view as their own preserve—by courting some of the countries, apparently with some success. One Saudi observer took President Rouhani to task for what he said was the latter's attempt to "satanize" individual Gulf states, namely Saudi Arabia, by bringing up the latter's support of Saddam Husayn during the Iran–Iraq War.[56] Saudi opinionmakers have always been critical of such cracks in a united stand that Riyadh views as vital in confronting Iran. For example, one Saudi academic scolded "those states who enjoy good relations with Tehran," telling them that they:

> must unify their policy vis-à-vis [Iran] with [the policy of] those states who do not have such confidence about [Iran]. A unified Gulf political stand, even if it does not prevent Iranian soft penetration in the Gulf [completely], will nevertheless delay it until new elements appear that will facilitate preventing such penetration or that will bring about new Iranian moderation, based on understanding that such interference in Gulf affairs is an obsolete and emotional idea that is useless for the future.[57]

As a counter to such emerging centrifugal forces and its own intensifying anxiety, Saudi Arabia periodically would re-energize its efforts in support of a unified GCC. In December 2013 a Saudi Foreign Ministry official, Nizar Madani, delivered an address at a security conference in Bahrain in which he stressed that, given the increasing threats, "transition from a phase of coordination and cooperation to one of integration and complete unification is no longer a luxury but has become an urgent imperative."[58] The Saudi media, likewise, carried on a parallel campaign on behalf of this goal. One editorial claimed that what was needed urgently for the GCC was "a unified armament purchasing effort, agreement on strengthening the Peninsula Shield [the GCC combined military force] with a single command structure, and initiating a joint industrialization program and military schools."[59] Another opinion article, pointing to Iran's continuing nuclear threat and announcing that "America is no longer what it once was" and that the Arab world was in a shambles, promoted GCC union as "the only logical solution."[60] Yet another pundit, citing the uncertainties in Iran's policy, and raising the possibility of unspecified secret clauses in any nuclear agreement with Iran, offered a unified GCC as an effective response to such concerns.[61] However, realistically, at that time, even less than before, there seemed to be virtually no chance of success for a GCC policy consensus on a nuclear threat, much less for organizational integration, especially after Riyadh's ostracism of Oman and the bitter flare-up between the Saudis and Qatar over the latter's support for the Muslim Brotherhood and competition for influence in Egypt, Syria, Libya, and other neighboring countries.

Nevertheless, citing the "urgent" need to confront the Iranian nuclear program, Saudi Arabia continued pressuring the other GCC states to at least have greater policy unity on Iran and, in April 2014, a senior officer in the Saudi Land Forces, Staff Major General Prince Nayif bin Ahmad, highlighting the continuing threats to the Gulf, promoted a unified GCC military.[62] While 2014 did see an announcement of the GCC's intention to create joint naval and police task forces and there was greater coordination on foreign policy, the Saudis viewed such measures as insufficient and continued to acknowledge "hesitation and reservations" by some of the states.[63] In fact, by early 2015, an impatient Saudi media was asking rhetorically:

> Will Saudi Arabia have to act forever as the elder brother, especially as the threat in the Gulf today is no longer diplomatic ... or has the time not come for the reservations that some have to end, and to announce unanimously the establishment of Gulf unification?[64]

In the revived emphasis on the need for GCC unification, the Saudis again put forward their own ability to protect the other GCC states as an inducement. One Saudi columnist called his country "a refuge" for the GCC because it had "power."[65] Another Saudi observer suggested to the UAE that it needed Saudi Arabia since Iran "knows that the UAE by itself cannot confront [Iran] because the latter will have nuclear weapons and intercontinental missiles, but [Iran] has forgotten that, God willing, the Kingdom is able to stand up to it as an equal."[66] A press editorial even posited as a selling point for unification to the other Gulf states that this would preclude "relying on protection by others."[67]

Saudi Arabia was able to convince at least some of the GCC states to become more supportive of Riyadh's position at least on the nuclear issue if not on unification. For example, in early 2015, seeking to cement a recent rapprochement with Saudi Arabia after a period of bitter rivalry, Qatar seemed prepared to agree with the Saudi position that if Iran acquired nuclear weapons then "others" could too, according to the Qatari Foreign Minister.[68] And Abu Dhabi's Crown Prince called Saudi Arabia "the backbone of the region's security."[69] Likewise, after the Kuwaiti ruler's visit to Saudi Arabia in February 2015, a Kuwaiti newspaper close to the government called Saudi Arabia the GCC's "beating heart" and openly acknowledged that "the time has come for [Saudi Arabia] to build its own atomic bomb."[70] And later the Kuwait representative to the GCC in June 2015 openly warned in a Saudi newspaper that if Iran did acquire nuclear weapons, then the GCC would also have the same right to do so.[71]

As will be seen later in greater detail, the GCC did attend the May 2015 Camp David Summit with the United States as a group. However, the greater openness to overtures from Iran after the July 2015 Nuclear Agreement by some of the GCC states probably represented the death knell for GCC unification under Riyadh's aegis, at least for the foreseeable future.

The long wait and mounting Saudi anxiety

As the negotiating process dragged on, Saudi frustration with the United States continued to grow amid fears that a deal would be reached at Riyadh's expense. What made the situation worse was that the results of the negotiations were largely inaccessible to Riyadh. Moreover, the Saudis voiced complaints to the effect that the U.S. media did not understand or appreciate the Gulf's concerns about Iran, and the Saudis were frustrated with what they felt was limited access to the U.S. media to explain their country's views.[72] At the same time, there was Saudi discontent with overall U.S. regional policy, and Saudis often claimed there was a linkage between the latter and the ongoing nuclear negotiations. For example, some believed that the United States was deliberately allowing Iran to play a significant role in Iraq and elsewhere in the Middle East as an inducement to Tehran to be more accommodating on the nuclear issue.[73] At the very least, Saudis interpreted President Obama's policy in the Middle East as being weak, thereby encouraging Iran to be more uncompromising on the nuclear issue.[74]

The aborted 2014 Iranian–Saudi détente

On the other hand, during 2014, there were indications that there might be hope for at least a cold détente between Riyadh and Tehran, to a considerable degree spurred by the mutual concern in both capitals about the unexpected and rapid rise of the Al-Qaida offshoot, Islamic State (often known as the "Islamic State in Iraq and Syria"—ISIS). Emerging from a schism within Al-Qaida in 2013, by the summer of 2014 this jihadist entity had become a significant threat not only to the Iraqi and Syrian governments, but also to other regional states, as well as to the international community. In the wake of resounding defeats that ISIS/Islamic State had been able to inflict on the Iraqi and Syrian military in 2014 and the ensuing political turmoil, a growing convergence of interests emerged at the time among Saudi Arabia, Iran, and the United States, all of whom began to view the looming Islamic State threat as central to their security concerns.

Iran, anxious to avoid at the hands of the anti-Shia Islamic State a defeat for the embattled Asad regime in Syria and for the Lebanon-based Shia Hizballah movement, as well as for the majority-Shia Iraqi government, seemed to become more flexible in its dealings with both the United States and its Arab neighbors, including on the nuclear issue. The United States, for its part, also anxious to avoid a further expansion of the Islamic State, with an ensuing threat to its friends and allies in the region and the resurgence of terrorism, also appeared interested to at least coordinate with Iran and Syria in the fight against Islamic State. Conversely, Iran perhaps believed that Washington would now also be more flexible in the ongoing nuclear talks. In addition, of course, Saudi Arabia had also become alarmed by the Islamic State's initial successes and Riyadh appeared prepared to modify its earlier regional policy in order to counter the growing threat to its own security. One Saudi commentator even posited at the time that "all expect a new Saudi–Iranian relationship."[75] Riyadh at the time even seemed willing to reconsider its earlier support for the Syrian opposition seeking to overthrow the Asad regime—a policy which now, however, facilitated the further expansion of the Islamic State—and seemed willing to envision if not a reconciliation with Iran, at least greater cooperation, as part of the fight against the common foe. Likewise, Saudi Arabia took steps to end the cold war in which it had been engaged against its Gulf neighbor Qatar, by sending a high-level delegation to the latter in August 2014.

Significantly, in August 2014, subordinating its deep-seated ideological distaste for Iran to overriding realpolitik concerns, Saudi Arabia, in the person of Foreign Minister Prince Saud Al-Faysal, held talks with Iran's Deputy Foreign Minister Hossein Amir Abdul Lahyan, which both sides described as "positive and constructive," while the Prince invited his Iranian counterpart for a visit to iron out existing differences.[76] More Iranian pilgrims were allowed into Saudi Arabia, the Saudis invited prominent political figure and member of the Assembly of Experts Hashemi Rafsanjani to visit, the two countries' UN ambassadors held frequent meetings, and the Saudi media began to accent the ties that bind the two neighbors, while the formerly common and virulent anti-Iranian rhetoric and anti-Iranian cartoons were greatly toned down in the Saudi press. The Iranian Foreign Ministry, for its part, also stressed the desirability of a dialogue and there seemed for a while to be the possibility of a thaw.[77]

Admittedly, many in Iran believed that the fall in oil prices that had occurred recently was part of a Saudi plot aimed at Iran, limiting the extent of any rapprochement.[78] However, while Saudi Arabia had continued its earlier production levels despite the fall in the price of oil in late 2014, this no doubt had more to do with Riyadh's interest in maintaining market share and in driving competing Western shale oil producers out of business. To be sure, the ancillary benefit of putting pressure on Iran (as well as on Iraq and Russia, of whose policy on Syria and Iran the Saudis were highly critical) was no doubt welcome in Riyadh, and Saudi analysts did openly link the reduction in oil income as a way to increase the pressure that the Iranian government already felt because of the existing nuclear-related sanctions. The Saudi media did label oil "a political weapon" and posited that a deteriorating economic situation would make Tehran more flexible in the nuclear talks or could even lead to destabilizing domestic social unrest and regime change.[79] While a genuine détente could have had a significant impact on Riyadh's outlook on Iran and on the latter's nuclear program, it is doubtful that the degree of rapprochement reached before it was reversed meant any change in Riyadh's continuing anxiety about Tehran's nuclear program, and very likely the thaw had only involved a temporary reordering of Riyadh's security priorities in response to the ISIS threat.

In effect, after the stemming of ISIS's original impetus, which was accompanied by an increased Iranian presence and influence in Iraq, as well as Tehran's continuing propping up of the Asad regime in Syria and increasing influence in Lebanon, Riyadh's earlier concerns about Iran's regional policy reasserted themselves. On the Saudi side, a renewed hardening had already appeared to be in the offing in October 2014, when Foreign Minister Prince Saud Al-Faysal demanded that Iran cease its "occupation" of Syria, which led Tehran in turn to accuse Riyadh of not being serious about developing the bilateral relationship.[80] Nevertheless, according to Tehran's ambassador to Beirut, it was still important for both countries to focus on common enemies such as ISIS and Israel, and symbolic gestures such as the Iranian Foreign Minister's attendance at King Abd Allah's funeral in January 2015 or the Saudi Ambassador's participation in Beirut in a celebration marking the anniversary of the Iranian Revolution that same month seemed to underline Tehran's expectations.[81] Tehran, in fact, seemed to remain optimistic about a rapprochement with Riyadh as late as February 2015, when Rafsanjani, in the immediate aftermath of King Salman's assumption of power, expressed an interest in reopening contacts, while an Iranian journalist was also allowed to call for a bilateral dialogue in the Saudi-controlled *Al-Sharq Al-Awsat* daily.[82]

However, growing Saudi concern about Iranian expansionism was also being fed by Saudi perceptions that a U.S.–Iranian nuclear deal would entail a new benevolence on Washington's part for Iran's regional role. In fact, by March 2015, Saudi conspiracy theories were becoming evident, with typical accusations that the United States was willing to form a strategic alliance with Iran as part of a plot to relinquish control of the Middle East to Tehran in exchange for the latter's agreeing to halt its nuclear program even if only temporarily.[83] Clearly, Saudi Arabia had come to view Iran as a greater danger than ISIS, especially once the latter no longer seemed as threatening.[84]

Now, in the atmosphere of uncertainty and anxiety surrounding the continuing nuclear negotiations, and with a new leadership team, as Crown Prince Salman had acceded to the throne following the death of King Abd Allah in January 2015, Riyadh embarked on a more assertive policy to counter what it interpreted as continuing Iranian expansionism that had been made possible thanks to Tehran's improved relationship with the United States. Riyadh augmented its involvement in Syria and, subsequently, even more visibly in Yemen, when—probably exaggerating an Iranian presence and threat—it launched Operation Decisive Storm in late March 2015 in the form of an air campaign, to be followed up by a ground operation. Predictably, the Saudi-led coalition's campaign against the Shia Houthi-led faction in Yemen, which Riyadh claimed was an Iranian puppet, not only led to a cancellation by Rafsanjani of his planned visit to Saudi Arabia but also resulted in a no-holds barred campaign of mutual vilification in the two countries' media. Perhaps more importantly, the Yemen War may also have served to confirm Iranian hardliners' belief that Saudi Arabia represents a continuing threat to the interests of Iran and its allies, a perception reinforced by Saudi Arabia's large-scale arms buys, which Tehran interpreted as posing an increasing danger to itself.[85]

Significantly, many Saudis openly interpreted Operation Decisive Storm as a direct consequence of their worry over the ongoing nuclear negotiations. One Saudi journalist explicitly linked the two issues, even claiming that the proclamation of the earlier Interim Agreement in November 2013 had "hastened" the launching of the Yemen War.[86] Specifically, the Saudis expressed a concern that the United States would diminish, or even end, its presence in the Middle East once it reached a nuclear agreement with Iran, mistakenly trusting in the latter to maintain stability in the region, while Tehran would be further emboldened to expand; therefore, for such observers, it was imperative for Saudi Arabia to show that it could take care of itself by dealing with Yemen.[87] Riyadh, in fact, viewed the Yemen operation as directed primarily against Iran, that is as a way to demonstrate Saudi Arabia's lack of fear of the latter and as a way of dealing a major blow to Tehran's prestige, and Yemen may have seemed a geographic theater where Riyadh believed it could have a military advantage. In the event, despite its ability to devastate largely unprotected targets and its insistent claims of victory, and despite the fact that by mid-2015, the Saudi-led coalition had succeeded in driving back the over-extended Houthi coalition from many Sunni areas, prospects for a decisive victory still appeared to remain elusive. Nevertheless, the Saudi media routinely portrayed the operation as a resounding success which had "bloodied Iran's nose" and had "shredded the Persian dream."[88] Some even saw the operation as a slap at the United States, as well as at the latter's "new allies [i.e. Iran]," with the intent of showing Riyadh's irritation with President Obama, whom the same journalist labeled as "the problem," even though, realistically, it is highly doubtful whether Saudi Arabia could have conducted such a campaign without significant support from the U.S. military and civilian contractors.[89]

Refocusing on the nuclear negotiations

In a way, Riyadh's launching of Operation Decisive Storm, at least at first, seemed to boost the Saudis' confidence in their country's influence on the international scene, with distinct echoes of their views on the nuclear situation. According to a professor at the Saudi Foreign Ministry's Diplomatic Institute, for example, the operation not only confirmed the Arabs' power but also made clear Saudi Arabia's position that its national security and, specifically, its right to acquire nuclear weapons were non-negotiable.[90] According to one unnamed Saudi official, Saudi Arabia felt that its operation in Yemen would have an impact on the ongoing nuclear negotiations with Iran, perhaps hoping that the negotiators would now be emboldened to harden their stance toward Tehran, while the resulting new-found confidence encouraged Riyadh to request greater concrete compensation in the nuclear field, specifically that "the Kingdom will consider anything that [Iran] gets from the Great Powers relating to facilities, technology, the degree of uranium enrichment allowed, and the number of centrifuges as also its right to acquire in order to develop its own nuclear program."[91]

This period also saw a return of harsh media criticism of U.S. policy toward Iran's nuclear program and of President Obama personally. For one columnist, the United States simply did not know how to use its power to defend its friends or its own interests, leading to, as that columnist feared, a nuclear agreement that would represent "the crowning act of a [U.S.–Iranian] alliance."[92] The editor of *Al-Sharq Al-Awsat* even put the situation in the form of a zero-sum game, claiming that the United States' desire to reach a nuclear agreement with Iran and at the same time retain its old alliances, was impossible.[93] Saudi observers dismissed Obama as the worst U.S. president of the twentieth and twenty-first centuries, called his Administration weak and vacillating, equating it to "a theater company that frightens no one," taxed American policy as "not to be taken seriously," and accused Secretary of State Kerry of being easy-going and of having "a weak personality."[94] Some critics accused President Obama of having "sold out most of the

United States' traditional allies" in order to make a deal with Iran so that he could point to one achievement for his presidency, while others attributed his eagerness to deal with Iran to a quest for "personal glory," accusing him of not appreciating the damage his actions caused to traditional alliances.[95] Still others taxed his policy as one based on dreams, delusions, and on "a blind, superficial vision," and accused President Obama of "political ignorance," of being naïve, and of having been duped by an Iran that was prostrate because of the sanctions.[96]

Conversely, Saudis viewed Israeli policy on the Iranian nuclear issue as mostly positive and welcomed the latter's opposition to an envisioned agreement with Tehran, both because it was thought Tel-Aviv might still use force against Iran's nuclear program and because of its perceived influence in the U.S. political system and media.[97] Not surprisingly, when Israeli Prime Minister Benjamin Netanyahu delivered a blistering speech to the U.S. Congress in March 2015 that was critical of the Obama Administration's handling of negotiations with Iran, many Saudis expressed their support, even if only grudgingly. Of course, the Saudi media was careful to underline that basic differences, such as on the Palestinian issue, still divided Saudi Arabia and Israel; and some Saudi journalists urged caution in embracing Israel and were anxious to avoid giving the impression that the Kingdom considered Israel a friend.[98] Nevertheless, most Saudi opinion focused on the utility of Israel's congruent opposition to Iran's potential acquisition of nuclear weapons and, as one journalist maintained, "even though [Netanyahu] is my enemy he compelled me to listen to him."[99] In fact, as another journalist asked rhetorically, "Is it embarrassing to admit a point of agreement with the Israeli enemy? … Netanyahu said what we say every day behind closed doors."[100] An academic, in fact, acknowledged openly that what Netanyahu had said was correct and repeated that Iran was now more dangerous than Israel.[101]

Intensifying activism abroad to influence the nuclear negotiations

As part of its strategy during this period of waiting, Riyadh also intensified its political activity abroad on several fronts both to influence the ongoing nuclear negotiations and to make provision for any potential outcome from those talks.

Courting the Great Powers

One aspect of this reinvigorated Saudi activism was a diplomatic effort to influence some players—France and Russia, in particular—on the 5+1 negotiating team. For example, in March 2015, while still Foreign Minister, Prince Saud Al-Faysal pressed his British counterpart to take a tough stand in the nuclear negotiations, telling him that Iran did not deserve a nuclear agreement.[102]

In the case of France, the Saudis had reportedly been building up their efforts for some time to convince Paris to adopt a harder line in the nuclear negotiations.[103] The courting of French support included praise in the Saudi media, closer political ties, the signing of weapons contracts (including financing one for Lebanon), and promises of participation in the Kingdom's civilian nuclear program.[104] Deputy Crown Prince Muhammad bin Salman's June 2015 European trip saw a firming of the Saudi–French relationship, with a Saudi arms buy worth billions of dollars and an agreement to participate in the building of two nuclear reactors in the Kingdom. And, on this occasion, Paris was said to also have expressed support for obliging Israel to relinquish its nuclear arsenal as part of a nuclear-free Middle East, an enduring Saudi demand.[105] To be sure, the Saudis recognized that it was Washington that had the decisive say in the negotiations, while the other negotiators on the 5+1 team ultimately would have to go along with the results.[106] More basically, rather than representing a realistic alternative to the United States, since neither France nor any other country would have the capability necessary to defend Saudi Arabia, this gambit may have been aimed instead at encouraging Paris to act as a tough negotiator with Iran on the nuclear issue and on other regional issues.[107]

As part of its diplomatic outreach, there was also an initiative by Riyadh to rebuild its relationship with Russia. Although Riyadh seems to have attempted a rapprochement with Moscow already in 2013, reportedly offering a lucrative arms deal in return for Russia's abandoning Syrian strongman Bashshar Al-Asad, it had been rebuffed at the time.[108] There were reports again in late 2014 of intensified Saudi overtures to Russia, with Riyadh offering the latter to limit Saudi oil production so that prices would rise, asking in return Moscow's support on Syria and in the nuclear negotiations with Iran; and the diplomatic effort continued and gathered momentum in 2015.[109] At the time, Saudi observers specifically linked a perceived greater Russian receptivity to stronger ties with Saudi Arabia to an opportunity to put pressure on Moscow to reduce its support for Iran's nuclear position.[110] In fact, by early 2015 Russia's economic situation had deteriorated in the wake of sanctions imposed by the West after Russia's aggression against Ukraine and due to the fall in oil prices, and apparently Moscow had become increasingly amenable to new Saudi overtures. Although significant differences between Riyadh and Moscow persisted over the latter's congruence with Iranian policy on Syria, Yemen, and Iraq, as well as because of its friendly ties with Iran, this Saudi approach seemed to bear fruit and culminated in the June 2015 visit by Deputy Crown Prince Muhammad bin Salman, when a series of bilateral agreements were reached. These deals provided significant inducements to Moscow in the form of massive arms contracts, cooperation on space projects, economic investment in Russia, and an agreement for Russia to be the main contractor for most of the nuclear reactors planned by the Kingdom, which some Saudi observers viewed as the centerpiece of all the agreements.[111] Furthermore, an apparent deal was also struck to review Saudi Arabia's oil production, which would address the low oil prices that had hurt Russia's oil export earnings.

Whatever the economic aspects of such diplomatic gambits, Saudi commentators interpreted their political and military significance as paramount, and viewed as their intent to send a signal to and exert pressure on the United States, as well as to influence other countries' policies on the Middle East and, specifically, their position on the still ongoing nuclear talks with Iran. As the Saudi media made clear, the visits to France and Russia were to be seen as a sign of Riyadh's displeasure with Washington's stand on the Iranian nuclear issue, which had caused the bilateral relationship to "languish" and had triggered the need for Riyadh to "seek other political and economic options."[112] One Saudi commentator even claimed that the rapprochement with Moscow was in retaliation for the United States' having "stabbed the Saudis in the back" with its surprise rapprochement with Iran, and that the expected nuclear agreement represented "an important political turning point" in the relationship.[113] For another Saudi columnist, Prince Muhammad's visits had marked "a turning point in U.S.–Saudi relations."[114] Specifically referring to the nuclear reactor deal with Moscow, this journalist observed that Riyadh was unhappy with how Washington had conducted the nuclear negotiations with Iran, and explicitly termed the Saudi–Russian nuclear agreement as "a strong message to America." Although he was quick to add that ties with the United States remained solid and that the Saudi–Russian rapprochement represented only one nail in the coffin of the Saudi–U.S. relationship and that many more would be needed to end that alliance, he nevertheless noted that doubts had arisen recently as to whether Washington understood Riyadh's security priorities, leading Riyadh to seek other options. However, all this might change yet again, he suggested, depending on how a new administration in Washington might view the situation. Saudi Arabia may also have hoped that the United States might now become more responsive to Saudi interests regarding Iran as a way to limit Riyadh's burgeoning relationship with Moscow. Indeed, some Saudis believed that re-emerging U.S. concern about Russian policy in what one Saudi political commentator claimed was a new cold war meant that any Iranian successes in the Middle East also represented a gain for Moscow, which would worry the West.[115]

How successful Riyadh's diplomacy was to be in affecting Russian and French policies was questionable, as shortly thereafter, for example, Moscow called for an end to the arms embargo on Iran and agreed to cooperate with Iran in the nuclear field, prompting the Saudi media to voice its surprise and disappointment.[116] Similarly, reports in the Saudi media suggested annoyance with what was portrayed as France's inordinate haste in normalizing relations with Tehran following the July 2015 Nuclear Agreement.[117]

Reviving the concept of a nuclear-free zone

Another of Riyadh's responses during this period was to revive what had become its moribund promotion of a WMD-free (essentially a nuclear-free) zone for the Middle East, both through official channels and in the Saudi media. For example, Foreign Minister Prince Saud Al-Faysal engaged in a wide-ranging diplomatic effort—focusing specifically on nuclear weapons—in October 2013 and again in April and May 2014.[118] As part of this campaign, Prince Turki Al-Faysal also hinted in 2013 at the possibility of accepting a nuclear umbrella if a nuclear-free zone could be arranged.[119] As the nuclear negotiations between the 5+1 Group and Iran progressed, Saudi Arabia intensified its traditional calls for a nuclear-free Middle East at every high-level meeting in which it participated.[120]

In the event, an international conference sponsored by the United Nations in May 2015, intended to address the possibility of a nuclear-free Middle East, proved unsuccessful, with U.S. representatives blaming Egypt and "other Arab states" of undermining the negotiations, as they had insisted also on Israel's compliance with any constraints as a defining condition.[121] However, as in earlier times, such gambits on the Saudis' part appear to have been largely a conscious public relations measure to gain "the moral high ground," since Riyadh had continued to insist on Israel's agreement to also relinquish its own nuclear arsenal as a sine qua non, fully aware that this was extremely unlikely for the foreseeable future.[122] In a way, this could be viewed not only as a way to put pressure on both Iran and Israel, but also as a means of justifying any steps Riyadh might take if, as is likely, such Israeli disarmament did not occur and if Iran eventually were to acquire nuclear weapons.

The April 2015 Framework Agreement and the May 2015 Camp David Summit

It is fair to say that, in light of the mounting Saudi criticism and skepticism, Washington felt the need to repair the bilateral relationship, as suggested by its intensified diplomatic activity targeted at Riyadh throughout early 2015—which was no doubt intended to reassure the Saudis about the ongoing negotiations—and included visits to Saudi Arabia by President Obama, the Commander of U.S. Central Command, and Secretary of State John Kerry (twice), as well as at least two telephone conferences between President Obama and King Salman. Officially, Riyadh sought to present a less dramatic and more positive public image of the U.S.–Saudi bilateral relationship which, of course, was still basically sound and of significant benefit to Riyadh, especially as there were no genuinely plausible alternative options. Typically, Saudi press summaries of President Obama's telephone conversation with King Salman in April 2015 underlined that the latter had termed relations between the two countries as being "solid," a theme that Saudi Foreign Minister Adil Al-Jubeir reiterated after Secretary of State Kerry's visit, when Al-Jubeir stressed the "strong … natural shared interests" between the two countries.[123] The Saudi media, however, was apparently allowed to characterize the results of Kerry's March 2015 visit less diplomatically as useless, with one editor dismissing it outright ("thanks for nothing"), another accusing Kerry of trying to "bamboozle us," while others assessed the visit's results as "very poor," and still others accused Kerry of "hypocrisy and lies," and again reproached Washington for having abandoned its old allies for Iran.[124]

From a Saudi perspective, the flurry of diplomatic activity with the United States, the other GCC states and beyond on the nuclear issue probably at least helped burnish the new ruling team's image by suggesting that Saudi Arabia was a significant player and, typically, one Saudi newspaper could now claim that "Riyadh is the political decisionmaking center for dealing with the region and even with many other areas of the world," while King Salman was "an exceptional monarch in every sense" who was "creating the required policy for the country and the region."[125] And, whatever the tangible results of such diplomacy, Saudi decisionmakers at least would have been seen at home and in the region as doing something, rather than being perceived as just passive observers, especially with a new king now on the throne. The Saudi media, in fact, praised the new Saudi administration's vigorous diplomatic activity, even claiming that now Saudi Arabia would shape the Middle East's history, and that the Kingdom now had developed such influence that it could change other countries' policies, including those of the Great Powers.[126]

A Framework Agreement which set the basic parameters for final agreement was reached on 2 April 2015, and included provisions to extend Iran's breakout time to one year for the next 10 years, reduce uranium stockpiles and enrichment for 15 years, limit the enrichment level and the number of centrifuges, and entail the inspection of major sites for 25 years, while an arms purchase embargo would apply for five years and for SSMs for eight years, and economic sanctions would be lifted in stages.[127] Although tough negotiations on implementation mechanisms remained, the clear implication from the Framework Agreement was that a final deal with Iran now would very likely become a reality, which only increased Saudi anxiety and triggered an even more intense outburst of Saudi discontent. At best, in fact, many Saudi commentators believed any agreement would just give Iran a "warrior's time out," as one academic termed it, with another observer positing that all Iran would do would be to place its nuclear quest "on the shelf temporarily," taking advantage of the opportunity to maintain its existing nuclear program while rebuilding its economy and preparing for a resumption of its quest for the bomb once the stipulated period had passed.[128] Typically, a Saudi columnist assessed the Framework Agreement as "not just bad but disastrous," taxed President Obama as being naïve and reckless if he believed Iranian promises, and accused him of gambling with U.S., Middle East, and international security.[129] Likewise, as one academic put it, for Iran "agreements are made to be broken" and the latter "will violate agreements before the ink dries."[130]

In fact, both Riyadh and Washington increasingly came to feel that more would need to be done to reassure the Saudis and to maintain the traditional relationship, and a summit, to be held at the presidential resort of Camp David, was called for mid-May 2015, one which the GCC states would attend as a group. Nevertheless, the Saudis remained skeptical about the upcoming summit, with one Saudi journalist warning that this event would be "perhaps the last chance for the White House Administration to clarify the nuclear agreement with Iran and to show greater resolve on Iranian interference in the region."[131] And, according to the Saudis, the GCC wanted to show the United States that "the Gulf's eggs are not all in one basket."[132] As the summit approached, an influential journalist, while terming it a positive step, nevertheless worried that the signing of a nuclear agreement would only embolden Iran, whom he characterized as "an active bacteria," since he expected an agreement would only "trim Iran's nuclear nails."[133]

Likewise, he wondered what guarantees would emerge from the summit, cautioning that increased U.S. arms sales and even a missile defense shield would not be enough, but that what was needed from Washington was "a clear line in the sand and the sea against any Iranian attack." Echoing these same concerns and arguments, another Saudi analyst recommended that at the upcoming summit "the GCC must demand the same political and technical rights as the ones that Iran will get in a nuclear agreement."[134] The Saudi security adviser to the Head of the GCC, for his part, asking what could be expected at the upcoming summit, noted that the United States would try to "sell" the agreement being negotiated with Iran, but that the key issues were whether the United States could reassure the GCC on Iran and to what extent Washington was prepared to defend the Gulf, questions on which, he claimed, "Gulf decisionmakers have major justifiable doubts." As he saw it, Iran and the United States were now cooperating and, with what he termed was a diminishing American presence in the region, Iran was bound to play a larger role. He did not expect the upcoming summit to produce any breakthroughs and his recommendation, therefore, was that even though the Gulf states could not find a realistic replacement for the United States, they should nevertheless also develop stronger ties with the other Great Powers.[135]

The summit, held on 13–14 May 2015, resulted in a joint U.S.–GCC statement in which the United States envisioned a new U.S.–GCC "strategic partnership" and committed itself to the GCC states' territorial integrity, promising to potentially use force in the event of aggression against those states, as well as offering assurances that America's intent was to deny Iran nuclear weapons, and promised to provide daily briefings until the expected agreement was reached.[136] A few days later, King Salman revealed that, in a phone conversation with President Obama, the "deep-rooted strategic and historical relationship between the two countries had been reaffirmed."[137]

It took a few days for the Saudi media to digest the results of the summit—or to receive official guidance—and then it appeared anxious to portray the event as a success for Saudi Arabia, probably as a way of convincing the domestic and regional publics that the Saudi leaders were influential and respected, not least by having obliged President Obama to convene the summit in the first place after what Saudi commentators described as public pressure by the GCC and "a diplomatic and media battle."[138] One Saudi commentator even insisted that the GCC leaders had met with President Obama from a position of strength, which showed that the GCC could not be ignored, and that this was due in great part to the efforts of the "charismatic" King Salman.[139] Some of the media sought to reassure their audience and, as one academic expressed confidently, "we told the world that neither Iran nor its nuclear weapons nor all its plots will succeed in marginalizing us or in frightening us."[140] Specifically, as an indication of success—and thanks to the GCC's power, which it was said the United States recognized—President Obama purportedly was now convinced of the threat that Iran posed and had been persuaded to reaffirm the use of U.S. military power to support America's Gulf allies, as well as to reiterate that Iran must not get nuclear weapons.[141] In fact, some portrayed the Camp David summit as a turning point, claiming that it had proved that the Gulf now had the initiative and that, while still cooperating with the United States, the GCC was now able to take matters into its own hands.[142]

However, even after the summit, as a prominent Saudi commentator noted, "there are still those who are skeptical."[143] And the Saudi media was soon concentrating on what it saw as the summit's shortcomings. Basic Saudi concerns remained unchanged before and after the summit to the effect that, at best, a nuclear agreement perhaps would provide a delay of a few years while Iran rebuilt its financial situation, after which it would even increase its expansionism.[144] One commentator continued to impute "political hypocrisy" as the basis for President Obama's policy, and claimed that the summit had forced the President to "reveal his cards and his contradictions."[145] Many were disappointed that President Obama had not linked the Iranian nuclear issue with a solution of other regional issues, with one critic terming the summit's results, therefore, as "nothing new."[146] Saudi columnists argued that the Gulf countries did not really get the reassurance they had wanted and asked why the GCC had not been granted the same status as Japan or South Korea in terms of U.S. nuclear guarantees, concluding that, since the United States had different political and ideological values than the GCC did, Congress would never have gone along with such an alliance with the GCC out of concern for Israeli interests, and complained that this indicated the United States had "little consideration for the Arabs."[147] Another observer remarked that there had already been defense cooperation even before the summit and that it would have been easy for the United States to formalize that relationship by means of a defense pact which would have served as a deterrent to Iran. The failure to do so, he concluded, put into doubt the reassurances President Obama had given at the summit, doubts which he claimed could increase as the U.S.–Iranian rapprochement developed and a nuclear agreement was signed, and which would encourage Iran to continue its current regional policy.[148] One commentator underlined that Saudi Arabia needed "more than just theoretical promises."[149]

Other Saudi commentators expressed their continued resentment at U.S. regional policies, with one even attributing Washington's alleged willingness to accept a continuing Iranian threat so that it could sell more arms to the GCC states, a traditional Saudi suspicion.[150] One Saudi journalist even appealed to Washington's self-interest, reminding the latter that "Saudi Arabia is more important to you than Iran is."[151] Another columnist claimed that "some" had believed the relationship with the United States would be eternal and unchangeable but, "it became clear that the repeated U.S. assurances to the Gulf states are no longer sufficient to compensate for the changes in its policy in the region, which has led to its position as a trusted ally to wobble." As the same columnist added, neither the United States nor the Gulf would end the alliance anytime soon but, nevertheless, he advised the Gulf countries to also look elsewhere for new allies and recommended that some distancing from Washington was desirable.[152] By late June 2015, a professor at the Saudi Foreign Ministry's Diplomatic Institute was prepared to conclude that "the traditional allies [i.e. the United States] are not interested in supporting security in our region and there is no consensus."[153] Some called into question what they saw as the Obama Administration's assumption that promoting a nuclear agreement would lead to a gradual regime change in Tehran, or at least that Iran would moderate its policies. The Saudi consensus was that the Iranian system would not change its character, with critics labeling such assumptions as "unrealistic."[154] Already by early 2015, in fact, Saudi critics had come to see little difference between Rouhani and his predecessors, and were convinced that any successor to Khamene'i would be the same as the latter.[155]

Reflecting their disappointment with President Obama, many Saudis now saw Congress—rather than the Administration—as a more conducive venue in which to address Gulf security and the nuclear issue (which constituted a reversal in the traditional Saudi approach, as Congress in the past had always been troublesome for Riyadh, whether in dealing with prospective arms deals, human rights, or allegations of softness on terrorism).[156] Saudis recognized that the GCC did not have the ability to stop an agreement from being concluded but, as it was not yet complete, they hoped that Israel or U.S. domestic opinion through Congress, or even France, might be able to do so.[157] One columnist, while ruing the fact that Camp David had provided only an American restatement of its traditional commitments and nothing more definite, as a consolation, expressed a faint hope that "perhaps when all is said and done, there will not be a nuclear agreement."[158] Yet another journalist believed that the GCC at least had succeeded in complicating President Obama's negotiations with Iran.[159] On the other hand, one Saudi commentator did worry that the U.S. Congress just might go along with the President on a nuclear agreement and therefore asked rhetorically "Will the Arabs act as just onlookers to an agreement or will they acquire a nuclear arsenal to balance Iran's power?"[160]

Riyadh's continuing nuclear warnings

As an underlying counterpoint throughout the period that the nuclear negotiations were in progress during the Rouhani era, the Saudi media often complemented its criticism with a repetition of its long-standing warnings that if Iran was allowed to acquire nuclear weapons then Saudi Arabia still retained the option of also doing so. Highlighting this reserve position very likely was meant to not only reassure the country's domestic constituency and to serve as leverage to influence the ongoing negotiations, but also to further develop and legitimate the environment in which—in a worst case scenario—if Iran did acquire nuclear weapons, Riyadh might best be prepared to follow suit.

Saudi opinionmakers continued to stress that Saudi Arabia had not abandoned its own nuclear option and that it would have recourse to that alternative if necessary. Sometimes the warning was expressed in general terms, with cautions that a changed regional balance resulting from a nuclear breakout by Iran "will oblige the other countries in [the region] to arm, precipitating a nuclear arms race."[161] At other times, the focus was clearly on Saudi Arabia. In particular, against a background of a perceived reduction in the United States' reliability, Saudi observers stressed more strongly than ever the need for self-defense. As one analyst saw it, Iran was "on the nuclear threshold," which would then "place the region on the threshold of hell" and, based on that, he emphasized the need for national self-reliance, noting that the new reality required "the increase of the components of the regional countries' own power in order to meet Iran's possible nuclear blackmail."[162] While indicating that Saudi Arabia would feel obliged to do something, some opinionmakers, though seeking to remain discreet, were nevertheless fairly transparent in their intent. For example, the head of the Shura Council's Foreign Affairs Committee noted coyly, "I believe that Saudi Arabia will also take steps if Iran takes steps to acquire nuclear weapons."[163] Others were more specific, as was one newspaper editor who remarked that a nuclear Iran would oblige Saudi Arabia to acquire "the same weapon."[164] Other journalists were still more explicit, with one highlighting the success and desirability of nuclear deterrence and asking rhetorically "Why shouldn't [Saudi Arabia] have the right to acquire nuclear weapons for deterrence?"[165] In fact, he suggested that Saudi Arabia take advantage of the ongoing negotiating process, as he claimed that Pakistan and Iran had done before, and try to acquire its own nuclear weapons.

Perhaps not surprisingly under the circumstances, in April 2014, at a conference on security held in Bahrain, Prince Turki Al-Faysal, while stressing that the GCC felt no hostility toward Iran, nevertheless expressed his concern with Iran's unclear position on nuclear weapons. As a result, he concluded, "The need to ensure our security forces us to work toward creating a balance with Iran in the field of nuclear knowledge and to prepare for any eventuality with Iran's nuclear program."[166] That same month, as if to underline the warning to Iran, as part of Saudi Arabia's "Sword of Abd Allah" exercise, when two nuclear-capable CSS-2 missiles were included in the final ceremonial parade, a Saudi journalist noted that there was "a message specifically for [Saudi Arabia's] Iranian neighbor, who seeks to acquire nuclear weapons," and he identified the CSS-2 as "a message to those forces that harbor evil for the security of Saudi Arabia and the Gulf."[167]

As noted already, skepticism continued in Saudi Arabia that even an agreement would not necessarily stop Iran's quest for nuclear weapons, and a retired Saudi military officer believed that even with an agreement "the Persian state will not abandon developing its first atomic bomb no matter what the cost, even if only after a delay."[168] Based on that assumption, the same officer was adamant that, in order to maintain the regional balance, "it will be necessary for Saudi Arabia to join the nuclear club."[169] Prince Turki Al-Faysal also expressed his pessimism again and predicted—or warned—in March 2015 that "any deal that comes out of Iran now will open the door for proliferation."[170] The Saudi media endorsed his statement, with one journalist adding that if Iran obtained nuclear weapons Saudi Arabia "as it has said clearly before ... will not just remain with its arms folded."[171] Other Saudi columnists also argued that the Kingdom must not be submissive to the United States and, instead, must rely on itself and "acquire a nuclear arsenal similar to that of Israel and Iran."[172] Voicing his concern about the April 2015

Framework Agreement, another commentator likewise warned that "the Middle East countries ... have the right to acquire a nuclear weapon that is at the same time both peaceful and a deterrent."[173] Official circles, too, continued to hint at a Saudi weapon, albeit discreetly, as was the case with then-Ambassador to Washington Adel Al-Jubeir who, when asked in March 2015 whether Riyadh would acquire nuclear weapons in response to a nuclear Iran, replied that "the kingdom of Saudi Arabia will take whatever measures are necessary in order to protect its security."[174] Local sources interpreted such statements as more definitive, with one academic, for example, explaining Al-Jubeir's reply in a tribal newspaper as indicating that "Saudi Arabia will develop its own nuclear program and will manufacture its own atom bomb in order to counter the military program in Iran."[175]

The Saudi media often expressed such demands in terms of equity and compensation for any concessions in the nuclear field granted to Iran as part of any agreement. For example, as a silver lining to the 2013 Geneva Interim Agreement, which he viewed as an inadequate brake on Iran, one Saudi analyst suggested that, at least, other regional powers, with Saudi Arabia being understood as one of them, could now demand equal rights for their own current or future nuclear programs.[176] Others, likewise, threatened that if Iran was allowed to acquire nuclear weapons then the "Gulf states" too had a right to the same capability "for an equivalent balance."[177] At the very least, the Saudis demanded strategic parity, claiming for their country exactly the same rights in the nuclear field as were to be given to Iran, for example the right to enrich uranium to a certain level, justifying such demands by highlighting the need to maintain a balance of power.[178]

Even after the May 2015 Camp David Summit, as before, some Saudis were open about the continuing need to acquire nuclear weapons, as was the case with an aerospace engineer who argued that "an observer cannot imagine how great the need is for the Kingdom and the GCC to acquire nuclear weapons to deter these two adversaries [i.e. Iran and Israel] and other enemies, both declared and undeclared, even if only by purchase initially."[179] Some feared that a future U.S. president could well opt for just containing a nuclear Iran, leading one analyst to conclude that it was therefore best for Saudi Arabia to rely on itself, with its own nuclear weapons.[180] As a retired Saudi general likewise concluded, "If Iran declares that it has an atom bomb, the following day we will also declare that we have one, since we must defend ourselves."[181] Another retired Saudi general also concluded, in June 2015, that Iran had succeeded in the international negotiations process, since it was expected that it would be able to maintain many nuclear facilities under the guise of a civilian program, which it could then use to develop nuclear weapons. Imputing to Iran the belief in the return of the occulted Mahdi that for him implied a willingness to kill to bring that about and a resulting disrespect for the Law of War on Iran's part and, "in the absence of credible guarantees on this score," he concluded that in that case only mutual deterrence would work and that "the time has come for serious action to acquire nuclear power and nuclear weapons."[182] Furthermore, in his view one could no longer rely on "our

American ally ... whose sugary promises have become disgusting," and Saudi Arabia would now have to rely on itself.[183] At the same time, he assessed a U.S. offer to provide an anti-missile defense shield as a positive defensive step. However, in his opinion, this was insufficient, since the system could be swamped and tricked by decoys and could not guarantee that it would stop all incoming missiles. Calling such an anti-missile defense shield "a trap lulling us and making us depend on others," he viewed it at best as a stopgap measure and held that it ought to be "a spur to improve our offensive and defensive capabilities and to acquire nuclear weapons."[184]

Notes

1 Ibrahim Al-Athimin, "Iran wa-mufawadat Kazakhstan" [Iran and the Negotiations in Kazakhstan], *Al-Yawm*, 27 February 2013, www.alyaum.com/News/art/73493.html.
2 Ayman Al-Hammad, "Dawr duwal al-taawun fi muhadathat al-milaff al-nawawi al-irani" [The Role of the GCC Countries in the Talks on the Iranian Nuclear Issue], *Al-Riyadh*, 21 February 2013, www.alriyadh.com/2013/02/21/article811918.html.
3 Fahd Al-Dhiyabi, "Saud Al-Faysal: Yajib tamkin al-shab al-suri min al-difa an nafsih, wa-Iran ghayr sadiqa hawl barnamijha al-nawawi" [Saud Al-Faysal: The Syrian People Must Be Empowered to Defend Themselves, and Iran Is Not Sincere about Its Nuclear Program], *Al-Sharq Al-Awsat*, 13 February 2013, www.aawsat.com/print.asp?did=717110&issueno=12496.
4 Abd Al-Munim Mustafa, "Ra'is nawawi fi Faris" [A Nuclear President in Persia], *Al-Madina*, 14 June 2013, www.al-madina.com/printhtml/459763.
5 Turki Al-Dakhil, "Wuud Ruhani—hal tusaddaq?" [Rouhani's Promises—Are They to Be Believed?], *Al-Riyadh*, 20 June 2013, www.alriyadh.com/2013/06/20/article845289.html, and Rashid Fahd Al-Rashid "Al-Ra'is al-irani al-sabi wa-duwal Al-Khalij" [Iran's Seventh President and the Gulf States], *Al-Riyadh*, 17 June 2013, www.alriyadh.com/2013/06/17/article844417.html.
6 Ali Al-Jahili, "Hal fihim mutadil?" [Are There any Moderates Among Them?], *Al-Iqtisadiya*, 20 June 2013, www.aleqt.com/2013/06/20/articl_764471.print (hereafter Al-Jahili, "Hal fihim").
7 Yusuf Al-Kuwaylit, "Ruhani: Hal yunhi marhalat al-thawra li-maslahat al-dawla?" [Rouhani: Will He End the Revolutionary Phase for Interest of State?], *Al-Riyadh*, 29 September 2013, and Yusuf Al-Kuwaylit, "Iran: al-wuduh fi al-ru'ya am mabda' 'al-taqiya'?!", [Iran: Clarity of Vision or a Fundamental Concept of "Taqiya"?!], *Al-Riyadh*, 3 June 2014, www.alriyadh.com/940991 (hereafter Al-Kuwaylit, "Iran: al-wuduh").
8 Al-Jahili, "Hal fihim."
9 Hamad bin Abd Allah Al-Luhaydan, "Hal yastati al-ra'is Ruhani lajm al-tatarruf al-irani?" [Can President Rouhani Rein in Iranian Extremism?], *Al-Riyadh*, 21 June 2013, www.alriyadh.com/2013/06/21/article845552.html, and Khalid Al-Dakhil, "Marhalat al-hudu' wa'l-hifazh ala al-siyasa al-kharijiya" [A Quiet Phase While Maintaining the [Same] Foreign Policy], *Anba'ukum*, 21 June 2013, www.anbacom.com/print?action=print&m=articlesm&id=16877.
10 Muhammad bin Abd Al-Latif Al Al-Shaykh, "Al-Iraniyun wa-Obama" [The Iranians and Obama], *Al-Jazira*, 27 September 2013, www.al-jazirah.com/2013/20130927/lp7.htm, and Ali Al-Ammari, "Iran takhsha al-sinariyu al-suri wa-amrika ta'mul idhanha talafiyan li-darba askariya" [Iran Fears a Syrian Scenario and America Hopes through Its Concessions to Obviate the Need for a Military Strike], *Al-Yawm*, 25 September 2013, www.alyaum.com/News/art/96016.html.
11 Mutlaq Saud Al-Mtiri, "Al-Ayn al-thalitha wa'l-tafawud ma Tihran" [Eyes in the Back of Your Head When Negotiating with Tehran], *Al-Riyadh*, 23 September 2013,

www.al-riyadh.com/2013/09/23/article869831.html (hereafter Al-Mtiri, "Al-Ayn al-thalitha").
12 Ibid.
13 Ali bin Hamad Al-Khashiban, "Hal takhsar Amrika shirakat muhimma fi Al-Sharq Al-Awsat?" [Will America Lose Important Partnerships in the Middle East?], *Al-Riyadh*, 28 October 2013, www.alriyadh.com/2013/10/28/article879060.html (hereafter Al-Khashiban, "Hal takhsar Amrika").
14 Prince Saud Al-Faysal, at the press conference with the Italian Foreign Minister, reported in Abd Allah Al-Hasani, "Saud Al-Faysal: Nurahhib bi-raghbat Tihran fi tahsin al-alaqat wa'l-ibra fi'l-ijra" [Saud Al-Faysal: We Welcome Tehran's Desire to Improve Relations But the Proof Is in the Pudding], *Al-Riyadh*, 4 October 2013, www.alriyadh.com/2013/10/04/article872730.html.
15 "Khamene'i yakshif nawaya al-nawawi al-haqiqiya" [Khamene'i Reveals the Nuclear Program's True Intent], *Makka*, 21 June 2014, www.makkahnewspaper.com/makka hNews/politics/55200.
16 Hasna' Al-Gunayir, "Iran wa-Isra'il wa'l-arab baynahuma" [Iran, Israel and the Arabs between Them], *Al-Riyadh*, 8 March 2015, www.alriyadh.com/1027977 (hereafter Al-Gunayir, "Iran wa-Isra'il"). The literal Arabic equivalent provided was that of "the devil getting into heaven."
17 Hasan Nasir Al-Zhahiri, "Al-Thalab al-irani" [The Iranian Fox], *Al-Madina*, 17 April 2015, www.al-madina.com/printhtml/601505.
18 "Iran wa-Amrika: Al-Hifazh ala ittifaq nawawi asab min iqrarih" [Iran and America: Preserving a Nuclear Agreement Is Harder than Reaching One], *Al-Iqtisadiya*, 15 March 2015, www.aleqt.com/2015/03/15/article_940126.print.
19 Muhammad Al-Uthaym, "Obama muharwilan" [Obama Is in a Rush], *Al-Iqtisadiya*, 2 October 2013, www.aleqt.com/2013/10/02/article_790042.print (hereafter Al-Uthaym, "Obama muharwilan").
20 For example, Bayyina Al-Milhim, "Al-Saudiya wa-Amirika allati taish daf Obama!" [Saudi Arabia and America Which Is Undergoing Obama's Weakness!], *Al-Riyadh*, 27 October, 2013, www.alriyadh.com/2013/10/27/article878766.html, Rakan Hasab, "Li-madha al-ghadab min Amrika?" [Why the Anger at America?], *Al-Watan*, 9 October 2013, www.alwatan.com.sa/Articles/Detail.aspx?ArticleID=13853, and Yusuf Abd Allah Makki, "Hawl al-taqarub al-amiriki al-irani" [About the American–Iranian Rapprochement], *Al-Watan*, 9 October 2013, www.alwatan.com.sa/Articles/Detail. aspx?ArticleID=18502.
21 Zuhayr Al-Harithi, "Al-Saudiya wa-Amrika wa-Iran … tara ma alladhi taghayyar?" [Saudi Arabia, America, and Iran; I Wonder What Has Changed?], *Al-Riyadh*, 29 October 2013, www.alriyadh.com/2013/10/29/article879495.html.
22 Al-Khashiban, "Hal takhsar Amrika."
23 Yusuf Al-Kuwaylit, "Amrika la tuhibbuna wa-la takrahuna!" [America neither Loves Us nor Hates Us], *Al-Riyadh*, 24 October 2013, www.al-riyadh.com/2013/10/24/a rticle878045.html.
24 Najib Al-Khunayzi, "Hal hunak mawqif irani jadid?" [Is There a New Iranian Position?], *Ukaz*, 6 October 2013, www.okaz.com.sa/new/Issues/20131006/PrinCon201310066 44868.htm, Ayman Al-Hammad, "Hisabat gharbiya istratijiya qad tuid 'shurti Al-Khalij'" [Western Strategic Calculations May Bring Back the "Gulf Policeman"], *Al-Riyadh*, 26 October 2013, www.alriyadh.com/2013/10/26/article878682.html (hereafter Al-Hammad, "Hisabat gharbiya"), and Ibrahim Al-Athimin, "Li-madha turid Iran al-taqarub ma Amrika?" [Why Does Iran Want a Rapprochement with America?], *Al-Yawm*, 18 October 2013, www.alyaum.com/News/art/999216.html.
25 Al-Mtiri, "Al-Ayn al-thalitha," Al-Uthaym, "Obama muharwilan," Mutlaq Saud Al-Mtiri, "Man tughatta bi'l-amrikan aryan" [He Who Uses the Americans as Clothing Is Naked], *Al-Riyadh*, 2 October 2013, www.alriyadh.com/2013/10/02/article872192. html, Yusuf Al-Kuwaylit, "Safaqat qad taksibha Iran" [Deals in Which Iran Could Be the Winner], *Al-Riyadh*, 25 September 2013, www.alriyadh.com/2013/09/25/a

rticle870345.html, and Hamad bin Abd Allah Al-Luhaydan, "Al-Yawm al-watani 83 quwwa wa-izza wa-istidad" [The 83rd National Day: Power, Pride, and Preparedness], *Anba'kum*, 20 September 2013, www.anbacom.com/print.php?action=print&m =articlesm&id=17541. (hereafter Al-Luhaydan, "Al-Yawm al-watani").

26 The Political Editor, "Al-Alaqat bayn Al-Riyadh wa-Washintun ... jawhar al-haqiqa wa-tafasil al-marhala" [Relations between Riyadh and Washington: The Essence of the State of Affairs and the Details about this Phase], *Al-Riyadh*, 25 October 2013, www.alriyadh.com/2013/10/25/article878375.html.

27 Ali Al-Khashiban, "Ma alladhi yumkin filah tujah Iran?" [What Can Be Done with Iran?], *Al-Riyadh*, 11 November 2013, www.alriyadh.com/2013/11/11/article882831.html.

28 "Al-Qabda al-rakhwa fi Janif" [Nailing Jello to the Wall in Geneva], *Al-Madina*, 9 November 2013, www.al-madina.com/printhtml/489906.

29 Interview with Prince Muhammad by Roger Boyes and Roland Watson, "Saudi Arabia Turns up Heat on the West over Possible Iran Nuclear Deal," *The Times*, 22 November 2013, www.thetimes.co.uk/tto/world/middleeast/article3929509.ece.

30 Adnan Kamil Salah, "Wad Iran wa-Isra'il taht mizhallat naz silah nawawi wahida" [Placing Iran and Israel under a Single Nuclear Disarmament Umbrella], *Al-Madina*, 17 December 2013, www.al-madina.com/printhtml/498590, and Al-Kuwaylit, "Iran: al-wuduh."

31 Muhammad Al Al-Shaykh, "Lan yaltazim al-iraniyun" [The Iranians Will Not Keep Their Promises], *Al-Jazira*, 1 December 2013, www.al-jazirah.com/2013/20131201/1p5.htm.

32 Al-Hammad, "Hisabat gharbiya."

33 Hamad Abd Allah Al-Luhaydan, "Qunbulat Iran al-nawawiya bayn al-mustawdi wa'l-raff" [Iran's Nuclear Weapon either in a Warehouse or on the Shelf], *Al-Riyadh*, 6 December 2013, www.alriyadh.com/2013/12/06/article890255.html.

34 Abd Al-Aziz Qasim, "Al-Qunbula al-nawawiya al-khalijiya wa'l-tirs al-sunni" [The Gulf Atom Bomb and the Sunni Shield], *Al-Watan*, 2 December 2013, www.alwatan.com.sa/Articles/Detail.aspx?ArticleId=19173.

35 Isa Sawadi, "Ittifaq nawawi hashsh" [A Fragile Nuclear Agreement], *Al-Watan*, 25 November 2013, www.alwatan.com.sa/Articles/Detail.aspx?ArticleID=19089.

36 Ibrahim Al-Athimin, "Ittifaq Janif: Al-Drama al-alamiya wa'l-ma'sat al-mash'uma" [The Geneva Agreement: The International Drama and the Calamitous Tragedy], *Al-Yawm*, 29 November 2013, www.alyaum.com/News/art/105934.html.

37 Yusuf Al-Kuwaylit, "Man kasab min jawlat al-nawawi al-irani?" [Who Came Out on Top in the Iranian Nuclear Round?], *Al-Riyadh*, 25 November 2013, www.alriyadh.com/886903.

38 Jamal Al-Khashogji, "Ayyuha al-saudi da al-qalaq wa-ibda' al-hayat" [Oh Saudis, Stop Worrying and Get On with Your Lives], *Al-Hayat*, 30 December 2013, http://alhayat.com/home/Print/577079?PrintPictures=0.

39 Abd Allah Al-Madani, "Min dawla sharira ila sadiqa li'l-shaytan al-akbar" [From Evil State to Friend of the Great Satan], *Al-Iqtisadiya*, 8 December 2013, www.aleqt.com/2013/12/08/article_805886.print, and Hamad bin Abd Allah Al-Luhaydan, "Iran wa-Isra'il wajhan li-umla wahida" [Iran and Israel: Two Sides of the Same Coin], *Al-Riyadh*, 14 February 2014, www.alriyadh.com/2014/02/14/article909987.html, and Yusuf Al-Kuwaylit, "Nadhhab li'l-Sharq ka-ma nadhhab li'l-Gharb" [We Go East Just as We Go West], *Al-Riyadh*, 19 February 2014, www.alriyadh.com/911378.

40 Interview with Prince Turki Al-Faysal by Edward Luce, "Lunch with the *FT*: Prince Turki al-Faisal," *Financial Times*, 14 March 2014, www.ft.com/cms/s/2/9eb2ba0c-a 9e0-11e3-adab-00144feab7de.html.

41 For example, Ghazanfar Ali Khan, "Obama Visit Gives Fresh Impetus to Saudi–US Ties," *Arab News*, 29 March 2014, www.arabnews.com/print/547636, Mohammed Fahad Al-Harthi, "Between the Lines: Obama Visit Affirms Strategic Alignment," *Arab News*, 2 April 2014, www.arabnews.com/print/549461, and Turki Abd Allah

Al-Sudayri, "Amrika ... wa-wuduh ghayatna" [America and Our Objective's Clarity], *Al-Riyadh*, 29 March 2014, www.alriyadh.com/922285.
42 Zuhayr Al-Harithi, "Washintun wa'l-Riyadh ... tajdid al-alaqa bi-tafahumat sariha!" [Washington and Riyadh: Renewing the Relationship with Frank Exchanges], *Al-Riyadh*, 1 April 2014, www.alriyadh.com/923075.
43 Ibid.
44 Abd Al-Aziz Al-Tuwayjiri, "Amirika wa-silah Iran al-nawawi" [America and Iran's Nuclear Weapons], *Al-Hayat* (Saudi edition), 19 April 2014, http://alhayat.com/Opinions/Writers/1880690.
45 Yusuf Al-Kuwaylit, "Iran wa'l-Gharb man yaqif ala khatt al-nar?" [Iran and the West: Who Is It That Is in the Line of Fire?], *Al-Riyadh*, 12 April 2014, www.alriyadh.com/926216.
46 Yusuf Al-Kuwaylit, "'Sayf Abd Allah' jahiziya askariya wa-difaiya" [The Sword of Abd Allah [Exercise]: Defensive Military Readiness], *Al-Riyadh*, 29 April 2014, www.alriyadh.com/931064.
47 Mutlaq Saud Al-Mtiri, "Musku tuarri marra thaniya al-daf al-amriki" [Moscow Exposes Once Again America's Weakness], *Al-Riyadh*, 8 March 2014, www.alriyadh.com/916328.
48 Zuhayr Al-Harithi, "Wa-hal thamma makan li-duwal Al-Khalij al-arabiya fiha?" [Is There Room for the Arab Gulf States in the Negotiations?], *Al-Sharq Al-Awsat*, 14 July 2014, http://classic.aawsat.com/print.asp?did=779356&issueno=13012.
49 Ayman Al-Hammad, "Al-Siyasa al-amirikiya fi Al-Khalij bayn 'lughat al-sawarikh' wa-'lughat al-masalih'" [U.S. Policy in the Gulf from the "Language of Missiles" to the "Language of Interests"], *Al-Riyadh*, 18 May 2014, www.alriyadh.com/936612.
50 Ayman Al-Hammad, "Al-Tahalufat al-saba" [Difficult Alliances], *Al-Riyadh*, 27 June 2014, www.alriyadh.com/947689, and Yusuf Al-Kuwaylit, "Amrika: Hal bada'at al-awda li-siyasat al-mahawir?" [America: Has It Initiated a New Policy of Polarity?], *Al-Riyadh*, 27 August 2014, www.alriyadh.com/964159.
51 "Al-Wajh al-khafi li'l-malaff al-nawawi ... iraniyun yatafawadun bi-ism al-bayt al-abyad" [The Hidden Aspect of the Nuclear Issue ... Iranians Negotiating in the Name of the White House], *Ajil* (Riyadh), 14 November 2014, www.burnews.com.
52 Yusuf Al-Kuwaylit, "Al-Safaqat wa'l-mutafarrijun" [Deals and Onlookers], *Al-Riyadh*, 24 November 2014, www.alriyadh.com/997044.
53 Sultan bin Abd Al-Rahman Al-Uthaym, "Bass wa-law" [It Isn't Over Yet], *Al-Arab* (Doha), 3 March 2014, www.alarab.qa/printarticle.php?artid=285144.
54 For example, as assessed by Qatar's representative at the IAEA, "Qatar: Hall al-khilafat hawl nawawi Iran bi'l-hiwar wa'l-diblumasiya" [Qatar: Resolving Differences over Iran's Nuclear [Program] by Means of Dialogue and Diplomacy], *Al-Arab*, 6 March 2014, www.alarab.qa/details.php?issueId=2278&artid=285578.
55 Al-Luhaydan, "Al-Yawm al-watani."
56 Muhammad Al-Silmi, "Ruhani wa-nazhrathu nahw Al-Khalij" [Rouhani and His View of the Gulf], *Al-Sharq Al-Awsat*, 19 March 2014, www.aawsat.com/print.asp?did=765240&issueno=12895.
57 Al-Mtiri, "Al-Ayn al-thalitha."
58 "Al-Mamlaka tu'akkid ahammiyat intiqal duwal Al-Khalij Al-Arabi min al-taawun ila al-ittihad" [The Kingdom Reiterates the Importance for the Arab Gulf Countries toTransition from Cooperation to Union], *Al-Riyadh*, 8 December 2013, www.alriyadh.com/2013/12/08/article890798.html.
59 Yusuf Al-Kuwaylit, "Tahaddiyat al-amn min al-raghba ila al-darura!" [Security Challenges from Option to Necessity!], *Al-Riyadh*, 17 October 2013, www.alriyadh.com/2013/10/17/article876179.html.
60 Khalaf Al-Harbi, "Al-Khaliji al-waqif ala al-bab" [The Gulf Individual Waiting at the Door], *Ukaz*, 8 December 2013, www.okaz.com.sa/new/Issues/20131208/PrinCon20131208660242.htm.

61 Abd Allah Abd Al-Karim Al-Sadun, "Wa-madha bad al-ittifaq?" [What Comes After the Agreement?], *Al-Riyadh*, 4 December 2013, www.alriyadh.com/2013/12/04/article889678.html.
62 Khalid Al-Sabii, "Al-Malaff al-nawawi al-irani wa-amn Al-Khalij" [The Iranian Nuclear Issue and Security of the Gulf], *Al-Sharq*, 8 February 2014, www.alsharq.net.sa/2014/02/08/1069174, editorial "Khalij muwahhad" [A Unified Gulf], *Al-Madina*, 9 November 2014, www.al-madina.com/printhtml/568351, William Maclean and Amena Bakr, "Saudi Arabia Leans on Gulf States to Close Ranks as Region Boils," *Reuters*, 19 November 2014, www.reuters.com/article/2014/11/19/us-gulf-dispute-idSKCN0J30H920141119, and Prince Nayif quoted in "Mu'tamar al-amn al-watani wa'l-iqlimi yabda' jalsatah bi-munaqashat tahaddiyat al-hadir amam Al-Khalij" [The Conference on National and Regional Security Begins Its Sessions with a Discussion of the Current Challenges Facing the Gulf], *Al-Iqtisadiya*, 24 April 2014, www.aleqt.com/2014/04/24/article_843667.print.
63 Mutlaq bin Saud Al-Mtiri, "Hazimat Iran 2015" [Iran's Defeat in 2015], *Al-Riyadh*, 3 January 2015, www.alriyadh.com/1009620.
64 Yasir Al-Ghaslan, "A-lam yahin waqt al-ittihad?" [Hasn't the Time Come for Unification?], *Al-Watan*, 22 January 2015, www.alwatan.com.sa/Articles/Detail.aspx?ArticleID=24793.
65 Bassam Al-Falih, "Al-Mamlaka wa-ta'thirha al-qawi" [The Kingdom and Its Powerful Influence], *Al-Sharq*, 19 February 2015, www.alsharq.net.sa/2015/02/19/1298809.
66 Ahmad Al-Maghluth, "Asifat Al-Hazm wa'l-hulm al-farisi" [Operation Decisive Storm and the Persian Dream], *Al-Yawm*, 2 April 2015, www.alyaum.com/article/4057692.
67 "Zaman al-ittihad" [Time for Unification], *Ukaz*, 19 May 2015, http://okaz.co/bwlexdo41.
68 Interview with Khalid bin Muhammad Al-Atiya by Jamil Al-Dhaylabi, "Wazir al-kharijia al-qatari lil'l-*Hayat*: 'Duwal Al-Khalij asiya ala al-thawrat'" [The Qatari Foreign Minister to *Al-Hayat*: "The Gulf States Are Immune to Revolutions"], *Al-Hayat*, 20 February 2015, http://alhayat.com/Articles/7537981.
69 Quoted in Mashari Al-Dhaydi, "Amud al-arab" [The Arabs' Backbone], *Al-Sharq Al-Awsat*, 18 February 2015, http://aawsat.com/home/article292141.
70 "Han al-waqt … al-qunbula al-nawawiya al-saudiya!" [The Time Has Come: A Saudi Atom Bomb!], *Al-Ra'i* (Kuwait), 19 February 2015, www.alraimedia.com/Articles.aspx?id=565201.
71 "Mas'ul khaliji: Duwal Al-Khalij bat mithalan yuhtadha bih fi tathbit daaim al-amn wa'l-aman" [A Gulf Official: The Gulf States Have Become an Example to Be Copied of How to Bolster Support for Security and Safety], *Al-Iqtisadiya*, 22 June 2015, www.aleqt.com/2015/06/21/article_967257.html.
72 "Safqa nawawiya iraniya muhtamila ma Al-Gharb … wa-radd al-fil al-khaliji al-muntazhar" [An Iranian Nuclear Deal with the West Is Possible … and the Expected Gulf Response], *Ukaz*, 7 November 2014, http://okaz.cbwFMJdeUo.
73 Abd Al-Munim Mustafa, "Qadhifat al-imam wa-suyuf Sulaymani" [The Imam's Bomber Aircraft and Sulaymani's Swords], *Al-Madina*, 5 December 2014, www.al-madina.com/node/573875.
74 Zuhayr Al-Harithi, "Al-Khalij wa-Iran wa'l-Gharb sadaqa la tanfa wa-adawa la tadurr!" [The Gulf, Iran, and the West: Friendship Is of No Use, While Hostility Does No Harm], *Al-Riyadh*, 23 December 2014, www.alriyadh.com/1006210.
75 Abd Al-Latif Al-Mulhim, "Al-Mamlaka wa-Iran hal hiya safha jadida?" [The Kingdom and Iran: Is It a New Page?], *Al-Yawm*, 18 May 2014, www.alyaum.com/News/art/139971.html.
76 "Iranian Official Hails Positive Saudi Talks," *Arab News*, 27 August 2014, www.arabnews.com/print/621481.

77 "Afkham: Min al-mufid al-hiwar ma duwal al-mintaqa wa-minha Al-Saudiya" [Afkham: A Dialogue with the Countries in the Region, to Include Saudi Arabia, Is Useful], *Al-Alam TV*, 20 August 2014, www.alalam.ir/print/1624525.
78 For example, "Ra'is al-jumhuriya: Taraju asar al-naft mu'amara min qibal bad al-duwal li-hisab duwal ukhra" [The President of the Republic: The Fall in Oil Prices Is a Plot by Some Countries Against Other Countries], *Kayhan* (Tehran), 10 December 2014, http://kayhan.ir/ar/print/11676.
79 "Al-Hulm al-khaliji al-nawawi—urubat al-munif" [The Gulf Nuclear Dream: The Arabness of a Majestic Individual], *Al-Jazira*, 29 November 2014, www.al-jazirah.com/2014/20141129/ar7.htm, and "Istimrar hubut al-naft yazid al-daght ala al-riyal al-irani" [The Continuing Decline in the Price of Oil Increases Pressure on the Iranian Riyal], *Al-Iqtisadiya*, 25 December 2014, www.aleqt.com/2014/12/25/article_917656.html, and Muhammad Al Al-Shaykh, "Hal tastati Iran an tasmud?" [Can Iran Hold Out?], *Al-Jazirah*, 6 January 2015, www.al-jazirah.com/2015/20150106/lp6.htm.
80 "Iran tarudd ala Al-Saudiya wa-tuhdhirha min mu'amarat al-aida'" [Iran Responds to Saudi Arabia and Warns It of Plots by Enemies], *Iran Radio in Arabic*, 14 October 2014, http://arabic.irib.ir/component/k2/item/149364?Itemid=38&tmpl=component&print=1, and [Iranian Deputy Foreign Minister] "Amir Abd Al-Lahyan: Mawqif Saud Al-Faysal min Iran adda ila awdat al-futur ila al-alaqat al-thuna'iya" [Amir Abd Al-Lahyan: Saud Al-Faysal's Position on Iran Has Led to a Cooling Again in the Bilateral Relationship], *Kayhan*, 4 January 2015, http://kayhan.ir/ar/print/13445.
81 "Iran Optimistic It Can Improve Ties with Saudi Arabia: Envoy," *Daily Star* (Beirut), 12 February 2015, www.dailystar.com.
82 "Rafsanjani: Laysat ladayna atma fi Suriya wa'l-Iraq wa'l-Bahrain wa-Lubnan wa'l-Yaman wa'l-tansiq ma Al-Riaydh yahill al-kathir min al-mashakil" [Rafsanjani: We Do Not Have any Designs on Syria, Iraq, Bahrain, Lebanon or Yemen and Coordination with Riyadh Will Solve Many Problems], *Kayhan*, 25 February 2015, http://kayhan.ir/ar/print/15717, and Ata' Allah Mahajarani, "Iran wa'l-Saudiya: Al-Haja li-istratijiya mushtaraka jadida" [Iran and Saudi Arabia: The Need for a New Joint Strategy], *Al-Sharq Al-Awsat*, 2 February 2015, http://aawsat.com/node/279736.
83 Al-Gunayir, "Iran wa-Isra'il," and Hamad bin Abd Allah Al-Luhaydan, "Al-Tanaghum al-irani al-isra'ili li'l-hirak al-mashbuh ala al-ard al-arabiya" [The Iranian–Israeli Harmony behind the Suspicious Move against Arab Lands], *Al-Riyadh*, 6 March 2015, www.alriyadh.com/1027476.
84 Abd Al-Rahman Al-Rashid, "Mashru hilf saudi turki ma Al-Asad" [The Plan for a Saudi–Turkish Alliance with Asad], *Al-Sharq Al-Awsat*, 7 July 2015, http://aawsat.com/node/401201.
85 "Al-Amid Jalali: Al-Saudiya tatahawwal min munafis iqlimi ila 'tahdid bi'l-niyaba' didd Iran" [Brigadier General Jalali: Saudi Arabia Has Transmuted from a Regional Competitor to a "Proxy Threat" against Iran], *Al-Wifaq* (Tehran), 27 June 2015, www.al-vefagh.com/export/print/80112?module=news.
86 Ma'mun Fandi, "Hal yasil al-ittifaq al-nawawi ila lahzhat al-tawqi?" [Will the Nuclear Agreement Reach the Signing Stage?], *Al-Sharq Al-Awsat*, 6 April 2015, http://aawsat.com/node/329661.
87 Asim Salih, "Asifat al-hazm fajr arabi jadid" [Operation Decisive Storm: A New Arab Dawn], *Al-Iqtisadiya*, 29 March 2015, www.aleqt.com/2015/03/29/article_944261.html, Jasir Abd Al-Aziz Al-Jasir, "Asifat al-hazm tuid al-tawazunat fi al-mintaqa" [Operation Decisive Storm Reestablishes the Balance in the Region], *Al-Jazira*, 29 March 2015, www.al-jazirah.com/2015/20150329/du12.htm, and Ayman Al-Hammad, "Khamene'i wa-mustasharu al-fitna" [Khamene'i and the Advisers of Turmoil], *Al-Riyadh*, 12 April 2015, www.al-riyadh.com/1038366.
88 "Iran wa-nuktat intisar iradat al-muqawama!" [Iran and Its Joke about the Victory of the Will to Resist!], *Al-Riyadh*, 30 April 2015, www.alriyadh.com/1043929.

89 Bayyina Al-Milhim, "Amrika al-daifa fi zaman quwwat al-hazm!" [A Weak America While There Is the Power of [Operation] Decisive [Storm]], *Al-Riyadh*, 13 April 2015, www.alriyadh.com/1038819.
90 Hamdan Al-Shihri, "Iran al-ta'ifiya ... sabruna nafadh wa-yakfi ahlaman tawassuiya" [Sectarian Iran, Our Patience Has Run Out and Enough Dreams of Expansion], *Al-Riyadh*, 14 April 2015, www.alriyadh.com/1038974.
91 Quoted in Jamal Khashogji, "5 za'id 1 ma bad Asifat Al-Hamz" [5+1+ Whatever Results from Operation Decisive Storm], *Al-Hayat*, 4 April 2015, http://alhayat.com/Opinion/Jamal-Khashoggi/8383460/5.
92 Mutlaq bin Saud Al-Mtiri, "Hal turid Washintun bay dawriha li-Iran?" [Does Washington Want to Sell Off Its Role to Tehran?], *Al-Riyadh*, 13 May 2015, www.alriyadh.com/1047655.
93 Salman Al-Dawsari, "Camp David khalijiya" [A Gulf Camp David], *Al-Sharq Al-Awsat*, 5 April 2015, http://aawsat.com/node/328831 (hereafter Al-Dawsari, "Camp David").
94 Abd Allah Al-Madani, "Obama yabhath amma yuawwid bi-fashlihi" [Obama Is Looking for Something to Compensate for His Failure], *Al-Iqtisadiya*, 7 December 2014, www.aleqt.com/2014/12/07/article_912474.html, Adnan Kamil Salah, "Al-Am al-hali: Hal yatanazal Obama aw Khamene'i?" [This Year: Will Obama or Khamene'i Back Down?], *Al-Madina*, 6 January 2015, www.al-madina.com/node/580256, Khalaf Al-Harbi, "Siyasat kiri miri" [A Policy That Is Not Serious], *Ukaz*, 21 March 2015, http://okaz.co/bwIbldlVQ, and Ahmad Al-Farraj, "John Kerry: Siyasat al-atifa al-mudammira!" [John Kerry: A Policy of Destructive Empathy!], *Al-Jazira*, 21 March 2015, www.al-jazirah.com/2015/20150321/ln40.htm.
95 Ahmad Al-Farraj, "Hal yatashayya Barak Obama?" [Will Barack Obama Take Sides?], *Al-Jazira*, 8 December 2014, www.al-jazirah.com/2014/20141208/ln37.htm, and Tariq Al-Humayyid, "Amrika wa'l-Khalij man tam'an al-akhar?" [America and the Gulf: Who Reassured Whom?], *Al-Sharq Al-Awsat*, 7 March 2015, http://aawsat.com/node/305536.
96 Khalid Al-Dakhil, "Obama yadfa al-mintaqa nahw al-hawiya" [Obama Is Driving the Region Toward the Abyss], *Al-Hayat*, 22 February 2015, http://alhayat.com/Opinion/Khaled-El-Dakheel/7577285, Abd Al-Rahman Ali Al-Fayfi, "Iran wa-labat al-mitraqa wa'l-sindan" [Iran and the Game of Hammer and Anvil], *Al-Riyadh*, 1 August 2015, www.al-riyadh.com/1069476, and Al-Dawsari, "Camp David."
97 Even as late as April 2015, some still believed that Israel would not accept a nuclear Iran, Turki Abd Allah Al-Sudayri, "Iran ila ayn wa-ma man?" [Iran: To Where and with Whom?], *Al-Riyadh*, 19 April 2015, www.alriyadh.com/1040468.
98 Badr Al-Rashid, "Iran wa-Isra'il hal aduww aduwwi sadiqi?" [Iran and Israel: Is My Enemy's Enemy My Friend?], *Al-Hayat* (Saudi edition), 7 March 2015, http://www.alhayat.com, and Muhammad Al-Tamihi, "Isra'il wa-Iran: Aduww aduwwi laysa sadiqi" [The Enemy of My Enemy Is Not My Friend], *Al-Riyadh*, 22 March 2015, www.alriyadh.com/1032175.
99 Ibrahim Ali Nasib, "Amrika wa-Iran al-nawawiya!" [America and a Nuclear Iran!], *Al-Madina*, 8 March 2015, www.al-madina.com/html/592847.
100 Amal Abd al-Aziz Al-Hazzani, "Khitab Netanyahu: Isra'il mana Iran diddana" [Netanyahu's Speech: Israel Is With Us, Iran Is Against Us], *Al-Sharq Al-Awsat*, 10 March 2015, http://aawsat.com/node/307901.
101 Al-Gunayir, "Iran wa-Isra'il."
102 Faris Al-Qahtani, "Sa-nattakhidh al-ijra'at li-himayat al-mintaqa ma lam yatimm inha' inqilab Al-Houthi" [We Will Take Steps to Defend the Region Unless Al-Houthi's Coup Ends], *Ukaz*, 24 March 2015, http://okaz.co/bwIbodl7t.
103 Muhammad Ballut, "Iran wa'l-Gharb: Tafahum nawawi mumaddad wa-siyasi mu'ajjal" [Iran and the West: The Nuclear Understanding Is Extended and the Political One Is Deferred], *Al-Safir* (Beirut), 24 November 2014, http://assafir.com/Articles/20/385979.

104 "After Scuttling Iran Deal, France Could Clinch Arms Deal," UPI, 12 November 2014, www.upi.com, and "France, Lebanon Sign Saudi-funded Arms Deal Worth $3 Bln," *Reuters*, 4 November 2014, www.reuters.com/assets/print?aid=USL6N0SU3TX20141104.
105 Ibrahim Mahmud Al-Nahhas, "Min ajl al-watan wa-nima'ih" [For the Country and Its Development], *Al-Riyadh*, 25 June 2015, www.alriyadh.com/1059775.
106 Adnan Kamil Salah, "Hal Obama muslim shii haqqan?" [Is Obama Really a Shia Muslim?], *Al-Madina*, 23 June 2015, www.al-madina.com/printhtml/615121 (hereafter Salah, "Hal Obama muslim").
107 Muhammad Al Al-Shaykh, "Luhmat al-khalijiyin wa-Camp David" [The Relationship between Those from the Gulf and Camp David], *Al-Jazira*, 10 May 2015, www.al-jazirah.com/2015/20150510/lp4.htm, (hereafter Al Al-Shaykh, "Luhmat al-khalijiyin") and Zuhayr Al-Harithi, "Faransa wa-duwal Al-Khalij ma maghza hudur Hollande li'l-qimma?" [France and the Gulf States: What Is the Meaning of Hollande's Presence at the Summit?], *Al-Riyadh*, 5 May 2015, www.alriyadh.com/1045379.
108 "Moscow 'Rejects' Saudi 'Offer' to Drop Assad for Rich Arms Deal," Russia Today (Moscow), 9 August 2013, http://rt.com/news/saudi-russia-arms-putin-239.
109 Turki Saqr, "Al-Nawawi al-irani wa'l-kayd al-saudi" [The Iranian Nuke and the Saudi Stratagem], *Al-Bina'* (Beirut), 24 November 2014, http://al-binaa.com/albinaa/?article=21251, and Mark Mazzetti, Eric Schmitt, and David C. Kirkpatrick, "Saudi Oil Seen as Lever to Pry Russian Support from Syria's Assad," *New York Times*, 3 February 2015, www.nytimes.com.
110 Ayman Al-Hammad, "Al-Riyadh wa-Musku taghayyur istratiji am marhali?" [Riyadh and Moscow: Strategic or Temporary Change?], *Riyadh*, 25 November 2014, www.alriyadh.com/997421.
111 Muhammad bin Yahya Al-Fal, "Al-Ziyara al-tarikhiya li-waliy waliy al-ahd ila Rusiya: Al-Tanmiya al-rabih al-akbar" [The Deputy Crown Prince's Historic Visit to Russia: Development Is the Biggest Winner], *Al-Jazira*, 2 July 2015, www.al-jazirah.com/2015/20150702/ar5.htm. The nuclear deal included a provision for 1,000 Saudis to study energy issues, including in the nuclear field, in Russia, Abd Al-Rahman Al-Rashid, "Al-Rus qadimun ila Al-Saudiya" [The Russians Are Coming to Saudi Arabia], *Al-Sharq Al-Awsat*, 20 June 2015, http://aawsat.com/node/387946 (hereafter Al-Rashid, "Al-Rus qadimun").
112 Al Al-Shaykh, "Luhmat al-khalijiyin," and Ali Al-Anazi, "Al-Saudiya wa-Rusiya wa'l-masalih al-mushtaraka" [Saudi Arabia and Russia and Shared Interests], *Al-Hayat* (Saudi edition), 27 June 2015, http://alhayat.com/Opinion/Ali-Anzi/96559284, and Ayman Al-Hammad, "Duwal Al-Khalij wa-Faransa akthar tahalufan" [A Closer Alliance Between the Gulf States and France], *Al-Riyadh*, 4 May 2015, www.alriyadh.com/1044945.
113 Al-Rashid, "Al-Rus qadimun."
114 Abd Allah Nasir Al-Utaybi, "Taharruk saudi qad yaqlib al-muadalat" [A Saudi Move That May Shift the Balance], *Al-Hayat*, 22 June 2015, http://alhayat.com/Opinion/Abdullah-nasser-Al-Othiabi/9603638.
115 Salman Al-Ansari, "Ma al-rabit bayn ibtila Rusiya Al-Qirim wa-ibtila Iran Al-Yaman?" [What Is the Link between Russia's Gobbling Up of the Crimea and Iran's Gobbling Up of Yemen?], *CNN Arabic*, 1 February 2015, http://arabic.cnn.com/middleeast/2015/0201/opinion-russia-iran-yemen.
116 Turki Abd Allah Al-Sudayri, "Madha yajdhib Amrika wa-Rusiya li-Iran" [What Attracts America and Russia to Iran?], *Al-Riyadh*, 12 July 2015, www.alriyadh.com/1064349, and Editorial "Al-Ta'yid al-rusi al-mutlaq li-Iran ghayr mubarrar" [Russia's Unqualified Support for Iran Is Not Justified], *Al-Watan*, 12 July 2015, www.alwatan.com.sa/Editors_Note/Default.aspx.
117 Michel Abu Najm, "Faransa tasa li-tatbi sari li-alaqatha ma Iran wa-tadu Ruhani li-ziyaratha" [France Seeks a Rapid Normalization of Relations with Iran and Invites Rouhani to Visit], *Al-Sharq Al-Awsat*, 30 July 2015, http://aawsat.com/node/418196.

118 Prince Saud Al-Faysal, at the press conference with the Italian Foreign Minister, reported by Abd Allah Al-Hasani, "Saud Al-Faysal: Nurahhib bi-raghbat Tihran fi tahsin al-alaqat wa'l-ibra fi'l-ijra'" [Saud Al-Faysal: We Welcome Tehran's Desire to Improve Relations But the Proof Is in the Pudding], *Al-Riyadh*, 4 October 2013, www.alriyadh.com/2013/10/04/article872730.html, and Prince Saud Al-Faysal quoted in Abd Allah Al-Hasani, "Al-Faysal: La yujad lada al-mamlaka siyasa aw mufawadat sirriya" [Al-Faysal: The Kingdom Does Not Have any Secret Policy or Negotiations], *Al-Riyadh*, 15 April 2014, www.alriyadh.com/927342, "Al-Mamlaka tadu ila taqyim wa-murajaat dawr Adam Al-Inhiyaz fi himayat wa-taziz al-silm al-alami" [The Kingdom Calls for Recognizing the Value and Revamping the Role of Non-Alignment in the Defense and Strengthening of World Peace], *Al-Riyadh*, 29 May 2014, www.alriyadh.com/939805?print=1.

119 Interview with Prince Turki Al-Faysal by Lally Weymouth, "Saudi Arabia's Prince Turki: 'American Policy Has Been Wrong'", *Washington Post*, 4 November 2013, www.washingtonpost.com.

120 "Al-Mamlaka tujaddid dawatha li-jal mintaqat Al-Sharq Al-Awsat khaliya min al-asliha al-nawawiya" [The Kingdom Renews Its Call to Make the Middle East a Nuclear-Free Zone], *Al-Riyadh*, 1 May 2014, www.alriyadh.com/931844, "Amam muntada al-arabi-al-rusi fi Al-Khurtum, Turki bin Muhammad: Alayna himayat mujamana min al-afkar al-haddama" [At the Arab-Russian Conference in Khartoum, [Prince] Turki bin Muhammad [Deputy Foreign Minister]: We Must Defend Our Society from Destructive Ideas], *Al-Riyadh*, 5 December 2014, www.alriyadh.com/10000680, and "Ilan Sharm Al-Shaykh: Al-Taharruk al-arabi anqadh Al-Yaman wa-sa-yastamirr hatta insihab al-milishiyat al-hawthiya wa-taslim aslihatha" [Announcement from Sharm Al-Shaykh: The Arab Initiative Saved Yemen and Will Continue Until the Houthi Militias Withdraw and Hand Over Their Weapons], *Al-Riyadh*, 30 March 2015, www.alriyadh.com/1034503.

121 Louis Charbonneau, "Dispute over Mideast Nuclear Arms Ban Torpedoes UN Conference," *Reuters*, 22 May 2015, www.reuters.com/article/2015/05/23/us-mideast-nuclear-un-idUSKBN072J220150523.

122 "Al-Kalima al-samiya allati alqaaha khadim al-haramayn … amam Majlis Al-Shura" [The Royal Speech that the Servant of the Two Holy Shrines Gave to the Shura Council], *Shura website*, 2007/08 legislative year, www.shura.gov, and "Al-Faysal: Al-Tafawud ma Iran khati' wa'l-mintaqa amam sibaq nawawi" [Al-Faysal: The Negotiations with Iran Are a Mistake and the Region Is Facing a Nuclear Arms Race], *Al-Watan*, 19 March 2015, http://alwatan.com.sa/Politics/News_Detail.aspx?ArticleID=217927&CategoryID=1.

123 "Al-Qalaq al-mushtarak min Tihran" [The Shared Concern about Tehran], *Saudi Opinion*, 8 May 2015, www.saudiopinion.net.

124 Salman Al-Dawsari, "Iran wa'l-Khalij bal huw ittifaq si'i" [Iran and the Gulf: Well, It's a Bad Agreement], *Al-Sharq Al-Awsat*, 9 March 2015, http://aawst.com/node/307456, Abd Allah Al-Nasir, "Bayn al-ama'im wa'l-qubbaat" [Between the Turbans and the Hats], *Al-Riyadh*, 6 March 2015, www.alriyadh.com/1027601, and Turki Al-Turki, "Fi al-tariq ila Camp David … Tadamun duwal Al-Khalij yaqwi mawqifha al-tafawudi" [On the Way to Camp David … The Gulf Countries' Solidarity Strengthens Their Negotiating Position], *Al-Iqtisadiya*, 10 May 2015, www.aleqt.com/2015/05/10/article_956492.html, and Jamil Al-Dhiyabi, "Inzau waraqat Tihran wa-tajahalu Obama" [Take away Tehran's Card and Ignore Obama], *Al-Hayat* (Saudi edition), 10 May 2015, http://alhayat.com/Editions/Print/9112893.

125 "Qimma ghayr adiya bi-kull al-maayir" [An Extraordinary Summit by any Measure], *Al-Iqtisadiya*, 6 May 2015, www.aleqt.com/2015/05/06/article_955349.html.

126 Hamdan Al-Shihri, "Waliy waliy al-ahd fi Musku wa-Baris: Shirakat al-hazm wa-tahalufat al-mustaqbal" [The Deputy Crown Prince in Moscow and Paris: Decisive Partnerships and the Alliances of the Future], *Al-Riyadh*, 27 June 2015, www.alriyadh.com/1060398 (hereafter Al-Shihri, "Waliy waliy al-ahd fi Musku").

127 Department of State, "Parameters for a Joint Comprehensive Plan of Action Regarding the Islamic Republic of Iran's Nuclear Program," 2 April 2015, www.state.gov/r/pa/prs/ps/2015/04/240170.htm.
128 Rashid Abanami, "Tadaiyat tahjim dawr Iran al-nawawi al-iqlimiya" [The Regional Consequences of Just Limiting Iran's Nuclear Role], *Al-Iqtisadiya*, 5 April 2015, www.aleqt.com/2015/04/05/article_946438.html, Amal Abd Al-Aziz Al-Hazzani, "La nawawi Iran la nawawi saudi" [If There Is No Iranian Nuclear Weapon, There Will Not Be a Saudi One], *Al-Sharq Al-Awsat*, 7 April 2015, http://aawsat.com/node/330426, and Rashid Muhammad Al-Fawzan, "Al-Ittifaq al-amiriki-al-irani iqtisadiyan mukhif" [The American–Iranian Agreement Is Frightening in Economic Terms], *Al-Riyadh*, 7 April 2015, www.alriyadh.com/1037037.
129 Tariq Al-Humayyid, "Sadhaja wa-tahawwur tasdiq khitabat al-murshid" [To Believe the Supreme Leader's Speeches Is Naïve and Reckless], *Al-Sharq Al-Awsat*, 12 April 2015, http://aawsat.com/node/334591.
130 Sufuq Al-Shammari, "Hal tusaddiqun Iran?" [Do You Trust Iran?], *Al-Riyadh*, 14 April 2015, www.alriyadh.com/1039006.
131 Turki Al-Turki, "Fi al-tariq ila Camp David ... Tadamun duwal Al-Khalij yaqwi mawqifha al-tafawudi" [On the Way to Camp David ... The Gulf Countries' Solidarity Strengthens Their Negotiating Position], *Al-Iqtisadiya*, 10 May 2015, www.aleqt.com/2015/05/10/article_956492.html.
132 Muhammad Maruf Al-Shaybani, "Qimmat Obama wa-majlis al-taawun" [The Obama–GCC Summit], *Al-Bilad*, 13 May 2015, www.albiladdaily.com.
133 Abd Al-Rahman Al-Rashid, "Hal Camp David li-taswiq ittifaq Iran?" [Is Camp David Intended Only to Sell the Iran Agreement?], *Al-Sharq Al-Awsat*, 9 May 2015, http://aawsat.com/print/355891.
134 Khalid Al-Dakhil, "Al-Mushkila fi Washintun wa-laysa Tihran" [The Problem Is in Washington Rather Than in Tehran], *Al-Hayat*, 10 May 2015, www.alhayat.com/edition/Print/9108003.
135 Khalid bin Nayif Al-Habbas, "Al-Qimma al-khalijiya-al-amrikiya nahw itar jadid li'l-taawun" [The Gulf-American Summit: Toward a New Framework for Cooperation], *Al-Sharq Al-Awsat*, 7 May 2015, http://aawsat.com/print/354091.
136 The White House, Office of the Press Secretary, "U.S.–Gulf Cooperation Council Camp David Joint Statement," 14 May 2015, www.whitehouse.gov/the-press-office/2015/05/14/us-gulf-cooperation-council-camp-david-joint-statement.
137 "Majlis al-wuzara' yushaddid ala tadammunih al-bayan al-khitami fi ijtima Camp David" [The Council of Ministers Underscores Its Support for the Final Communiqué from the Camp David Meeting], *Al-Riyadh*, 18 May 2015, www.alriyadh.com/1049220.
138 Abd Al-Rahman Al-Rashid, "Al-Khalij wa-amrika: Man la yatlub la yuta" [The Gulf and America: If You Don't Ask You Don't Get], *Al-Sharq Al-Awsat*, 15 May 2015, http://aawsat.com/node/361326.
139 Abd Allah bin Muhammad Al-Rifai, "Min asifat al-hazm ila Camp David makasib wa-makasib" [From Operation Decisive Storm to Camp David: From Success to Success], *Al-Riyadh*, 16 May 2015, www.alriyadh.com/1048586.
140 Talal bin Sulayman Al-Harbi, "Iran bad al-an" [Iran from Now On], *Al-Riyadh*, 14 May 2015, www.alriyadh.com/1048060.
141 Ali Al-Qahis, "Al-Ra'is al-amriki: Akinn ihitiraman wa-taqdiran kabirayn li'l-malik Salman alladhi dakhkh dima' al-shabab fi sultat al-hukm" [The American President: I Feel Great Regard and Respect for King Salman Who Injected Fresh Blood into the Government], *Al-Riyadh*, 17 May 2015, www.alriyadh.com/1048770.
142 For example, "Nataawan ma Amrika am natamid alayha?" [Should We Cooperate with or Depend on America?], *Ukaz*, 16 May 2015, http://okaz.co/bwleudoUM.
143 Abd Al-Rahman Al-Rashid, "Hal baqiyat asrar fi mufawadat Iran?" [Are There Still Some Secrets Remaining in the Negotiations with Iran?], *Al-Sharq Al-Awsat*, 17 June 2015, http://aawsat.com/node/385616.

144 For example, Jasir Abd Al-Aziz Al-Jasir, "Al-Malaff al-nawawi al-irani ala tawulat Camp David" [The Iranian Nuclear Program on the Table at Camp David], *Al-Jazira*, 12 May 2015, www.al-jazirah.com.sa/2015/20150512/dul2.htm, and Muhammad Al-Mukhtar Al-Fal, "Muqtadayat al-alaqa al-istiratijiya" [The Requirements for a Strategic Relationship], *Ukaz*, 16 May 2015, http://okaz.co/bwleudoUR.

145 [Prince] Badr bin Saud, "Nifaq Obama" [Obama's Hypocrisy], *Ukaz*, 18 May 2015, http://okaz.co/bwlewdo1w.

146 Nasir Al-Shihri, "Intahat Camp David wa-baqiya mismar Juha" [Camp David Is Over but the U.S. Excuse to Interfere Remains], *Al-Bilad*, 17 May 2015, www.albila ddaily.com.

147 Khalid Al-Dakhil, "Li-madha al-itimad ala Washintun awwalan?" [Why the Reliance on Washington as the First Option?], *Al-Hayat*, 17 May 2015, http://alhayat.com, and Abd Al-Salam Al-Yamani, "Tabyid al-siyasa al-iraniya ala al-tariqa al-amrikiya" [Whitewashing Iranian Policy the American Way], *Al-Hayat* (Saudi edition), 18 May 2015, http://alhayat.com/Opinions/Abdulsalam-Al-yamani/9213298/.

148 Muhammad Al-Mukhtar Al-Fal, "Muahadat difa" [A Defense Treaty], *Ukaz*, 18 May 2015, http://okaz.co/bwlewdo1z, and Abd Al-Rahman Al-Habib, "Ayyuhuma akhtar al-tawassu am al-nawawi al-irani?" [Which Is the More Dangerous of the Two: Iranian Expansionism or Its Nuclear Weapons?], *Al-Jazira*, 18 May 2015, www.al-jazirah. com.sa/2015/20150518/ar2.htm.

149 Bayyina Al-Milhim, "Camp David: Kayf yatimm al-ittifaq ma dawla raiyat al-irhab" [Camp David: How an Agreement Will Be Concluded with a State Sponsor of Terrorism], *Al-Riyadh*, 18 May 2015, www.alriyadh.com/1048953 (hereafter Al-Milhim, "Camp David").

150 Zaynab Ghasib, "Madha law wafaq al-kunghras?" [What If Congress Agrees?], *Al-Hayat* (Saudi edition), 22 May 2015, http://alhayat.com/Opinion/Zinab-Ghasab/9275184 (hereafter Ghasib, "Madha law wafaq").

151 Husayn Shubukshi, "Al-Saudiya ahamm min Iran" [Saudi Arabia Is More Important than Iran], *Al-Sharq Al-Awsat*, 15 May 2015, http://aawsat.com/print/360541.

152 Saud Katib, "Al-Ibtiad bad al-shay' an Amrika" [A Little Distancing from America], *Al-Madina*, 20 May 2015, www.al-madina.com/printhtml/608219.

153 Al-Shihri, "Waliy waliy al-ahd fi Musku."

154 Muhammad Al Al-Shaykh, "Li'l-ra'is Obama an Iran aqul" [I Am Telling President Obama about Iran], *Al-Jazira*, 2 June 2015, www.al-jazirah.com/2015/20150602/lp7. htm, and Salah, "Hal Obama muslim."

155 Editorial "Hal Rouhani ra'is islahi?" [Is Rouhani a Reformist President?], *Al-Riyadh*, 29 March 2015, www.alriyadh.com/1033322.

156 Mutlaq bin Saud Al-Mtiri, "Obama wa-muallimuh al-irani" [Obama and His Iranian Instructor], *Al-Riyadh*, 6 May 2015, www.alriyadh.com/1045702, Al-Milhim, "Camp David," and Fadila Al-Jaffal, "Bada'il al-ittifaq al-nawawi ma Iran" [Alternatives to a Nuclear Agreement with Iran], *Al-Iqtisadiya*, 21 April 2015, www.aleqt.com/2015/04/21/article_951280.html.

157 Tariq Al-Humayyid, "Ma alladhi faalhu al-khalijiyun fi Camp David?" [What Did Those from the Gulf Accomplish at Camp David?], *Al-Sharq Al-Awsat*, 17 May 2015, http://aawsat.com/node/361886., and Ma'mun Fandi, "Wartat Obama wa'l-ittifaq al-irani" [Obama's Dilemma and the Iranian Agreement], *Al-Sharq Al-Awsat*, 18 May 2015, http://aawsat.com/node/362716 (hereafter Fandi, "Wartat Obama").

158 Ayman Al-Hammad, "Camp David shiraka jadida la hilf jadid" [Camp David Is a New Partnership, Not a New Alliance], *Al-Riyadh*, 16 May 2015, www.alriyadh.com/1048575.

159 Fandi, "Wartat Obama."

160 Ghasib, "Madha law wafaq."

161 Jamil Al-Dhiyabi, "Najah al-shaytan al-akbar wa-ghab Al-Khalij!" [The Great Satan Has Succeeded and the Gulf Is Absent!], *Anba'akum*, 25 November 2013, www. anbacom.com/print.php?action=print&m=articlesm&id=18291, and Abd Al-Munim

Mustafa, "Iran nawawiya ... ayn al-arab?" [A Nuclear Iran: Where Are the Arabs?], *Al-Madina*, 22 November 2013, www.al-madina.com/printhtml/492857.

162 Abd Al-Munim Mustafa, "Iran fawq al-ataba al-nawawiya" [Iran Is on the Nuclear Threshold], *Al-Madina*, 27 September 2013, www.al-madina.com/printhtml/480894, Hamad Abd Allah Al-Luhaydan, "Al-Matami wa'l-tawajjuhat al-askariya al-iraniya" [Iranian Military Appetites and Hostility], *Al-Riyadh*, 6 September 2013, www.alriya dh.com/2013/09/06/article865450.html, and Yusuf Al-Kuwaylit, "Tahaddiyat al-amn min al-raghba ila al-darura!" [Security Challenges from Option to Necessity!], *Al-Riyadh*, 17 October 2013, www.alriyadh.com/2013/10/17/article876179.html.

163 "Adw bi'l-Shura: Al-Nawm sa-jujafi al-mintaqa bad al-ittifaq al-irani" [A Member of the Shura: The Region Will Lose Sleep following the Iranian Agreement], *Al-Yawm*, 25 November 2013, www.alyaum.com/News/art/105119.html.

164 Yusuf Al-Kuwaylit, "Nam lasna ala wifaq ma Amrika!" [That's Right, We Do Not Agree with America!], *Al-Riyadh*, 3 November 2013, www.alriyadh.com/2013/11/03/article880633.html.

165 Fahd Amir Al-Ahmadi, "Wa-ma alladhi yamna imtilakna silahan nawawiyan?" [What Prevents Us from Acquiring Nuclear Weapons?], *Al-Riyadh*, 18 February 2014, www.alriyadh.com/2014/02/18/article911241.html, and Ali Sad Al-Musa, "Li-madha ghab su'al al-silah al-nawawi al-saudi?" [Why Has the Question of a Saudi Nuclear Weapon Been Absent?], *Al-Watan*, 23 February 2014, www.alwatan.com.sa/Articles/Detail.aspx?ArticleId=20259.

166 "Turki Al-Faysal: Siyasat Iran munaghghisa li-amn Al-Khalij" [Turki Al-Faysal: Iran's Policies Are Disruptive to the Gulf's Security], *Al-Watan* (Manama, Bahrain), 23 April 2014, www.alwatannews.net.

167 Nayif Al-Asimi, "Sayf Abd Allah risala saudiya li-quwa al-sharr" [The Sword of Abd Allah Is a Saudi Message to the Forces of Evil], *Al-Watan*, 29 April 2014, www.alwatan.com.sa/Local/News_Detail.aspx?ArticleID=186428&CategoryID=5.

168 Ibrahim bin Sad Al Mari, "Natijat al-mufawadat al-gharbiya al-iraniya sa-tughayyir mizan al-quwa fi Al-Sharq Al-Awsat" [The Results of the Western–Iranian Negotiations Will Change the Balance of Power in the Middle East], *Markaz Al-Sharq Al-Arabi* (London), 25 November 2014, www.asharqalarabi.org.uk.

169 Ibrahim bin Sad Al Mari, "Al-Rad al-nawawi" [Nuclear Deterrence], *Al-Riyadh*, 5 January 2015, www.alriyadh.com/1010214.

170 Interview with Prince Turki by Christiane Amanpour, *CNN*, 17 March 2015, http://edition.cnn.com/TRANSCRIPTS/1503/17/ampr.01.html.

171 "Al-Faysal: Al-Tafawud ma Iran khati' wa'l-mintaqa amam sibaq nawawi" [Al-Faysal: The Negotiations with Iran Are a Mistake and the Region Is Facing a Nuclear Arms Race], *Al-Watan*, 19 March 2015, http://alwatan.com.sa/Politics/News_Detail.aspx?ArticleID=217927&CategoryID=1, and Khalid Al-Sulayman, "Li-madha yanjadhib Al-Gharb li-Iran?" [Why Is the West Attracted to Iran?], *Ukaz*, 18 March 2015, http://okaz.co/bwlbidlMy.

172 Zaynab Ghasib, "Amrika wa'l-lib ala al-hablayn" [America: Playing Two Sides of the Street], *Al-Hayat* (Saudi edition), 16 May 2015, http://al-hayat.com, also Tariq Al-Buaynayn, "Shukran Iran ... al-nawawi al-saudi qariban" [Thank You Iran: A Saudi Nuke Is Coming Soon], *Al-Sharq*, 10 April 2015, www.alsharq.net.sa/2015/04/10/1325731.

173 Asim Hamdan, "Ittifaq Lausanne yuid al-thiqa al-mafquda bayn Al-Gharb wa-Iran" [The Lausanne Agreement Restores Trust between the West and Iran], *Al-Madina*, 7 April 2015, www.al-madina.com.

174 Interview with Adel Al-Jubeir, by Alexandra Jaffe, "Saudi Ambassador to U.S. Won't Rule Out Building Nukes," *CNN*, 26 March 2015, www.cnn.com/2015/03/26/politics/saudi-open-to-nuclear-bomb; also statement by Prince Muhammad bin Nawwaf, Ambassador to the United Kingdom, Con Coughlin, "The Kingdom's Ambassador to London Tells *The Telegraph* that 'All Options Are on the Table' if Talks Fail to Keep

Iran in Check," *The Telegraph*, 8 June 2015, www.telegraph.co.uk/news/world news/middleeast/saudiarabiba/11658338/The-Saudis-are-ready-to-go-nuclear.html.

175 Zhafir bin Hubayyib, "Al-Qunbula al-nawawiya al-saudiya" [The Saudi Atom Bomb], *Sahifat Bani Amr* (Saudi Arabia), 31 March 2015, http://news.bani3mro.com/bani3mro/955.

176 Ali bin Hasan Al-Tawani, "Al-Tafkir al-ijabi fi al-safqa al-nawawiya al-iraniya" [Thinking Positively about the Iranian Nuclear Deal], *Ukaz*, 4 December 2013, www.okaz.com.sa/new/Issues/20131204/PrinCon20131204659329.htm.

177 Hashim Abdu Hashim, "Al-Quwwa wa-lays al-daf tuhaqqiq al-istiqrar fi al-mintaqa" [Strength, Not Weakness, Will Create Stability in the Region], *Al-Riyadh*, 13 May 2015, www.alriyadh.com/1047615, and Hasan Basuwayd, "Muhallilan li-*Ukaz*: Al-Matlub taharruk khaliji li-waqf tahdidat al-nawawi al-irani" [Two Analysts to *Ukaz*: What Is Needed Is a Gulf Initiative to Stop the Threat of Iranian Nuclear Weapons], *Ukaz*, 29 January 2015, http://okaz.co/bwH8fdje4.

178 Prince Turki Al-Faisal quoted in Barbara Plett Usher, "Saudi Warning on Iran Nuclear Deal," *BBC News*, 16 March 2015, www.bbc.com/news/world-middle-east-31901961, and Ayman Al-Hammad, "Hal tukhassib Al-Mamlaka al-yuraniyum?" [Will the Kingdom Enrich Uranium?], *Al-Riyadh*, 4 April 2015, www.alriyadh.com/1036014.

179 Sami Said Habib, "Al-Rad al-nawawi awjab wajibat al-marhala" [A Nuclear Deterrent Is the Most Important Requirement at This Juncture], *Al-Madina*, 23 May 2015, www.al-madina.com/printhtml/608920.

180 Khalid Al-Dakhil, "Obama wa-'aqlaniyat' Iran 'al-istitrajiya'" [Obama and Iran's "Strategic Rationality"], *Al-Hayat*, 24 May 2015, www.alhayat.com/Opinion/Khaled-El-Dakheel/9284916.

181 Interview with Staff Major General Anwar Majid Ishqi (Ret.) by Walid Diyab and Ahmad Abd Al-Hamid, "Ra'is Markaz Al-Sharq Al-Awsat Li'l-Dirasat Al-Istratijiya: Iran nimr min waraq" [The Director of the Middle East Center for Strategic Studies: Iran Is a Paper Tiger], *Akhbar Al-Khalij* (Manama), 20 May 2015, www.akhbar-alkhaleej.com/13182/article_touch/19174.html.

182 Major General Salama bin Hadhdhal Bin Saidan (Ret.), "Tabadul al-istiqrar ma Iran bayn ida'ha al-mawruth wa-ahdiha al-mankuth" [Mutual Stability with Iran in Light of Its Historical Enmity and Its Broken Promises], *Al-Jazira*, part 2, 3 June 2015, www.al-jazirah.com/sa/2015/20150603/ar7.htm.

183 Ibid.
184 Ibid.

11

COMING TO TERMS WITH THE 14 JULY 2015 NUCLEAR AGREEMENT

Saudi anxiety overcome?

The July 2015 Nuclear Agreement: initial Saudi reactions

Despite long-held preparation in Saudi Arabia for a nuclear agreement, nevertheless the final Nuclear Agreement of 14 July 2015 still came as a major challenge, forcing a reappraisal of the country's interests and strategy not only with respect to nuclear weapons but also to its broader regional and foreign policy and, specifically, to re-evaluating the key variable of Iran. The Saudi authorities perhaps had felt that allowing the media to vent frustration and disappointment after the Camp David summit was a way to prepare the public for an inevitable agreement and, even before the July Agreement was announced, in fact, many were already casting doubts about the expected outcome. For example, one analyst, who teaches at the Foreign Ministry's Institute of Diplomatic Studies, used the authority of the recently-deceased iconic Foreign Minister, Prince Saud Al-Faysal, to claim that the impending Agreement would be a bad deal, noting that while Prince Saud had been in favor of an agreement, it was not one where so many concessions would be made to Iran as was now said to be the case.[1]

Essentially, the July 2015 Nuclear Agreement followed the guidelines set by April's Framework Agreement, although negotiating the relevant details proved anything but easy.[2] The initial official Saudi reaction to the Nuclear Agreement was diplomatically anodyne, with King Salman stating in a telephone conversation with President Obama that Saudi Arabia "supports any agreement that guarantees that Iran will be prevented from acquiring nuclear weapons."[3] Subsequent official reactions continued to be muted and conditional. Typically, the Saudi Ambassador to the United Nations expressed his hope that Iran would see the Agreement as a new page in its regional and international policy and hoped that now the situation in the Middle East would improve.[4] Likewise, Foreign Minister Al-Jubeir was reported in the western media as having said that "the kingdom has been reassured by Washington" and that the Agreement "generally seems to have achieved these objectives," referring to effective inspections and the possibility of "snap-back" sanctions if Iran should violate the Agreement's provisions.[5] However, the version of his interview reported in the local press was far from a ringing endorsement, as it was made conditional, stressing that Riyadh welcomed any agreement, but only one that prevented nuclear weapons, and not explicitly saying that this was the case with the present Agreement.[6] Saudi press analyses, moreover, clarified such conditionality, noting that Saudi Arabia would welcome the Agreement, but only if it actually prevented Iran's acquisition of nuclear weapons, and that this had to be viewed against a background of Iran as a liar whom one could not trust.[7]

At the same time, the GCC foreign ministers as a group—following a telephone conference call with U.S. Secretary of State John Kerry—likewise expressed their hope that the new Agreement would "lead to a removal of the fears related to the Iranian nuclear program."[8] However, individually, some GCC states were considerably more receptive. The UAE was the first in the GCC to respond, sending a message the same day that the Agreement was announced to Iran's President Rouhani, expressing the hope that the Agreement would contribute to the region's security and stability, all the more striking as on the same day—perhaps in a reflexive reaction—an unnamed Saudi official source termed the Agreement "a historic error" arrived at by means of a "stage play."[9] Predictably, given its special relationship with Tehran, Oman's ruler, Sultan Qabus, in a telephone call to President Rouhani, characterized the Agreement as "good for the region and the world," while the Omani media called it "a historic agreement."[10] Qatar, too, through its Foreign Minister, termed the Agreement as "positive not only for the world but for the region as well."[11]

Such reactions, and the subsequent reaching out by Iran to some of the GCC countries, predictably, upset Riyadh, as was the case with one academic who fumed about "the GCC's weak response."[12] Saudi observers were especially furious that Tehran was approaching GCC states individually, fearing this would divide and weaken the GCC—and Saudi influence—and warned that "it is hard to imagine, much less accept" Tehran's approach, and proposed that to counter the "Iranian plots" it was necessary for the GCC to finally unify.[13] In fact, in the wake of the Agreement, there were renewed calls in the Saudi media for GCC unification. For example, one Saudi columnist claimed that "evil Iran" wanted to "erase the Gulf's Arab identity" and that "the Iranian enemy" could never become a friend whatever agreements were signed. In her view, the only solution was GCC unification, which allegedly was being demanded urgently by the people of the GCC countries, and which should be carried out immediately since there was "no need to listen to what America says."[14]

The Saudi media: "debating" the Agreement

Significantly, the Saudi media contributed at least a version of a debate—more of an indirect discussion really—assessing the Nuclear Agreement and Saudi options in its wake. Expressing differences in public on an issue such as the Agreement was in itself unusual and may have indicated a leadership initially in disarray, deeply uncertain, or even split as to the meaning of the Agreement and of its implications. At the same time, the Saudi media also went out of its way to rebut Iranian claims that there were divisions in Saudi Arabia, dismissing outright any suggestion that there were "hawks and doves" in the country.[15] Rather than a direct engagement of opposing views, commentators usually focused on different aspects of the Agreement and on its potential repercussions or varied in their degree of skepticism or hope. Nevertheless, two main trends in opinion did emerge. In this case, some media balance may not have been unwelcome in official circles, as damage-control to mitigate any appearance of weakness by the Saudi government, while at the same time still voicing criticism of the Agreement.

The doubters

Those who articulated a negative opinion were clearly in the majority and more blunt and consistent in their criticism than those who were more positive, although all commentators invariably stressed that they did not oppose an agreement with Iran per se. Prince Bandar bin Sultan set the tone for the doubters, although given his marginalized position under the new monarch, he had to express his views in a foreign newspaper (albeit one owned by Saudi interests), while the Saudi media did not give him the publicity he would have garnered in the past.[16] Very bluntly, he concluded that as the result of the Agreement, "chaos will engulf the Middle East," and he blamed President Obama personally. Moreover, his self-promotion as someone who uniquely understood the American political system and its players and the highlighting of his role as adviser to previous monarchs also contained implicit criticism of the current Saudi ruling team, given his portrayal of the Agreement as an unalloyed calamity. However, one Saudi commentator did remind Prince Bandar that it was he who was responsible for the present situation, and wondered how "we could be deceived by America," since Prince Bandar had been Ambassador to Washington for so many years and had remained a key player in Saudi policy even later. Asking "why did we remain at America's mercy?" this critic remarked sarcastically that the country would have expected to learn much earlier of such American duplicity "from our ambassadors [i.e. Prince Bandar] who are best-informed about U.S. policy and its swings!"[17] To criticize a royal so openly—even one no longer in favor—was very unusual, and suggests official encouragement in reaction to Prince Bandar's own criticism.[18]

However, criticism in the Saudi media of the Nuclear Agreement was no less severe, and extended over a range of issues. President Obama was often held directly responsible, as only the United States was seen to really matter, with critics not shying away from leveling opprobrium at him personally. President Obama was said to have desired an agreement "at any price" and had acted in "haste," achieving only "a disaster."[19] One prominent analyst called the whole negotiating process "a farce," claiming that President Obama could have achieved a better deal instead of being in a hurry for a political triumph, and concluded that Iran's leaders probably were smiling, unable to believe they had secured such favorable terms and that, in the process, he had strengthened the hardliners in Tehran.[20] Indeed, Iran was supposedly rewarded with "undreamed-of concessions," and President Obama was compared in the media to British Prime Minister Neville Chamberlain and the latter's unsuccessful 1930s policy of appeasement of Hitler, and he was taxed with having become "the registered trademark" for bad judgment.[21] While U.S. pressure might have forced Iran to make certain concessions, the overall results, from the Saudis' point of view, were not seen as positive, as they often felt that they would pay the price in terms of a strengthened and emboldened Iran, which might well acquire nuclear weapons anyhow in the long term.

On the purely technical aspect, many Saudis voiced concern that sufficient inspection and verification provisions were lacking, warning that an agreement that depends, as they saw it, solely on trust and goodwill would not last, as "no one trusts Iran's word or any agreement."[22]

A member of the Shura Council, for his part, feared that Iran would certainly not abide by the Agreement's provisions.[23] And, even in that case, it was said that Russia and China would oppose the envisioned "snap-back" sanctions.[24] Others complained that Iran had been allowed to retain its nuclear infrastructure as well as its SSM sector, while Iran's military facilities would also avoid inspection. In fact, developments in Iran's SSM arsenal had always been viewed in Saudi circles as an indicator of Tehran's undiminished intent to acquire nuclear weapons. In that vein, Saudi observers were concerned that although Iran had been willing to negotiate on its nuclear program it had refused adamantly to do so as far as its SSMs were concerned.[25]

Often, commentators—including a member of the Shura Council's Foreign Affairs Committee—remarked that the Agreement would only delay, but not prevent for good, Iran's acquisition of nuclear weapons and, for him, only the complete shutdown of all of Iran's nuclear facilities would have been effective. According to this view, permission for Iran to continue its civil nuclear program would enable it to develop its nuclear technology and experts during the pause, which it could then transfer to a military program once the Agreement had lapsed, if not before.[26] For one academic, Iran was already very close to developing a bomb ("the last 100 meters"), while for another pundit, in fact, Iran had already achieved "half an atom bomb" thanks to its nuclear know-how and the permission that had it received in the Agreement to continue enriching uranium.[27] At best, there would be a postponement of when Iran would achieve a nuclear weapon which, as one Saudi commentator put it, would be at a time when President Obama was retired in his rocking chair on the porch of his mansion in Chicago.[28] In fact, according to some observers, Iran had now been recognized as a nuclear state in all but name.[29]

Of course, for Riyadh, the nuclear negotiations had always encompassed more than just the strictly nuclear aspect that was enshrined in the July 2015 Agreement.[30] That is, what mattered critically for Riyadh was also any agreement's impact on Iranian policy in the region, and it had always sought to include a direct linkage in any agreement. Although commentators suggested that the Agreement could be positive if it led to an end to what Riyadh termed Iran's expansionism and interference in the other countries in the region and to a domestic focus instead, almost all concluded that this was not likely. On the contrary, the overwhelming consensus was that the Agreement instead would facilitate a continuation and an intensification of Iran's policy, as the West would view that as a fair trade-off in exchange for Iran's concessions on the nuclear issue and for the lure of economic gains, and would be reluctant to jeopardize the Agreement by confronting Tehran over its regional policy.[31] Supporters of such views, ultimately, believed that Iranian policy would not change or, as one journalist put it, "Iran will be Iran."[32] If anything, many Saudi commentators felt that the Agreement granted de facto recognition to Iran as a regional power and awarded Tehran "a free hand" in the Middle East or even believed that President Obama had given Tehran "a green light."[33] Moreover, a lifting of economic sanctions would provide more money to Iran with which the latter could finance its clients and, as the Saudis termed it, promote even more "terrorism and instability."[34]

Such consequences in and of themselves were enough for one typical Saudi columnist to conclude that the Agreement was "a bad deal," while another even added that the West wanted to use Iran to frighten the Arabs so that it could sell the latter more arms.[35] Some remarked that the Agreement signaled a shift from a U.S. alliance with the Gulf states to one with Iran, and still others went so far as to see the Agreement as a turning point in Middle East history, changing the regional balance of power forever and with worse yet to come, including even the partition of the Arab world into mini-states.[36] How the Agreement had been negotiated only added fuel to the fire, and some felt that the United States "had never given a second thought to the interests of its [Gulf] allies."[37] Critics spoke in terms of the Arabs having succumbed to "sweet words" and "bogus assurances," and disparaged "false friends" who had "betrayed" their allies.[38] One commentator interpreted the Agreement as "the last warning to anyone who believes in 'the American ally's' honesty."[39]

The positivists

As noted, there was also a parallel strand of analysis that saw the Agreement in more positive—or at least in less negative—terms. This view did not replace the more negative one but continued to run parallel to it, even if distinctly a very much weaker alternative in terms of frequency and intensity. In general, this trend gathered adherents later, perhaps as a corrective after the realization by the authorities that too strong a focus on attributing success to Iran might validate Tehran's ongoing trumpeting of the Agreement as a victory. In fact, at times, Iran projected in its Arabic-language media a sense of having achieved a victory over Saudi Arabia thanks to the Nuclear Agreement, aware of the discomfiture that this would cause Riyadh, which no doubt made the latter feel even more acutely the need to avoid giving the impression that it too saw the Agreement as an Iranian victory over the Saudis.

A perceived Iranian advantage must have been galling to the Saudis, who no doubt felt that Tehran had stolen a march on them, not least in terms of relations with the West. Moreover, an image of a successful Iran could have enhanced the latter's prestige among Middle Eastern audiences for whose loyalty both countries were vying, and would also result in encouraging Tehran to act more boldly. Perhaps equally importantly, any perception of an Iranian victory might make those in power in Saudi Arabia look inept or impotent in the eyes of the domestic or regional publics for having failed to prevent or even influence the Agreement, thus affecting the Saudi rulers' image and legitimacy negatively. In fact, the Saudis were very sensitive to suggestions that the Agreement represented a defeat for Saudi Arabia or was an indication of the latter's weakness, and one could detect an effort at damage-control. When the iconic Arab pundit, Egypt's Muhammad Hasanayn Heikal, suggested in a July 2015 interview in a Lebanese daily—along with numerous criticisms of Saudi policy—that Saudi Arabia (and the other Gulf states) were too weak to do anything about the Nuclear Agreement, apart from complaining to the Americans, and that the Saudis were all living in fear of the Iranians, it sparked a firestorm in Saudi Arabia. Variously attributing his remarks to such factors as hatred of Saudi Arabia, senility, or pique that the Saudi leaders did not value his views or consult him, the Saudi media castigated him bitterly for weeks thereafter, with journalists accusing him of "inflating Iran as compared to us," of "making propaganda for Iran after the Nuclear Agreement," and of belittling Saudi Arabia.[40] A Saudi academic, in fact, contended that Iran had been forced to sign the Agreement as a result of King Salman's assertive regional policy, which had forced Tehran to "get on America's and the West's good side."[41] Some Saudis stressed that it was Iran that was the loser, as it had made major concessions, including suspending its nuclear ambitions, to the international community and had even "sold its sovereignty."[42] Others dismissed outright Iranian claims of victory as propaganda.[43]

Typical of the optimists, a Saudi political scientist early on concluded that the Agreement would contain Iran and would prevent it from acquiring nuclear weapons and that the Agreement on the whole was "good for everyone."[44] Observers in this camp were often hopeful, arguing that the Agreement would boost reformist trends within Iran and that domestic demands inside Iran would now rise and undermine the current regime, and often pointed out that, in any case, Iran could not behave any worse in the region than it had been doing already.[45] An editor calculated that it was an exaggeration to think of the Agreement as "the end of the world," citing Iranian concessions in terms of oversight of its nuclear program, and seeing the results as at least mixed.[46] Another observer, in fact, was distinctly positive, certain that Iran's nuclear program would be frozen and that the United States would monitor it closely, that Iran would not be able to import SSMs for years, that Tehran would now follow a more cautious foreign policy and that, besides, any alternative would have been worse.[47] Still others went out of their way to admonish their fellow-countrymen that in the wake of the Nuclear Agreement it was sufficient, in any case, "to have faith in ourselves and in our decisive and prudent leaders."[48] Some at least softened their analysis of the Agreement with less negative assessments, as was the case with one analyst who noted that Iran would continue to have significant economic problems even after the sanctions were lifted in the wake of the Agreement.[49] Moreover, despite the now-permitted oil sales, it would take a long time for Iran to be able to raise its production and compete with Saudi Arabia.[50] Another journalist noted that the Agreement might be beneficial to Saudi Arabia as the latter could now justifiably request compensation in the form of written international security guarantees, advanced weaponry, and a recognition of Saudi interests and right to exert influence in the region.[51]

Perhaps as a way to diminish Tehran's pride and take the pressure off the Saudi government, at times, the Saudi media sought to suggest an air of indifference or at least to belittle Iran's nuclear pretensions. A cartoon in the daily *Al-Riyadh*, for example, portrayed the existing nuclear club countries as a modern warship alongside a small decrepit tugboat (Iran) giving itself self-delusional airs of having become an equal member of an elite group. However, in light of the widespread apprehension to be found in the Saudi media, such bravado often rang hollow.

The less alarmist trend may have received official encouragement and confirmation at one juncture when Abd Al-Rahman Al-Rashid—whom many consider the dean of Saudi commentators—moderated his own rhetoric, even though just a few days earlier he had been one of the Agreement's harshest critics. In a 26 July 2015 commentary reflecting a more balanced view, he reversed himself on virtually every point of criticism he had made up to then, when he had labeled the negotiating process "a farce" and the Agreement "a gift from the sky" for Tehran, and had argued that the Agreement would only provide a pause in Iran's nuclear quest, allow Tehran a free hand in the region, and strengthen the position of Iran's hardliners.[52] In his revised view, on the contrary, he now stressed that the United States had forced Iran to submit, that Iran's nuclear threat would now be limited, that the GCC states would not suffer negative consequences, and even that Iran might change. Moreover, Saudi relations with the United States would not be much affected as a result of the Agreement.[53] After all was said and done, as one observer pointed out, the economic, political, and security ties between the two countries were still of such a magnitude that it was "extremely unlikely" that the bilateral relationship would end.[54]

The positivists overshadowed

Although all the GCC states—including Saudi Arabia—publicly endorsed the Agreement when Secretary of State John Kerry visited the Gulf in early August 2015, Saudi Arabia was still convinced that Iran intended to develop nuclear weapons.[55] And, Riyadh was on its way to concluding that Iran would not abandon its positions on Syria, Iraq, Lebanon, or Yemen and had become concerned about Tehran's courting of some of the GCC states, resulting in an escalation in the anti-Iranian rhetoric in the Saudi media aimed at Iran's political leaders and their foreign policy. As a corollary of such conclusions about Iranian foreign policy, there was a resurgence of Saudi negative assessments of the Nuclear Agreement's reliability and expected impact, and anything positive about the Agreement was soon overshadowed again by negative assessments in the media. Indeed, one academic concluded that "Anyone who has a positive assessment of the Nuclear Agreement, I believe, is delusional!"[56] As another academic now argued, the Nuclear Agreement was "half-baked" and "not worth the ink in which it was written," and was not based on principles but motivated by the West's interests to sell arms and technology and to have access to Iran's oil. And, he believed that while the United States would ensure that Israel was compensated, he assumed at the same time that Washington would ignore the interests of its other Middle East allies.[57] Others dismissed the entire negotiating process as "political comedy," claiming that if the United States had really been serious it would have destroyed Iran's nuclear capability once and for all or at least insisted on a better deal.[58]

Senior pundit Abd Al-Rahman Al-Rashid, reversing himself once again, now claimed to believe that those optimists who were unable to distinguish between "facts and fairytales" and who had predicted that the Nuclear Agreement would lead to a change in Iran's regional policy were completely mistaken, and that Tehran's verbal declarations and wooing of the GCC states were only "diplomatic gestures" intended to facilitate acceptance of the Agreement in the United States, that Iran would not abide by the Agreement, and that the Agreement would have no positive impact in the Middle East.[59] In fact, one Saudi academic dismissed anything Iran said as being simply deception—using the Shia religious term for dissimulation, *taqiya*—and stressed the need for "the Arabs" to respond with all available means.[60] Even after Secretary Kerry's August 2015 visit to Riyadh that was intended to reassure the Saudis, one journalist concluded that "the Nuclear Agreement is part of the problem, not of the solution."[61] Still others expressed a sense of resentment at what they now felt was U.S. pressure on Riyadh to engage in a dialogue with an unregenerate Tehran.[62] In effect, a growing consensus had coalesced that Iran would not change despite the Agreement.[63] Paradoxically, those expounding alarmist views in the United States—who were featured prominently in the Saudi media—may have contributed to Saudi anxiety and encouraged Saudis to view the Agreement and the Obama Administration in negative terms.

The way forward

Many, and perhaps most, informed Saudis continued to view Iran's nuclear potential as a threat to their country, Agreement or no Agreement. In this uncertain environment, what Saudi Arabia should do in concrete terms in the wake of the Agreement, not surprisingly, elicited considerable commentary, especially on the part of those who viewed the Agreement in negative terms. One cleric, Salman Al-Awda, included some implicit criticism when, in contrast to what he saw as

Iran's having a vision and a plan, he asked "the Arab governments" where their counter-plans were.[64] Some now saw the challenge as either to "remain passive observers or to become players in the game," and often the stress now was on self-reliance.[65] As part of the fallout from the Agreement, there was an increase of proposals for a more proactive policy, including enlisting anti-Iranian proxies in other countries as well as minorities and dissidents within Iran in what was viewed as a new post-Agreement Cold War.[66] Iran had accused Riyadh of supporting subversion—including by supporting jihadist groups—already for a number of years, and any increase could raise tensions even further.[67] Other observers suggested that Saudi Arabia in the future should use its economic investments abroad more actively to influence other countries' policies, while still others blamed the Tehran government and sought to appeal to the Iranian population against the latter.[68]

In terms of the implications for Saudi Arabia's nuclear options, many appeared to be in agreement with the Saudi columnist who claimed that the Nuclear Agreement "launches a nuclear weapons race in the region," giving every state in the region the same right to its own defense and that this was the beginning of the end of the NPT.[69] Although the United States was now willing to sell even more arms to the Gulf states, that was not seen as equivalent to having a "deterrent" and, according to some commentators, "the only option" for Saudi Arabia or for the GCC was to acquire a nuclear weapon equivalent to that of Iran.[70] The focus remained clearly on Iran, as an academic held that since it was best to carry on a dialogue from a position of strength, then Saudi Arabia should acquire nuclear weapons, as well as advanced conventional ones, so that "Iran will think long and hard before doing anything."[71]

A columnist, for his part, made the veiled threat that either the Middle East become a nuclear-free zone—to include Israel, of course—or that Saudi Arabia should leave the NPT and acquire nuclear weapons.[72] Given the assumed likelihood that Iran would cheat on the Agreement, one Saudi newspaper concluded that "the only thing that can be relied upon to face Iran is a nuclear weapon."[73] In fact, one commentator accused the United States of having changed its priorities and its friends in the Middle East, resulting in an erosion of trust in U.S. security guarantees and that, as a consequence, Saudi Arabia needed to reassess its own strategy, especially since nuclear proliferation was now certain to ensue.[74] A journalist, who stated in no uncertain terms that it was "guaranteed" that Iran would get nuclear weapons, even if only later, saw that as automatically entailing Saudi Arabia's acquisition of the same capability too.[75] A political scientist was equally direct, confirming the views that Saudi commentators had introduced over the years, as he stated bluntly that "the decision to acquire a nuclear deterrent is, basically, a national sovereign one."[76] As he stressed, "It is senseless to speak of an Arab or a Gulf atom bomb, and it is only possible to speak instead of a Saudi, Egyptian, or Algerian one." Moreover, in his view, a nuclear umbrella from regional allies—i.e. Pakistan—would not be enough. Neither would reliance on the United States, as even during the Cold War Britain and France allegedly did not believe their ally would risk New York City for London or Paris in a nuclear exchange. And, of course, ultimately, if one decided to acquire such a deterrent, a corollary decision would follow, that of being willing to "use it, or to be prepared to use it, or to threaten to use it."

For the moment, some supported developing Saudi Arabia's own civilian nuclear capabilities in preparation for when Iran did officially go nuclear. Specifically, they suggested building Saudi Arabia's civilian nuclear infrastructure, with nuclear reactors and research, as Saudi Arabia was said to have a right to demand the same rights in the nuclear field as those granted to Iran and, in particular, in terms of enriching uranium.[77] One editor linked the establishment of a Saudi civilian nuclear program with "the beginning of a nuclear arms race," coinciding with "anxiety ... about Iran's nuclear ambitions and the Agreement reached between the 5+1 countries and Iran."[78] As another editor put it, in the wake of the Agreement it was now necessary for Saudi Arabia to strengthen itself, and he even believed that the Agreement provided "a green light for the Gulf states—and foremost for Saudi Arabia—to develop a nuclear program that would enable them to acquire nuclear fuel, and that will produce a deterrent to guarantee stability in the balance of power."[79] A Saudi academic, in fact, argued that as a response to Iran it was now "imperative to act decisively and quickly to transfer nuclear technology to the Gulf states." Although she called for the process to be undertaken under the supervision of the IAEA, that is as part of a civilian program, the underlying implications were clearly viewed from a security standpoint.[80]

Those who may have held less alarmist views, for their part, were hard-put to offer any tangible suggestions, apart from a passive "wait-and-see," weakening their position in comparison with those calling for greater activism. One journalist suggested that the Agreement need not be an Iranian victory if others made judicious use of diplomatic démarches and by "participating in monitoring the Nuclear Agreement's provisions."[81] Other commentators, while expressing their concern about continuity in Iran's regional policy, offered to see if the United States would fulfill its guarantees to the GCC with respect to the Nuclear Agreement and Iran's policy of expansion.[82] A rare individual even suggested attempting co-existence with Iran.[83] However, as noted above, Riyadh's views had hardened over the summer and such suggestions soon ceased to appear. In fact, many Saudis continued to harbor hopes that opponents of the Agreement, whether Israel, American legislators, or hardliners in Iran, might scuttle it, and the Saudi press would give wide coverage of any instances of opposition as an indication that this might occur. In particular, Saudis pinned their hopes on the U.S. Congress—and especially on the Republican Party—to reject the Agreement.[84] Some reports suggested that, to that end, Saudi financing contributed to one lobbying firm's use of TV ads that aired in the United States to oppose the Agreement.[85]

Who's to blame?

Some Saudis viewed the developments connected with the Iranian nuclear issue and its culmination in a disappointing Nuclear Agreement as an intelligence and policy failure for Riyadh, blaming poor information and analysis that resulted in an inability to predict or shape events. Tellingly, after the Agreement, some Saudis engaged in a post-mortem to identify and remedy such shortcomings, and one Saudi academic compared the GCC during the preceding negotiating process to "midgets playing volleyball against giants who are professionals."[86] He faulted the GCC's poor intelligence and analytical capabilities, describing as self-deception such predictions as the one that Iran would fall apart, or misunderstanding the developing U.S.–Iranian relationship, and decried the failure to generate strategies that could have countered Iran's success. He also excoriated the political pundits, although acknowledging that they had "lacked information" with which to work. In particular, he rued the fact that there are no effective research institutes in the Gulf. While such criticism was directed at "the Gulf," implicitly Saudi Arabia's own shortcomings were also to be understood. Others were more explicit, grumbling that there were no research institutes in Saudi Arabia specifically for Iranian studies or for strategic studies, and that the country had to depend on foreign research centers or governments for its information and analysis.[87]

Other media pundits, for their part, launched blistering attacks on Saudi Arabia's diplomats, most of whom (with the explicit exception of the Ambassador to Great Britain—a prince) were taxed as woefully ineffective in representing their country's interests or in influencing foreign decisionmakers, while embassies were said to be staffed with inept cronies.[88] Critics, in particular, blamed the lack of a presence by Saudi representatives in the foreign media as a way to influence foreign public opinion.[89] In fact, observers barely concealed their envy of what they believed was Iran's diplomatic effectiveness on the nuclear issue, citing the role of Iranian–American academics in paving the way to negotiations, and even giving Iran credit for supposedly having penetrated U.S. think tanks with its supporters, thus allegedly allowing Tehran to feed inaccurate information to U.S. policymakers as the latter grappled with the nuclear challenge.[90] While Riyadh reportedly has devoted significant amounts of money in an effort to influence U.S. policy, the focus apparently has been on lobbying firms and what one Saudi observer called "mercenary writers," which he concluded was ineffective.[91]

Closing the circle—King Salman's September 2015 visit to Washington

While the September 2015 de facto ratification by Congress of the Nuclear Agreement can be said to mark the culminating point for the United States in the quest to prevent Iran's acquisition of the atom bomb, for Saudi Arabia that circle was closed with King Salman's visit to Washington earlier that same month for a summit with President Obama although, of course, in both cases the final resolution of the Iranian nuclear issue remains a work in progress. Clearly, for the Saudis, the catalyst and centerpiece of the summit held on 3–4 September 2015 was the Nuclear Agreement and its potential security and political consequences, as Foreign Minister Al-Jubeir and other officials pointed out; and in most cases, the summit's ensuing conclusions and agreements all related back to Iran.[92]

Adapting to a new reality

The King's visit came as a number of developments placed Riyadh in an uncomfortable position. It was becoming evident that any hoped-for leverage to be gained from Riyadh's courting of Russia had not borne fruit, given Moscow's continuing—and even increasing—military and political support for the Asad regime and good relations with Iran, and realization that there was no realistic replacement for the United States as a guarantor of Saudi security.[93] It was also becoming increasingly clear to Saudi observers over time that President Obama would likely be able to muster sufficient support in Congress and in public opinion to make possible an official acceptance of the Nuclear Agreement. The Saudis were becoming disenchanted by the Republican Party not only because of its failure to prevent the Nuclear Agreement, but also because that party was seen as a strong supporter of Israel, had plans to remake the Middle East in a way detrimental to the Arabs, and wanted "puppets" to govern in the region, so that a Republican successor to President Obama might be even less favorable to Saudi interests.[94] And, at the same time, the Saudis apparently concluded that Israel and the "Zionist" lobby, too, would not succeed in opposing the Agreement and that Riyadh had overestimated their influence in this matter.[95]

Moving toward a resigned acceptance

Gradually, Saudi commentators adopted a sense of resignation to a situation that could not be changed, as one did when he stated that it was no use asking the United States to change its Iran policy even though the Agreement was "a stinging slap and … a psychological shock."[96] The local media interpreted the message from Secretary of Defense Ashton Carter's 2015 Riyadh visit as that "the allies must understand that the Agreement with Iran is a fact and they must deal with it."[97] One journalist, for his part, noted that despite the fact that the Middle East would pay the price of the Agreement, "it is unavoidable that we deal with [its] consequences rather than rejecting it."[98] Another commentator portrayed the Agreement as not being a victory for Iran, and characterized those who claimed that it was as "enemies of the Gulf governments," while concluding that it was best for the GCC to deal with the situation as given, since to do otherwise was "a waste of time," and advising critics to "stop spreading rumors."[99] An academic who admitted he had "significant doubts" whether the Agreement would really prevent Iran from acquiring nuclear weapons or whether it would simply acknowledge that fact when it happened, nevertheless also recognized that it was difficult for Riyadh to change its existing alliances and hoped that President Obama's successor would return to more traditional policies.[100] Some interpreted the 2 September 2015 article by pundit Thomas Friedman in which he supported the Nuclear Agreement (and also criticized Saudi Arabia's backing of hardline Islamists) as having signaled U.S. pressure on Riyadh at the upcoming summit in Washington to go along with the Agreement, a conclusion fueled by the Saudi assumption that Friedman has close ties to the White House.[101] Significantly, according to a well-informed Saudi writing on the eve of King Salman's departure for Washington, the Saudi ruler was said to be taking the same message there that the Saudis had given to visiting Secretary of Defense Carter in August 2015 to the effect that, while Saudi Arabia would support the Agreement, it doubted whether Iran would actually abide by it.[102]

King Salman and the Americans: objectives and results

In particular, Riyadh may have felt the need to pull back from the criticism of and distancing from the United States that both official circles and the media had displayed in expressing Saudi displeasure and doubts about the direction of the bilateral relationship and, specifically, about the Nuclear Agreement and its implications for U.S. policy in the region. This self-imposed Saudi alienation may have fed concerns that, if it continued unchecked, a self-fulfilling prophecy of an expanding U.S.–Iranian rapprochement and increasing U.S. reliance on Iran in the region might actually come to pass by default. Not surprisingly, one of the stated Saudi objectives for the summit was to counter media "speculation" about problems in the U.S.–Saudi bilateral relationship.[103]

Clearly, the intent of the visit was also to burnish the image of the ruling family domestically and in the region, as the impression may have taken hold that Saudi Arabia and, by extension, the royal family had been bested by Iran with the latter's rapprochement with the United States. Moreover, Riyadh's apparent inability to affect, much less derail, the Nuclear Agreement despite its opposition, may have suggested weakness and ineptitude by the Saudi rulers, factors with both psychological and potentially tangible repercussions. Very likely, the sizeable delegation that accompanied the King to Washington, and which included editors, journalists, academics, businessmen and intellectuals, was designed to convey a forceful message upon their return to counter potentially negative impressions that had built up over the past few months. And indeed, the coverage which the Saudi media supplied was not only copious and repetitive, but also standardized, and when the prevalent themes are identified here, there is no need to indicate specific sources, as all the media presented a uniform portrait.

Riyadh now conveniently forgot its previous doubts and snubs (such as King Salman's refusal to attend the May 2015 Camp David Summit), as well as the earlier unflattering assessments of U.S. policy and the vituperative language that the Saudi media had been allowed to use in describing President Obama and other U.S. officials. Saudi officials and the country's media characterized the summit as extremely important, pivotal, historic, and extraordinary, and exceptionally warm— even the body language was said to indicate this—and King Salman was quoted as saying "We love America."[104] Understandably, even the blistering Saudi media response to Friedman's article would be delayed until after the summit. Of course, it was also in the Obama Administration's interest to smooth over differences, especially in light of the continuing instability and threats in the region.[105]

Saudi officials stressed the importance of the relationship with the United States, which the Saudi media now characterized as stable and robust, and assured its public that any superficial differences and minor details on secondary issues would not have an impact, and that Saudi Arabia was not thinking of replacing the United States with other allies. Conversely, as Riyadh was anxious to prevent Iran from moving closer to the United States, much less replacing Saudi Arabia as the latter's key partner in the region, Saudi Arabia was also eager to prove to Washington that it was a more valuable partner than Iran would be. Even the extensive economic agreements concluded at the summit, involving an unprecedented opening of the country to U.S. business and which the Saudis claimed could be worth $300 billion, were geared with that in mind, and also portrayed as giving Riyadh additional leverage over the United States.[106]

The Saudi side declared itself more than satisfied with the summit's results. The leadership team briefed the accompanying Saudi journalists using such terms—some of which eventually also appeared in the final joint communiqué—as positive, productive, a "resounding success," and a victory for Riyadh, with a consensus on all regional issues, as well as on the Nuclear Agreement, due in great part to the personal role of the King and of his son, Deputy Crown Prince Muhammad. In fact, the summit had "raised the relationship to new levels," and the negotiators had achieved a "new strategic partnership for the twenty-first century." Indicative of the summit's significance that the Saudi government wished to portray to the public was the local media's coverage and commentary that continued for weeks after the event, with the media equating the summit's importance as equal to the original establishment of the bilateral relationship by the country's founder, King Abd Al-Aziz, and President Franklin Roosevelt in 1945, and with King Salman portrayed as "the man of the hour" and "the architect of a new era for the region."[107]

The emphasis in the Saudi media was also on showcasing Saudi Arabia's strength and importance as a factor in the summit. The Saudi media insisted that it was not their country that had changed its policy, which was described as steadfast and constant, but rather that events had forced President Obama to review his position.[108] In fact, the onus for past problems was placed on the Obama Administration for allegedly having taken "an enemy state [i.e. Iran] … as a friend in order to balance or to compete with the Kingdom of Saudi Arabia."[109] On this occasion, it was Saudi Arabia that had "set the agenda" and had come not as a supplicant, since the King stressed to his hosts that his country "does not need anything." Indeed, Saudi Arabia's "wise leaders" were said to "circle the globe not to listen but to speak," and "it was necessary for someone to ring the bell and tell the United States that we were no longer infants and that we would no longer accept being treated as subordinates."[110] In fact, Saudi Arabia had imposed itself on the international scene "because it is an important player who cannot be ignored."[111] King Salman was reported to have told President Obama that "the Kingdom does not need anyone to defend it or to help it," but had only requested the provision of advanced weaponry before the visit "in order not to be prisoners of any hypothetical and not binding assurances."[112] The King was said to have made a compelling impression on the U.S. Administration and the world, while the Americans "paid rapt attention to every word Salman spoke" and saw that he is strong and decisive.[113]

The Saudi media stressed that during the summit Washington had dealt with Riyadh as an equal, while the reception afforded to the King was said to have been unprecedented.[114] The Saudi media portrayed King Salman as representing "a great and capable regional power" playing a key role in the international balance and Prince Muhammad briefed the Saudi media to the effect that the summit showed that Saudi Arabia was "the most powerful and the most important country in the region."[115] Not surprisingly, an influential Saudi pundit now reiterated earlier claims that Riyadh was able to defend the Gulf and the rest of the Arab world.[116] Moreover, the United States had recognized Riyadh's importance and leadership role in the Muslim and Arab worlds, and that Saudi Arabia remained central for regional security, including in countering Russian influence.[117] Indeed, King Salman was said to represent all the Arabs.[118] President Obama was even said to have needed Saudi support for the Nuclear Agreement in his struggle to gain approval for the deal in Congress.[119] In fact, one academic claimed that now the United States needed Saudi Arabia more than the other way around.[120] Significantly, King Salman was portrayed as having succeeded in "extracting" from the United States the commitment to stand up to Iran that was to appear in the final communiqué.[121] Riyadh also sought to give the impression that its earlier gambit with France and Russia "might have raised some questions with the Americans about losing traditional allies in the Gulf region," thereby making the United States more anxious to retain Saudi Arabia's friendship.[122] The Saudis certainly were relieved that the improved U.S.–Saudi relationship would preclude a closer rapprochement between Washington and Iran and viewed this aspect as a victory over Tehran. Perhaps as way to deflate Saudi claims of success and power, frequent Iranian statements to the effect that it was Iran that was the strongest regional power coincided with the summit and its aftermath.[123]

Deep down, the Saudis' conviction that Iran's intent was and would continue to be to acquire nuclear weapons probably had not changed, as King Salman had affirmed to President Obama during the latter's visit to Saudi Arabia in January 2015.[124] Bowing to realism, however, the Saudis had clearly downsized their objectives on the nuclear issue for the Washington summit. As one senior journalist acknowledged, it was unlikely that President Obama in his last few months in office would have been willing to alter the Nuclear Agreement in any case, "otherwise, we would be saying that the Nuclear Agreement with Iran was subject to modification," and the Saudis had gone to Washington "with their eyes wide open."[125] Riyadh expressed its satisfaction that President Obama had assured the King that the Nuclear Agreement would prevent Iran from acquiring nuclear weapons, as well as promising to speed up the sale of advanced weaponry, deploy a joint missile defense shield, and continue to protect its Gulf allies, while all the agreements concluded at the summit were said to help ensure stability. A key point, of course, was Riyadh's acceptance of the Nuclear Agreement, as highlighted in the final joint communiqué. However, even here there may have been a lingering tinge of skepticism and conditionality. While the English-language version notes more positively that the King expressed his support for the Agreement, "which once fully implemented will prevent Iran from obtaining a nuclear weapon," the Arabic-language version can also suggest a degree of conditionality or doubt, as the term used may be understood as "in the event that" or "in case"—that is, *if*—the Agreement is implemented fully (*hal tatbiqihi*).

Encapsulating what the Saudis might view as the uncertain future implications of the Nuclear Agreement, a Saudi academic, while acknowledging that it will be good if Iran is prevented from acquiring nuclear weapons for the next 15 years, also raised doubts as to whether Iran would adhere to the Agreement's provisions and wondered what the American reaction might be to any violations. And, while raising the possibility that President Obama's successor might even abrogate the Agreement, he also questioned whether U.S. policymakers understood that it was impossible for a regime such as Iran's to submit to the international system.[126]

Notes

1 Hamdan Al-Shihri, "Al-Faysal jaal Al-Mamlaka hajar zawiya li'l-amn wa'l-silm al-dawliyayn" [Al-Faysal Made the Kingdom the Cornerstone of International Security and Peace], *Al-Riyadh*, 12 July 2015. www.alriyadh.com/1064393.
2 The White House, "The Iran Deal," https://medium.com/the-iran-deal, and "Crucial Provisions of the Accord," *New York Times*, 14 July 2015, www.nytimes.com/live/iran-nuclear-deal-live-updates/key-provisions-of-the-accord.
3 "Al-Malik Salman fi ittisal ma Obama: Nu'ayyid ayy ittifaq yamna Iran min al-husul ala al-silah al-nawawi wa-yudammin aliyat taftish li-kaffat al-mawaqi" [King Salman in a Conversation with Obama: We Support Any Agreement That Prevents Iran from Acquiring Nuclear Weapons and That Guarantees a Mechanism for Inspecting All the Sites], *Al-Riyadh*, 15 July 2015, www.alriyadh.com/1065264.
4 To CNN, cited in "Al-Muallimi: Ala Iran an takun adwan muhtaraman fi al-mujatama al-duwali" [Al-Muallimi: Iran Must Be a Responsible Member of the International Community], *Al-Madina*, 18 July 2015, www.al-madina.com/printhtml/619734.
5 "Saudi FM: Iran Deal May Stop Tehran from Getting Nuke Weapons," *Associated Press*, 23 July 2015, httop:hosted.ap.org/dynamic/stories/m/ml_saudi_iran_nuclear_1st_ld_writethru?site=ap&section=home&template=default.
6 "Al-Jubayr: Nahnu ma al-ittifaq alladhi yamna imtilak Iran li'l-silah al-nawawi" [Al-Jubeir: We Support an Agreement That Prevents Iran from Acquiring Nuclear Weapons], *Al-Madina*, 24 July 2015, www.al-madina.com/printhtml/620808.
7 Ibrahim Ali Nasib, "Obama wa-ahlam al-yaqzha!" [Obama and Daydreaming!], *Al-Madina*, 21 July 2015, www.al-madina.com/printhtml/620084.
8 "Duwal Al-Khalij: Kerry atlana ala tafasil al-ittifaq al-nawawi wa-akkad al-iltizam bi-nata'ij Camp David" [The Gulf States: Kerry Informed Us of the Details of the Nuclear Agreement and Reaffirmed a Commitment to the Provisions of Camp David], *Al-Iqtisadiya*, 15 July 2015, www.aleqt.com/2015/07/15/article_973676.html.
9 "Al-Imarat tuhanni' Iran ala al-ittifaq al-nawawi wa-masdar Saudi li-CNN: Al-Mamlaka sa-yakun laha radd qawi" [The UAE Congratulates Iran on the Nuclear Agreement While a Saudi Source to CNN: The Kingdom's Response Will Be a Strong

One], *CNN Arabic*, 14 July 2015, http://arabic.cnn.com/middleeast/2015/07/14/pol-iran-nuclear-deal-uae-ksa.

10 "Qabus: Al-Ittifaq al-nawawi li-salih al-mintaqa wa'l-alam wa-hall al-azmat mumkin bi-musaadat Iran" [Qabus: The Nuclear Agreement Is Good for the Region and the World and the Crises Can Be Resolved with Iran's Help], *Al-Quds*, 17 July 2015, www.alquds.com/news/article/view/id/565667, and "Ra'y *Al-Watan*: Ittifaq tarikhi li-salih al-mintaqa wa'l-alam" [In *Al-Watan's* Opinion: A Historic Agreement Good for the Region and the World], *Al-Watan* (Muscat), 15 July 2015, http://alwatan.com/details/69060.

11 "Al Attiyah: Qatar among First Countries to Encourage Settling Iran Nuclear Issue through Peaceful Means," Qatar News Agency, 16 July 2015, www.qna.org.

12 Hamad Abd Allah Al-Luhaydan, "Al-Abth wa'l-ghatrasa al-iraniya yumkin lajmuhuma bi'l-muwajaha wa'l-hiwar" [It Is Possible to Curb Iranian Recklessness and Arrogance by Confrontation and Dialogue], *Al-Riyadh*, 31 July 2015, www.alriyadh.com/1069286. Iran's ambassador to Kuwait had even hinted that Tehran would be willing to share its nuclear technology with its Gulf neighbors, "Safir Iran lada Al-Kuwayt yu'akkid istidad biladih li-naql al-taknulujiya al-nawawiya li-jiranha" [Iran's Ambassador to Kuwait Confirms His Country's Willingness to Transfer Nuclear Technology to Its Neighbors], *Al-Wifaq*, 27 July 2015, www.al-vefagh.com/export/print/82912?module=news.

13 Da'ud Al-Shiryan, "La budd min muawadat tashkil majlis al-taawun" [Reconfiguring the Structure of the GCC Is Needed], *Al-Hayat*, 28 July 2015, http://alhayat.com/Opinion/Dawood-Al-Sheryan/10246885, Jasir Abd Al-Aziz Al-Jasir, "Mukhattat millali Iran li'l-mintaqa al-arabiya" [Iran's Nationalist Plan for the Arab Region], *Al-Jazira*, 19 July 2015, www.al-jazirah.com/2015/20150719/du5.htm, and Abd Al-Ilah bin Saud Al-Sadun, "Ittihadna wa'l-ta'amur al-irani al-mustamirr" [Our Union and the Continuing Iranian Plotting], *Al-Jazira*, 29 July 2015, www.al-jazirah.com/2015/20150729/du6.htm.

14 Saygha Al-Shammari, "Dawlat Al-Khalij al-uzhma" [The Great Gulf State], *Al-Jazira*, 10 August 2015, www.al-jazirah.com/2015/20150810/ar4.htm.

15 Tariq Al-Humayyid, "Hal fi Al-Saudiya suqur wa-hama'im?" [Are There Hawks and Doves in Saudi Arabia?], *Al-Sharq Al-Awsat*, 27 July 2015, http://aawsat.com/node/415696.

16 Letter from Prince Bandar, "Al-Amir Bandar bin Sultan yakhruj an samtih" [Prince Bandar bin Sultan Emerges from His Silence], *Ilaf*, 15 July 2015, http://elaphjournal.com/Web/News/2015/7/1024252.html. Likewise, reflecting his diminished status, when Prince Bandar submitted the same text (less the self-promoting portion about his understanding of American presidents) to the *Washington Post*, the latter published it on 17 July 2015 only as a short easy-to-miss letter to the editor, whereas when he had been a public figure such an intervention on his part would surely have garnered a prominently-featured op-ed.

17 Musaid Al-Asimi, "Ila al-amir Bandar bin Sultan: Ta'akhkharna kathiran" [To Prince Bandar bin Sultan: We Are Very Late], *Al-Watan*, 22 July 2015, www.alwatan.com.sa/Articles/Detail.aspx?ArticleID=27176.

18 As a TV host and his guest found out when they were arrested in 2015 after having criticized a past monarch in a very minor way on the air. "Bi-amr al-malik: Muhakamat Al-Awaji wa'l-Mudayfir wa-manuhuma min al-zhuhur al-ilami" [By Order of the King: Legal Proceedings against Al-Awaji and Al-Mudayfir and a Ban on Their Appearing in the Media], *Sabq*, 2 July 2015, http://sabq.org/8XAgde.

19 Talal Salih Bannan, "Adw fi al-nadi al-nawawi!" [Member of the Nuclear Club!], *Ukaz*, 21 July 2015, http://okaz.co/bwlhNdsko, Ali Al-Anazi, "Al-Ittifaq al-nawawi wa-inikasatuh" [The Nuclear Agreement and Its Impact], *Al-Hayat* (Saudi edition), 18 July 2015, http://alhayat.com/Opinion/Ali-Al-Anzi/10042259 (hereafter Bannan, "Adw fi al-nadi"), and Rashid Muhammad Al-Fawzan, "Al-Ittifaq al-irani al-amiriki

bi-manzhur iqtisadi" [The Iranian–U.S. Agreement from an Economic Perspective], part 2, *Al-Riyadh*, 22 July 2015, www.alriyadh.com/1066709.

20 Abd Al-Rahman Al-Rashid, "Al-Ittifaq al-irani al-gharbi wa-nahnu" [The Iranian–Western Agreement and Us], part 1, *Al-Sharq Al-Awsat*, 16 July 2015, http://aawsat.com/node/407491.

21 Abu Lajin Ibrahim Al Dahman, "Al-Ittifaq al-nawawi ma Iran huw ma yaqra'hu al-alam fa-qat!" [The Nuclear Agreement with Iran Is Only What the World Interprets It As!], *Sabq*, 14 July 2015, http://sabq.org/7L1aCd, and Abd Al-Munim Mustafa, "Al-Nawm min al-qunbula!" [Sleeping with the Bomb!], *Al-Madina*, 17 July 2015, www.al-madina.com/printhtml/619573.

22 Rashid Muhammad Al-Fawzan, "Al-Ittifaq al-irani al-amiriki bi-manzhur iqtisadi" [The Iranian–U.S. Agreement from an Economic Perspective], part 1, *Al-Riyadh*, 21 July 2015, www.alriyadh.com/1066707, and Ahmad bin Muhammad Al-Jamia, "Al-Nawawi al-irani: Al-Ittifaq sabaq thawrat al-jia!" [Iran's Nuclear Program: The Agreement Headed Off a Revolution by the Hungry!], *Al-Riyadh*, 15 July 2015, www.alriyadh.com/1065148.

23 Abd Allah Al-Askar quoted in Radwa Abd Allah, Iyad Abd Allah, and Tharwat Al-Battawi, "Duktur Al-Askar: Al-Ittifaq yumahhid li-uqala' Iran kal iba'at al-tatarruf wa'l-ta'ifiya" [Dr. Al-Askar: The Agreement Makes It Possible for Those Who Are Wise in Iran to Free Themselves of the Burden of Extremism and Sectarianism], *Al-Madina*, 16 July 2015, www.al-madina.com/printhtml.619406 (hereafter "Duktur Al-Askar").

24 Sufuq Al-Shammari, "Ittifaq nawawi aswa' min al-si'i!" [A Nuclear Agreement That Is Worse Than Bad!], *Al-Riyadh*, 21 July 2015, www.alriyadh.com/1066541 (hereafter Al-Shammari, "Ittifaq nawawi"), and confirmed to Saudi audiences in the statement by Russian Deputy Foreign Minister Sergei Rybakov reported in Sami Ammara, "Zharif fi Musku bad ghad" [Zareef in Moscow the Day after Tomorrow], *Al-Sharq Al-Awsat*, 15 August 2015, http://aawsat.com/node/430006.

25 Mustafa Al-Tarhuni, "Muhadathat Iran al-nawawiya wa-aqabat al-sawarikh" [Iran's Nuclear Negotiations and the Missile Obstacle], *Al-Madina*, 13 April 2014, www.al-madina.com/printhml/524239, and Jasir Abd Al-Aziz Al-Jasir, "Al-Uyun al-ghar-biya tughammad an al-ghubar al-nawawi al-irani" [The West's Eyes Are Blinded by Iran's Nuclear Dust], *Al-Jazira*, 23 February 2014, www.al-jazirah.com/2014/20140223/du6.htm.

26 Quoted in Nayif Al-Rashid, "Khabir Saudi: Laysa mustabdan tamalluk Tihran li-silah nawawi fi al-mustaqbal" [A Saudi Expert: Tehran's Acquisition of Nuclear Weapons in the Future Is Not to Be Excluded], *Al-Sharq Al-Awsat*, 15 July 2015, http://aawsat.com/406881, Da'ud Al-Shiryan, "Ittifaq Vienna yu'ajjil al-musiba wa-la yam-naha" [The Vienna Agreement Will Postpone the Calamity, But Not Prevent It], *Al-Hayat* (Saudi edition), 15 July 2015, http://alhayat.com/Opinion/Dawood-Al-Sheryan/9985479, Jasir Abd Al-Aziz Al-Jasir, "Iran al-irhabiya badalan min Iran al-nawawiya" [A Terrorist Iran Instead of a Nuclear Iran], *Al-Jazira*, 15 July 2015, www.al-jazirah.com/2015/20150715/du9.htm, and Hammad Al-Salimi, "Al-Nawawi yu'annis 'Shaytan Bazrag': madha bad?" [Nuclear Weapons Humanize "the Great Satan": What Next?], *Al-Jazira*, 2 August 2015, www.al-jazirah.com/2015/20150802/ar3.htm.

27 Ali bin Hamad Al-Khashiban, "Hal yumkin al-sulh ma Iran?" [Is Reconciliation Possible with Iran?], *Al-Riyadh*, 24 August 2015, www.alriyadh.com/1075826, and Abd Al-Munim Mustafa, "Ruznamat sayf sakhin wa-kharif multahib" [The Calendar of a Hot Summer and a Torrid Autumn], *Al-Madina*, 21 August 2015, www.al-madina.com.sa/printhtml/625857.

28 Ali Sad Al-Musa, "Bi'l-Qanun: Iran dawla nawawiya" [It Is Now Legal: Iran Is a Nuclear State], *Al-Watan*, 15 July 2015, www.alwatan.com.sa/Articles/Detail.aspx?ArticleId=27097, and Sami Said Habib, "Al-Ittifaqiya al-gharbiya-al-iraniya istifaf alami bi-tawqit madrus!" [The Western–Iranian Agreement Is an International

Arrangement with a Planned Timeline!], *Al-Madina*, 18 July 2015, www.al-madina.com/printhtml/619738.
29 Hashim Abdu Hashim, "Sibaq al-tasalluh al-nawawi khiyar la badil lahu" [A Nuclear Arms Race Is the Only Viable Option], *Al-Riyadh*, 18 July 2015, www.alriyadh.com/1065874, Bannan, "Adw fi al-nadi," and Hammad Al-Salimi, "Al-Nawawi yu'annis 'Shaytan Bazrag': madha bad?" [Nuclear Weapons Humanize "the Great Satan": What Next?], *Al-Jazira*, 2 August 2015, www.al-jazirah.com/2015/20150802/ar3.htm.
30 One academic, in fact, noted that "It is both erroneous and foolish to view the recent Agreement … in isolation from Iran's agenda for expansionism in the region," Abd Al-Majid Muhammad Al-Jallal, "Al-Mamlaka qaidat mashru al-arab li-waqf al-tamaddud al-farisi" [The Kingdom Is the Mainstay of the Arabs' Strategy to Stop the Persian Expansionism], *Al-Riyadh*, 1 August 2015, www.al-riyadh.com/1069475.
31 For example, Salman Al-Dawsari, "Al-Ittifaq al-nawawi yaftah abwab al-sharr" [The Nuclear Agreement Opens the Floodgates to Disaster], *Al-Sharq Al-Awsat*, 15 July 2015, http://aawsat.com/node/406761, Hani Wafa, "Al-Duwal al-arabiya maniya bi'l-ittifaq al-nawawi al-irani wa-lakin laysa ala hisab amniha wa-istiqrarha wa-tanmiyatha" [The Arab States Respect the Iranian Nuclear Agreement But Not at the Price of Their Security, Stability, and Development], *Al-Riyadh*, 15 July 2015, www.alriyadh.com/1065137, Muhammad Al-Asimi, "Al-Istikbar al-irani!" [Iranian Arrogance!], *Ukaz*, 16 July 2015, http://okaz.co/bwlhldr5T, and Mazin Al-Sudayri, "Iran: Innahu al-iqtisad ya dhaki" [Iran: It's the Economy, Stupid], *Al-Riyadh*, 22 July 2015, www.alriyadh.com/1066857.
32 Hani Salim Mashur, "Iran lan takhla imamatha abadan" [Iran Will Never Remove Its Turban], *Al-Jazira*, 30 July 2015, www.al-jazirah.com/2015/20150730/du5.htm.
33 For example, Jasir Abd Al-Aziz Al-Jasir, "Al-Tarikh sa-yadhkur muwajahat al-hazm li-jinat al-ghadar" [History Will Remember Operation Decisive Storm's Resistance to the Genes of Treachery], *Al-Jazira*, 21 July 2015, www.al-jazirah.com.sa/2015/20150721/du16.htm, Husayn Shabkashi, "Al-Ittifaq ma baltagi al-mintaqa!" [The Agreement with the Region's Bully!], *Al-Sharq Al-Awsat*, 16 July 2015, http://aawsat.com/node/407536, and Hasna' Abd Al-Aziz Al-Gunayir, "Kayf al-sabil ila al-taayush aw al-tahawur ma dawla min shiyamha al-makr wa'l-ghadar?" [How Can One Have Coexistence and Dialogue with a State in Whose Nature Are Deception and Treachery?], *Al-Riyadh*, 23 August 2015, www.alriyadh.com/1075626.
34 "Duktur Al-Askar."
35 Mutlaq bin Saud Al-Mtiri, "Al-Mashru al-nawawi al-ta'ifi ila ayna?" [Where Is the Sectarian Nuclear Project Headed?], *Al-Riyadh*, 18 July 2015, www.alriyadh.com/1065848, Ali bin Hamad Al-Khashiban, "Li-madha yasna Al-Gharb Iran?" [Why Does the West Build Up Iran?], *Al-Riyadh*, 20 July 2015, www.alriyadh.com/1066308, and Rayyan bin Ali Al-Tamimi, "Hazima wa-intisar" [Defeat and Victory], *Al-Riyadh*, 23 July 2015, www.alriyadh.com/1067087.
36 Salman Al-Dawsari, "Tahaluf Al-Gharb ma Al-Saudiya laysa minha" [The West's Alliance with Saudi Arabia Is Not Free], *Al-Sharq Al-Awsat*, 20 July 2015, http://aawsat.com/node/410661, Mishari Al-Dhaydi, "Shaghaf Obama al-khatir" [Obama's Dangerous Infatuation], *Al-Sharq Al-Awsat*, 20 July 2015, http://aawsat.com/node/410676, Jasir Abd Al-Aziz Al-Jasir, "Al-Tarikh sa-yadhkur muwajahat al-hazm li-jinat al-ghadar" [History Will Remember Operation Decisive Storm's Resistance to the Genies of Betrayal], *Al-Jazira*, 21 July 2015, www.al-jazirah.com.sa/2015/20150721/du16.htm, Yusuf Al-Dayni, "McDonalds fi Tihran: Li'l-Gharb al-nawawi wa-lana al-thawri" [McDonalds in Tehran: For the West the Nuclear Iran and for Us the Revolutionary One], *Al-Sharq Al-Awsat*, 28 July 2015, http://aawsat.com/node/416721, and Adil Al-Harbi, "'Junun al-tarikh': Bi-wasfih mashruan amirikiyan" ["A Historical Folly": He Sees It as an American Plan], *Al-Riyadh*, 22 July 2015, www.alriyadh.com/1066871.

37 Al-Shammari, "Ittifaq nawawi," and Sultan Al-Amir, "Al-Ittifaq al-nawawi: Ma al-amal?" [The Nuclear Agreement: What Is to Be Done?], *Al-Hayat* (Saudi edition), 28 July 2015, http://alhayat.com/Opinionn/Sultan-El-Amer/10246952.
38 Salih Al-Diwani, "Nahnu wa'l-ittifaqiya al-nawawiya" [The Nuclear Agreement and Us], *Al-Watan*, 23 July 2015, www.al-watan.com.sa/Articles/Detail.aspx?ArticleID=27194, and Jasir Abd Al-Aziz Al-Jasir, "Al-Tarikh sa-yadhkur muwajahat al-hazm li-jinat al-ghadar" [History Will Remember Operation Decisive Storm's Resistance to the Genes of Betrayal], *Al-Jazira*, 21 July 2015, www.al-jazirah.com.sa/2015/20150721/du16.htm.
39 Fadl bin Sad Al-Buaynayn, "Bina' al-iqtisad am al-silah al-nawawi?" [To Develop the Economy or Nuclear Weapons?], *Al-Jazira*, 21 July 2015, www.al-jazirah.com/2015/20150721/ar5.htm.
40 Abd Allah Salih Al-Qarni, "Haykal wa'l-ilam al-misri al-khass wa-lanat al-markaz!" [Heykal and the Private Egyptian Media and the Curse of the Center!], *Al-Madina*, 29 July 2015, www.al-madina.com.sa/printhtml/627406, Editorial, "Al-Maliki wa-Haykal wa-tali ittifaq nawawi Tihran" [Al-Maliki, Heykal, and the Burnishing of Tehran's Nuclear Agreement], *Al-Yawm*, 23 July 2015, www.alyaum.com/article/4079811.
41 Abd Allah Al-Muflih, "Ma alladhi ala Al-Saudiya an tafalhu li-tashih al-awda fi Misr?" [What Must Saudi Arabia Do to Fix the Situation in Egypt?], *Shu'un Khalijiya*, 23 July 2015, http://alkhaleejaffairs.org/c-22792.
42 Salim Makhashin, "Inikasat al-ittifaq al-nawawi" [The Consequences of the Nuclear Agreement], *Al-Sharq*, 31 July 2015, www.alsharq-net.sa/2015/07/31/1382226.
43 Mutlaq Al-Anazi, "Ka'aba amma: Al-Khamene'i sawf yabtali 'al-wali al-muntazar'" [General Depression: Khamene'i Will Have to Swallow the "Awaited Mahdi"], *Al-Yawm*, 31 July 2015, www.alyaum.com/article/4081058.
44 Ibrahim bin Mahmud Al-Nahhas, "Hal min ijabiyat li'l-ittifaq al-nawawi al-irani ala Al-Sharq Al-Awsat?" [Are There Any Positive Aspects of the Iranian Nuclear Agreement for the Middle East?], *Al-Riyadh*, 16 July 2015, www.alriyadh.com/1065523.
45 Tawfiq Al-Sayf, "Ta'thir al-ittifaq al-nawawi ala buniyat al-sulta fi Iran" [The Impact of the Nuclear Agreement on the Government's Foundation in Iran], *Al-Sharq Al-Awsat*, 22 July 2015, http://aawsat.com/print/412161, and Aql Al-Aql, "Li-madha nartaib min al-ittifaq al-nawawi al-irani?" [Why Are We Terrified by the Iranian Nuclear Agreement?], *Al-Hayat* (Saudi edition), 21 July 2015, http://alhayat.com/Opinion/Akel-Il-Akel/10098131.
46 Sultan Al-Amir, "Al-Ittifaq al-nawawi: Ma al-amal?" [The Nuclear Agreement: What Is to Be Done?], *Al-Hayat* (Saudi edition), 28 July 2015, http://alhayat.com/Opinionn/Sultan-El-Amer/10246952.
47 Ahmad Al-Hinaki, Al-Ittifaq al-nawawi ma Iran li-maslahat al-salam" [The Nuclear Agreement with Iran Is in the Interest of Peace], *Al-Hayat* (Saudi edition), 18 July 2015, http://alhayat.com/Opinion/Ahmad-AlHinaki/10042261.
48 Major General Muhammad Bin Mari Al-Amri (Ret.), "Wa-saqat al-qina al-majusi al-gharbi" [The Zoroastrian and Western Masks Have Come Off], *Sahifat Bani Amr* (Saudi Arabia), 1 August 2015, http://news.bani3mro.com/bani3mro/3209.
49 Muhammad Sulayman Al-Anqari, "Iran taht al-wisaya al-dawliya" [Iran Is under International Guardianship], *Al-Jazira*, 19 July 2015, www.al-jazirah.com/2015/20150719/ec17.htm.
50 Abd Allah Al-Fayfi, "Mukhtassun: Raf intaj al-naft al-irani yahtaj li-sanawat wa-la ta'thir fili bi'l-aswaq" [Specialists: Raising Iran's Oil Production Will Take Years and Not Have a Significant Impact on the Market], *Al-Riyadh*, 16 July 2015, www.alriyadh.com/1065446, and Usama Sulayman, "Suq al-naft tattajih li'l-irtifa wast tawaqquat bi-ann awdat sadirat Iran sa-tastaghriq bad al-waqt" [The Oil Markets Are Heading Higher on the Basis of Expectations that Iran's Exports Will Need Some Time], *Al-Iqtisadiya*, 16 July 2015, www.aleqt.com/2015/07/16/article_973839.html.

51 Usama Yamani, "Hisab al-arbah wa'l-khasa'ir fi al-ittifaq al-nawawi" [A Calculus of Gains and Losses from the Nuclear Agreement], *Al-Bilad*, 12 August 2015, www.albiladdaily.com.
52 Abd Al-Rahman Al-Rashid, "Al-Ittifaq al-irani al-gharbi wa-nahnu" [The Iranian–Western Agreement and Us], part 1, *Al-Sharq Al-Awsat*, 16 July 2015, http://aawsat.com/node/407491, and Abd Al-Rahman Al-Rashid, "Al-Ittifaq al-irani al-gharbi wa-nahnu" [The Iranian–Western Agreement and Us], part 2, *Al-Sharq Al-Awsat*, 17 July 2015, http://aawsat.com/node/408546.
53 Abd Al-Rahman Al-Rashid, "Khilaf Al-Khalij ma al-amirikan tafasil" [The Gulf's Differences with the Americans Only Concern Minor Details], *Al-Sharq Al-Awsat*, 26 July 2015, http://aawsat.com/node/415201, and Abd Al-Rahman Al-Rashid, "Hal al-alaqa ma Washintun khata' tarikhi?" [Is the Relationship with Washington a Historic Error?], *Al-Sharq Al-Awsat*, 27 July 2015, http://aawsat.com/node/415691.
54 Fahd Al-Dughaythir, "Al-Malik Salman fi Washintun" [King Salman in Washington], *Al-Hayat* (Saudi edition), 30 August 2015, http://alhayat.com/Opinion/Fahad-Al-Dgheter/10868710.
55 As noted by Foreign Minister Adil Al-Jubeir on his visit to Germany, "Al-Saudiya harisa ala tatwir al-alaqat ma Iran sharitat taghyirha li-siyasat al-tadakhkhul fi al-mintaqa" [Saudi Arabia Desires to Develop Its Relations with Iran on Condition that the Latter Change Its Policy of Meddling in the Region], *Al-Sharq Al-Awsat*, 10 August 2015, http://aawsat.com/node/426606.
56 Abd Al-Majid Muhammad Al-Jallal, "Al-Mamlaka qaidat mashru al-arab li-waqf al-tamaddud al-farisi" [The Kingdom Is the Mainstay of the Arabs' Strategy to Stop the Persian Expansion], *Al-R iyadh*, 1 August 2015, www.alriyadh.com/1069475.
57 Muhammad bin Abd Allah Al Abd Al-Latif, "Obama al-hawi wa'l-arbaun thubanan" [Obama the Snake Charmer and the Forty Snakes], *Al-Jazira*, 11 August 2015, www.al-jazirah.com/2015/20150811/ar2.htm.
58 Abd Allah Al-Nasir, "Bayariq al-majus" [The Flags of the Magi], *Al-Riyadh*, 21 August 2015, www.alriyadh.com/1075135, and Mutlaq Al-Anazi, "Lanat al-ittifaq wa-ma yasturun!" [The Curse of the Agreement and What They Are Planning], *Al-Yawm*, 14 August 2015, www.alyaum.com/article/4083388.
59 Abd Al-Rahman Al-Rashid, "Li-ladhina bashsharu bi'l-taghyir" [To Those Who Optimistically Predicted a Change], *Al-Sharq Al-Awsat*, 16 August 2015, http://aawsat.com/node/430606, and Abd Al-Rahman Al-Rashid, "Wujuh al-hukuma al-iraniya al-mubtasima!" [The Smiling Faces of the Iranian Government!], *Al-Sharq Al-Awsat*, 23 August 2015, http://aawsat.com/node/435991; likewise, see Ali bin Hasan Al-Tawati, "Hal kan haflan li'l-istslam wa'l-taslim" [Was It Just a Performance of Surrender and Capitulation?], *Ukaz*, 13 August 2015, http://okaz.co/bwIjhdtuW, Abd Al-Munim Mustafa, "Mufaja'a: al-mawlud yashbih al-qabila" [Surprise: The Newborn Resembles the Midwife], *Al-Madina*, 14 August 2015, www.al-madina.com.sa/printhtml/624407, and Khalid Al-Dakhil, "Rasa'il Zareef bayn al-tadhaki wa'l-tahdid" [Zareef's Messages of Sweet-Nothings and Threats], *Al-Hayat*, 16 August 2015, http://alhayat.com/Opinion/Khaled-El-Dakheel/10601971.
60 Hasna' Abd Al-Aziz Al-Gunayir, "Iran aduww li-arab Al-Khalij wa-quwwat ihtilal yajib al-taamul maha ala hadha al-asas" [Iran Is an Enemy of the Gulf Arabs and an Occupation Force that Must Be Dealt with on that Basis], *Al-Riyadh*, 16 August 2015, www.alriyadh.com/1073411 (hereafter Al-Gunayir, "Iran aduww li-arab Al-Khalij").
61 Imad Al-Mudayfir, "Al-Irhab al-irani yantaish ma raf al-uqubat al-dawliya" [Iranian Terrorism Has a New Life with the Lifting of the International Sanctions], *Al-Jazira*, 19 August 2015, www.al-jazirah.com/2015/20150819/ar6.htm.
62 Abd Allah Al-Shammari, "Hal asbah al-hiwar al-saudi al-irani matlaban amrikiyan?" [Has a Saudi–Iranian Dialogue Become an American Demand?], *Al-Yawm*, 4 August 2015, www.alyaum.com/article/4081760,
63 Editorial "Nizham Tihran udwani qabl al-ittifaq wa-badu" [The Tehran Regime Was One of Aggression Before and After the Agreement], *Al-Yawm*, 28 July 2015, www.

alyaum.com/article/4080634, Hani Salim Mashur, "Hadaya Iran al-mufakhkhakha" [Iran's Boobytrapped Gifts], *Al-Jazira*, 18 August 2015, www.al-jazirah.com/2015/20150818/du7.htm, Hammud Abu Talib, "Hakadha tuhawirna Iran" [That Is How Iran Dialogues with Us], *Ukaz*, 20 August 2015, http://okaz.co/bwljodtSv, and Muhammad Al-Mukhtar Al-Fal, "Iran lam tataghayyar" [Iran Has Not Changed], *Ukaz*, 23 August 2015, http://okaz.co/bwljrdt3o.

64 Salman Al-Awda quoted in "Al-Awda yualliq ala al-ittifaq al-nawawi ma Iran wa-yatasa'al an mashru al-hukumat al-arabiya li-muwajaht al-tahaddi" [Al-Awda Comments on the Nuclear Agreement with Iran and Wonders about the Arab Governments' Plan to Meet the Challenge], *Al-Marsad*, 14 July 2015, http://al-marsd.com/c-120374.

65 Salih Al-Diwani, "Nahnu wa'l-ittifaqiya al-nawawiya" [The Nuclear Agreement and Us], *Al-Watan*, 23 July 2015, www.al-watan.com.sa/Articles/Detail.aspx?ArticleID=27194, and Ali Al-Jahli, "Ittifaq Obama al-nawawi" [Obama's Nuclear Agreement], *Al-Iqtisadiya*, 25 July 2015, www.aleqt.com/2015/07/25/article_976035.html.

66 For example, Abd Al-Muhsin Hilal, "Nahnu wa-Iran" [Iran and Us], *Ukaz*, 27 July 2015, http://okaz.co/bwlhTdsBL, and Al-Gunayir, "Iran aduww li-arab Al-Khalij."

67 "Tihran tattahim al-muthallath al-amiriki al-isra'ili al-saudi bi-dam al-irhab fi Iran" [Tehran Accuses the American–Israeli–Saudi Triangle of Supporting Terrorism in Iran], *ABNA* (Tehran), 18 September 2010, http://ar.abna24.com/196183/print.html, "Kowsari: Iran sa-tuaqib khatifi junudha idha lam taqum Bakistan bi-wajibatha" [Kowsari: Iran Will Punish Those Who Kidnapped Its Soldiers If Pakistan Does Not Do Its Duty], *Al-Alam TV* (Tehran), 25 March 2014, www.alalam.ir/print/1578987?img=0, "Man huwa al-rajul al-thani fi Jaysh Al-Adl al-irhabiya al-ladhi qutil mu'akhkharan?" [Who Is the Number-Two Man in the Terrorist Jaysh Al-Adl Who Was Killed Recently?], *Al-Alam TV*, 26 April 2015, www.alalam.ir/print/1698164?img=0. Indeed, the leader of the Jaysh Al-Adl, a Sunni extremist anti-regime armed group in Iran, was featured in an interview in the Saudi press; interview with Salah Al-Din Faruqi by Ahmad Al-Ahmad, "Khasa'ir Iran fi Al-Yaman inakasat ala al-dakhil al-irani wa-nunadil min ajl huquq shabna al-mudtahad" [Iran's Losses in Yemen Have Been Reflected on the Domestic Scene and We Fight for the Rights of Our Oppressed People], *Al-Riyadh*, 15 August 2015, www.alriyadh.com/1073264.

68 Abd Allah Mughram, "Bina' al-qudrat huw al-hall!" [Developing Capabilities Is the Solution!], *Al-Riyadh*, 19 July 2015, www.al-riyadh.com/1066038, and Usama Al-Qahtani, "Ila uqala' al-shab al-irani al-jar" [To the Wise Ones Among the Neighboring Iranian People], *Al-Watan*, 14 August 2015, www.alwatan.com.sa/Articles/Detail.aspx?ArticleID=27495.

69 Da'ud Al-Shiryan, "Ittifaq Vienna yu'ajjil al-musiba wa-la yamnaha" [The Vienna Agreement Will Delay the Calamity, But Not Prevent It], *Al-Hayat* (Saudi edition), 15 July 2015, http://alhayat.com/Opinion/Dawood-Al-Sheryan/9985479, Said Al-Farha Al-Ghamdi, "Al-Nawawi al-irani, wa-madha an Isra'il?" [The Iranian Nuke, and What About Israel?], *Al-Madina*, 20 July 2015, www.al-madina.com/printhtml/620016, Hashim Abdu Hashim, "Marhalat al-difa an al-masir" [The Phase in Defense of the Future], *Al-Riyadh*, 20 July 2015, www.alriyadh.com/1066340, "Ittifaq mashrut" [A Conditional Agreement], *Al-Madina*, 15 July 2015, www.al-madina.com/printhtml/619246, and Talal Salih Bannan, "Adw fi al-nadi al-nawawi!" [Member of the Nuclear Club!], *Ukaz*, 21 July 2015, http://okaz.co/bwlhNdsko.

70 Al-Shammari, "Ittifaq nawawi," Abd Al-Aziz Al-Jar Allah, "Li-madha la yuammam barnamaj Iran?" [Why Should Iran's Program Not Be Extended to Others?], *Al-Jazira*, 25 July 2015, www.com/2015/20150725/ln43.htm, and Said Al-Farha Al-Ghamdi, "Al-Nawawi al-irani, wa-madha an Isra'il?" [The Iranian Nuke, and What About Israel?], *Al-Madina*, 20 July 2015, www.al-madina.com/printhtml/620016.

71 Hamdan Al-Shihri, "Al-Hiwar ma Tihran ala tariqatna la ala tariqatha" [Dialogue with Tehran Our Way, Not the Latter's Way], *Al-Riyadh*, 22 August 2015, www.alriyadh.com/1075354.

72 Brigadier General Ali bin Hasan Al-Tawati (Ret.), "Hal falan tukhifna al-harb al-nawawiya?" [Does Nuclear War Really Frighten Us?], *Ukaz*, 30 July 2015, http://okaz/bwlhWdsKw.
73 Editorial "Iran wa-awham al-nufudh" [Iran and the Delusions of Influence], *Al-Bilad*, 30 August 2015, www.albilad.com.
74 Abd Al-Munim Mustafa, "Washintun taghayyar wa-nahnu aydan" [Washington Is Changing and So Are We], *Al-Madina*, 7 August 2015, www.al-madina.com.sa/printhtml/623251.
75 Abd Al-Muhsin Hilal, "Al-Hass al-gha'ib" [The Missing Sense], *Ukaz*, 5 August 2015, http://okaz.co/bwli9ds3V.
76 Talal Salih Bannan, "Qarar imtilak al-radi al-nawawi" [The Decision to Have a Nuclear Deterrent], *Ukaz*, 4 August 2015, http://okaz.co/bwli8ds0A.
77 Jasir Abd Al-Aziz Al-Jasir, "Hatta la nakun dahiyat al-khida al-nawawi" [So That We Do Not Become Victims of Nuclear Deception], *Al-Jazira*, 20 July 2015, www.com/2015/20150720/du9.htm, Abd Al-Rahman Al-Awmi, "Ittifaq al-saffah bayn Amrika wa-Iran" [The Killer's Agreement between America and Iran], *Al-Yawm*, 19 July 2015, www.alyaum.com/article/4079304, and Sadaqa Yahya Fadil, "Al-Siyasa al-nawawiya al-saudiya" [Saudi Nuclear Policy], *Ukaz*, 2 August 2015, http://okaz.co/bwli6dsTa.
78 Ayman Al-Hammad, "Dalalat al-hudur al-nawawi al-rusi fi al-mintaqa" [Indications of the Russian Nuclear Presence in the Region], *Al-Riyadh*, 27 August 2015, www.alriyadh.com/1076788.
79 Ayman Al-Hammad, "Al-Nadi al-nawawi yuid siyaghat shurutih" [The Nuclear Club Revises Its Requirements], *Al-Riyadh*, 15 July 2015, www.alriyadh.com/1065088.
80 Al-Gunayir, "Iran aduww li-arab Al-Khalij."
81 Khalaf Al-Harbi, "Lan nahzim Iran bi'l-shata'im" [We Will Not Defeat Iran with Insults], *Ukaz*, 9 August 2015, http://okaz.co.bwljddthB.
82 Jamal Al-Qahtani, "Mukhrajat al-ittifaq al-nawawi takshifha bu'r al-mintaqa al-mushtaila" [Excerpts from the Nuclear Agreement Reveal the Abyss of a Region in Flames], *Al-Riyadh*, 15 July 2015, www.alriyadh.com/1065155.
83 Muhammad Abd Allah Al-Khazim, "Ma bad al-ittifaq al-nawawi: Hadith ghayr siyasi" [What after the Nuclear Agreement? An Impolitic Discussion], *Al-Jazira*, 26 July 2015, www.al-jazirah.com/2015/20150726/ln34.htm.
84 "Jumhuriyun munasirun li-Isra'il yashinnun hamla mudadda li-rafd al-ittifaq al-nawawi ma Iran" [Republican Supporters of Israel Mount a Campaign to Oppose the Nuclear Agreement with Iran], *Al-Sharq Al-Awsat*, 23 July 2015, http://aawsat.com/home/article/413206, Ranim Hannush, "DAISH waraqat ibtizaz bi-yad Bush fi intikhabat al-ri'asa al-amirikiya" [ISIS Is an Ace in the Hole for Bush in the American Electoral Campaign], *Al-Sharq Al-Awsat*, 13 August 2015, http://aawsat.com/node/428136, Shaykha Al-Dawsari, "Ghiyab al-thiqa bi-Tihran yuharrik zuama' al-hizb al-jumhuri li-ihbat al-ittifaq al-nawawi" [A Lack of Trust of Tehran Motivates the Leaders of the Republican Party to Defeat the Nuclear Agreement], *Al-Sharq Al-Awsat*, 5 August 2015, http://aawsat.com/node/422596, "Al-Kungras al-amriki yattajih li-rafd al-ittifaq al-nawawi ma Iran" [The U.S. Congress Is Leaning Toward Rejecting the Nuclear Agreement with Iran], *Al-Yawm*, 8 August 2015, www.alyaum.com/article/4082413, Hiba Al-Qudsi, "Na'ib dimuqrati bariz yuhrij Obama bi-azmih al-taswit didd al-ittifaq al-nawawi" [A Prominent Democratic Senator Embarrasses Obama by Resolving to Vote against the Nuclear Agreement], *Al-Sharq Al-Awsat*, 8 August 2015, http://aawsat.com/node/424656, and "Obama bayn al-murawagha wa'l-wuduh amam al-kunghras li-tamrir al-ittifaq al-nawawi" [Obama Combines Evasiveness and Clarity before Congress in Order to Pass the Nuclear Agreement], *Al-Sharq Al-Awsat*, 9 August 2015, http://aawsat.com/node/425571.
85 Lee Fang, "Wave of TV Ads Opposing the Iran Deal Organized by Saudi Arabian Lobbyist," *The Intercept*, 20 August 2015, https://firstlook.org/theintercept/2015/08/

20/wave-anti-iran-deal-tv-ads-organized-saudi-arabian-lobbyist. To be sure, other opponents of the Agreement were also clients of that same lobbying firm.

86 Abd Al-Rahman Al-Turayri, "Hal najal ittifaq al-nawawi sadmat ifaqa lana?" [Will We Use the Nuclear Agreement As a Shock to Wake Us Up?], *Al-Iqtisadiya*, 30 July 2015, www.aleqt.com/2015/07/30/article_977385.html.

87 Abd Al-Latif Al-Duwayhi, "Iran wa'l-Saudiya wa-marakiz al-dirasat" [Iran and Saudi Arabia and Research Centers], *Ukaz*, 21 July 2015, http://okaz.co/bwlhNdskr.

88 Jamal Khashogji, "Al-Ghiyab al-saudi al-kabir" [The Big Saudi Absence], *Al-Hayat*, 1 August 2015, http://alhayat/Opinion/Jamal-Khashoggi/10325439 (hereafter Khashogji, "Al-Ghiyab al-saudi"), and Ahmad Al-Farraj, "Lubi al-masalih al-saudi!" [A Saudi Interest Lobby!], *Al-Jazira*, 10 September 2015, www.al-jazirah.com/2015/2015/0910/ln44.htm (hereafter Al-Farraj, "Lubi al-masalih"). The Ministry of Foreign Affairs may be a vulnerable target because although princes remain well represented at the deputy minister level, they are holdovers from the previous monarch.

89 Muhammad Al-Mukhtar Al-Fal, "Diblumasiyat al-ilam" [Media Diplomacy], *Ukaz*, 14 September 2015, http://okaz.co/bwIkUdvkA.

90 Abd Allah Al-Shammari, "Hal asbah al-hiwar al-saudi al-irani matlaban amrikiyan?" [Has a Saudi–Iranian Dialogue Become an American Demand?], *Al-Yawm*, 4 August 2015, www.alyaum.com/article/4081760, Imad Al-Mudayfir, "Al-Ittifaq al-nawawi al-irani nasr am rudukh?" [The Iranian Nuclear Agreement: Victory or Capitulation?], *Al-Jazira*, 5 August 2015, www.al-jazirah.com/2015/20150805/ar4.htm, and Khashogji, "Al-Ghiyab al-saudi."

91 Al-Farraj, "Lubi al-masalih," and Lee Fang, "The Saudi Lobbying Complex Adds a New Member: GOP Super PAC Chair Norm Coleman," *The Nation*, 18 September 2014, www.thenation.com/article/saudi-lobbying-complex-adds-new-member-gop-super-pac-chair-norm-coleman/.

92 Al-Jubeir quoted in Muhammad Al-Maddah, "Liqa' al-malik-Obama mustawa jadid min al-shiraka al-istratijiya" [The King–Obama Meeting: A New Level in the Strategic Partnership], *Ukaz*, 5 September 2015, http://okaz/co/bwIklduRe, and Khidr Al-Qurayshi, Head of the Shura Council's Foreign Policy Committee, quoted in Muhammad Al-Aklabi, "Ada' al-shura: Ziyarat al-malik li-Amrika sa-tadfa bi'l-taawun ila fada'at ijabiya" [Shura Members: The King's Visit to America Will Drive Cooperation to Positive Spheres], *Al-Iqtisadiya*, 5 September 2015, www.aleqt.com/2015/09/05/article_988338.html.

93 Eventually, Riyadh came to openly question the desirability of its rapprochement with Moscow, with the media asking "Is there any utility for the Arabs to continue their policy of opening to Moscow?" Hashim Abdu Hashim, "Safaqat iraniya rusiya ghamida" [Murky Iranian–Russian Deals], *Al-Riyadh*, 16 September 2015, www.alriyadh.com/1082092.

94 Abd Allah Bakhashwin, "Al-Hizb al-jumhuri wa'l-istimar al-dimuqrati!" [The Republican Party and Democratic Imperialism!], *Al-Jazira*, 14 September 2015, www.al-jazirah.com/2015/20150914/ln330.htm.

95 Ma'mun Fandi, "Hal yubarrar 'al-tawahhud al-istratiji' al-arabi?" [Is Arab "Strategic Autism" Justified?], *Al-Sharq Al-Awsat*, 14 September 2015, http://aawsat.com/node/451881.

96 Muhammad Al-Mazini, "Azmat Al-Khalij fi muwajahat al-waq al-murr" [The Gulf Crisis in the Face of Bitter Reality], *Al-Hayat* (Saudi edition), 29 July 2015, http://alhayat.com/Opinion/Mohammed-Al-Mzini/10267249.

97 Usama Al-Salim, "Al-Risala al-amrikiya bad al-ittifaq al-nawawi bayn tahaluf yatawakka' wa-akhar yatatalla" [The American Message after the Nuclear Agreement: A Stagnant Coalition or a Dynamic One], *Al-Iqtisadiya*, 18 August 2015, www.aleqt.com/2015/08/18/article_982746.html.

98 Ma'mun Fandi, "Al-Ittifaq al-nawawi: Yaqzha kadhiba" [The Nuclear Agreement: False Consciousness], *Al-Sharq Al-Awsat*, 20 July 2015, http://aawsat.com/node/410571.

99 Ahmad Al-Farraj, "Hal al-ittifaq al-nawawi si'i?" [Is the Nuclear Agreement Bad?], *Al-Jazira*, 25 July 2015, www.al-jazirah.com/2015/20150725/ln45.htm.
100 Ali bin Hamad Al-Khashiban, "Khamas istratijiyat siyasiya muhimma!" [Five Important Political Strategies!], *Al-Riyadh*, 27 July 2015, www.alriyadh.com/1068090.
101 Ahmad Al-Farraj, "Iqra'u Thomas Friedman jayyidan!" [Read Thomas Friedman Carefully!], *Al-Jazira*, 5 September 2015, www.al-jazirah.com.sa/201520150905\ln43.htm. The article in question was Thomas Friedman, "Our Radical Islamic BFF, Saudi Arabia," *New York Times*, 2 September 2015, www.nytimes.com.
102 Fahd Al-Dughaythir, "Al-Malik Salman fi Washintun" [King Salman in Washington], *Al-Hayat* (Saudi edition), 30 August 2015, http://alhayat.com/Opinion/Fahad-Al-Dgheter/10868710.
103 Salman Al-Dawsari, "Al-Malik Salman fi Washintun" [King Salman in Washington], *Al-Sharq Al-Awsat*, 4 September 2015, http://aawsat.com/node/444586, and Editorial "Al-Shiraka al-istratijia damanat al-alaqat al-qawiya al-mutajaddada" [The Strategic Partnership Is a Guarantee for Strong Renewed Relations], *Ukaz*, 9 September 2015, http://okaz.co/bwIkPdu35.
104 Abd Allah bin Bijad Al-Utaybi, "Al-Malik Salman fi Amrika" [King Salman in America], *Al-Sharq Al-Awsat*, 6 September 2015, http://aawsat.com/node/446081.
105 Greg Jaffe, "As Saudi King Visits, Obama's Focus Is on Common Ground," *Washington Post*, 5 September 2015, A8.
106 As Saudi Arabia's Minister for Economics and Planning responded when asked whether his country was worried about U.S. investments in Iran: "We are confident about what we are offering to international investors." "Al-Turayfi: Ziyarat Washintun naqla nawiya fi al-alaqat al-iqtisadiya" [Al-Turayfi: The Visit to Washington Is a Qualitative Step in Economic Relations], *Al-Arabiya TV*, 6 September 2015, www.alarabiya.net, and Saud Al-Riyas, "Al-Saudiya hin tatakallam!" [When Saudi Arabia Speaks!], *Al-Hayat* (Saudi edition), 10 September 2015, http://alhayat.com/Opinion/Saud-Il-Rias/11082288 (hereafter Al-Riyas, "Al-Saudiya").
107 Editorial "Khadim al-haramayn al-sharifayn wa-Obama yadaan malamih hiqba jadida min al-alaqat al-istratijiya bayn al-baladayn" [The Servant of the Two Holy Places and Obama Set the Outline for a New Era in Strategic Relations Between the Two Countries], *Al-Jazira*, 14 September 2015, www.al-jazirah.com/2015/20150914/ar1.htm.
108 Jasir Abd Al-Aziz Al-Jasir, "Qimmat Salman–Obama" [The Salman–Obama Summit], *Al-Jazira*, 7 September 2015, www.al-jazirah.com/2015/20150907/du10.htm.
109 Ibid.
110 Al-Riyas, "Al-Saudiya," and Talal bin Sulayman Al-Harbi, "Asdiqa' la sada" [Friends, Not Masters], *Al-Riyadh*, 10 September 2015, www.alriyadh.com/1081219.
111 Major General Jamal Mazhlum, Chair of Political and Strategic Studies at the country's Nayif Arab University for Security Sciences, quoted in Ahmad Al-Ahmad, "Siyasiyun wa-akadimiyun li'l-*Riyadh*: Al-Qimma al-saudiya al-amirikiya sa-tu'assis li-masar thabit li'l-alaqat" [Officials and Academics to *Al-Riyadh*: The Saudi–U.S. Summit Will Set a Solid Path for Relations], *Al-Riyadh*, 4 September 2015, www.alriyadh.com/1079428.
112 Abd Al-Muhsin Hilal, "Waqfa ma sadiq" [Sitting Down with a Friend], *Ukaz*, 7 September 2015, http://okaz.co/bwIkNduW8 (hereafter Hilal, "Waqfa").
113 Nasir Al-Shihri, "Salman yuwajih Obama wa'l-alam" [Salman Confronts Obama and the World], *Al-Bilad*, 6 September 2015, www.albiladdaily.com, Mina Yusuf Hamdan, "Ziyara malakiya wa-qararat tarikhiya" [A Royal Visit and Historic Decisions], *Al-Madina*, 10 September 2015, www.al-madina.com.sa/printhtml/629867, Khalid Bu Ali, "Al-Malik Salman … Huna Washintun" [King Salman … Washington Calling], *Al-Sharq*, 7 September 2015, www.alsharq.net.sa/2015/09/07/1401564, and Ahmad Al-Jumaya, "Al-Malik Salman fi Washintun … al-risala wasalat" [King Salman in Washington: Message Received], *Al-Riyadh*, 9 September 2015, www.alriyadh.com/1080817 (hereafter Al-Jumaya, "Al-Malik Salman fi Washintun").

114 Abd Allah Al Hayda, "Ziyarat al-malik Salman al-ula ila Amrika: Al-Taawun al-amni awwal al-tafahumat" [King Salman's First Visit to America: The First Agreement Is on Security Cooperation], *Al-Sharq Al-Awsat*, 3 September 2015, http://aawsat.com/node/444051.

115 Editorial "Al-Riyadh-Washintun … al-musaraha wa'l-tafahum" [Riyadh-Washington: Frankness and Mutual Understanding], *Al-Yawm*, 6 September 2015, www.alyaum.com/article/4087497, Amal Abd Al-Aziz Al-Hazzani, "Al-Alaqat al-saudiya al-amirikiya al-thabat wa'l-istidama" [Saudi–U.S. Relations: Endurance and Continuity], *Al-Sharq Al-Awsat*, 8 September 2015, http://aawsat.com/node/447711, and Khalid bin Abd Allah Al-Malik, "An al-ziyara al-malakiya li-Amrika" [On the Royal Visit to America], part 4, *Al-Jazira*, 11 September 2015, www.al-jazirah.com/2015/20150911/ria1.htm.

116 Hashim Abdu Hashim, "Malahim mustaqbal al-mintaqa al-amin tarsumha ziyarat al-malik Salman li-Amrika" [The Outline of a Secure Future for the Region which King Salman's Trip to America Delineates], *Al-Riyadh*, 3 September 2015, www.alriyadh.com/1078933.

117 Bayyina Al-Milhim, "Ziyarat al-malik li-Washintun wa-thabat al-siyasa al-saudiya" [The King's Visit to Washington and the Steadfastness of Saudi Policy], *Al-Riyadh*, 7 September 2015, www.alriyadh.com/1080238.

118 Muhammad Abd Allah Al-Uwayn, "Al-Malik Salman fi Washintun: Rataq futuq al-alaqat al-istratijiya" [King Salman in Washington: He Mended the Rips in the Strategic Relationship], part 2, *Al-Jazira*, 7 September 2015, www.al-jazirah.com/2015/20150907/ln36.htm.

119 Al-Riyas, "Al-Saudiya."

120 Al-Jumaya, "Al-Malik Salman fi Washintun."

121 Tariq Al-Humayyid, "Al-Malik wa'l-ra'is 'La nahtaj ila shay' … yahimmuna istiqrar al-mintaqa'" [The King and the President: "We Do Not Need Anything … What Interests Us Is the Region's Stability"], *Al-Sharq Al-Awsat*, 7 September 2015, http://aawsat.com/node/446976.

122 Yusuf Al-Kuwaylit, "Al-Itar wa'l-mana fi ziyarat al-malik Salman li-Amrika" [The Framework and Meaning of King Salman's Visit to America], *Al-Yawm*, 12 September 2015, www.alyaum.com/article/4088551 (hereafter Al-Kuwaylit, "Al-Itar"), Hilal, "Waqfa."

123 For example, by the Commander of the Iranian Revolutionary Guard, Major General Mohammad Ali Jafari, "Al-Liwa' Jafari: Iran tuadd al-yawm al-quwwa al-iqlimiya al-kubra wa-munjazatna al-sarukhiya amil rad" [Major General Jafari: Today Iran Is Considered the Strongest Regional Power and Our Missile Achievements Are a Deterrent Factor], *Kayhan*, 1 September 2015, http://kayhan.ir/ar/print/25243, or by the Deputy Foreign Minister Morteza Sarmadi, "Sarmadi: Iran tahawwalat ila quwwa faqat mustawa al-mintaqa raghm al-dughut" [Sarmadi: Iran Has Become More Than a Regional Power Despite the Pressures], *Kayhan*, 7 September 2015, http://kayhan.ir/ar/issue/391/2.

124 Jasir Abd Al-Aziz Al-Jasir, "Ula qimam al-asr al-jadid" [The First Summit of the New Era], *Al-Jazira*, 29 January 2015, www.al-jazirah.com/2015/20150129/du8.htm.

125 Al-Kuwaylit, "Al-Itar."

126 Ahmad Al-Farraj, "Ma bad al-ittifaq al-nawawi" [What Comes after the Nuclear Agreement], *Al-Jazira*, 17 September 2015, www.al-jazirah.com/2015/20150917/ln50.htm.

12

CONCLUSIONS AND IMPLICATIONS

This study suggests several conclusions and potential implications applicable not only to Saudi Arabia and the Middle East but also more broadly to the issue of nuclear proliferation.

A Saudi nuclear path is likely … if …

First, this study concludes that if Iran were to continue to develop its nuclear program and achieved a nuclear breakout at whatever time in the future, there is a very strong likelihood that Saudi Arabia would seek to also acquire nuclear weapons. To be sure, at this juncture, the Saudi case is one of non-proliferation. However, this result is potentially only temporary and conditional, depending as it does on the key variable of future Iranian conduct. As one Saudi pundit summed it up, in case of an Iranian breakout, "There is one thing on which we will not disagree … and that is that the Gulf will become a nuclear one."[1] The sheer quantity of hints, overt warnings, and analyses emanating from senior policymakers and from the overriding atmosphere in the civilian and military media, as well as the development of the supporting infrastructure, all indicate that Saudi Arabia would indeed very likely acquire nuclear weapons under certain circumstances and, in particular, if Iran did so.

Reflecting this implicit conditionality, Saudi reservations about the nuclear issue seem to have continued in the background despite the Nuclear Agreement and the September 2015 summit in Washington, stemming from, as a senior pundit termed it, "significant doubts" whether Iran would change, and this conditionality was characterized by continuing warnings that if Iran is allowed to acquire nuclear weapons that would spark a regional nuclear arms race.[2] Specifically, according to one academic, "if Iran has a nuclear [weapons] capability, then the Arabs too must strive to acquire their own nuclear capability," in order to ensure "a deterrent balance."[3] Calling Iran "evil," a professor at the Foreign Ministry's Diplomatic Institute likewise warned that Iran's acquisition of nuclear weapons would lead to the entire region following suit since it was "a legitimate right of these countries to strengthen themselves in order to defend their territories."[4] Another academic, for his part, now promoted the unification of the GCC states' militaries, and specified that "perhaps the only [appropriate] response to the policies, interests, and fears stemming from the Nuclear Agreement is for the Gulf to become the rising defensive military and nuclear power."[5]

In fact, as a result of the nuclear negotiations leading up to the Agreement, the Saudis also came to conclude that just being able to brandish the threat of a potential nuclear capability can result in substantial leverage with the international community or, as one academic put it, "the nuclear [program] gave Iran some extra cards to play."[6] Specifically, the Saudis highlighted what they believed was the political power of nuclear weapons, claiming that even wielding just the prospect of nuclear weapons had been sufficient to enable Iran to negotiate and break out of its isolation and to end the sanctions.[7] Alluding to the U.S.–Iranian rapprochement accompanying the nuclear negotiations with Tehran, and underlining the clout that the potential acquisition of nuclear weapons conferred on a state, a Saudi editorial concluded that "America only shakes hands with others who have a strong hand" and a columnist maintained that it was Iran's nuclear potential that had forced the West to deal with Tehran.[8] Significantly, one Saudi journalist stressed that Iran was able to increase its regional activity after the nuclear negotiations began.[9] In fact, another columnist maintained that the United States' reluctance to confront Iran and thereby risk failure in the nuclear talks with the latter had even led at one point to a modification in Washington's policy toward the Syrian regime, to the latter's benefit.[10] Of course, the Iranians fueled such perceptions in their Arabic-language media, with Ali Khamene'i's military adviser, Major General Yahya Safavi, for example, boasting with respect to the nuclear talks then still in progress that "the Americans have been forced to negotiate and to recognize that Iran is a regional power."[11]

Moreover, in a sense, Saudi Arabia's continuing adherence to nonproliferation is only partial. That is, now, unlike in the past, Riyadh may likely feel some comfort in having already thought the problem through conceptually and of having developed or being well on its way to developing some supporting components necessary to becoming a nuclear power. In a way, in fact, Saudi Arabia could now already be considered a "latent" nuclear power, that is one for whom the time needed to acquire nuclear weapons could be short. To be sure, as Scott D. Sagan highlighted convincingly, latency is a vague term and, admittedly, as he put it, "any general measure of 'nuclear latency' is likely to be a chimera," given the different and imprecise criteria that are used to gauge it.[12] The case of Saudi Arabia would be an unusual form of a breakout. That is, if, as the present study posits, Riyadh would likely have recourse to a transfer of ready-made nuclear warheads rather than to domestic development, then a breakout could be relatively quick, with little or no warning, bypassing indicators connected to a traditional development process, while key components of a supporting infrastructure—such as the preparation of domestic and regional public opinion, religious legitimacy, a missile delivery capability, and perhaps soon also a civilian nuclear cadre and facilities—will have already been put into place.

True, Saudi Arabia could change—whether in its cultural outlook, view of nuclear weapons, or in its political system—over the next 15 years, that is the time that Iran is mandated to refrain from acquiring nuclear weapons, provided Tehran adheres to the full moratorium period stipulated in the Nuclear Agreement. However, no such macro-level change in Saudi Arabia is apparent, barring unlikely societal upheaval. As long as the royal family remains in control, Saudi Arabia's outlook on Iran and the nuclear issue is not likely to evolve significantly. And, even with a successor government either in Riyadh or Tehran or in both, as long as Riyadh believes that Iran intends to pursue a nuclear weapons capability, its outlook is not likely to change either.

Significantly, the nuclear vector in Saudi Arabia's policy is not a phenomenon attributable to a single driven political leader or even to a small nationalistic core, but seems to reflect a more stable and wider elite and popular consensus. Although it is difficult to judge conclusively, even the limited evidence available suggests that there is probably broad-based public support for the official depiction of the foreign threat and for pursuing a nuclear capability in response to that threat, and that there is little opposition even in dissident circles to such an option. Saudi Arabia almost assuredly will maintain and continue to develop at least the supporting infrastructure built up over the years for a nuclear weapon of its own as a hedge against any potential future nuclear breakout by Iran. As Prince Turki Al-Faysal counseled at a conference in Dubai in April 2014—alluding to the GCC states, but no doubt intending Saudi Arabia—in light of the ambiguity of Iran's nuclear policy "the need to preserve our security compels us to work to establish a balance with [Iran], including in [the area of] nuclear knowledge and to be prepared for any possibility regarding the Iranian nuclear program."[13]

In Saudi Arabia's case, the decisionmakers' assessment of the threat posed by the blatant challenge that a nuclear-armed Iran poses to Saudi Arabia's perceived vital interests would very likely override any other international relations considerations. Decisionmakers, moreover, may interpret threats not only in strictly speaking military terms, but also in terms of the fear and impact on the regional political balance and on regime credibility that nuclear weapons would have, which the Saudi rulers appear to view as primary. According to one Saudi military writer, in fact, the quest for "political and economic blackmail and [the ability] to impose [one's] political conditions both nearby and further afield" is a key motivator for a country's acquisition of nuclear weapons.[14] It will be difficult to remove such lingering Saudi doubts about Iran, especially given the enduring antipathy prevalent in Saudi policy circles toward the Shia, which will reinforce Riyadh's resolve to monitor closely and be prepared to respond to any future Iranian developments in the nuclear field, and all the more so if Iran does not seriously curtail its current policy of supporting fellow-Shia regimes and communities in the region, which is also a policy red line for Riyadh.

While possible, a failure to follow through with long-standing warnings if an actual Iranian nuclear threat did materialize would entail a loss of prestige and credibility for Saudi decisionmakers, and might be prejudicial to the ruling family's legitimacy. Since state–society relations involve an interactive process even in an authoritarian system such as that of Saudi Arabia, the media, while functioning as an information mechanism that the decisionmakers can use, also can heighten public demand and generate pressure on the decisionmaker. That is, decisionmakers may feel a greater need to actually deliver on the expectations that have been actively encouraged from above in case of the fruition of the Iranian nuclear threat as Riyadh has publicized over the years. In particular, what at times has been the strident support for the acquisition of nuclear weapons by Saudi Arabia's religious establishment could put pressure on the Saudi decisionmakers and open up the latter to charges of being remiss if they fail to meet a nuclear challenge needed to protect the Umma, especially since the threat is portrayed as emanating from Shia Iran, as well as from Israel, countries that the clerics depict as enduring dangers from a religious perspective.

Saudi Arabia and proliferation models: commonalities and uniqueness

Second, in terms relating to broader theoretical considerations, the Saudi case offers some empirical data to test a number of assumptions. While Saudi Arabia's non-proliferation stance may seem to confirm the assumptions basic to some models, including in cases where Riyadh does not conform to the indicators of a proliferating state in such models, this situation, as the present study argues, may not be permanent but, rather, conditional, and dependent in particular on Iran's future nuclear policy.

Does the realist model apply?

At first glance, Saudi Arabia would appear to constitute a classic example of the realist security model, with a state acting in response to a perceived nuclear threat and in light of an assessment that there is no credible alternative, buttressed by doubts about reliable foreign support. Arguably, the Saudi perception that an unacceptable potential nuclear threat cannot be countered except by an equivalent nuclear capability is perhaps the most widely-held common variable at play in this framework. However, as posited here, such threat-based realism must be evaluated within the parameters of the Saudi security culture framework. The case of Saudi Arabia, in particular, confirms the significance of a country's identity, political and ideological foundation, and national interests, in shaping threat perceptions, objectives, and policy and, in particular, in stimulating and legitimizing the need to acquire nuclear weapons.

That is, while Saudi Arabia shares commonalities with some other cases on certain aspects of this realist perspective, one has to be cautious to not conclude that this case confirms the validity of a quasi-deterministic response by countries faced by such a threat. For example, even though at least some of the other GCC states would seem to face a similar, though not identical, potential security threat from Iran, their responses have not necessarily been the same as that of Riyadh, given the differences in their situations, whether in terms of their human resources, geographic constraints, complex demographic composition, or definition of national interest. The multiplicity of responses to a shared threat in the GCC underlines the importance of understanding the specific characteristics of a country's socio-political system and of its decisionmaking process. Identifying and appreciating the individuality of a country's threat perceptions, interpretation of lessons learned from other cases, calculus of perceived costs and benefits, assumptions about the envisioned modes of employment of nuclear weapons (political and military), and the legal/ethical considerations involved, as well as each country's strategic culture and political decisionmaking process, are key to understanding and evaluating how actual and potential regional nuclear powers may decide on the nuclear issue.

Moreover, Saudi thinking has clearly also been tied to domestic considerations of systemic legitimacy, as well as to narratives about the country's essential identity. The more expansive "nuclear mythmaking" model need not conflict with the realist model in the Saudi case, but may instead enrich and help explain the Saudis' analysis of and the decisionmaking process on the nuclear issue. However, the "nuclear mythmaking" approach, too, bears adjustment to specific countries, some of which may not be amenable to all the components normally associated with this approach. For example, it would be difficult to recognize in Saudi Arabia a key step in Lavoy's model, namely that in which a country's national elites (or, as he terms them, the "nuclear mythmakers") seek "to convince senior decisionmakers to accept and act on these views," that is to adopt a nuclear option.[15] In the Saudi system, it is more likely that the promotion of such a dynamic would be the result of a top-down process, with nuclear mythmaking national elites—not easily defined in this case, in any event, given the overlapping of personal, family, and institutional allegiances—as the executors rather than the initiators of such policies generated by the senior decisionmakers.

In addition, the Saudi case does not seem to conform to certain aspects or assumptions of some other proliferation models, indicating that while some variables in such models may be applicable, others may be irrelevant for understanding specific countries. For example, a model by Sonali Singh and Christopher R. Wray, which proposes indicators (or "stages") to determine when countries are proceeding toward becoming nuclear powers, includes as one of the four stages to monitor that of a country's "substantial efforts to develop weapons."[16] Yet, there probably would be little development to detect if the judgment is correct that Riyadh would most likely bypass attempts at indigenous development and, instead, acquire such weapons outright by purchase. In this case, there appear to be at least ample verbal indications and warnings, but in some cases even that may be missing. For example, with the dissolution of the Soviet Union, discussions reportedly occurred in 1992 between Qaddafi and Kazakhstan's president, Nursultan Nazarbaev, about cooperating on retaining that country's nuclear arsenal, with perhaps a possible transfer at a subsequent date.[17] Likewise, the Singh-Wray model also proposes a set of "explanatory variables," including a country's industrial capacity index.[18] Yet, in Saudi Arabia's case, while some of the variables used are applicable, others are not, and negative results could suggest misleading conclusions. For example, Saudi Arabia has no real industrial infrastructure, as is assumed to be a variable by this model, even though this factor may not serve as a retardant in Saudi Arabia's case as the model would suggest. The outcome of calculating such variables, which would indicate that Saudi Arabia is highly unlikely to acquire nuclear weapons, however, may be questionable and a decision need not really be dependent on the results stemming from applying the variables in that model.

Nor would a focus on the psychology of an individual decisionmaker, as suggested by Jacques E. C. Hymans, necessarily be very informative in Saudi Arabia's case, given the group-based decisionmaking characteristic of that country's political system, despite the fact that, as is true in any human collective, the Saudi royal family contains members who may be outspoken and assertive and others who are retiring and reticent. While K. P. O'Reilly, like Hymans, also provides a valid corrective in highlighting the need to "bring the human factor into our analysis" as the O'Reilly terms it, in the case of Saudi Arabia there has been no identifiable single individual in the royal family who could be seen as the champion or opponent of nuclear weapons.[19] Moreover, Hyman's specific emphasis on an "oppositional nationalist" personality is also not likely to be useful here, as this type is the antithesis of the country's cautious royal elite taken as a whole, who display continuity over time and where a more or less diffuse consensus-making process is not necessarily dependent on any one individual or on changes of individual position holders.[20] King Abd Allah, who died in his 90s in 2015, as a case in point, was a modest, cautious, and pragmatic individual far from the stereotypical hardline strident personalities one has come to identify with oppositional nationalists, such as Saddam Husayn.[21] Neither does his successor, 80-year-old King Salman, fit in the oppositional nationalist mold. To be sure, the latter's son, Prince Muhammad, as Defense Minister and Deputy Crown Prince, reportedly is an assertive activist in security and foreign policy matters, but he, too, has not emerged as a promoter of nuclear weapons, at least publicly. Rather, in the Saudi case, it has been more a case where leadership in this arena has been exercised by a narrow elite within the royal family in the form of a consensus buttressed by a guided but receptive society.

The models of restraint

To be sure, as other models supported by multiple studies have shown, a number of countries have declined to undertake a nuclear program—while others have denuclearized or reversed their progress in the nuclear field—due to the influence of domestic and international factors.

The domestic focus

Etel Solingen's stimulating study, for example, focused attention on the domestic nature of states in forecasting which ones were most likely to seek nuclear weapons, in terms of their relationship with the international system. Solingen posited that the degree of a country's integration in the international community is key and, specifically, she identified whether national elites were inward-looking or outward-looking as a key discriminant in this regard. That is, models "regarding integration in the global political economy have created different constraints, incentives, receptivity, and compliance patterns and have conditioned the role that international power, institutions, and democracy played in nuclear decisions."[22] As she concluded, based on her comparison of the experience of the Middle East and East Asia, it has been "inward-looking" national leaders promoting models "less dependent on external markets, investments, capital, and technology" who "have had greater tolerance—and in some cases strong incentives—for developing nuclear weapons."[23] And, conversely, "nuclearization has been less attractive and much more costly for leaders and coalitions pursuing internationalization into the global economy in order to advance domestic, regional, and international objectives."[24]

In many ways, however, the Saudi case may run counter to the principal conclusion in Solingen's work if, as the present study posits, Saudi Arabia is likely to pursue nuclear weapons if Iran does so. Of relevance to Solingen's hypothesis, Saudi Arabia—despite the uniqueness of its socio-political system, much less the cosmetics of the country's national clothing or customs—is integrated into the international community to a remarkable degree, and this is particularly true of its elite, however it is defined, apart perhaps from the religious establishment.

In fact, it would be difficult to find a country whose economy is more highly integrated in the international economy than is the case with Saudi Arabia.[25] In economic terms, oil, of course, is key, accounting for 88 percent of total exports in a foreign trade totaling $521 billion in 2014.[26] Beyond that, Saudi Arabia is a significant player in international financial and economic institutions such as the World Bank, the International Monetary Fund, and the G-20 Forum that brings together the world's countries with the largest economies, not to mention its membership in numerous regional political and economic groupings. Major international companies have a presence in virtually every sector of Saudi Arabia's economy and service sector. Foreign investment in Saudi Arabia totals some $242 billion (and measures were enacted in 2015 to open the country's markets to foreign investors), while Saudi investments abroad total over $800 billion.[27] The number of outlets of consumer landmark names—whether McDonald's, Honda, or IKEA, or hundreds of others—in virtually every Saudi town is striking evidence of international integration and is visible even to the ordinary citizen.

In human terms, Saudi Arabia is also remarkably integrated and outward-looking. In 2014, there were 147,046 Saudis studying abroad, a number that is impressive and adds up over the years, and one that is likely to grow as new groups of students were sent abroad in 2015 on exploratory visits related to future nuclear studies.[28]

What is perhaps even more significant than the raw numbers is the fact that many of today's Saudi economic, bureaucratic, media, and intellectual elite—including many individuals from the royal family—have studied abroad. This foreign exposure includes the Saudi military, both commoners and princes. Saudi tourists abroad also numbered over 10 million and spent over $70 billion abroad in 2014, even if most (apart those from the elite who can afford the West or Asia) go to other Middle East countries, not least for quick weekend getaways in less restrictive Bahrain or the UAE.[29] Likewise, by 2014, the number of foreign workers in Saudi Arabia had grown to over 10 million, representing one third of the country's population and an estimated 80 percent of the labor force.[30] That number includes foreigners who would be difficult to replace and without whom vital sectors, such as defense, health, the oil sector, and higher education, would grind to a halt.[31] Foreign contractors and military personnel provide irreplaceable support functions for the country's defense sector. Although the U.S. government has always refused to release numbers of those working on defense contracts in Saudi Arabia, it likely runs into the thousands, in addition to personnel from countries such as Pakistan.[32] And, significantly, there is a reciprocal international integration or dependence on Saudi Arabia, specifically in terms of energy. To be sure, the advent of U.S. shale oil on the market and the appearance of other oil producers have led some to question whether Saudi Arabia would be forced to relinquish, or at least share, its traditional role of swing producer, along with the clout that this role has provided. However, despite the current turbulence in the world oil market both Saudi and foreign analysts expect Saudi Arabia to remain a key player in the global energy market for the foreseeable future.[33]

The relationship between the domestic policymakers and the international system, as illustrated by the Saudi case, may thus suggest that, in certain instances, rather than serving as a disincentive, the high degree of international integration and the dependence of the world's economy on a particular country may provide a degree of immunity and a buffer for a country such as Saudi Arabia to cross the nuclear threshold, under certain circumstances, with tolerable costs, given the world's mutual dependence on that country. Thus, it may act as a neutral factor, if not as an incentive.

The internationalist focus

Maria Rost Rublee, for her part, in a thought-provoking study, proposed that international nonproliferation norms and institutions—such as the Treaty on the Non-Proliferation of Nuclear Weapons (NPT), other treaties and agreements, nuclear-free zones, or cooperation with the International Atomic Energy Agency (IAEA)—increasingly over time have developed into a factor discouraging countries from proliferating. Specifically, as she posited:

> the international social environment, supported by first an emergent and then a full-fledged nuclear nonproliferation regime, has helped to provide that systemic

impetus toward nuclear nonproliferation ... Over time, nuclear nonproliferation became more costly—economically, technically, and diplomatically—whereas nuclear nonproliferation became more rewarding.[34]

She also posits as a key corollary that once a country has adhered to this international regime, it is very likely to maintain its observance:

> once states accede to the regime, they are tethered to it in a number of ways: a domestic bureaucracy is created and empowered to advocate for the NPT, nuclear decisionmaking becomes no longer solely a function of security advisors but also involves those in the foreign ministry, and elites fear that breaking out of the NPT would result in a loss of international credibility and legitimacy.[35]

In fact, for Egypt and Libya, the desire to acquire and maintain such international legitimacy "redefined what it means to be a successful state, a vision that does not include nuclear weapons."[36] Despite the intellectual and practical validity of such concepts in many cases, the experience of Saudi Arabia suggests that such assumptions may not be universal, or at least may be influenced by other contributing factors.

Quite apart from the justification for acquiring nuclear weapons based on security concerns, the Saudis also routinely have raised the issues of justice and effectiveness in thinking on proliferation. The perceived effectiveness of nonproliferation has long been compromised to some extent, as the Saudi media frequently has addressed the flaunting of such norms by Israel, Pakistan, or North Korea. In fact, as one academic concluded after the 2015 Nuclear Agreement with Iran, which he believed was ineffective and would only postpone an Iranian nuclear breakout, "that Agreement represents a new nail in the coffin of the NPT."[37]

Saudis have also long objected to what they see as a double standard on the part of the United States and the West, who are said to ignore Israel's nuclear arsenal while denying similar weapons to others, thus undercutting respect for the NPT and other international norms—a concern that some Western authors have also highlighted.[38] Typically, as a well-placed former royal adviser complained with some intensity to the author in 2000, "The United States did not criticize Israel for its nuclear weapons, but now it criticizes Pakistan [just] because it is a Muslim state."[39] A Saudi pundit, likewise, lamented the fact that "it is permissible (*halal*) for it [i.e. Israel] to possess weapons to destroy, obliterate, and kill us, [yet] it is forbidden (*haram*) for others to possess arms for self-defense."[40] Praising in ironic terms Israel for its determination in developing its nuclear arsenal, another Saudi criticized the pressure exerted on the Arabs to sign the NPT while at the same time not doing so with Israel.[41] Yet another Saudi analyst even accused the United States itself of being one of the biggest nonproliferation violators because of its support for Israel's nuclear program.[42] Likewise, a Saudi columnist alleged that the United

States had turned a blind eye to Iran's pursuit of nuclear weapons and had even given "a green light to Iran" while shortchanging the Arabs and the Turks on that score.[43] A Saudi editorial, in fact, blamed this double standard for complicating the international community's ability to deal with Iran, since the latter could argue that Israel's nuclear weapons are permitted.[44]

Characteristically, Saudi audiences initially interpreted President Obama's 2009 landmark speech in Cairo as heralding a new U.S. effort to halt nuclear proliferation the Middle East, but were soon expressing their disappointment with what they came to view as the traditional double standard by the United States towards Israel's nuclear weapons. Typically, one commentator noted with respect to the continuing U.S.–Israeli nuclear cooperation that "barely a year passed since Obama's speech before he was forced to eat his words and he appeared before the entire world bereft of any power and ability to make decisions freely when faced by Israeli Prime Minister Benjamin Netanyahu" and took the U.S. president to task for "flip-flopping … on his 'firm' position."[45]

There has also been enduring Saudi resentment about what is viewed as the double standard and hypocrisy exercised by the Great Powers in general toward smaller powers wishing to join their exclusive nuclear club, with one military journal arguing that:

> the Great Powers who possess these [nuclear] weapons talk about steps to prevent nuclear arms and participate in international conferences on this topic. They even sign treaties to limit nuclear arms and confront and contest any step to acquire nuclear weapons by states outside the nuclear club. However, when it comes down to the actual situation, we find a different standard.[46]

Other commentators have criticized specifically the United States for retaining its own nuclear arsenal while condemning other countries for trying to also acquire that capability, and for exploiting the NPT in order to maintain its own nuclear superiority.[47]

In that vein, although the focus of Saudi policy in the past was to put its faith in a nuclear-free zone in the Middle East and although such appeals by policymakers and the media have continued, with somewhat of a revival after the U.S.–Iranian rapprochement in 2013, these calls appear to be largely pro-forma nowadays. To be sure, such a public position provides an opportunity to elicit praise in the local media for the efforts by the Saudi authorities on behalf of commendable goals. As one Saudi writer enthused, Saudi Arabia had "left no stone unturned" in its efforts to promote a nuclear-free region, and its efforts were proof of the principled, noble, and bold character of Saudi diplomacy.[48] However, in practical terms, the intent seemed designed to generate diplomatic pressure on Israel and Iran, as a consensus had emerged in Saudi Arabia that such proposals had been a failure and were unrealistic. The issues of fairness and of a nuclear-free zone, in fact, intersect, as a Saudi writer declared that "it is logical for the Arabs to … to reject double standards," noting that "for every action there is a reaction … and the Arabs can be called to account for their attempt to acquire nuclear weapons only once there is the removal of weapons of WMD from the entire region."[49] Saudi Arabia's policymakers came to believe, as Prince Turki Al-Faysal expressed it, that "our efforts and the world's efforts to convince Israel to relinquish its WMD and now Iran, too, with respect to the same weapons have failed."[50] A corollary was that the effort to promote a WMD-free Middle East "has resulted in failure," as one newspaper editor assessed it.[51] As a military study likewise concluded, "there is no possibility of making the Middle East region free of WMD in the near future."[52]

At base, Saudis were skeptical about the likelihood of nuclear disarmament in general. One typical Saudi press article reflecting such an outlook termed nuclear disarmament "a dream for some, a nightmare for others," and argued that "it will never happen" unless underlying political issues are resolved first. Indeed, the same writer concluded that it was not realistic that the Great Powers would de-nuclearize and predicted that "all states will seek to assure their security and their effectiveness by acquiring nuclear weapons, even if only in small quantities."[53] Moreover, some Saudis believed that even if the international community is well-intentioned about non-proliferation, the IAEA, as the monitoring and enforcing mechanism, is ineffective and has limited enforcement powers. In that vein, one academic saw North Korea as an object lesson of how easily the international community could be deceived, and warned that Iran was also likely to cheat.[54]

Saudi Arabia: a complex case

Ultimately, the Saudi case, in many ways, may conform most closely to, and confirm the validity of, Sagan's concept of "multicausality." As such, it reinforces the perception that searching for a single theory of proliferation that will explain the complexity of the phenomenon for all cases may be impractical, given the numerous unique features that may characterize a country's socio-political system and processes and culture, as in the case of Saudi Arabia. Instead, it may be more productive to accept the reality of a multiplicity of possible factors and, rather than expecting a single theory to provide ready-made answers, to accept that not all theoretical constructs or constituent elements may be applicable or relevant to every case. Furthermore, such an outlook underlines the utility of Jasper's approach in providing analytical flexibility to accommodate such real-world complexity, as it sheds light on how the actors themselves interpret threats and potential solutions.

As in Karl von Clausewitz's conception of war, with respect to the phenomenon of nuclear proliferation, too, perhaps there may be questions to ask related to the phenomenon's "nature"—unchanging, general shared attributes—but also a recognition that each case has an individual "character"—that is having distinctive features that are unique and not mere replications, with minor differences, of other cases. Multiple theoretical constructs, of course, are useful tools in the analytical toolbox, and provide a variety of questions to ask that one can select as appropriate to particular cases. The only commonalities as causes for nuclear proliferation to look at may be such general truisms as that a state faced by a nuclear threat will seek to maximize its national interest, that it will strive to provide for its security, and that it will strive to ensure that its government is be able to project an appearance of success—concepts that can then be applied to specific cases, with benefits to be weighed against political and economic costs and alternative defense solutions in considering a nuclear option. Individual motivations or causes, as well as the calculus for these common factors, may vary considerably from case to case and must be understood within each country's context. As such, the analyst's overall experience and knowledge of an individual case and of the subject country's perspectives are indispensable in selecting and applying the appropriate models and questions as guides and, most importantly, in developing the answers.

International leverage on proliferation may sometimes be limited

Third, the case of Saudi Arabia suggests that in some instances the international community's leverage to prevent nuclear proliferation may be limited. The perceived need to respond to threat assessments in a starkly realist mode may well trump other considerations, including nuclear nonproliferation norms, and may subordinate international opinion to what in the Saudi case may be perceived in existential terms. What is more, as noted earlier, the Great Powers' credibility as allies may have decreased in Riyadh's eyes, and that handicap may translate into a reduced ability to exert moral suasion in any attempt to persuade Saudi Arabia not to pursue a nuclear option. In addition, as also noted, the Saudis resent what they see as a double standard on the part of the United States and the West with respect to their acceptance of Israel's nuclear arsenal while denying similar weapons to the Arabs, thereby not only undercutting the legitimacy of international norms on nonproliferation but the international community's persuasiveness.

As Sagan points out, the choice of the model that one believes is the most appropriate one to explain nuclear proliferation will have a bearing on what counter-proliferation policies are selected.[55] However, in general, to be able to deter proliferation requires an overmatch in tools such as political, economic, and military and, ultimately, the ability to convince a country that to forgo, or at least delay, acquiring a nuclear capability will yield greater security and greater benefits than pursuing it—a daunting task in most instances, and especially so with Saudi Arabia.

Saudi policymakers probably expect that the international reaction to Riyadh's acquisition of nuclear weapons would be muted, and they may quite possibly be correct, depending on the timing. Since Saudi Arabia would likely take such a momentous step only if Iran actually acquired a nuclear weapon, international opinion at that point might be so incensed against Iran and understanding of the need of other countries to respond for self-defense that there might not be an outcry, as one might expect otherwise. Indicative of this factor, as one Saudi academic concluded based on what he believed was Washington's more accepting attitude toward civilian nuclear projects in the Arab countries, "the United States in the past used to prohibit the Arab countries from developing nuclear technology, but now has become more open to such an option, out of fear that Iranian influence will increase, potentially leading to a sort of hegemony over political developments in the region."[56] Ultimately, the Saudis might argue that if Iran, for whatever reason, one day does announce a nuclear breakout, they would have given the international community a fair chance to do something to prevent Iran's acquisition of nuclear weapons, and that Riyadh had taken a decision to go nuclear only after the international community had failed to meet its implied obligations to act effectively. Again, the Saudis are likely to also see this as an issue of fairness if an Iranian nuclear breakout is accepted by the international community.

Political considerations may indeed have a deciding impact on the international community's reaction to a specific country's acquisition of nuclear weapons. Thus, international reactions to Pakistan's progress on nuclear research in the 1980s were muted, no doubt because of the need for that country's support in the war of resistance to the Soviet presence in Afghanistan. Likewise, after September 2001, the United States lifted the sanctions it had imposed on Pakistan after the latter had tested a nuclear device in 1998. Again, Pakistan's support for U.S. access to Afghanistan was vital and served to neutralize any negative international reaction. In India's case, too, not only did the country's size and geo-political importance play a role in a relatively benign international reaction to its acquisition of nuclear weapons, but also the fact that India is not seen as an aggressively revisionist state. In part, many Saudis may also believe that a reaction by the United States, in particular, would be influenced by the latter's political ties with the proliferating country and that Saudi Arabia could rely on its close relationship with Washington and other countries in the West for a limited reaction. As a senior military officer writing in the SANG journal posited, the United States was willing to exercise a selective double standard on proliferators, depending on its political relationship with the country, thus condemning North Korea's nuclear program while accepting those in India and Pakistan.[57] Likewise, an editorial in *Al-Riyadh* also concluded that the West opposed the nuclear programs in North Korea and Iran principally for political reasons, that is because those two countries were outside the West's orbit, whereas it had accepted Israel's nuclear program.[58] In addition, Riyadh may be hoping that its substantial conventional arms purchases, which are usually accompanied by significant numbers of foreign civilian advisers, may strengthen security and political bonds with seller countries and reduce the impact of potentially negative reactions when and if it actually did acquire nuclear weapons. Moreover, it would be very difficult to isolate Saudi Arabia in the same way that one could isolate North Korea or even Iran, which do not form part of larger political and socio-cultural systems. Saudi Arabia is part of a wider system in the form of the Arab world, as well as being the focus of the Muslim world, and achieving system-wide agreement for such a regime of isolation would be impractical, all the more so that Saudis believed that "Washington understands Riyadh's importance in the region and that it cannot do without it."[59]

Certainly, in Iran's case, robust economic and political sanctions and the potential for a military strike appear to have been effective in convincing Tehran to reconsider its nuclear policy at least temporarily and, admittedly, to what extent remains to be seen. Of course, as seen above, Saudi Arabia may be a special case, due to its own considerable leverage with the international community thanks to its energy resources. Given Saudi Arabia's unique position in the world oil market, with no credible alternative source able to replace its production without major and perhaps fatal disruptions in the international economy, significant sanctions would simply not be realistic. In particular, if the smaller oil and gas-producing Gulf states such as the United Arab Emirates, Kuwait, and Qatar were unwilling to replace even part of any lost Saudi production, either out of solidarity with Riyadh or due to the latter's pressure, any threat of effective economic sanctions against Saudi Arabia would be untenable. Likewise, other countries, too, whether for political or economic reasons, may also be able to resist or avert altogether outside pressure on the nuclear issue.

More broadly, this case study reinforces the assumption that a state's interpretation of its national interests and reading of the threat environment can be expected to be the decisive consideration in decisionmaking and will outweigh outside admonitions or pressures against acquiring nuclear weapons if—as seems to be the case with Saudi Arabia—a state feels that its vital interests are at stake and that it has no other reliable means to counter the threat. In effect, justifying Riyadh's purchase of the CSS-2—after the missiles had been discovered by U.S. intelligence in 1988—King Fahd had maintained that "Our country's orientation is determined by our national interests; we are not with anyone, but only with our interests."[60] In that vein, according to a 2014 editorial, if Iran goes nuclear, Saudi Arabia would have no choice but to follow suit "without regard to world opinion or pressure from others."[61]

Modifying the threat environment can help

Fourth, a key approach to alleviate the pressure to proliferate is that of modifying the regional threat environment by the international community. Of course, analysts and policymakers have often proposed political, economic, legal, and military measures that could help address individual countries' security concerns as a way to reduce the perceived need for acquiring nuclear weapons.[62] In particular, what the international community can do in such cases is to try to remove or diminish the source of perceived insecurity, as others have suggested.[63]

Ultimately, of course, if the international community can convince Riyadh that the 2015 Nuclear Agreement has been effective in stopping Iran's progress toward nuclear weapons, that would preclude the need for Riyadh to also follow suit and acquire a corresponding nuclear capability. However, any positive outcome from the Agreement with Iran would have to be enduring and carry solid guarantees that the Saudis would find convincing. That is, even if Iran does forgo producing a nuclear device at this time, there need to be safeguards that it would not develop the components that could be used for a breakout in the future once the stipulated period of the moratorium ends or if there were a change in policy in Tehran.

Otherwise, if there should be a future Iranian nuclear breakout, Saudi Arabia would again be faced with the same security dilemma as it has faced up to now.

Even if the international community only succeeds in preventing Iran from taking the final steps toward developing further and weaponizing a nuclear capability, that would be a significant achievement, since such a respite could be very useful in preparing international security and political safeguards for other countries in the region. Moreover, during such a delay, selected countries in the international community could also help develop relevant expertise in allied and partner nations—with an emphasis on technical issues, such as the safety risks associated with nuclear establishments, the instability of deterrence, and the perils of proliferation—that could decrease the attractiveness of nuclear weapons to potential proliferators such as Saudi Arabia. Visits to U.S. academic and scientific institutions, participation in seminars, diplomatic contacts, scientist exchanges, or coursework in professional military education for military officers could all contribute to such an effort. Given a potential gap in credibility, perhaps an indirect approach through academia or private firms might be more effective than an effort emanating only from official sources. Such educational efforts may be directed to and tailored for the academic, technocratic, religious, media, and military sectors—players who would shape any proliferation process over the long term by translating guidance into policy on safety or operational military doctrine, especially if Saudi Arabia evolves into a more open political system.

Of course, the perceived nuclear threat may be only a symptom or subset of root causal threats—in Saudi Arabia's case of the perceived hegemonic threats with religious undertones from Israel and especially Iran. In general, the resolution, or at least genuine progress toward the resolution, of political conflicts and the threats they generate may reduce or at least slow down, if not eliminate, further proliferation. Specifically, in the Middle East, a just resolution of the Arab–Israeli issue would contribute to this effort by decreasing the perception of insecurity and the deep-seated sense of injustice stemming from the current political situation as well as from the sense of unfairness at the international community's acceptance of Israel's nuclear arsenal but opposition to one for any Arab country. Likewise, if the international community could convince Iran that there is no intent of engineering regime change from the outside, that the cost of expansion and interference in neighboring countries is too high a price to pay, and that integration into the international community is preferable, that too could have a positive effect in improving regional atmospherics and threat perceptions. While perhaps there is no automatic and direct linkage, de-escalating the key sources of tension in the region would probably make decisionmakers in Saudi Arabia less concerned about the need to confront Israel or Iran and, therefore, perhaps less prone to proliferation.

Opening the door to further proliferation?

Fifth, if Saudi Arabia did acquire nuclear weapons in the wake of Iran's having done so, this could well be the prelude to an additional, even if not immediate, spate of proliferation in the region, with consequences that may be difficult to foresee. Turkey, Egypt, or Algeria—for various security reasons of their own, not always tied to an Iranian threat—might also be tempted to follow Saudi Arabia's lead, especially if the international community appeared to express an understanding for and acceptance of Riyadh's actions. One Saudi academic saw such a process as likely, in particular, given the fact that the Middle East can be viewed as a system ("we live in a single region," as he put it) where such processes are hard to isolate.[64] To be sure, some, such as Philipp Bleek or Francis J. Gavin, who has spoken of "nuclear alarmism" in overstating the likelihood of proliferation, have seen such nuclear cascading—or "domino-effect proliferation"—as unlikely.[65] Others, however, such as Nicholas L. Miller and Nuno P. Monteiro and Alexandre Debs, have suggested that the probability of nuclear proliferation may in fact be an interactive variable dependent on what other states do.[66]

The present study, in fact, suggests that Saudi Arabia may represent such a case of reactive proliferation, with Iran's actions a key variable in Riyadh's decisions on the nuclear issue. Indicative of Iran as a direct stimulus is the fact that all the discussions in Saudi Arabia about a possible nuclear path in recent years have focused on Iran and on the latter's potential nuclear threat. Were it not for Iran, it is extremely unlikely that Saudi Arabia—a basically status-quo state—would have even considered the possibility of itself acquiring nuclear weapons, not only because of the potential international political cost but also because of the risk of thereby provoking Iran, in particular, into embarking on a nuclear path if the latter had otherwise not intended to do so. Nor would Saudi officials and the Saudi civilian and professional media have engaged in such frequent warnings and discussions about a potential Saudi acquisition of nuclear weapons over the years without the Iranian stimulus. While concerned about Israel's nuclear arsenal, the Saudis by and large have not seen that as a direct threat to the Gulf and would very likely have continued to react to that concern by promoting the concept of the Middle East as a nuclear-free zone. Whatever arguments have been made for a nuclear capability to deter Israel or a Western foreign intervention, or for national pride, have been as an ancillary general justification bolstering the case for the central objective of any Saudi nuclear initiative, that is in response to a perceived Iranian nuclear threat. This is not to say that the relationship is a symmetric one, for Iran's principal motivation for pursuing a nuclear capability has not been any perceived Saudi threat. Rather, for Iran, the more plausible impetus has been the perceived need to deter the United States and Israel.

Saudi nuclear proliferation: does it matter?

But, in the end, would the acquisition of nuclear weapons by Riyadh really matter, apart from the negative example that this might provide to other countries? Objectively, in terms of regional stability and of the possibility of a nuclear mishap or even nuclear use in war (though the latter would be remote), the overall impact of Saudi Arabia's acquisition of nuclear weapons would likely be negative.

True, some "optimists" view the possession of nuclear weapons as a positive factor, thanks to a perceived stabilizing effect of deterrence, with proponents of this view often relying on the superpower experience during the Cold War. Beginning perhaps most forcefully with Kenneth N. Waltz, others have followed suit, with Martin van Creveld making perhaps the most eloquent case for this approach with respect to the Middle East.[67] A countering "pessimist" view, however, not only holds that the role of nuclear weapons was a less significant factor in the preservation of peace during the Cold War than assumed, but also stresses the complexity and ambiguity of the historical record and the instability of the deterrence experience even during that era.[68] Or, even when accepting the more traditional view of the earlier period, skeptics have been less sanguine about the possibility of replicating such a phenomenon elsewhere in the post-Cold War era, pointing to the significance of the specific context of the Cold War.[69] More recently, even those who would categorize themselves as realists have also made cogent policy arguments in favor of nonproliferation.[70]

Some, in particular, have highlighted the differences between the Middle East and other cases, calling into question the validity of the deterrence analogy for that region.[71] Of course, a key consideration for the stability of nuclear deterrence may be a country's basic political outlook, with a status-quo one such as Saudi Arabia less likely to represent a danger to nuclear stability than a blatantly revisionist one seeking to redress perceived injustices. Even so, the possibilities of miscalculations or accidents by countries with limited intelligence and early warning capabilities, small vulnerable nuclear arsenals, and imperfect command and control could easily invalidate assumptions about an optimistic replication of the Cold War deterrence experience in other parts of the world. Given the high stakes, and whatever the obstacles and limitations, counterproliferation efforts by the international community, both in general and tailored to specific situations such as Saudi Arabia, are still important and must continue in order to promote genuine stability and to reduce the risk of unintended consequences. Such counterproliferation efforts must include the control of missile technology from potential suppliers as well as recipients, as this delivery capability represents an instrumental aspect of emerging nuclear programs, and such efforts must rely on the panoply of political, economic, information, and military instruments available.

Notes

1. Abd Al-Rahman Al-Turayri, "Al-Khalij arabi am farisi?" [The Gulf: Arab or Persian?], *Al-Iqtisadiya*, 23 August 2011, www.aleqt.com/2011/08/23/article_572330.print.
2. Abd Al-Rahman Al-Rashid, "Hal yughayyir al-mal wa'l-infitah al-iraniyyin?" [Will Money and the Opening Change the Iranians?], *Al-Sharq Al-Awsat*, 11 September 2015, http://aawsat.com/node/449931, and Ali Al-Khashiban, "Ma alladhi yajri bayn Al-Saudiya wa-Amrika?" [What Is Happening between Saudi Arabia and America?], *Al-Riyadh*, 7 September 2015, www.alriyadh.com/1080144.
3. Muhammad Abd Allah Al-Uwayn, "Al-Malik Salman fi Washintun: Rataq futuq al-alaqat al-istratijiya" [King Salman in Washington: He Mended the Rips in the Strategic

Relationship], part 2, *Al-Jazira*, 7 September 2015, www.al-jazirah.com/2015/20150907/ln36.htm.
4 Hamdan Al-Shihri, "Iran la tata' ardan illa wa-tudannisha ya sayyid Friedman" [Iran Does Not Set Foot in Any Land Without Contaminating It, Mr. Friedman], *Al-Riyadh*, 12 September 2015, www.alriyadh.com/1081813.
5 Mutlaq bin Saud Al-Mtiri, "La badil an al-jaysh al-khaliji al-wahid" [There Is No Alternative to a Unified Gulf Army], *Al-Riyadh*, 7 September 2015, www.alriyadh.com/1080255.
6 Abd Al-Wahid Al-Hamid, "Mufailat nawawiya saudiya li-ma la?" [Saudi Nuclear Reactors: Why Not?], *Al-Jazira*, 18 April 2015, www.al-jazirah.com.sa/2015/20150418/ln52.htm.
7 Hammad Al-Salimi, "Al-Nawawi yu'annis 'Shaytan Bazrag': madha bad?"[Nuclear Weapons Humanize "the Great Satan": What Next?], *Al-Jazira*, 2 August 2015, www.al-jazirah.com/2015/20150802/ar3.htm, and Imad Al-Mudayfir, "Al-Ittifaq al-nawawi al-irani nasr am rudukh?" [The Iranian Nuclear Agreement: Victory or Capitulation?], *Al-Jazira*, 5 August 2015, www.al-jazirah.com/2015/20150805/ar4.htm.
8 "Iran DAISH al-kubra!" [Iran Is the Great ISIS!], *Al-Riyadh*, 3 November 2014, www.alriyadh.com/990630.
9 Abd Al-Aziz Al-Uwayshiq, "Al-Tajahul al-amiriki li'l-tamaddud al-irani fi al-mintaqa" [America's Disregard for Iran's Expansionism in the Region], *Al-Watan*, 12 March 2015, www.alwatan.com.sa/Articles/Detail.aspx?ArticleID=25443, and Ali bin Hasan Al-Tawati, "Ma taht khaymat Iran al-nawawiya" [What Is Inside Iran's Nuclear Tent], *Ukaz*, 9 April 2015, http://okaz.co/bwlcLdmU9.
10 Ahmad Al-Ahmad, "Ta'yid Kerry li'l-tafawud ma Al-Asad yuthir jadalan hawl taghayyur mawqif Washintun min nizham Dimashq" [Kerry's Support for Dialogue with Al-Asad Stokes Controversy about a Change in Washington's Position on the Damascus Regime], *Al-Riyadh*, 17 March 2015, www.alriyadh.com/1030590.
11 Major General Yahya Safavi speech reported in "Law-la damna li'l-Iraq wa-Suriya la-kunna nuqatil al-irhabiyin ala hudud Iran" [Were It Not for Our Support to Iraq and Syria We Would Have Been Fighting the Terrorists on Iran's Border], *Shabestan News Agency* (Tehran), 29 June 2015, http://ar.shabestan.ir/detail/News/34935.
12 Scott D. Sagan, "Nuclear Latency and Nuclear Proliferation," in William C. Potter with Gaukhar Mukhatzhanova, eds, *Forecasting Nuclear Proliferation in the 21st Century: The Role of Theory*, vol. 1 (Stanford, CA: Stanford University Press, 2010), 80–101.
13 "Turki Al-Faysal yadu duwal Al-Khalij ila ijad 'tawazun nawawi' li-muwajahat al-tumuhat al-iraniya" [Turki Al-Faysal Calls on the Gulf States to Establish a "Nuclear Balance" in Order to Counter Iran's Ambitions], *Al-Riyadh*, 24 April 2014, www.alriyadh.com/929960.
14 Staff Brigadier Zayd bin Muhammad Al-Amri, "Dawafi imtilak al-qudrat al-istratijiya al-sarukhiya al-fada'iya wa'l-nawawiya" [The Incentives for Acquiring Strategic Rocket, Space, and Nuclear Capabilities], *Al-Difa Al-Jauwi*, December 2010, 14.
15 Peter R. Lavoy, "Nuclear Proliferation over the Next Decade: Causes, Warning Signs, and Policy Responses," *The Nonproliferation Review*, xiii, 3, November 2006, 435.
16 Sonali Singh and Christopher R. Wray, "The Correlates of Nuclear Proliferation: A Quantitative Test," *Journal of Conflict Resolution*, xlviii, 6, December 2004, 866 (hereafter Singh and Wray).
17 The information came from a Kazakhstani diplomat, Renat Tashkinbaev, "Kaddafi predlagal Nazarbaevu sokhranit' yadernyi potentsial" [Qaddafi Suggested to Nazarbaev That He Retain a Nuclear Capability], *Tengri News Agency* (Almaty, Kazakhstan), 29 November 2012, http://tengrinews.kz/kazakhstan_news/kadda-=predlagal-nazarbaevu-sohranit-yadernyiy-potentsial-224323. However, a UAE source claimed that the initiative had come from Kazakhstan rather than from Libya, "Ra'is Kazakhstan sawam Al-Qadhdhafi ala asliha nawawiya liqa'an milyar dular sanawiyan" [The President of Kazakhstan Bargained with Qaddafi Over Nuclear Weapons in Return for a Billion Dollars a Year], Al-Arabiya TV, 4 December 2011, www.alarabiya.net/articles/2011/12/04/180827.html. On the other hand, well-publicized reports of an attempt by

Qaddafi to buy an atom bomb from China in 1970 appear to have been inventions spread by Egyptian sources, and were denied by the regime's number-two man, Abd Al-Salam Jallud—although he admitted having sought China's cooperation on nuclear development; interview with Abd Al-Salam Jallud by Ghassan Sharbal, "Al-Rajul al-thani ala mustawa Libiya yakshif haqa'iq ajiba an tahawwurat Al-Qadhdhafi fi adad min al-qarrat" [The Number-Two Man in Libya Reveals Amazing Facts about Qaddafi's Bizarre Behavior on Several Continents], originally in *Al-Hayat*, republished in *Ikhbariyat Arar* (Arar, Saudi Arabia), 2 November 2011, www.ararnews.com/124481.html.
18 Singh and Wray, 867–70.
19 K. P. O'Reilly, *Nuclear Proliferation and the Psychology of Political Leadership: Beliefs, Motivations and Perceptions* (Abingdon: Routledge, 2015), 2.
20 As Hymans posited, "the decision to acquire nuclear weapons is not only a means to the end of getting them; it is also an end in itself, a matter of self-expression … The oppositional nationalist's emotional impulses in this direction are so strong that the mere arrival in power of such a leader is practically a sufficient condition to spark a decision to build the bomb." Jacques E. C. Hymans, *The Psychology of Nuclear Proliferation: Identity, Emotions, and Foreign Policy* (Cambridge: Cambridge University Press, 2006), 35–36. Alexander L. George had also made the case for such an approach, "The Need for Influence Theory and Actor-Specific Behavioral Models of Adversaries," in Barry R. Schneider and Jerrold M. Post, eds, *Know Thy Enemy: Profiles of Adversary Leaders and Their Strategic Culture* (Maxwell Air Force Base, AL: USAF Counterproliferation Center, July 2003), 271–310.
21 On Saddam Husayn, see Jerrold M. Post and Amatzia Baram, "'Saddam Is Iraq, Iraq Is Saddam' (Until Operation Iraqi Freedom)," in Barry R. Schneider and Jerrold M. Post, eds, *Know Thy Enemy: Profiles of Adversary Leaders and Their Strategic Culture* (Maxwell Air Force Base, AL: USAF Counterproliferation Center, July 2003), 163–220.
22 Etel Solingen, *Nuclear Logics: Contrasting Paths in East Asia and the Middle East* (Princeton, NJ and Oxford: Princeton University Press, 2007), 285.
23 Ibid., 276.
24 Ibid., 277.
25 Unless otherwise noted, all economic data here is drawn from the CIA's *World Factbook*, (Washington, DC: CIA, 2015), https://www.cia.gov/library/publications/the-world-factbook/geos/sa.html.
26 Ernst & Young, *Understanding the Opportunities and Challenges for Businesses in the GCC* (London: Ernst & Young Global Limited, 2014), 11. International integration, using the share of international trade as a per cent of GDP (2013) as an indicator, was 83 percent for Saudi Arabia (compared to 35 percent for Japan, 30 percent for the United States, and 62 percent for the UK), The World Bank, Table: Trade (percent of GDP), *World Trade website*, http://data.worldbank.org/indicator/NE.TRD.GNFS.ZS.
27 *World Factbook* and Abdullah Saddiq Dahlan, "Why Shouldn't Expats Send Money Abroad When Saudis Do the Same?" *Saudi Gazette* (Jeddah), 24 October 2014, www.saudigazette.com.sa/index.cfm?method=home.regcon&contentid=20141024222137.
28 Ministry of Higher Education, *Al-Talim al-ali fi Al-Mamlaka Al-Arabiya Al-Saudiya* [*Higher Education in the Kingdom of Saudi Arabia*] (Riyadh: Ministry of Higher Education, 2014), 151, and Nayif Al-Wayil, "Al-Nawawi al-saudi hulm mashru li-mustaqbal taqa akthar ishraqan wa-aminan" [The Saudi Nuclear Program Is a Dream for a Program for a More Brilliant and More Secure Energy Future], *Al-Riyadh*, 22 June 2015, www.alriyadh.com/1058888.
29 Yusuf Al-Muhaymid, "Min ayn ja' ha'ula'i al-saudiyun?" [Where Did Those Saudis Come From?], *Al-Jazira*, 14 July 2015, www.al-jazirah.com/2015/20150714/ms6.htm.
30 "30.8 miliyun nasamat sukkan Al-Saudiya thulthuhum ajanib" [The Population of Saudi Arabia Is 30.8 Million, of Whom One Third Are Foreigners], *Al-Iqtisadiya*, 29 January 2015, www.aleqt.com/2015/01/29/article_926837.html, and *World Factbook*. And in 2015, the Saudi authorities announced plans to recruit an additional 1.2 million foreign workers, Abdullah Al-Qahtani, "Go Ahead Given for Hiring 1.2 Million Workers for

Saudi Arabia," *Saudi Gazette*, 9 July 2015, www.saudigazette.com.sa/index.cfm?method=home.regcon&contentid=20150709249906.
31 For example, the majority of health personnel in Saudi Arabia are expatriates, M. Almalki, G. Fitzgerald, and M. Clark, "Health Care System in Saudi Arabia: An Overview," *Eastern Mediterranean Health Journal* (Cairo: World Health Organization Regional Office for the Eastern Mediterranean), xvii, 10, 2011, 789.
32 "Troops Already in Saudi Arabia, Says Minister," *Dawn* (Karachi), 11 April 2015, www.dawn.com/news/1175231.
33 John Sfakianakis, "Saudi Arabia's Essential Oil: Why Riyadh Isn't Worried About the U.S. Gas Revolution," *Foreign Affairs*, 8 January 2014, www.foreignaffairs.com/articles/saudi-arabia/2014-01-08/saudi-arabias-essential-oil, Bassam Fattouh and Anupama Sen, *Saudi Arabia Oil Policy: More than Meets the Eye?* (Oxford: Oxford Institute for Energy Studies, June 2015), www.oxfordenergy.org/wpcms/wp-content/uploads/2015/06/MEP-13.pdf, Steve Levine, "If OPEC Is Dead, How Is Saudi Arabia Still Calling the Shots in the Oil Market?" *Quartz* (New York), 27 April 2015, http://qz.com/391283, and Anwar Abu Al-Ala', "Khurafa: Al-Mamlaka tatakhallas min bitrulha li-tawaqquha intiha' asr al-bitrul" [Myth: The Kingdom Is Jettisoning Its Oil Because It Expects the End of the Oil Era], *Al-Riyadh*, 1 March 2015, www.alriyadh.com/1026053, and interview with Fatih Birol by Mehreen Khan, "United States Will Not Become the 'New Saudi Arabia' of Global Energy," *Telegraph*, 26 February 2015, www.telegraph.co.uk/finance/newsbysector/energy/oilandgas/11436337/United-States-will-not-become-the-new-Saudi-Arabia-of-global-energy.html. Birol is Executive Director of the International Energy Agency.
34 Maria Rost Rublee, *Nonproliferation Norms: Why States Choose Nuclear Restraint* (Athens, GA and London: University of Georgia Press, 2009), 202.
35 Ibid.
36 Ibid., 203.
37 Abd Al-Ghaffar Al-Duwayk, "Iran al-nawawiya" [A Nuclear Iran], *Ukaz*, 30 August 2015, http://okaz.com/bwljzduxj. Although Al-Duwayk is an Egyptian, he teaches at the Saudi Ministry of the Interior's Prince Nayif University for Security Studies.
38 Timothy Miklos, "Unraveling the Myth of Opacity: How Israel's Undeclared Nuclear Arsenal Destabilizes the Middle East," *International Affairs Review*, xxii, 1, Fall 2012, 43–61.
39 As told to the author in Riyadh during a visit to Saudi Arabia under the auspices of The National Council on U.S.-Arab Relations, 2001.
40 Muhammad Abd Al-Wahid, "Sunna al-mawt" [Architects of Death], *Al-Yawm*, 6 May 2011, www.alyaumonline.com/News/art/10731.html.
41 Al-Juhani, "Hal yufiq al-arab."
42 Sami Said Habib, "Qira'a fi qimmat al-junun al-nawawi al-alami" [An Analysis of the International Nuclear Madness Summit], *Al-Madina*, 17 April 2010, www.al-madina.com/print/240768.
43 Jasir Abd Al-Aziz Al-Jasir, "Daqq jaras sibaq al-tasalluh al-nawawi fi al-mintaqa" [The Starting Bell for the Nuclear Arms Race in the Region Has Sounded], *Al-Jazira*, 16 April 2009, www.al-jazirah.com.sa/20090416/du1.htm.
44 "Iran al-nawawiya" [A Nuclear Iran], *Al-Madina*, 13 July 2010, www.al-madina.com/print/256294.
45 Sami Said Habib, "Safat Obama al-nawawiya li'l-umma al-islamiya" [Obama's Nuclear Slap to the Islamic Umma], *Al-Madina*, 10 July 2010, www.al-madina.com/printhtml/255964.
46 Salih Sulayman, "Al-Silah al-nawawi inhisar am mazid min al-intishar?" [Nuclear Weapons: Rollback or Further Proliferation?], *Al-Haras Al-Watani*, October–November 2007, 34 (hereafter Sulayman, "Al-Silah al-nawawi").
47 "Al-Rad al-nawawi ... ustura za'ifa" [Nuclear Deterrence Is a Spurious Myth], *Shams* (Riyadh), 6 February 2011, www.shms.com.sa/html/story.php?-124218, Sulayman, "Al-Silah al-nawawi," 30–35, and Abd Al-Jalil Zayd Al-Marhun, "Al-Alam al-thalith wa-mudilat al-intishar al-nawawi [The Third World and the Problem of Nuclear

Proliferation], *Al-Riyadh*, 15 June 2001, www.alriyadh.com/2001/06/15/article32562.html.
48 Malha Abd Allah in "Al-Siyasa al-saudiya tahkumha al-mabadi' wa-qiyam al-haqq" [Saudi Policy Is Governed by Principles and Just Standards], *Al-Yawm*, 18 April 2013, www.alyaum.com/News/art/79481.html.
49 Yusuf Makki, "Al-Arab wa'l-tiknulujiya al-nawawiya" [The Arabs and Nuclear Technology], *Al-Khalij*, 15 March 2009, www.alkhaleej.ae/portal/ab1b80b2-b23b-4e70-8021-a8af70d022d4.aspx.
50 Salim Al-Sharif, "Turki Al-Faysal: Al-Alam fashal fi iqna Isra'il wa-Iran min 'al-nawawi' wa-khiyaratna maftuha" [Turki Al-Faysal: The World Failed to Convince Israel and Iran on the Nuclear [Issue] and Our Options Are Open], *Al-Madina*, 6 December 2011, www.al-madina.com/print/343006.
51 Jasir Abd Al-Aziz Al-Jasir, "Naam li-silah nawawi khaliji" [Yes to a Gulf Nuclear Weapon], *Al-Jazira*, 7 December 2011, www.al-jazirah.com/2011/20111207/du8.htm. Likewise, another opinion piece also concluded that this objective was "impractical," Abd Al-Munim Mustafa, "Kull shay' lam yaud kafiyan" [All of That Is Not Enough], *Al-Madina*, 14 February 2010, www.al-madina.com/print/224041.
52 Hay'at Al-Tahrir [Editorial Board], "Hal yusbih Al-Sharq Al-Awsat mintaqa khaliya min aslihat al-damar al-shamil?" [Will the Middle East Become a Region Free of Weapons of Mass Destruction?], *Majallat Kulliyat Al-Malik Khalid Al-Askariya*, March 2004, 45.
53 Muhammad Al-Zawawi, "Naz al-silah al-nawawi min al-alam hulm li'l-bad wa-kabus li-akharin" [Global Nuclear Disarmament—A Dream for Some and a Nightmare for Others], *Majallat Al-Jazira*, 18 July 2006, www.al-jazirah.com.sa/magazine/18072006/almlfsais4.htm.
54 Abd Al-Rahman bin Ali Al-Fayfi, "Taaddadat al-tasa'ulat wa'l-jawab wahid" [There Are Many Questions But Always the Same Answer], *Al-Riyadh*, 30 August 2015, www.alriyadh.com/1077706.
55 Scott D. Sagan, "Why Do States Build Nuclear Weapons? Three Models in Search of a Bomb," *International Security*, xxi, Winter 1996/97, 83.
56 Salih Abd Al-Rahman Al-Mani, "Al-Tiqniya al-nawawiya fi Al-Khalij" [Nuclear Technology in the Gulf], *Ukaz*, 16 December 2006, www.okaz.com.sa/okaz/osf/20061216/PrinCon2006121671686.htm.
57 Major General Ali Muhammad Rajab, "Qira'a fi al-barnamij al-amriki li-hazr intishar aslihat al-damar al-shamil" [Assessing the U.S. Strategy to Prevent WMD Proliferation], *Al-Haras Al-Watani*, March-April 2005, 53.
58 Editorial "Al-Mamnu wa'l-masmuh fi intishar al-silah al-nawawi!" [Forbidden and Permitted Nuclear Proliferation!], *Al-Riyadh*, 7 October 2006, www.alriyadh.com/2006/10/07/article192609.html.
59 Editorial by Salman Al-Dawsari, "Obama: 4 saat fi Al-Riyadh" [Obama: Four Hours in Riyadh], *Al-Sharq Al-Awsat*, 28 January 2015, http://aawsat.com/node/276066.
60 Interview with King Fahd by Ahmad Jar Allah, "Al-Fahd: Anayt ka-ma law ann al-ta'ira al-makhtufa saudiya" [Fahd: I Was As Concerned As If the Hijacked Aircraft Had Been a Saudi One], *Al-Siyasa*, 28–29 April 1988, 7.
61 Yusuf Al-Kuwaylit, "Al-Khalij al-ari wa-Iran al-nawawiya" [The Exposed Gulf and a Nuclear Iran], *Al-Riyadh*, 26 November 2014, www.alriyadh.com/997663.
62 An especially comprehensive inventory of such potential measures is contained in James E. Goodby and Steven Pifer, "Creating the Conditions for a World without Nuclear Weapons," in George P. Shultz and James E. Goodby, eds, *The War That Must Never Be Fought: Dilemmas of Nuclear Deterrence* (Stanford, CA: Hoover Institution Press, 2015), 473–501.
63 For example, Joseph Cirincione, *Bomb Scare: The History and Future of Nuclear Weapons* (New York: Columbia University Press, 2007).
64 Yusuf Makki, "Hawl tadaiyat ittifaq Lausanne" [On the Consequences of the Lausanne Agreement], *Al-Watan*, 15 April 2015, www.alwatan.com.sa/Articles/Detail.aspx?ArticleID=25901. On the concept of the Middle East as a system, see F. Gregory Gause III,

"Systemic Approaches to Middle East International Relations," *International Studies Review*, i, 1, Spring 1999, 11–31.

65 Francis J. Gavin, "Same As It Ever Was: Nuclear Alarmism, Proliferation, and the Cold War," *International Security*, xxxiv, 3, Winter 2009/10, 7, 17–19, and Philipp Bleek, "Why Do States Proliferate? Quantitative Analysis of the Exploration, Pursuit, and Acquisition of Nuclear Weapons," in William C. Potter with Gaukhar Mukhatzhanova, eds, *Forecasting Nuclear Proliferation in the 21st Century: The Role of Theory*, vol. 1 (Stanford, CA: Stanford University Press, 2010), 159–76.

66 Nicholas L. Miller, "Nuclear Dominoes: A Self-Defeating Prophecy?" *Security Studies*, xxiii, 1, 2014, 33–73, and Nuno P. Monteiro and Alexandre Debs, "The Strategic Logic of Nuclear Proliferation," *International Security*, xxxix, 2, Fall 2014, who posit that "The likelihood of proliferation, we contend, is largely determined by the strategic interaction between a state deciding whether to acquire nuclear weapons and its adversaries" within "the context of the strategic interaction that takes place between the potential proliferator, its adversaries, and, when present, its allies," 9.

67 Kenneth Waltz, "The Spread of Nuclear Weapons: More May Be Better," *Adelphi Papers*, no. 171 (London: International Institute for Strategic Studies, 1981), and Martin van Creveld, *Nuclear Proliferation and the Future of Conflict* (New York: The Free Press, 1993), 97–153, especially the chapter "Nuclear Weapons in the Middle East".

68 See John Mueller, "The Essential Irrelevance of Nuclear Weapons: Stability in the Postwar World," *International Security*, xiii, 2, Autumn 1988, 55–79, John Mueller, "Epilogue: Duelling Counterfactuals," in John Lewis Gaddis, Philip Gordon, Ernest May and Jonathan Rosenberg, eds, *Cold War Statesmen Confront the Bomb: Nuclear Diplomacy Since 1945* (Oxford: Oxford University Press, 1999), 272–83, and George H. Quester, *Nuclear Monopoly* (Edison, NJ: Transaction Publishers, 2000). Others, while accepting the significance of nuclear weapons in the Cold War, have also stressed the unique features which made deterrence successful, despite the risks of inadvertent war and escalation, and have highlighted the inadequacy of the Cold War as a deterrence model for more recent situations, Stephen J. Cimbala, "Proliferation and Peace: An Agnostic View," *Armed Forces and Society*, xxii, 2, Winter 1995/96, 211–233.

69 For example, Keith B. Payne, *The Fallacies of Cold War Deterrence and a New Direction* (Lexington, KY: University of Kentucky Press, 2001), Matthew Woods, "Reflections on Nuclear Optimism: Waltz, Burke, and Proliferation," *Review of International Studies*, xxviii, 2002, 169–89, and Henry D. Sokolski, "Nuclear 1914: The Next Big Worry," in Henry Sokolski, ed., *Taming the Next Set of Strategic Weapons Threats* (Carlisle Barracks, PA: U.S. Army War College Strategic Studies Institute, June 2006), 41–50. For an insightful analysis of such countervailing positions, see Barry R. Schneider, "Nuclear Proliferation and Counter-Proliferation: Policy Issues and Debates," *Mershon International Studies Review*, xxxviii, 1994, 209–34.

70 George P. Shultz, William J. Perry, Henry A. Kissinger and Sam Nunn, "Toward a Nuclear-Free World," *Wall Street Journal*, January 15, 2008, http://online.wsj.com/article/SB120036422673589947.html, and Steven Pifer, "A Realist's Rationale for a World without Nuclear Weapons," in George P. Shultz and James E. Goodby, eds, *The War That Must Never Be Fought: Dilemmas of Nuclear Deterrence* (Stanford, CA: Hoover Institution Press, 2015), 81–107.

71 See Yair Evron, *Israel's Nuclear Dilemma* (Ithaca, NY: Cornell University Press, 1994), Richard L. Russell, *Weapons Proliferation and War in the Greater Middle East: Strategic Contest* (New York: Routledge, 2005), and, based on the Iraqi experience, Cigar, *Saddam Hussein's Nuclear Vision*, 52–57.

Bibliography

Bleek, Philipp, "Why Do States Proliferate? Quantitative Analysis of the Exploration, Pursuit, and Acquisition of Nuclear Weapons," in William C. Potter with Gaukhar

Mukhatzhanova, eds, *Forecasting Nuclear Proliferation in the 21st Century: The Role of Theory*, vol. 1 (Stanford, CA: Stanford University Press, 2010), 159–176.

Cigar, Norman, *Saddam Hussein's Nuclear Vision: An Atomic Shield and Sword for Conquest* (Quantico, VA: Marine Corps University Press, 2011).

Cimbala, Stephen J., "Proliferation and Peace: An Agnostic View," *Armed Forces and Society*, xxii, 2, Winter 1995/96, 211–233.

Cirincione, Joseph, *Bomb Scare: The History and Future of Nuclear Weapons* (New York: Columbia University Press, 2007).

Evron, Yair, *Israel's Nuclear Dilemma* (Ithaca, NY: Cornell University Press, 1994).

Fattouh, Bassam and Anupama Sen, *Saudi Arabia Oil Policy: More than Meets the Eye?* (Oxford: Oxford Institute for Energy Studies, 2015), available at: www.oxfordenergy.org/wpcms/wp-content/uploads/2015/06/MEP-13.pdf.

Gause III, F. Gregory, "Systemic Approaches to Middle East International Relations," *International Studies Review*, i, 1, Spring 1999, 11–31.

Gavin, Francis J., "Same As It Ever Was: Nuclear Alarmism, Proliferation, and the Cold War," *International Security*, xxxiv, 3, Winter 2009/10, 7–37.

George, Alexander L., "The Need for Influence Theory and Actor-Specific Behavioral Models of Adversaries," in Barry R. Schneider and Jerrold M. Post, eds, *Know Thy Enemy: Profiles of Adversary Leaders and Their Strategic Culture* (Maxwell Air Force Base, AL: USAF Counterproliferation Center, 2003), 271–310.

Goodby, James E. and Steven Pifer, "Creating the Conditions for a World without Nuclear Weapons," in George P. Shultz and James E. Goodby, eds, *The War That Must Never Be Fought: Dilemmas of Nuclear Deterrence* (Stanford, CA: Hoover Institution Press, 2015), 473–501.

Hymans, Jacques E. C., *The Psychology of Nuclear Proliferation: Identity, Emotions, and Foreign Policy* (Cambridge: Cambridge University Press, 2006).

Jasper, Ursula, *The Politics of Nuclear Non-Proliferation: A Pragmatist Framework for Analysis* (Abingdon: Routledge, 2015).

Lavoy, Peter R., "Nuclear Proliferation over the Next Decade: Causes, Warning Signs, and Policy Responses," *The Nonproliferation Review*, xiii, 3, November 2006, 434–454.

Miklos, Timothy, "Unraveling the Myth of Opacity: How Israel's Undeclared Nuclear Arsenal Destabilizes the Middle East," *International Affairs Review*, xxii, 1, Fall 2012, 43–61.

Miller, Nicholas L., "Nuclear Dominoes: A Self-Defeating Prophecy?" *Security Studies*, xxiii, 1, 2014, 33–73.

Monteiro, Nuno P. and Alexandre Debs, "The Strategic Logic of Nuclear Proliferation," *International Security*, xxxix, 2, Fall 2014, 7–51.

Mueller, John, "The Essential Irrelevance of Nuclear Weapons: Stability in the Postwar World," *International Security*, xiii, 2, Autumn 1988, 55–79.

Mueller, John, "Epilogue: Duelling Counterfactuals," in John Lewis Gaddis, Philip Gordon, Ernest May, and Jonathan Rosenberg, eds, *Cold War Statesmen Confront the Bomb: Nuclear Diplomacy Since 1945* (Oxford: Oxford University Press, 1999), 272–283.

O'Reilly, K. P., *Nuclear Proliferation and the Psychology of Political Leadership: Beliefs, Motivations and Perceptions* (Abingdon: Routledge, 2015).

Payne, Keith B., *The Fallacies of Cold War Deterrence and a New Direction* (Lexington, KY: University of Kentucky Press, 2001).

Pifer, Steven, "A Realist's Rationale for a World without Nuclear Weapons," in George P. Shultz and James E. Goodby, eds, *The War That Must Never Be Fought: Dilemmas of Nuclear Deterrence* (Stanford, CA: Hoover Institution Press, 2015), 81–107.

Post, Jerrold M. and Amatzia Baram, "'Saddam Is Iraq, Iraq Is Saddam' (Until Operation Iraqi Freedom)," in Barry R. Schneider and Jerrold M. Post, eds, *Know Thy Enemy: Profiles of Adversary Leaders and Their Strategic Culture* (Maxwell Air Force Base, AL: USAF Counterproliferation Center, 2003), 163–220.

Quester, George H., *Nuclear Monopoly* (Edison, NJ: Transaction Publishers, 2000).

Rost Rublee, Maria, *Nonproliferation Norms: Why States Choose Nuclear Restraint* (Athens, GA and London: University of Georgia Press, 2009).

Russell, Richard L., *Weapons Proliferation and War in the Greater Middle East: Strategic Contest* (New York: Routledge, 2005).

Sagan, Scott D., "Why Do States Build Nuclear Weapons? Three Models in Search of a Bomb," *International Security*, xxi, Winter 1996–1997, 54–86.

Schneider, Barry R., "Nuclear Proliferation and Counter-Proliferation: Policy Issues and Debates," *Mershon International Studies Review*, xxxviii, 1994, 209–234.

Singh, Sonali and Christopher R. Wray, "The Correlates of Nuclear Proliferation: A Quantitative Test," *Journal of Conflict Resolution*, xlviii, 6, December 2004, 859–885.

Sokolski, Henry D., "Nuclear 1914: The Next Big Worry," in Henry Sokolski, ed., *Taming the Next Set of Strategic Weapons Threats* (Carlisle Barracks, PA: U.S. Army War College Strategic Studies Institute, 2006), 41–50.

Solingen, Etel, *Nuclear Logics: Contrasting Paths in East Asia and the Middle East* (Oxford and Princeton, NJ: Princeton University Press, 2007).

van Creveld, Martin, *Nuclear Proliferation and the Future of Conflict* (New York: The Free Press, 1993).

Waltz, Kenneth, "The Spread of Nuclear Weapons: More May Be Better," *Adelphi Papers*, no. 171 (London: International Institute for Strategic Studies, 1981).

Woods, Matthew, "Reflections on Nuclear Optimism: Waltz, Burke, and Proliferation," *Review of International Studies*, xxviii, 2002, 169–189.

INDEX

Abd Al-Aziz, King 16, 18–19, 199
Abd Allah, King 7, 17–18, 20–1, 26–9, 65, 81, 140–1, 144, 217
Ahmadinejad, Mahmoud 25, 150, 154
Al-Jubeir, Adil 66, 119, 166, 172, 186–87, 196
Al-Marashi, Ibrahim 5
Al-Rashid, Abd Al-Rahman 192–3
Al Saud 17–19; 25, 27–8
Al-Walid bin Talal, Prince 13 n33, 68

Bahrain 139, 142, 144
Bandar bin Sultan, Prince 20, 94, 188
Betts, Richard K. 16
Bin Ladin, Usama 26–7

Camp David summit 66, 134, 168–70
Carter, Ashton 197–8
civil nuclear program: Saudi 130–5, 165, 196; Saudi view of Iran's 49
clerics 10, 86–8, 133, 193–4, 214
Clinton, Hillary 63
Consultative Council see Shura

Desch, Michael C. 15
deterrence, Saudi views of 52–3, 72, 84–5, 102–10, 114–17, 155
Dubai 142–4

Fahd, King 7, 26, 28–9, 39, 78, 106, 118, 120
France 163–5, 170, 200
Friedman, Thomas 197–8

GCC see Gulf Cooperation Council
Geneva Interim agreement 152–4, 161
Gulf Cooperation Council 50–1, 64, 66, 80, 137–45, 149, 154, 156–8, 167–70, 187, 192, 195–7, 213, 216

Hagel, Chuck 155
Heikal, Muhammad Hasanayn 191
Husayn, Saddam 39, 55, 106, 115, 157
Hyman, Jacques E. C. 3, 11 n1, 217

International Atomic Energy Agency 38, 92, 150, 195, 219
Iran 1–2, 29; and Saudi views of 20–3, 42–5, 52, 159–61
Iraq 39, 110–11; see also Husayn, Saddam
Israel 29; and nuclear weapons 39–41, 43–4, 54–5, 63–5, 68–70, 83–4, 106, 109, 155, 163, 166, 169–70, 197, 220–1

Jasper, Ursula 4–6, 21, 222
Jervis, Robert 16
Johnston, Alastair Iain 15
Joint Comprehensive Plan of Action 2, 10–11, 20, 65, 162–4, 187; and Saudi view of 186–201, 220

Kerry, John 20, 154, 162, 166, 187, 192–3
Khalid, King 39
Khalid bin Sultan, Prince 81, 92, 104, 107, 115–16, 120
Khamene'i, Ali 150–1, 153, 170

Kroenig, Matthew 93
Kuwait 139, 141–2, 144, 157

Lavoy, Peter R. 3–4, 215
Leverage, international 223–5
Libya 40, 42; *see also* Qaddafi, Muammar

missile defense shield 65–6, 156, 168, 173, 200
Mitib, Prince 17, 20, 27
Mubarak, Husni 64–5
Muhammad bin Salman, Prince 20–1, 164, 199–200, 217
Muqrin, Prince 40, 80–2

Nayif, Prince 40
Netanyahu, Benjamin 70, 163
Non-Proliferation Treaty 40, 64, 105, 115, 194, 219–20
North Korea 70–1, 83, 111–14, 151, 222
Nuclear Agreement *see* Joint Comprehensive Plan of Action
nuclear-free zone 78, 80, 131, 164–6, 194, 221–2
nuclear theory: cascading 227; domestic politics 4–5; idealism 3, 15; internationalist 219–22; latency 213–23; multicausality 4–5, 222; mythmaking 3–4, 216; norms 4–5; pragmatism 4, 6; realism 3, 15–16, 216
nuclear umbrella *see* umbrella, nuclear

Obama, Barack 65–6, 69–70, 150, 154–5, 162–3, 166–70, 187–90, 196–201, 221
Oman 56, 142, 144, 156–7, 187
O'Reilly, K. P. 3, 217

Pakistan 63, 79, 83, 90; and Saudi Arabia 91–4, 109

Qaddafi, Muammar 40, 110, 217; *see also* Libya
Qatar 143–4, 156–8, 187

Rafsanjani, Hashemi 160–1
religion *see* clerics
Rost Rublee, Maria 3, 219–20
Rouhani, Hassan 11, 149–50, 153, 156, 170, 187
Russia 8, 164–5, 189, 197, 200

Sagan, Scott D. 4–5, 213, 222–3
Salman, as Crown Prince and Minister of Defense 7, 18, 92, 140; as King 20–1, 25, 28, 93, 161, 166–8, 187, 191, 196–201, 217

SANG *see* Saudi National Guard
Saud Al-Faysal, Prince 42, 54, 62, 78, 81, 140, 143, 149, 151, 160, 165
Saudi Arabia: aborted détente with Iran 159–62; acquisition options 90–4; decisionmaking process 7, 15–21; deterrence 52–3, 83–4; economy 29–30, 56; media 8–9; nuclear warfighting 53–6, 94, 105–7, 109, 114–15; policy toward Iran 61–72; public opinion 43–4; regime legitimacy 24–30, 56; proliferation models, relation to 215–23 ; shaping regional opinion 44–5; space 116, 119; strategic culture 6, 15–30; view of Iran's nuclear threat 38–5, 48–57, 116–17; view of nuclear weapons 53–4, 78–9, 83–7, 89, 103–5, 107–11, 170–3, 194–5, 212–3, 223–5; view of U.S. Congress 170, 195, 197, 200; view of U.S. double standard 220–1; view of U.S.-Iranian relations 66–7; view of U.S. policy 40, 42, 64–5, 66, 71–2, 86, 93, 108–10, 151–2, 154, 164–9, 172–3, 219–20, 192–3; view of U.S.-USSR Cold War 65, 69, 80–1, 103, 194, 228; *see also* Iran
Saudi National Guard 10, 17–18, 21
Shia 21–2, 48, 54, 68, 214
Shura 6, 19, 27, 40, 43, 171, 189
Sing, Sonali 216
Solingen, Etel 3, 218–9
Sultan, Prince 10, 13n33, 19, 26, 29, 78–9, 91–92, 106, 118

Talal, Prince 109
Tannenwald, Nina 53
threat environment, impact of 225–6
Turki Al-Faysal, Prince 43–4, 64–5, 68–9, 79–82, 140, 143–4, 154, 165, 171, 214

UAE *see* United Arab Emirates
umbrella, nuclear 63–6, 80, 138–9, 143, 145, 158, 165, 194
United Arab Emirates 143, 158, 187

Van Creveld, Martin 228
Varisco, Andrea 103

Waltz, Kenneth N. 228
Washington summit 198–201
Wray, Christopher R. 216

Yemen 56, 161–2

Zakaria, Fareed 90